HABITATS OF THE BASILEIA

New Testament Monographs, 46

HABITATS OF THE BASILEIA
ESSAYS IN HONOUR OF
ELAINE M. WAINWRIGHT

edited by
Robert J. Myles, Caroline Blyth
and Emily Colgan

SHEFFIELD PHOENIX PRESS
2024

Copyright © 2024 Sheffield Phoenix Press
Published by Sheffield Phoenix Press
University of Sheffield, S10 2TN

www.sheffieldphoenix.com

A CIP catalogue record for this book
is available from the British Library

Typeset by the HK Scriptorium

ISBN: 978-1-914490-39-2

CONTENTS

Habitats of Matthew

Habitats beyond Matthew

Legacies

LIST OF CONTRIBUTORS

Vicky Balabanski, Uniting College for Leadership and Theology, University of Divinity

Caroline Blyth, Wollaston Theological College, University of Divinity

Alan H. Cadwallader, Australian Centre for Christianity and Culture, Charles Sturt University

Warren Carter, Phillips Theological Seminary, Tulsa, OK

Emily Colgan, College of St John the Evangelist, Auckland

Elizabeth Dowling, Institute of Sisters of Mercy of Australia and Papua New Guinea. Formerly Australian Catholic University

Anne Elvey, Pilgrim Theological College, University of Divinity, Monash University

Norman Habel, Flinders University

James Harding, University of Otago

Veronica Lawson, Institute of Sisters of Mercy of Australia and Papua New Guinea. Formerly Australian Catholic University

Tat-siong Benny Liew, College of the Holy Cross, Worcester, MA

Kathleen McPhillips, University of Newcastle

Anita Monro, University of Queensland

Robert J. Myles, Wollaston Theological College, University of Divinity

Vaitusi Nofoaiga, Malua Theological College

Anne Pattel-Gray, School of Indigenous Studies, University of Divinity

Carlos Olivares, Universidade Adventista de São Paulo

Barbara Reid, Catholic Theological Union, Chicago, IL

Kathleen P. Rushton, Independent Biblical Interpreter, Trinity Methodist Theological College

Nāsili Vaka'uta, Trinity Methodist Theological College, Auckland

ABBREVIATIONS

AAWW	*Anzeiger der philosophisch-historischen Klasse der Österreichischen Akademie Wissenschaften*
AB	Anchor Bible
AHB	*Ancient History Bulletin*
Ann.	Tacitus, *Annales*
Ant.	Josephus, *Antiquities of the Jews (Antiquitates judaicae)*
ANTC	Abingdon New Testament Commentaries
Apol.	*Apology*
ASAA	*Annuario della R. Scuola di Archaeologia di Atene*
ASV	American Standard Version
AusBR	*Australian Biblical Review*
b.	Babylonian Talmud
b. Ḥull.	Babylonian Talmud tractate *Ḥullin*
BARev	*Biblical Archaeology Review*
BCAR	*Bullettino della Commissione Archeologica Comunale di Roma*
BDAG	Walter Bauer, Frederick W. Danker, William F. Arndt and F. Wilbur Gingrich, *A Greek-English Lexicon of the New Testament and Other Early Christian Literature*, 3rd edn (revised and edited by Frederick W. Danker; Chicago: University of Chicago Press, 2000)
BDB	Francis Brown, S.R. Driver and Charles A. Briggs, *A Hebrew and English Lexicon of the Old Testament* (Oxford: Clarendon Press, 1907)
BETL	Bibliotheca ephemeridum theologicarum lovaniensium
BGU	*Berlin griechische Urkunden*
Bib	*Biblica*
BibInt	Biblical Interpretation Series, Brill
BJS	Brown Judaic Studies
BMC Phrygia	*Coins of the British Museum: Phrygia*
BMW	Bible in the Modern World
BTB	*Biblical Theology Bulletin*
BZNW	*Beihefte zur Zeitschrift für die neutestamentliche Wissenschaft*

CBQ	*Catholic Biblical Quarterly*
CBQI	*Catholic Biblical Quarterly* Imprints
C. Cels.	Origen, *Contra Celsum*
C. Chr.	Porphyry, *Contra Christianos*
CEB	Common English Bible
CIIP	*Corpus inscriptionum Iudaeae/Palaestinae*
CIRB	*Corpus inscriptionum regni Bosporani*
ClAnt	*Classical Antiquity*
CR	*Critical Review of Books in Religion*
DCH	David J.A. Clines (ed.), *The Dictionary of Classical Hebrew* (8 vols.; Sheffield: Sheffield Phoenix Press, 1993–2011)
Dec.	Philo, *De decalogo*
Did.	*Didache*
Digest	*Digest of Justinian*
EDNT	*Exegetical Dictionary of the New Testament* (ed. Horst Robert Balz and Gerhard Schneider; Grand Rapids, MI: Eerdmans, 1990–1994)
ESV	English Standard Version
Eth. Nic.	Aristotle, *Ethica nichomachea*
ETL	*Ephemerides theologicae lovanienses*
FCNTECW	Feminist Companion to the New Testament and Early Christian Writings
Geo.	Virgil, *Georgica* (*Georgics*)
GNB	Good News Bible
Gos. Thom.	*Gospel of Thomas*
HALOTSE	Ludwig Koehler and Walter Baumgartner, *The Hebrew and Aramaic Lexicon of the Old Testament: Study Edition* (rev. W. Baumgartner and J. J. Stamm; trans. and ed. M.E.J. Richardson; Leiden: E.J. Brill, 2001)
HTS	*Hervormde Teologiese Studies*
ICC	International Critical Commentary
ICNT	International Commentary on the New Testament
I.Ephesos	*Die Inschriften von Ephesos*
IGR	*Inscriptiones graecae ad res romanas pertinentes*
IG	*Inscriptiones graecae*
ILS	*Inscriptiones latinae selectae* (ed. Hermann Dessau; 5th edn, Berlin: Weidmann, 1997)
Int	*Interpretation*
I.Parion	*Die Inschriften von Parion*
I.Portes du desert	*Les portes du désert. Recueil des inscriptions grecques d'Antinooupolis, Tentyris, Koptos, Apollonopolis Parva et Apollonopolis Magna*

Harding considers the nature of the bird mentioned in Job 39.13-18, asking what its role might be within the wider context of this divine speech. Why, he asks, does the LORD seem to take such pride and delight in a bird who appears to have neither wisdom nor understanding? And what is Job to learn from such a creature? Following a detailed exegetical analysis of the text, Harding argues that the ostrich serves to illustrate a valuable lesson for Job about the nature of wisdom. Job learns that, rather than burying his head in the sand, he must embrace the freedom to encounter God, and all living creatures, with a sense of wonder and faith rather than anxiety and dread.

Taking further inspiration from Elaine, several chapters in this section bring an ecological focus to their critical engagements with the biblical text. This was already evident in Rushton's chapter noted earlier and continues in Emily Colgan's chapter, 'An Eco-Rhetorical Reading of Jeremiah 2.1-9 and its Colonial Reverberations'. Here, Colgan uses an ecological hermeneutic and a rhetorical methodology to critically examine this passage from Jeremiah, in which the binary between fertile field and desert land is particularly pronounced. She then traces intertextual echoes of this biblical imagery, noting the role such imagery may have played in dictating the terms of encounter between British settlers and the land of Aotearoa New Zealand.

Alan Cadwallader's chapter, 'The Young Man and the Sea: Reconceiving Ancient Water Resources', carries on this ecological focus by discussing the renaming of Lake Gennesaret as 'the Sea of Galilee' in Mark's Gospel. Cadwallader attempts to reconfigure ecological hermeneutics by tracing the origins of anthropocentric toxicity to early imperial intensification of agricultural and aquacultural practices for material gain. His reading therefore imbues the early Jesus movement with a nascent ecological concern, albeit one that is conscious of the socio-economic disruption occurring under the 'avaricious watch' of first-century tetrarch Herod Antipas.

The next three chapters bring ecological-critical insights to Luke's Gospel. Anne Elvey's chapter, 'Thinking the Divine Animal? A Braided Reading of Luke 2.7', considers the concept of 'habitat' in this Gospel location and beyond. Focusing particularly on Lk. 2.1-20, Elvey hones in on the symbol of the manger as a focus for the habitat into which the infant Jesus is born. Practicing a 'braided reading' of various texts, she explores how the manger conjures a point of intersection between humans, other-than-human-animals and the divine. She concludes that this braided reading might prompt the reader to listen to the voices of contemporary creatures.

In 'Feeding 5,000 in the Slums of Bethsaida (Luke 9.10-17)', Robert J. Myles considers Jesus's catering miracle within the context of Herodian urbanization projects that were transforming the environment in the early decades of first-century CE Palestine. Myles notes Luke's unique localization of the feeding event within both 'a deserted place' (v. 12) and 'a city called Bethsaida' (v. 10). Analysing this tension, Myles argues that the 'desolate' habitat of the urbanized Bethsaida exposes both the damaging cycle of economic and environmental exploitation by this newly raised *polis* and also the inherent contradiction of a *polis* that cannot adequately provide for its own mass of inhabitants.

In the next chapter, titled '"Giving her All": An Ecological Feminist Reading of Luke 21.1-4', Elizabeth Dowling and Veronica Lawson use an ecological approach to analyse the Lukan story about the needy widow who gives two coins as a temple offering. They suggest that the widow's actions can be understood as prophetic in nature, highlighting the 'vast inequality' between the gifts and donations offered by the rich and the poor, as pointed out by Jesus in Lk. 21.3-4. Reading this text in the current global context of wars, pandemics and ecological crisis, Dowling and Lawson suggest that this widow who 'gives her all' demonstrates a power that is neither exploitative nor unjust; instead, like Jesus, she demonstrates a non-violent power that is much needed in the world today.

Finally, this section of the volume concludes with Caroline Blyth's chapter, '"The Place that Men Call Paradise": Emily Dickinson's Earthly Engagement with the Apostle Paul'. Blyth argues that Dickinson's references to Paul in her letters and poetry thoroughly unbalance the apostle's spiritual and heaven-centred gaze, thrusting it earthward to bring new and unexpected meaning to matters such as friendship, love, suffering and desire. By taking a closer look at some of Dickinson's writings, Blyth maps out how the poet rejects certain features of Pauline theology in favour of her own earth-centred spirituality, where paradise can be encountered amidst the flowers in the garden, the birds and trees, and the company of loving family and friends.

Legacies

The volume rounds out with three chapters concerning 'legacies', both the legacy of Elaine's lifework, including her organizing and encouragement of emerging theological scholarship in the Oceanic region, as well as the broader trends and avenues in current biblical scholarship that have been impacted by Elaine's touch in some way.

First, Nāsili Vaka'uta's chapter, 'Moana Hermeneutics: Charting a Niu Direction', assesses the state and future direction of 'Moana hermeneutics', by which he means the ongoing *talanoa* or conversation concerning biblical interpretation among the diverse islanders of the Pacific. Moana, meaning sea or ocean, decentres the ideologies obsessed with land ownership that are implicit (or even explicit) within colonial and biblical discourses. As is well known, Elaine has been a champion of contextual biblical methods in general and has supported and offered guidance in the development of Moana hermeneutics in particular. Vaka'uta's chapter is something of a manifesto for the next phase of Moana hermeneutics; he seeks to ensure what he labels '*niu*-ness' in this approach, as well as further movement beyond malestream and Eurocentric orientations entangled within dominant 'Western' methods of biblical scholarship.

Second, Vaitusi Nofoaiga pays homage to Elaine's feminist work on Matthew's Gospel, using it as a launching pad for his own Samoan contextual exploration of the women disciples at the cross. In his chapter titled 'Professor Elaine Wainwright's *Silasila Mamao* (Watching from a Distance) and Matthew 27.55-56: Biblical Studies and Women in the Samoan Christian World', Nofoaiga emphasizes the need to recognize that the women disciples who 'watch from a distance' at the crucifixion of Jesus embody faithful action. Specifically, he reads these women's actions through the Samoan concept of *Silasila Mamao*, which understands watching from a distance as a form of profound wisdom.

The final chapter in this volume is by Kathleen McPhillips and is titled 'SeaChanges: Creating and Sustaining a Community of Women Scholars of Feminism, Religion and Theology in the Pacific 1990–2016'. McPhillips offers a 'herstory' of Elaine's contributions to the fields of feminist studies in religion and theology, as well as the research and collegiality that she facilitated among the women academics and graduate students located in and around the Pacific region. The chapter focuses in particular on Elaine's leadership of the Women Scholars of Religion and Theology association (WSRT), which offered an important and creative space for women in academia to discuss theological and academic issues. The chapter thus pays tribute to Elaine's vision for a diverse community of women scholars who could offer one another support and inspiration.

It has been a privilege to collaborate with so many important scholars in putting together this collection. We (the editors) also wish to give special thanks to Anne Elvey, Kathleen Rushton and Nāsili Vaka'uta, who greatly assisted with bringing this project together, especially in its early stages. The volume would not have existed were it not for their initial input. Further, we wish to thank all the contributors to this volume. Each chapter testifies to the significant impact Elaine has had in her academic life and beyond. We are grateful to Glenn Loughrey for his generous permission to include his artwork on the cover of this volume. Finally, we wish to thank the team at Sheffield Phoenix Press for wholeheartedly backing the project. It occurred to us early on during the planning stage that Sheffield Phoenix Press would be the most appropriate habitat for a volume to honour Elaine given that the press had published Elaine's most recent contributions to the field.

We hope that readers of this volume are engaged and inspired to continue Elaine's work of imagining new ways and habitats where the *basileia* can flourish and thrive, and to bear witness to the transformation of the world—including its messy social structures and layers of oppressions—so that 'all members of the Earth community might live in right-relationship toward not only the survival but the enhancement of Earth'.[8]

8. Wainwright, *Women Healing/Healing Women*, p. 189.

flight from Pharaoh (LXX Exod. 2.15) and David's flight from Saul (LXX 1 Sam. 19.10), showing how the term is 'richly layered with intertextual significance that intensifies the sub-theme of displacement within the Matthaean text; especially so when it recurs around instances of political instability and turmoil in the infancy narrative'.[18] Of particular significance to the current study is Myles's suggestion that withdrawal can be a 'subversive political act'.[19] He connects it with the insight of Slavoj Žižek that, in the face of socio-political violence, the 'truly difficult thing is to step back, withdraw'.[20] The significance of stepping back from aggression, and the fact that this can be a powerful and subversive act, is important for this study.

Matthew's portrayal of Jesus as Wisdom/Sophia is of particular significance to Wainwright, especially as refracted through Mt. 11.16-19.[21] She points out that in Mt. 11.19, 'Wisdom/Sophia is justified not by her children, but by her *deeds*'.[22] How Jesus as Wisdom/Sophia *acts* is just as significant as what s/he *says*. The multiple instances of Jesus withdrawing from conflict are a narrative demonstration of this saying.

Wainwright argues that Jesus's identification with both Sophia and Christos is demonstrated through the deeds of Jesus Christos (Mt. 11.2) and Jesus Sophia (Mt. 11.19) paralleling one another.[23] This identification breaks boundaries, both conceptually and in practice:

> Jesus is Jesus Sophia and, like Sophia, unites the human and the divine by way of theological evocation that breaks open gender distinctions. ... For those Matthean households whose storytelling shaped a community identity that was inclusive of genders, ethnicities, and classes, the image of Jesus Sophia may have functioned as boundary-breaking and been linked intimately with the boundary-breaking aspects of the works of the *basileia*.[24]

The verb ἀναχωρέω is part of this Matthaean depiction that calls gender distinctions into question and redraws what it means to proclaim Jesus as

---

Jesus' "Decision" to Go Rogue', in Bruce Worthington (ed.), *Reading the Bible in an Age of Crisis: Political Exegesis for a New Day* (Minneapolis, MN: Fortress Press, 2015), pp. 217-43.

18. Myles, 'Echoes of Displacement', p. 34.

19. Myles, 'Homelessness, Neoliberalism, and Jesus', p. 225.

20. Slavoj Žižek, *Violence* (London: Profile Books, 2008), p. 183.

21. See, e.g., Elaine M. Wainwright, 'But Who Do You Say That I Am? An Australian Feminist Response', *Pacifica* 10.2 (1997), pp. 156-72; *idem, Shall We Look for Another? A Feminist Rereading of the Matthean Jesus* (Maryknoll, NY: Orbis Books, 1998), pp. 76-79.

22. Wainwright, 'But Who Do You Say That I Am?', p. 171. Emphasis mine.

23. Wainwright, *Shall We Look for Another?*, p. 76.

24. Wainwright, *Shall We Look for Another?*, p. 77.

Christos. In the Graeco-Roman world, as today, courage was often understood as pursuing conflict. Indeed, the Greek term for 'to be courageous',
ἀνδρίζομαι, literally means 'behave like a man'.[25] But in the Matthaean narrative, Jesus demonstrates a different type of courage—Žižek's 'truly difficult thing' mentioned above—and in doing so, offers the sort of boundary-
breaking Wisdom to which Wainwright refers.

From this short review, it is clear that the nuances of the verb ἀναχωρέω
shift according to the reading context and method. The emphasis in this
study is on the Matthaean narrative depiction of Wisdom as withdrawing,
indeed disengaging, from conflict situations, and in doing so, crossing
boundaries. I will now review the usage of this verb.

Reviewing the Verb ἀναχωρέω in Matthew's Gospel

The ten instances of this verb in Matthew's Gospel are listed here according
to the chronology of the narrative:

> Mt. 2.12 The Magi withdrew (from Herod the King)
> Mt. 2.13 When they (the Magi) had departed/withdrawn …
> Mt. 2.14 Joseph withdrew (to Egypt with the child and his mother)
> Mt. 2.22 Joseph withdrew to the region of Galilee to avoid Archelaus
> Mt. 4.12 Jesus withdrew (at the arrest of John)
> Mt. 9.24 Jesus tells the crowds around the little girl (who is 'not dead but
> sleeping') to go away, depart, withdraw
> Mt. 12.15 Jesus withdrew (from Pharisees)
> Mt. 14.13 Jesus withdrew (at the death of John)
> Mt. 15.21 After conflict with the Pharisees and scribes, and after teach-
> ing the crowd about what defiles, Jesus withdraws to the region of
> Tyre and Sidon
> Mt. 27.5 And Judas, having tossed the pieces of silver into the sanctuary,
> withdrew/departed and hanged himself.

All of these uses of ἀναχωρέω are distinctive to Matthew, belonging
either to the Special M material or to Matthaean redaction. Together they
let us build a picture of actions taken by various characters in the face of
conflict that are endorsed by the evangelist.

In the following section, I set out the ten uses of ἀναχωρέω in four
groupings:[26] (1) Mt. 2.12, 13, 14 and 22; (2) Mt. 4.12 and 14.13; (3) Mt.
12.15; 15.21 and 9.24; and (4) Mt. 27.5. In my study of these four groups of

---

25. Cf. the use of this verb in 1 Cor. 16.13.
26. This differs from Deirdre Good's seven groupings. Good excludes discussion
of Mt. 9.24.

The upshot of Jesus's 'deeds' in Mt. 12.1-8, namely his defence of his followers' actions of plucking and eating grain on a Sabbath when they are hungry, reveals divine priorities in favour of the weary and burdened, or specifically in this case, the hungry. Jesus's interpretation offers scriptural precedents—the actions of David and his followers and the actions of priests in the Temple—and invites his opponents to perceive a different set of priorities, where mercy rather than sacrifice is the fundamental value. The evangelist does not say whether these arguments bear any fruit, but immediately shows Jesus departing from there and going to their synagogue. Here the verb is not ἀνεχώρησεν, but μεταβὰς ... ἦλθεν (having departed ... he went, Mt. 12.9). Verse 9 forms a redactional bridge to the next conflict situation, this time in 'their' synagogue. Jesus has moved locations, but has not yet disengaged from the conflict with the Pharisees.

In the next section, Mt. 12.10-14, the conflict over the Sabbath intensifies. This time it is not precipitated by a healing but by a question about whether it is legitimate to heal on the Sabbath. Jesus's opponents present him with a man who has a withered hand as a case in point, 'so that they might accuse him' (Mt. 12.10). If they had been genuinely concerned about preserving the sanctity of the Sabbath, they could have saved their question for another day. Jesus once again gives the opponents a precedent from the law, signifying that it is indeed right to do good on the Sabbath.[33] And to ensure that Wisdom is demonstrated not only by words but by deeds, Jesus tells the man to stretch out his hand. The man does so, and enables his own healing to ensue. Now the Pharisees, going out (ἐξελθόντες), 'conspired against him, how to destroy' Jesus (Mt. 12.14).

On hearing of this, Jesus now withdraws from the confrontation (ἀνεχώρησεν). We can see that this is no sign of weakness or capitulation, but rather a decision that enables divine Wisdom to be more fully understood. It leads to another formula quotation, this time from Isa. 42.1-4, setting out the logic of G-d's servant as one who both proclaims justice to the Gentiles (Mt. 12.18) and brings justice to victory (Mt. 12.20). Withdrawing from conflict is in keeping with the sort of servant described in this quotation, who will not quarrel or cry out (Mt. 12.18).

Matthew 15 is another context where the Pharisees and scribes from Jerusalem are shown to pit the 'tradition of the elders' against the practices of Jesus, this time with regard to purity and defilement. Again, the issue is framed as a criticism of the behaviour of Jesus's followers rather than of

33. Exercising care of animals is a precept of the law (Exod. 23.5 and Deut. 22.4); however, the right action on the Sabbath was contested. Lifting an animal out of a pit on the Sabbath was deemed to be work, according to the Damascus Document (CD 11.13-14). Note that Jesus does not physically touch the man here, but calls on him to stretch out his own hand. Neither action was necessarily work.

Jesus himself: 'Why do your disciples break the tradition of the elders'?
(Mt. 15.1). Jesus's response follows a similar pattern to the conflict in ch.
12, drawing on Scripture to demonstrate how their interpretation is self-
serving and inadequate, and concluding with a quotation from Isa. 29.13
that names their apparent piety as hypocrisy. The conflict is quite intense;
although Jesus does not start the quarrel, he responds decisively and with
authority.

The conflict is not an end in itself but leads to further teaching. In Mt.
15.10, Jesus challenges the crowds to listen and understand more deeply the
significance of the purity commandments—that they are not for external
compliance but internal integrity (Mt. 15.17-20). In Mt. 15.12, the disciples point out that the Pharisees have taken offence at what Jesus has said.
Jesus does not resile from his description of them as hypocrites—indeed,
he heightens the critique, calling them 'blind guides leading the blind' (Mt.
15.14). Nevertheless, he takes the decision to leave that place and disengage
from the conflict (ἀνεχώρησεν, Mt. 15.21). This sets him on the path to the
district of Tyre and Sidon, where he will have his own challenging encounter with the Canaanite woman. Just as Gentiles featured prominently in ch.
12, and again in ch. 15, the withdrawal from conflict takes Jesus into Gentile territory. In neither instance is the withdrawal a retreat or a return home.
Both become opportunities for Wisdom to be more clearly understood by
the disciples, the crowds, the Gentiles and by Jesus himself.

Another instance of the verb ἀναχωρέω is in Mt. 9.24, this time on the
lips of Jesus, in the form of a present imperative (ἀναχωρεῖτε): Go away!
The context is the intercalated stories of the synagogue leader's daughter
who was on the point of death, and the woman suffering from hemorrhages
(Mt. 9.18-26). Instead of sending away the woman who has surreptitiously
seized her own healing by touching his cloak, Jesus has encouraged her to
'take heart', and publicly validated her action as faith. However, time with
her has delayed Jesus reaching the synagogue leader's house. There, public displays of grief—flute players and a crowd making a commotion—are
already under way for the girl's death (Mt. 9.23).

It is to these people that Jesus addresses the command to 'go away!',
adding that the girl is not dead but sleeping. Unlike the other eight usages
we have already examined, this could simply be a charge to go away or go
home.[34] However, Matthaean usage so far could imply the further nuance
of 'disengage with this situation'. Immediately after Jesus's words, we are
told that they (the flute players and the crowd of mourners) were laughing
at him (κατεγέλων αὐτοῦ).[35] This verb, stronger and more negative than

---

34. Deidre Good excludes discussion of this instance as not being part of the Matthaean pattern that her article is considering ('The Verb ΑΝΑΧΩΡΕΩ', p. 5).

35. The imperfect tense of καταγελάω indicates an ongoing and repeated action.

the translation 'laughing' can convey, could be more accurately translated as mocking, ridiculing, deriding or jeering. This attitude may be linked to the fact that Jesus had not yet seen the 'corpse' and yet presumed to know better than they did that the girl was not dead. It could also mean that they thought their livelihoods as flute players and professional mourners were being threatened.

There is a conflict situation here, though one that is subtler than Jesus's conflict with the Pharisees and scribes. By putting the command ἀναχωρεῖτε on Jesus's lips, the evangelist implies that the crowds need to disengage from their certainty about their own perception, particularly about life and death, and open themselves to the possibility that something greater is here than they realize.[36] The use of this verb indicates that there is divine Wisdom in stepping away from this situation and changing their attitude to Jesus's words.

ἀναχωρέω in Mt. 27.5

Throwing down the pieces of silver in the temple, [Judas] departed (ἀνεχώρησεν); and he went and hanged himself.

The final usage of ἀναχωρέω is the most difficult to interpret. When compared with the other instances of this verb in Matthew's Gospel, there does not appear to be a g-dly person withdrawing from a conflict situation, as with the Magi, Joseph and Jesus, or a challenge to the crowds to behave in such a way, as in Mt. 9.23.

The story of Judas's suicide forms part of the Matthaean Passion Narrative.[37] The evangelist places it immediately after Jesus is handed over to Pilate and before Jesus is interrogated, condemned and executed. The account is, in fact, a story of repentance, complete with various scriptural allusions and a formula quotation. The evangelist makes it clear that Judas realizes and rejects what he has done. He brings back the thirty pieces of silver to the chief priests and the elders, and confesses that he has sinned by betraying innocent blood (Mt. 27.3-4). His words and actions indicate that he wants to distance himself from his act of betraying Jesus to the authorities. When the authorities refuse to receive the money back, Judas throws it down in the inner sanctuary of the Temple (εἰς τὸν ναὸν), the place where the veil would be torn from top to bottom (Mt. 27.51).

---

36. Compare Mt. 11.11; 12.6, 41, 42, which affirm that something greater than John the Baptist, the Temple, Jonah and Solomon is here.

37. This account is unique to Matthew's Gospel. For a non-suicide story of Judas's death, see Acts 1.18-20.

At this point, of course, nothing Judas can do will change the course of events for Jesus, but the account reveals how the blood money returns to the control of those who have been plotting to kill Jesus (Mt. 22.15). The words of the chief priests about the treasury imply that they are more concerned about its 'purity' than about the purity of the inner sanctuary, or how a repentant sinner can be restored. There is a profound conflict within Judas himself as to what he has done, and there is also conflict between Judas and the chief priests. Judas took the path that seemed the only one he could bear: he withdrew (ἀνεχώρησεν), and having gone away, hanged himself (ἀπελθὼν ἀπήγξατο) (Mt. 27.5). By including two words that mean 'depart', the evangelist suggests that the first has more significance than simply movement. Judas withdrew from this ugly situation of conflict, internal and external, before knowing what would become of Jesus. Whether this—and his act of ending his own life—is viewed as an act of despair or an attempt at repentance is a topic that lies beyond the scope of this study.[38] However, Jesus's words in Mt. 11.20-24 suggest that it may be more tolerable for Judas on the Day of Judgment than for the chief priests. His repentance matters.

In summary, we can affirm that eight of the ten usages of the verb ἀναχωρέω in Matthew's Gospel are the actions of g-dly people, and of Jesus himself, withdrawing from conflict situations and thereby demonstrating divine Wisdom. I have argued that, in Mt. 9.24, Jesus's command to the crowd can be interpreted in a similar way. The use of the verb in Mt. 27.5, which refers to Judas's withdrawal from the Temple and its authorities, can be seen also as a kind of disengagement from the machinations of those determined to put Jesus to death. The verb ἀναχωρέω is therefore theologically significant, and gives greater depth to the saying that Wisdom— understood through the actions of Jesus Sophia—is vindicated by her deeds (Mt. 11.19).

Recognizing that Wisdom is also known in and through other cultures and traditions, I now turn to the most ancient continuously living culture today, namely that of the First Peoples of Australia. Indigenous Wisdom includes the practice of choosing to disengage and withdraw from situations where conflict or lack of respect are present. By doing so, First Nations people demonstrate their disagreement and dissociate themselves from situations that are potentially harmful. Knowing when to disengage and when to persevere is an important aspect of Indigenous Wisdom.

---

38. Ulrich Luz (*Matthew 21–28: A Commentary on Matthew 21–28* [Minneapolis, MN: Fortress Press, 2005], p. 469) argues that 'the remorse of Judas, his declaration of Jesus' innocence, and the reactions of the chief priests and elders … are of particular theological importance for Matthew'.

*Indigenous Perspectives on Disengaging
from Conflict Situations*

Indigenous elder and theologian Rev. Dr Aunty Denise Champion puts it this way: 'When people stop listening, I stop talking. I take lessons from dormancy. Things that are planted need time to grow. That's true for thoughts and ideas too. Silence and space need time to grow. We reserve the right to step back when we're not heard.'[39]

One of the features of communication in Aboriginal cultural settings is the expectation that real communication will take time. There is no substitute for sitting down together, listening and being listened to and taking all the time that is needed to find common ground.[40] However, even once the speaking and listening have been done, agreement may not have been reached. One or more of the parties may choose to disengage and withdraw from the conversation, not as a sign of weakness or capitulation, but as acknowledgment that—for the time being—there is no common ground.

This cultural value was visible on 13 February 2008—the day when Kevin Rudd, as prime minister of Australia, apologized to the stolen generations of Aboriginal people. This apology was very significant to many First and Second Peoples. It was, however, followed by a response from the opposition leader, Brendan Nelson, in which he defended the intentions of those who had removed Aboriginal children from their families and spoke of Indigenous Australians as 'living lives of existential aimlessness'. Many Australians were offended and responded in their thousands by turning their backs on the screens that projected this response. As one journalist reported, 'In Melbourne, the 8,000-strong crowd at Federation Square turned its back on the screen during Dr Nelson's speech, amid chants of "get him off".'[41] The reports quite reasonably do not distinguish between Indigenous and non-Indigenous responses, but the symbolic act of disengagement from the offence of the moment was a distinctively Indigenous action, which Second Peoples joined in to show solidarity.

There was another example of the Indigenous value of disengaging and leaving a situation of conflict at the National Assembly of the Uniting Church in Australia (UCA) in 2009. A proposal endorsed by the National Uniting Aboriginal and Islander Christian Congress (UAICC / 'Congress')

---

39. Personal communication, Adelaide, 3 March 2022. The concept for this study arose from an earlier conversation with Aunty Denise, who observed that it was important that Jesus stepped back and took time out.

40. This sits uncomfortably with contemporary political and administrative processes, which are characterized by fixed agendas and tight schedules.

41. See Staff Reporters, 'Fury over Nelson's 'sorry' response', *The Age*, 14 February 2008. https://www.theage.com.au/national/fury-over-nelsons-sorry-response-2008 0214-ge6q1r.html.

was presented to the Assembly. It concerned the UCA formally adopting a carefully crafted preamble to its constitution acknowledging the spiritual heritage of the First Peoples and the complicity of churches in dispossessing First Peoples of their land and heritage.[42] Chris Budden describes what took place during the debate:

> [S]omeone asked whether it was really true that First Peoples under-stood God as Christians understood God. I think this was intended to be a respectful question, an attempt not to absorb Indigenous spirituality into church categories. Congress leaders heard the question differently, as suggesting that they were godless. The Congress Chairperson said that the meeting had become unsafe for them, and they wished to withdraw for some time. He said the rest of the Assembly could continue to discuss the issues if it wanted to. This ability for Congress to withdraw and discuss issues on their own was (and is) part of the agreed Assembly processes.[43]

The fact of this decision to withdraw and the recognition in UCA Assembly processes that First Peoples' representatives have this option to withdraw both acknowledge the cultural value of withdrawing from a conflict situation as part of Indigenous cultural Wisdom. As Budden points out, the choice to withdraw can in fact lead to a renewal of relationship:

> The withdrawal of Congress was a deeply painful moment for members of the Assembly; it spoke of a failure of relationships. The Assembly stopped working. Some time later Congress said they wished to return. The members of the Assembly left the room, and came back in with Congress members, who then led a time of prayer as people knelt all around the meeting space. Decisions were made the next day.[44]

One of the Australian Indigenous languages, Yolŋu Matha, which is spoken in Arnhem Land, Northern Territory, has some words and phrases that communicate this ancient Wisdom of withdrawing from conflict. In particular, the reflexive verb *gänaŋ 'maranhamirr* means 'make oneself separate, isolate, alone, segregated from'. It is used in the Yolŋu translation of Rom. 16.17 ('I urge you, brothers and sisters, to keep an eye on those who cause dissensions and offences, in opposition to the teaching that you have learned; avoid them'), meaning 'stay away from, avoid involvement in'.[45]

---

42. See 'The Uniting Church in Australia Revised Preamble to the Constitution', 2011, https://assembly.uca.org.au/images/stories/covenanting/PreamblePoster-web.pdf.

43. Chris Budden, 'Preamble Discussion' (Notes for a Post-Assembly Presentation on the Preamble), Uniting Church in Australia, Assembly Archives, Box 60 (UAICC, Chris Budden's Papers, U-I-8), File 2, Document 60a.

44. Budden, 'Preamble Discussion'.

45. I thank Howard Amery for this information (personal communication). He points out that the source word is *gäna* (adj.)—isolated, alone, separate, distinct. Other words close in meaning / having a fairly close fit: *ganarrtham* and *gunharra 'yun* (verb)—avoid, don't touch, avoid, abandon, desert; *raypirri 'yunmirr*—exercise self-discipline.

The now famous Yolŋu word *makarrata* ('coming together after a struggle') indicates that a struggle or conflict can indeed lead to the parties separating, but that it is not the end of the matter. There can also be a healing movement of drawing together again and finding common ground. This is why the 'Statement from the Heart'[46] calls for the establishment of a First Nations Voice enshrined in the Constitution, a Makarrata Commission to supervise a process of agreement-making between governments and First Nations, and truth-telling about history.[47]

In conclusion, I affirm that Wisdom among Australian Indigenous peoples seeks to give every opportunity for mutual understanding, while recognizing that there are times when staying away from or quitting a situation of conflict may be necessary to preserve safety or respect. Withdrawing from conflict is not the ultimate goal; it can enable more effective listening to happen.

Matthew's Gospel shows Wisdom expressed by the verb ἀναχωρέω in the actions of g-dly people, and by Jesus himself, when he disengages from conflict with his opponents. While withdrawing from conflict is not the only posture in keeping with Jesus's life and ministry, the repeated depiction of ἀναχωρέω as Wisdom calls into question any theology that justifies pre-emptive aggression. May we learn afresh how to prioritize Wisdom by disengaging from conflict in the present time, and every time that conflict arises.

In the form of conventional advice, sagacity and adages: *Yaka bondi wapthurr*—refrain from reacting too early and from being partial or taking sides; *buthuru-bitjurr ŋäthil ga yaka bondi buku-bakmaraŋ*—first listen and refrain from replying too quickly; *gurrum'thun waŋi*—talk softly, gently, carefully (also placate); *mayali'kurr waŋa*—talk in a meaningful way, talk indirectly, talk respectfully so as not to offend; *galipum waŋa*—talk indirectly, respectfully so as not to offend.

46. https://ulurustatement.org/the-statement.

47. At the time that this chapter goes to press, the Federal Government's endeavour to institute constitutional reform based on the call issued in the 2017 'Uluru Statement from the Heart' has been rejected by the majority of voters in all Australian states and territories except the ACT. Finding a way forward in Wisdom toward justice and self-determination rather than confrontation and conflict is now more crucial than ever.

2

(Not) Swearing Oaths and Negotiating Imperial Power? Matthew 5.33-37

Warren Carter

'Do not swear at all … Let your word be "Yes, Yes" or "No, No"' (Mt. 5.34, 37).[1] In Mt. 5.33-37, the Matthaean Jesus speaks out against perjury, the root of which is swearing oaths.

Scholars have explored numerous aspects of this enigmatic pericope (5.33-37). What is the origin of the teaching that Jesus attributes to those of ancient times—Torah texts[2] or mostly Hellenistic Jewish wisdom traditions?[3] How do vv. 33bc and 34a relate,[4] and how does v. 34a connect

---

1. In honour of Professor Elaine Wainwright's excellent work, especially on gender and ecology, in Matthew's Gospel.

2. See Alexander Sand, *Das Evangelium nach Matthäus* (Regensburg: Friedrich Pustet, 1986), p. 117. According to Donald Hagner, *Matthew 1–13* (WBC, 33A; Dallas, TX: Word Books, 1993), p. 127, Jesus's teaching on oaths and perjury in this Matthaean pericope reflects 'a crystallization of the OT teaching on the subject'. Robert Gundry, *Matthew* (Grand Rapids: Eerdmans, 2nd edn, 1994), p. 93, suggests it is 'an extrapolation from the strictures put on oaths in the OT'. W.D. Davies and Dale Allison, *A Critical and Exegetical Commentary on the Gospel According to Saint Matthew. Volume 1. Introduction and Commentary on Matthew I–VII* (ICC; Edinburgh: T. & T. Clark, 1988), p. 533, list Exod. 20.7 (the misuse of the divine name); Lev. 19.12 (prohibition on swearing falsely by the divine name); Num. 30.3-15 (concerning vows made by women); Deut. 23.21-23 (warning against not fulfilling a vow made to God); Matthias Konradt, *The Gospel According to Matthew* (Waco, TX: Baylor University Press, 2020), p. 89, suggests there is 'a Pentateuchal basis' for Jesus's teaching here.

3. Hans Dieter Betz, *The Sermon on the Mount: A Commentary on the Sermon on the Mount, Including the Sermon on the Plain (Matthew 5.3–7.27 and Luke 6.20-49)* (Hermeneia; Minneapolis, MN: Fortress Press, 1995), pp. 263-65, cites LXX Zech. 5.3-4; 1 Esdr. 1.46; Wis. 14.25; *T. Ash.* 2.6; Philo, *Spec. leg.* 1.235; 2.26-27; 4.40; *Dec.* 88; Josephus, *War.* 1.260; 2.135; *Ant.* 5.169-70; 8.20; 14.348; 18.335; *Life* 21. He especially highlights *Ps.-Phoc. sent.*16: 'Do not commit perjury'. Ulrich Luz, *Matthew 1–7: A Commentary* (trans. James E. Crouch; Hermeneia; Minneapolis, MN: Augsburg Fortress Press, 2007), p. 261, notes that Mt. 5.33b does not derive from the conventionally cited Hebrew Bible texts, but from Hellenistic Jewish parenesis.

4. Betz, *Sermon*, p. 266; Davies and Allison, *Matthew*, p. 533. W.C. Allen, *Gospel*

with the four examples in vv. 34b-36, which may or may not involve swearing by the divine name?[5] What role do Hellenistic traditions about perjury and speech play in framing the section?[6] Is the teaching to be understood literally or is it a more modified polemic?[7] And if it is a blanket negation, how is it to be read in relation to Jesus's apparent tolerance of oaths in Mt. 23.16-22?[8]

The discussions of these intertextual, textual and contextual issues are rich and important. Yet while scholarly work has focused on oaths made to the divine, oaths and perjury are not only a matter of interaction with the divine, and interpretation is not only a matter of the intellect.[9] Oaths and perjury involve bodies that interact with other bodies in the body politic. The interpretive discussions reference some everyday contexts such as speech in daily life,[10] legal matters[11] and religious oaths,[12] yet interpreters rarely develop how Jesus followers might negotiate these situations.

Early interpreters of Mt. 5.33-37 regard the instruction as a general ban on oaths: 'Do not swear at all'. James 5.12 omits any reference to religious oaths (cf. Mt. 5.33) in favour of a general command not to swear at all (cf. Mt. 5.34a) and an exhortation to let one's yes or no be sufficient (cf. Mt. 5.37). Justin (*Apol.* 1.16.5) follows suit in the mid-second century. Previously, Philo of Alexandria, living in a large, ethnically complex, and imperially strategic city, complains about pervasive oath-taking that marked everyday life:

> There are some who without even any gain in prospect have an evil habit of swearing incessantly and thoughtlessly about ordinary matters where there is nothing at all in dispute, filling up the gaps in their talk with oaths, forgetting that it were better ... to be silenced altogether, for from much swearing springs false swearing and impiety ... For I know full well that

According to Matthew (ICC; New York; Charles Scribner's Sons 1910), p. 53, declares, 'In its present connection the sequence of thought is confused'.

5. Betz, *Sermon*, pp. 267-70; Davies and Allison, *Matthew*, p. 533.

6. Betz, *Sermon*, pp. 259-74.

7. Davies and Allison, *Matthew*, pp. 535-36; Luz, *Matthew*, p. 266.

8. Hagner, *Matthew 1-13*, p. 127; Luz, *Matthew 1–7*, p. 268; Donald Senior, *Matthew* (ANTC; Nashville, TN: Abingdon, 1998), p. 79, comments, 'later in the Gospel both Herod (14.7) and Peter (26.72) will take oaths with disastrous consequences'.

9. See the excellent, wide-ranging discussion in John Fitzgerald, 'The Problem of Perjury in Greek Context: Prolegomena to an Exegesis of Matthew 5:33; 1 Timothy 1:10; and *Didache* 2.3', in *The Social World of the First Christians: Essays in Honor of Wayne Meeks* (ed. Michael White and Larry Yarbrough; Philadelphia: Fortress Press, 1995), pp. 156-77.

10. Davies and Allison, *Matthew*, p. 536 (citing Jeremias); Luz, *Matthew 1–7*, pp. 263-64.

11. Konradt, *Matthew*, p. 90.

12. Betz, *Sermon*, p. 265.

there are persons who … swear at length and make whole speeches consisting of a string of oaths. (*Dec.* 92, 94)[13]

If Jesus-followers believed that Jesus banned all oaths (and the accompanying risk of perjury) in Mt. 5.33-37, could they participate in socio-economic
interactions in business and trades, social/relational dealings, legal matters,
religious obligations and political demands where oath-taking was custom-
ary? And what would be the socio-economic, relational and political consequences for Jesus-followers of taking the Matthaean Jesus's words literally?
Is the prohibition against swearing oaths/committing perjury practicable
for Jesus-followers in the late first-century world of, for example, a major
multi-ethnic, imperially strategic city such as Antioch in Syria, a commonly
suggested provenance for Matthew's Gospel?

Such questions are too extensive for this one chapter, so I limit the exploration to an intertextuality neglected in Matthaean scholarship: namely,
intertextuality between the Matthaean prohibition and the practice of swearing political-imperial oaths of loyalty.[14] The absence of any consideration of
the pericope's intertextuality with imperial oath-taking—both oaths to the
emperor and swearing by the emperor's name—reflects the long-standing
scholarly avoidance in NT studies of examining interactions between NT
texts and imperial-political structures and practices.

Two factors encourage this exploration. First there is some evidence that
Jesus-followers did swear certain oaths by the emperor. Without referring to
the Matthaean section, around 200 CE, Tertullian attests to Christians swearing oaths by the emperor. He says that Christians refuse to swear by 'the
genii of the Caesars' because it treats them as divine. Christians, though, do
swear by the emperors' safety or health (*Apol.* 32). Rhona Beare explains the
force of these oaths: 'Perjury would endanger the emperor … when (a person)
swore by the emperor's safety he meant: "May the emperor fall ill if I am
lying"'.[15] This practice of swearing represents a significant departure from the
Matthaean prohibition, ignoring it in favour of a pragmatic instruction.

Second, the Matthaean pericope's language of swearing falsely or com-
mitting perjury (ἐπιορκέω, and cognates ἐπιορκία ['perjury'] and ἐπίορκος
['perjured']) commonly appears in a long tradition of imperial-political dis-

---

13. In *Philo, Volume 7* (trans. F.H. Colson; LCL, 320; Cambridge, MA: Harvard
University Press, 1984).

14. Peter Herrmann, *Der römische Kaisereid: Untersuchungen zu seiner Herkunft
und Entwicklung* (Göttingen: Vandenhoeck & Ruprecht, 1968); Søren Lund Sørensen,
'Herod's Oath of c. 6 BCE', *Religion in the Roman Empire* 4 (2018), pp. 260-72; D. Clint
Burnett, *Studying the New Testament through Inscriptions: An Introduction* (Peabody,
MA: Hendrickson, 2020), pp. 97-120.

15. Rhona Beare, 'The Meaning of the Oath by the Safety of the Emperor', *American Journal of Philology* 99.1 (1978), pp. 106-110 (esp. 106, 108).

course. Both Greek and Roman traditions attest oaths of loyalty to ruling and imperial figures with punishment for perjury.[16] I argue that, viewed in relation to the imperial-political practice of taking oaths of loyalty and the widespread disapproval of perjury,[17] the Matthaean command urging pure speech without oaths offers an ideal that is largely impractical for the pragmatic demands of imperial-political life.

Political/Imperial Oath-Taking and Perjury

The use of the word group for perjury, just named, goes back at least to Herodotus in the fifth century BCE. Frequently, these terms occur in contexts of political conflicts and threats to civic and political order. In *Persian Wars* 4.68, for example, the verb ἐπιορκέω appears four times when Herodotus narrates a scene in which the king of the Scythians falls ill.[18] The cause of the illness is said to be perjury after someone swore by the 'king's hearth' (his person or life).[19] The diviners are to identify the culprit who is to be executed. The scene illustrates the danger that perjury causes to both the one swearing falsely as well as to the one by whom the oath is sworn. More specifically, perjury politically threatens the security and stability of the state personified in the figure of the king.[20]

The comic playwright Aristophanes (d. 386 BCE) employs the word group in several plays. In *Birds,* the Athenium Pisthetaerus/Peisetaerus promotes the power and sovereignty of the birds who, in creating a city in the sky, could re-establish their position as the original gods if Zeus would return the sceptre to them. One advantage of rule by the birds is that the raven will be able quickly to peck out the eye of a perjurer:

> Won't you gods actually have greater power if birds are sovereign down below? At present, mortals can hide beneath the clouds, and with bowed heads swear false oaths (ἐπιορκοῦσιν) in your names; but if you have the birds for allies, whenever anyone swears 'by the Raven and by Zeus', the

16. Herrmann (*Der römische Kaisereid*) traces the origin and development of oaths of loyalty in Greek (pp. 21-49) and Roman (pp. 50-89) traditions.

17. Fitzgerald, 'Problem of Perjury', p. 157.

18. Herodotus, *The Persian Wars, Volume II: Books 3–4* (trans. A.D. Godley; LCL, 118; Cambridge, MA: Harvard University Press, 1921).

19. Beare, 'The Meaning of the Oath', pp. 108-110.

20. In her discussion of whether people swore by Julius Caesar during his lifetime, Rhona Beare ('The Imperial Oath under Julius Caesar', *Latomus* 38.2 [April-June 1979], pp. 469-73) demonstrates that this habit, and its risk of perjury, was well known by Tertullian (*Apol.* 32) and into the third century by Dio Cassius (44.6.1; 47.18.5). Seneca (*De ira* 3.30.5) recognizes that perjury endangers the emperor. See Seneca. *Moral Essays, Volume I: De providentia. De constantia. De ira. De clementia* (trans. John W. Basore; LCL, 214; Cambridge, MA: Harvard University Press, 1928).

> Raven will happen by and swoop down on that perjurer before he knows
> it, and peck out his eye like a shot. (*Birds* 1609)[21]

Perjury threatens the human order, it is often disguised, and perjurers need instant punishment to secure just socio-political dealings.

In Aristophanes's play *Clouds*, Socrates questions the conventional wisdom that Zeus hurls thunderbolts against perjurers (lines 397-402). The word group appears four times in the scene. Strepsiades observes that 'It's quite obvious that Zeus hurls [a lightning bolt] against perjurers', but Socrates is not persuaded:

> If he really strikes perjurers (τοὺς ἐπιόρκους), then why hasn't he burned
> up Simon or Cleonymus or Theorus, since they're paramount perjurers
> (ἐπίορκοι)? On the other hand, he strikes his own temple, and Sunium
> headland of Athens, and the great oaks. What's his point? An oak tree
> certainly doesn't perjure itself (ἐπιορκεῖ)! (*Clouds*, 397-402)[22]

Socrates complains that too much perjury goes unpunished, and by failing to punish perjurers, Zeus has failed to uphold the socio-political order.

In his *Anabasis* (c. 370 BCE), Xenophon narrates the attempt of an army of Greek mercenaries led by Cyrus the Younger to take the throne of Persia from his brother Artaxerxes II in 401 BCE. Clearchus led a contingent of Greek mercenaries. After Cyrus is killed, the king pledges to assist the Greeks in returning to Greece. But many of the Greeks do not trust the king and advocate attacking him. In reply, Clearchus argues that the king's oath is to be trusted because he is unlikely to commit perjury in public before the gods, Greeks and barbarians:

> Furthermore, in case fighting becomes necessary, we have no cavalry
> to help us, whereas the enemy's cavalry are exceedingly numerous and
> exceedingly efficient; hence if we are victorious, whom could we kill?
> And if we are defeated, not one of us can be saved. For my part, there-
> fore, I cannot see why the King, who has so many advantages on his side,
> should need, in case he is really eager to destroy us, to make oath and give
> pledge and forswear himself [ἐπιορκῆσαι] by the gods and make his good
> faith unfaithful in the eyes of Greeks and barbarians. (*Anabasis* 2.4.7)[23]

The king is trustworthy, Clearchus argues, because oaths are the currency of international military diplomacy and because perjury is too public, costly and damaging.

---

21. Aristophanes, *Birds. Lysistrata. Women at the Thesmophoria* (ed. and trans. Jeffrey Henderson; LCL, 179; Cambridge, MA: Harvard University Press, 2000).

22. Aristophanes, *Clouds. Wasps. Peace* (ed. and trans. Jeffrey Henderson; LCL, 488. Cambridge, MA: Harvard University Press, 1998).

23. Xenophon, *Anabasis* (trans. Carleton L. Brownson; revised by John Dillery; LCL, 90; Cambridge, MA: Harvard University Press, 1998).

Moving to internal Athenian politics (c. 324 BCE), nine leading politicians were prosecuted for misappropriating funds and taking bribes from Harpalus, the treasurer of the rapacious Alexander 'the Great'. Dinarchus, an Athenian speechwriter, prosecuted the politician Demosthenes:

> On his past record he ought to have been put to death, and he is liable to all the curses known to the city, having broken the oaths [ἐπιωρκηκὼς] he took on the Areopagus, in the names of the holy goddesses and the other deities by whom it is customary to swear there, and making himself accursed at every sitting of the Assembly. He has been proved to have taken bribes against Athens, has cheated the people and the council in defiance of the curse, professing views he does not hold, and in private has recommended to Aristarchus a course both cruel and unlawful. For these misdeeds, if there is any power to exact a just punishment from perjurers (ἐπιόρκων) and criminals—as there surely is—this man shall pay to-day. (*Against Demosthenes*, 47)[24]

Dinarchus names Demosthenes's failings as twofold. He has committed perjury and has taken bribes, rendering him a perjurer and a criminal. He therefore poses a double threat to the civic and political body.

From the first centuries BCE and CE, there are numerous instances of oaths of loyalty to figureheads within the (mostly) Roman imperial-political sphere. Some involve troops, while others relate to the populace in civic-political contexts.

- 44 BCE: legionary and veteran military units as well as 'nearly the whole senate, and most of the equestrian order … as well as the most distinguished of the plebeians … voluntarily' swore an oath of allegiance to Mark Antony at Tibur. They swore 'that they would not abandon their goodwill and loyalty to him' (Appian, *Bellum civile* 3.46).[25]
- c. 40 BCE: Parthians arrest Phasael, the brother of Herod, the Rome-appointed puppet ruler of Judea (Josephus, *Ant.* 15.194-201; 20.247), along with the former chief priest Hyrcanus, after swearing oaths for their safety: 'The prisoners curs[ed] them bitterly for their perjury (τὴν ἐπιορκίαν) and breach of faith' (Josephus, *War* 1.260).[26]

---

24. Lycurgus, Dinarchus, Demades, Hyperides, *Minor Attic Orators, Volume II: Lycurgus. Dinarchus. Demades. Hyperides* (trans. J.O. Burtt; LCL, 395; Cambridge, MA: Harvard University Press, 1954).

25. Appian, *Roman History, Volume V: Civil Wars, Books 3–4* (ed. and trans. Brian McGing; LCL, 543; Cambridge, MA: Harvard University Press, 2020).

26. Josephus, *The Jewish War, Volume I: Books 1–2* (trans. H. St.J. Thackeray; LCL, 203; Cambridge, MA: Harvard University Press, 1927). Josephus subsequently notes that an initiate into the Essenes 'is made to swear tremendous oaths' (*War* 2.139).

- In his *Res gestae* (3.3), Augustus claims 'the number of Roman citizens who bound themselves to me by military oath (ὅρκον) was about 500,000'.[27]
- 32 BCE: in his war against Antony, Octavian/Augustus declares that 'the whole of Italy voluntarily took an oath of allegiance to me and demanded me as its leader in the war in which I was victorious at Actium. The provinces of the Spains, the Gauls, Africa, Sicily, and Sardinia took the same oath of allegiance' (*Res gestae* 25.2). Dio (50.6.6) adds that 'such was the zeal of both sides alike that the alliances which they made with the two leaders were cemented by oaths of allegiance'.[28]
- c. 21–20 BCE: Herod imposed harsh restrictions and punishments on a resistant populace and required an oath of loyalty: 'As for the rest of the populace, he demanded that they submit to taking an oath of loyalty (ὅρκοις), and he compelled them to make a sworn declaration that they would maintain a friendly attitude to his rule. Now most of the people yielded to his demand out of complaisance or fear, but those who showed some spirit and objected to compulsion he got rid of by every possible means' (Josephus, *Ant.* 15.368-69).[29] Josephus notes that Herod exempted the Essenes from taking this oath (*Ant.* 15.371), explaining elsewhere that 'any word of theirs has more force than an oath; swearing they avoid, regarding it as worse than perjury (τῆς ἐπιορκίας)' (*War* 2.135).[30] This reported attitude of the Essenes strongly resembles the teaching of the Matthaean Jesus.
- c. 6 BCE: Josephus narrates an oath of loyalty to Augustus when 'the whole Jewish people affirmed by an oath (ὅρκων) that it would be loyal to Caesar and to the king's government'. Some, whom Josephus identifies as Pharisees, 'over six thousand in number, refused to take this oath, and … the king punished them with a fine' (*Ant.* 17.42).[31]

27. Velleius Paterculus, *Compendium of Roman History. Res Gestae Divi Augusti* (trans. Frederick W. Shipley; LCL, 152; Cambridge, MA: Harvard University Press, 1924).

28. Rosalinde Kearsley, 'Triumviral Politics, the Oath of 32 B.C. and the Veterans', *Classical Quarterly* 63 (2013), pp. 828-34.

29. Josephus. *Jewish Antiquities, Volume VI: Books 14-15* (trans. Ralph Marcus and Allen Wikgren; LCL, 489; Cambridge, MA: Harvard University Press, 1943).

30. In *Ant.* 8.17-20, Josephus narrates the story of Shimei, whose submission and obedience King Solomon binds with an oath. When Shimei commits perjury, Solomon orders his death.

31. Josephus. *Jewish Antiquities, Volume VII: Books 16-17* (trans. Ralph Marcus and Allen Wikgren; LCL, 410; Cambridge, MA: Harvard University Press, 1963). For further discussion, see Sørensen, 'Herod's Oath'.

- 6/5 BCE or 3/2 BCE: the inhabitants of the island of Samos in the eastern Aegean swear an oath to Augustus in gratitude for his gift of freedom to the island (Dio 54.9.7).[32]
- 6/5 BCE: 'an oath to Augustus and the male members of his family' was sworn in the 'western part of the empire' in the town of Conobaria in Baetica, one of the three provinces in Hispania.[33] González argues that the oath recognizes the introduction of Augustus's sons, Gaius and Lucius, to political life, and expresses the population's 'willingness to fight for the *salus*, *honos*, and *victoria* of its Emperor and his sons and heirs'.[34]
- 3 BCE: Paphlagonia, specifically Phazimon, on the southern shore of the Black Sea, with Galatia to the south, Pontus to the east and Bithynia in the west, was absorbed into Roman rule in 65 BCE by Pompey Magnus. In 3 BCE, Paphlagonia became a province. Representatives from its cities swore allegiance to Augustus in the capital and then dispersed to administer the oath to 'all throughout the regions in the countryside at the temples to Augustus by the altars to Augustus'. The oath in Greek to be loyal 'all through my life, both in word and deed and thought' is sworn to 'Zeus, Earth, Sun, all the gods and goddesses, and to Augustus himself'.[35]
- 11 CE: the people of Narbonese in Gaul took a vow to Augustus, his wife, children and clan, and committed to his honouring in various cultic activities including an annual sacrifice and offerings of incense and wine.[36]
- 2/17 CE: Livy attributes the following oath-taking scene to Scipio Africanus before his defeat of Hannibal in 202 BCE:

> With a few accompanying him, Scipio then made for Metellus' quarters. Finding there in a meeting the young men about whom he been told, he held his unsheathed sword over their heads as they conferred and exclaimed: 'I swear that I shall not myself abandon the republic of the Roman people nor will I allow any other Roman citizen to do so, either. If I knowingly lie, then, Jupiter Optimus Maximus, visit the most terrible destruction on my home, my family and my possessions! I demand that you ... take this oath using these words of mine. Anyone not swearing—let him know that this sword is drawn against him!' Just as frightened as if they were looking

---

32. Herrmann, *Der Kaisereid*, pp. 95-96, 125-26.

33. Julián González, 'The First Oath Pro Salvte Avgvsti in Baetica', *Zeitschrift für Papyrologie und Epigraphik* 72 (1988), pp. 113-27 (114).

34. González, 'First Oath', pp. 122-23, 125.

35. For the Greek text, see *ILS* 8781; Herrmann, *Der Kaisereid*, pp. 123-24, 128; English translations in Robert Sherk, *The Roman Empire: Augustus to Hadrian* (Translated Documents of Greece and Rome, 6; Cambridge: Cambridge University Press, 1988), p. 31; Tim Parkin and Arthur Pomeroy, *Roman Social History: A Sourcebook* (London: Routledge, 2007), p. 9; for further discussion, see Herrmann, *Der Kaisereid*, pp. 96-99.

36. Sherk, *Roman Empire*, pp. 12-13.

upon the victorious Hannibal, they all took the oath and put themselves in
Scipio's charge. (Livy, 22.53.10-12).[37]

- 14 CE: A Greek inscription in Palaipaphos, Cyprus, begins with the names
of numerous gods and goddesses including Aphrodite and Caesar Augustus. Plural language signifies the communal nature of the oath, whereby
'we, ourselves and our children swear' obedience and loyalty to Tiberius Caesar Augustus and 'the sons of his blood'. It concludes by curs-
ing those who commit perjury. Mitford proposes the oath marks Tiberius
becoming emperor in 14 CE.[38]
- 14 CE: Tacitus (*Ann* 1.7.1)[39] writes that on Tiberius's accession, 'the con-
suls, Sextus Pompeius and Sextus Appuleius, first took the oath of allegiance to Tiberius Caesar … The senators, the soldiers, and the populace
followed.'
- 37 CE: the Roman governor of Syria, Vitellius, 'administered to the people an oath of loyalty (ὥρκισεν) to Gaius' after Tiberius's death (Josephus, *Ant* 18.124).
- 37 CE: Aritium in the Iberian province of Lusitania (contemporary Por-
tugal) swears an oath of allegiance in Latin to emperor Gaius Caligula.[40]
They swear to be enemies of those who are Gaius's enemies and utter a
curse on themselves if they commit perjury.
- 37 CE: the inhabitants of Assos, also known as Apollonia, in the Troad
region on the coast of Asia Minor (contemporary Turkey), swear an oath
of allegiance in Greek to Gaius Caligula.[41] Preceding this oath is a decree
passed by the local senate and approved by the local Roman authorities.
- 37-41 CE: in Sestinum in Umbria, an undated oath in Latin probably
expresses loyalty to Gaius.[42]
- 69 CE: Suetonius (*Galba* 16)[43] narrates that the army in Upper Germany
refused to swear the annual oath of loyalty to Galba but swore instead to

---

37. Livy. *History of Rome, Volume V: Books 21–22* (ed. and trans. J.C. Yardley;
LCL, 233; Cambridge, MA: Harvard University Press, 2019).

38. T.B. Mitford, 'A Cypriot Oath of Allegiance to Tiberius', *Journal of Roman
Studies* 50 (1960), pp. 75-79 (79); Herrmann, *Der Kaisereid*, pp. 124-25.

39. Tacitus, *Histories: Books 4-5. Annals: Books 1-3* (trans. Clifford H. Moore and
John Jackson; LCL, 249; Cambridge, MA: Harvard University Press, 1931).

40. For the Greek text, see E. Mary Smallwood, *Documents Illustrating the Principates of Gaius, Claudius and Nero* (Cambridge: Cambridge University Press, 1967),
pp. 28-29; Herrmann, *Der Kaisereid*, p. 122; for the English translation, see Sherk, *The
Roman Empire*, pp. 78-79.

41. For the Greek text, see Smallwood, *Documents*, p. 29; Herrmann, *Der Kaisereid*,
p. 123.

42. Herrmann, *Der Kaisereid*, p. 122.

43. Suetonius, *Lives of the Caesars, Volume II* (trans. J.C. Rolfe; LCL, 38; Cambridge, MA: Harvard University Press, 1914).

the senate. Tacitus attests similar instability concerning military oaths to both Galba (*Hist.* 1.12.1; 55; 56.2) and Otho (*Hist.* 1.76).[44]

- c.70 CE: in Corsica, leaders and the populace swear a (short-lived) oath of allegiance to Vitellius (Tacitus, *Hist.* 2.16).

- 82–84 CE, the incomplete municipal charter of Salpensa in Baetica, one of the three provinces in Hispania, includes instructions for the leading magistrates of the town, the duoviri, aediles and quaestors to swear an oath 'before the public assembly by Jupiter and the deified Augustus and the deified Claudius and the deified Vespasianus Augustus and the deified Titus Augustus and the tutelary deity of Domitianus Augustus and the Penates gods' to govern in accordance with the charter.[45]

- 110–113 CE: Pliny, imperial governor of the provinces of Bithynia and Pontus, informs the emperor Trajan that 'We have made our annual vows, Sir, to ensure your safety and thereby that of the State, and discharged our vows for the past year, with prayers to the gods'. Trajan replies, 'I was glad to hear from your letter, my dear Pliny, that you and the provincials have discharged your vows to the immortal gods on behalf of my health and safety, and have renewed them for the coming year' (*Letters* 10.35-36).[46] Subsequently. Pliny assures Trajan that he has administered 'the oath of allegiance to your fellow-soldiers in the usual form, and found the provincials eager to take it, too, as a proof of their loyalty' (10.52). The exchange attests an annual oath of loyalty to the emperor taken by the inhabitants of Bithynia and Pontus, along with a separate oath of loyalty taken by soldiers.[47]

---

44. Tacitus, *Histories: Books 1-3* (trans. Clifford H. Moore; LCL, 111; Cambridge, MA: Harvard University Press, 1925).

45. For the English text, see Sherk, *The Roman Empire*, pp. 138-40; for the Greek text, see M. McCrum and A.G. Woodward, *Select Documents of the Principates of the Flavian Emperors* (Cambridge: Cambridge University Press, 1961), pp. 123-26.

46. Pliny the Younger, *Letters, Volume I: Books 1-7* (trans. Betty Radice; LCL, 55; Cambridge, MA: Harvard University Press, 1969).

47. Should Acts 17.7—'(of) the decrees of the emperor' (τῶν δογμάτων Καίαρος)—be included? Burnett (*Studying the New Testament*, pp. 97-120) thinks not, arguing that the phrase refers to 'imperial decrees or letters from Roman emperors … confirming' the privilege of being a 'free' city (p. 97) that was granted by Antony c. 42 BCE. This argument, though, is questionable. Burnett cannot produce any evidence from Thessalonica for such letters across some 100–140 years ('must have' and 'it is probable' dominate the discussion, pp. 118-19). If the Greek phrase was translated as an objective genitive ('decrees concerning Caesar'), it would refer to practices of honouring the emperor fostered by the city's elites. What might such decrees require? Sacrifices? Games? Oaths of loyalty? The lack of a material record neither confirms nor negates the possibility of oaths.

These instances of oath-swearing, often with punishments for perjury, attest a lengthy tradition of swearing political-military oaths of loyalty. By historical accident, the scripts of some of these oaths have survived. The scripts are not uniform in wording or content, but three features commonly occur.[48] First, oaths usually begin by detailing the gods and goddesses along with the imperial figures by and to whom the oath is sworn. Second, the oath of loyalty follows. And third, those who swear the oath curse themselves and their descendants with destruction if they commit perjury.

These three elements are evident, for example, in the oath taken in Paphlagonia to Augustus in 3 BCE.[49] First, the oath is sworn to 'Zeus, Earth, Sun, all the gods and goddesses, and to Augustus himself'. Next, the swearer pledges, 'I will be loyal to Caesar Augustus, his children and descendants all through my life, both in word, deed, and thought, holding as friends those they hold as friends and considering those as enemies whom they judge to be such'. The swearer then promises to report any plotting against the emperor and to defend the emperor's household 'with arms and steel'. Finally, the swearer declares grave consequences for perjury: 'If I should do anything contrary to this oath or fail to follow up what I have sworn, I impose a curse on myself encompassing the destruction and total extinction of my body, soul, life, children, my entire family, and everything essential ... and may neither earth nor sea receive the bodies of my family and descendants nor bear fruit for them'.

The same three elements comprise the oath of loyalty to the new emperor Tiberius, sworn in 14 CE at Palaipaphos, Cyprus. First, the list of deities by whom the oath is sworn is extensive. It includes local gods and goddesses, identified by the adjective 'our own', along with imperial Roman figures 'the God Caesar Augustus, Rome the Everlasting, and all other Gods and Goddesses'. Second, the oath itself promises 'to harken unto and to obey alike by land and sea, to regard with loyalty and to worship Tiberius Caesar Augustus ... and to the sons of his blood—to these only together with the other gods, and to none other at all'. The same commitment is made to have the same friends and foes as Tiberius. Finally, the oath ends with the concern for perjury: 'If we keep this oath, may prosperity be ours; if we break it, may the opposite befall us'.[50]

There are, of course, variations. The example cited above from Livy concerning Scipio Africanus lacks the first item but includes items two and three. The concern about perjury calls on 'Jupiter Optimus Maximus' to visit destruction on 'my home, my family, and my possessions'. This is similar to the oath made to Gaius Caligula taken at Aritium, with various gods and

---

48. González, 'First Oath', p. 126; Mitford, 'Cypriot Oath', p. 76.
49. Citing Parkin and Pomeroy, *Roman Social History*, p. 9.
50. Mitford, 'Cypriot Oath', p. 79.

goddesses evoked in relation to perjury.[51] Swearers declare to be enemies of Gaius Caligula's enemies and promise to pursue anyone who threatens him 'with armed might and war of extermination'. The concern with perjury follows: 'If knowingly I swear or will swear falsely, may Jupiter Best and Greatest and the deified Augustus and all the other immortal gods deprive me and my children of our motherland, our safety and all our fortunes'.

This discussion has established two points of intertextuality with the Matthaean Jesus's ban of oaths and perjury. First, it has demonstrated a lengthy and widespread practice of political oath-taking, particularly in the form of oaths of loyalty sworn both to and by emperors. The surviving materials confirm political oaths of loyalty taken across the empire, spanning over a century, sometimes involving soldiers and often involving the whole populace. Occasions for the oaths involve aligning with one party in power struggles; acknowledging transitions in power and expressing loyalty to a new ruler; renewing loyalty to the emperor perhaps annually; and signalling appreciation for imperial benefactions.

Second, this imperial tradition of oaths of loyalty foregrounds the danger and risks of perjury. Swearers announce severe curses of destruction on themselves, family members and descendants if they fail to keep their oaths and if they should ally with the ruler's enemies. This concern with perjury is a standard feature in the texts of political oaths of loyalty.

While the historical record (both literary references and material artifacts) attests this political practice of oath-taking, questions remain. It is not clear if such oaths were occasional and associated only with liminal moments of transitions of power and rule. Nor is it clear if they were widely and regularly (perhaps annually?) taken by inhabitants across the empire. Pliny indicates an annual event not only in his provinces of Bithynia and Pontus, but, as he assures Trajan, 'everywhere the oath is being taken for you' (*Pan.* 68.5-6).[52] Does Pliny reflect an actual practice here, or does he engage in a rhetorical performance to enhance his standing with the emperor? It is unclear if the practice of Pliny's provinces was normative for (all) other regions of the empire. The partial nature of the material and literary record might reflect sporadic oath-taking practices, or it might indicate a practice so normative, common and pervasive as to be unremarkable in surviving inscriptional and literary sources.

Nevertheless, the surviving record, surely partial after several millennia, reasonably points to a common cultural practice with which hearers of Matthew's Gospel would be familiar.

---

51. Sherk, *The Roman Empire*, pp. 78-79.
52. Pliny the Younger, *Letters, Volume II: Books 8-10. Panegyricus* (trans. Betty Radice; LCL, 59; Cambridge, MA: Harvard University Press, 1969).

Intertextuality with Matthew's Prohibition of Oaths

What, then, might be the intertextuality between the Matthaean Jesus's prohibition of oaths and perjury and this cultural-imperial practice? What are the societal or practical implications of the prohibition? Is it politically practical or naïvely idealistic? How are Jesus-followers to engage the body politic where oath-swearing is commonplace? Were they required to swear oaths of loyalty on the accession of new emperors: Titus (79 CE), Domitian (81 CE), Nerva (96 CE) and Trajan (98 CE)? Pliny assures the emperor Trajan that 'everyone' swore the annual oaths of loyalty; did Jesus-followers participate? In the considerable tumult in Syrian Antioch after 70 CE, there was widespread hatred of and violence against Jews, accusations against Jews for plotting to burn the city, demands that Jews sacrifice (to whom is not specified), and demands for their exclusion from the city and for the abolition of their rights (Josephus, *War* 7.47-61, 103, 108-11). In this fraught context, was an oath of loyalty to the emperor administered? If so, what did Jewish Jesus-followers do? Did Jesus-followers swear oaths of loyalty in trade associations while offering sacrifices or participating in the associations' meals?[53]

We do not have definitive answers though we might suggest possible strategies. Perhaps some Jesus-followers favoured social cooperation and therefore disregarded the teaching of the Matthaean Jesus, instead swearing oaths to the emperor without perceiving any incongruity and offering heartfelt allegiance. Perhaps others also disregarded the teaching by approaching oath-swearing pragmatically as necessary for maintaining neighbourly relationships, complying outwardly but with no commitment of heart to the empire. Perhaps some adopted the sorts of practices Philo commends:

> The oath should be by a father and mother, their good health and welfare if they are alive, their memory if they are dead. (*Spec. Leg.* 2.1.2)
> Some, if they are ever forced to swear, raise qualms not only in the spectators but even in those who are administering the oath; such people are in the habit of saying 'Yes, by—' or 'No, by—' and add nothing more, and by thus breaking off suggest the clear sense of an oath without actually making it. (*Spec. Leg.* 2.1.4)

We cannot assume a monolithic practice for negotiating oath-taking. Whichever political-imperial options were taken, the Gospel's author in idealistic mode prohibits them. Whenever oaths to and by the emperor are required, Jesus-followers are not to swear and thereby avoid perjury. Matthew does not give consideration to the dangers or penalties that might await the nonswearer.

---

53. Philip Harland, *Associations, Synagogues, and Congregations: Claiming a Place in Mediterranean Society* (Minneapolis, MN: Augsburg Fortress, 2003), pp. 115-36.

The Gospel offers at least two justifications for this idealized prohibition. First is the factor of allegiance. Jesus-followers are to live from (4.17) and to (6.33) the empire of the heavens. Swearing loyalty to and by the emperor entangles Jesus-followers in the divinely sanctioned imperial claims and powers of sovereignty and rule that are contrary to the present and future empire of heaven manifested by Jesus. Heaven is the throne or centre of God's rule (5.34). Jesus-followers who swear oaths by the emperor and the imperial gods express loyalty where it does not belong. They engage in idolatry and polytheism.

A second justification consists of an argument from character. This section of the pericope finally dismisses oaths and perjury with the appeal to practice truthful, nondeceptive, and authentic speech. A 'yes' is to be yes; a 'no' is to be no (5.37). Such 'purity' of speech is possible only for those with purity of heart, whose very beings are centred on God, and whose souls have renounced evil (Mt. 5.5; cf. Ps. 24.1-6). The heart signifies a person's commitments or treasure (Mt. 6.21). From the heart proceeds evil (15.21) or good fruit (7.15-20). Such commitment, the basis for integrity of character, renders oath-taking and perjury redundant. Whether an imperial agent is going to accept such an idealized approach to political-imperial discourse is not known.

It is significant to note that the pericope does not forbid involvement in the imperial body politic but shapes how involvement is to be conducted. Forbidding oaths does not mean rejection of the imperial body politic, nor does it urge a life of retreat and disengagement. Rather, Jesus-followers can participate, with integrity of character, with truthful speech *and* without oaths. There is no textual recognition of the impracticability of the prohibition on political-imperial oath-swearing. Yet an important task remains: negotiating the oath-swearing imperial world and determining appropriate practices for followers of one crucified by the empire and one who announced an alternative empire (βασιλεία). While the Matthaean prohibition aligns with various aversions to oaths and perjury,[54] the discourse of the Jesus-movement regarding participation in imperial culture and taking oaths is diverse.

The writer of Revelation, for example, is extreme in urging the impractical solution of retreat from all imperial involvements. The writer forbids eating food offered to idols and uses the metaphor of 'fornication' found for

---

54. For example, Cicero values character over a ritualized oath (*Pro Balbo* 5), Ps.-Phoc. (*Sent.* 16) declares 'Do not commit perjury, neither ignorantly nor willingly; the immortal God hates a perjuror' (trans. P.W. Van Der Horst; in James H. Charlesworth (ed.), *The Old Testament Pseudepigrapha. Volume 2. Expansions of the 'Old Testament' and Legends, Wisdom and Philosophical Literature, Prayers, Psalms, and Odes, Fragments of Lost Judeo-Hellenistic Works* [New York: Doubleday, 1985], p. 574). According to Josephus, Essenes do not swear oaths (*War* 2.135).

example in Ps. 106.35-39 to signify forbidden participation in Gentile/impe-
rial idolatrous cultures. The writer calls Jesus-followers to 'come out' from
an imploding and condemned empire (Rev. 6.1-8; 18, esp. 18.4).[55] Revelation also attacks the woman who leads the church in Thyatira for her apparent active support of participation in imperial society (Rev. 2.18-29). Yet
other writings take a vastly different approach. They assume and endorse
active participation in imperial society, including praying for (1 Tim. 2.1-
2) and being subject and obedient to rulers (Tit. 3.1). The epistle of 1 Pet.
2.14-17 goes further by urging Jesus-followers to participate in all practices
(without exception!) that honour the emperor.[56]

In Mt. 5.33-37, the Matthaean Jesus is somewhere in-between these
divergent positions. This idealized ban on oaths and perjury suggests a
retreat that is in line with Revelation's advocacy. But by urging integrity of
speech, the Matthaean scene is more permissive (and challenging) in that it
allows for participation in the body politic even though it does not engage
with the problematic pragmatics of this ban. The rest of Matthew 5 recognizes continuing socio-political interaction (5.21-26, marriage, sex and
divorce; 5.27-32, 38-48, engagements with oppressive power and conflict)
as do subsequent chapters, such as the double references to taxes (17.24-27;
22.15-22).

Conclusion

This chapter has examined possible intertextualities between the Matthaean
Jesus's ban on oaths and perjury and the participation of Jesus-followers in
the body politic. A long tradition attests oaths of loyalty to rulers and emperors that include severe punishment on those who commit perjury. As part of
this discourse, the Matthaean prohibition on oath-swearing and perjury is
idealistic without regard for its pragmatic implications in the body politic.
The chapter explores possible ways in which Jesus-followers might have
negotiated such a situation.

---

55. Anna Bowden, *Revelation and the Marble Economy of Roman Ephesus: A
People's History* (Lanham, MD: Lexington Fortress Academic; Rowman & Littlefield,
2021); Warren Carter, *What Does Revelation Reveal? Unlocking the Mystery* (Nashville,
TN: Abingdon, 2011).

56. Warren Carter, 'Going all the Way? Honoring the Emperor and Sacrificing Wives
and Slaves in 1 Peter 2:13–3:6', in *A Feminist Companion to the Catholic Epistles and
Hebrews* (ed. Amy-Jill Levine; Sheffield: Sheffield Academic Press, 2004), pp. 13-43.

3

WHEN MASTERS LIE DOWN WITH DOGS: BEING CHURCH IN A POST-SECULAR SOCIETY

Anita Monro

Introduction

There are two mentions of dogs in the Gospel of Matthew. Toward the end of the Sermon on the Mount, the crowds are exhorted not to 'give what is holy to dogs' (Mt. 7.6);[1] and at the heart of the Gospel, the Canaanite woman challenges Jesus on whether or not it is 'fair to take the children's food and throw it to the dogs' (Mt. 15.26-27). Both passages are concerned with determining what is appropriate for which people. Both passages have long histories of interpretation considering these questions and the way in which Jesus's particular approach(es) should be understood.[2]

My consideration of these passages occurs in the context of a society that is largely regarded as secular, or at least operating on secular principles given a multi-faith and multi-perspectival population. The first results of the 2021 Australian census data reveal a decrease in religiosity and specifically in Christian affiliation. No religious affiliation is reported by 38.9% of the population, an increase from 30.1% recorded in the 2016 census. Only 43.9% of the population identify as Christian, a decrease from 52.1% recorded in the 2016 census. After Christianity, the next five most significant religious affiliations are Islam, Hinduism, Buddhism, Sikhism and Judaism.[3]

---

1. All biblical quotes are from the NRSV.
2. See, e.g., Nancy Klancher, *Constructing Christian Identities, One Canaanite Woman at a Time: Studies in the Reception of Matthew 15:21-28* (PhD diss., University of Pittsburgh, 2012).
3. Australian Bureau of Statistics, 'Snapshot of Australia: National Data Summary', 28 June 2022, https://www.abs.gov.au/statistics/people/people-and-communities/snapshot-australia/2021#religious-affiliation.

In this context, the question of power and identity between religious and non-religious, Christian and non-Christian, and secular and non-secular people is somewhat fraught. As a society whose laws and institutions are still largely based in Western traditions, Australian cultural norms and values have been significantly influenced and formed by and through Christianity. In the face of significant contemporary issues, including climate justice, recognition of Indigenous peoples, and diversity of gender identity and sexual expression, Christians locate themselves across the spectrum of attitudes toward these concerns. In a democratic society, the contributions of all citizens to public debate is imperative. In contemporary Australian public life, then, the primacy of the church's voice cannot be claimed. Yet even more anomalous from certain Christian perspectives is the judgment of public debate and scrutiny that the church's witness is not necessarily virtuous, preferred or correct, and not without reason.[4]

The two mentions of dogs in the Gospel of Matthew and the context of their concerns about who is 'in' and who is 'out', or what is appropriate and what is not, lend themselves to a contemporary theological exploration of the church's role in secular society for two reasons. First, the passages themselves appear to be at odds with each other. Matthew 7.6 enjoins listeners not to 'give what is holy to dogs', while Mt. 15.26-27 appears to allow exactly that. This juxtaposition complicates the interpretation of the idea of people being 'in' or 'out', and the nature of what is appropriate or not in the Gospel. Second, the Christian church finds itself in an ambiguous place in secular Australian society. In previous times since European colonization, the church held considerable political and moral authority. The Sunday sermons of prominent Christian leaders were reported weekly in Australian newspapers, and Christian leaders featured in public debate. In the early days of the European colonization of Australia, Christian clergy also functioned as judicial authorities. In more recent times, the church's presence has often been received as outdated at best, largely hypocritical and outright abusive and destructive at worst. Those who were once received as 'masters' have become 'dogs' in certain social and political contexts, and the church cast as a 'dog' often struggles to regain mastery of itself let alone mastery of a public voice.

Riffing on the two key mentions of dogs in the Gospel of Matthew, then, this article considers interpretations of these passages by feminist, postmodern, postcolonial, intersectional and queer scholars to explore this ambiguous role of the Christian church in secular society. Who are the 'masters' and who are the 'dogs'? What is each entitled to? Who needs to rethink

---

4. See, e.g., Commonwealth of Australia, Royal Commission into Institutional Responses to Child Sexual Abuse, *Final Report* (Barton: Attorney-General's Department, 2017), https://www.childabuseroyalcommission.gov.au/final-report.

their approach(es) to the other? Where does each go from here in an increasingly diversified society that refuses to treat some as 'masters' and some as 'dogs'? That riffing occurs over the bass line of a poststructuralist understanding of identity formation and assignment as inherently dualistic. The disruption and destabilization of dualistic identities is therefore required for more adequate understandings of the 'real' complexity of both individual subjectivity and social relationships. The riffing culminates in an integration of the role of divine scapegoating in Christian theology as outlined by René Girard and supplemented by Martha Reineke, who draws on the work of Julia Kristeva. This integration highlights that an ecclesial recognition of shared animality is essential both to respectful involvement by the church in public debate and to an effective participation in post-secular contexts.

Defining the Secular and Considering the Post-Secular

Jürgen Habermas notes that an understanding of secularism as concomitant with modernization is underpinned by a trifold assessment of the nature of the secular. First, meaning-making is anthropocentric and devoid of metaphysical explanations. Second, social subsystems are functionally differentiated, with religion and related metaphysical understandings being relegated to the private domain. Finally, the existential need for metaphysics is diminished in the face of 'a reduction of risks in life' due to scientific advances.[5] Notwithstanding the threats of climate change and pandemics, these three criteria, particularly the last, rest on a population believing that it has some scientific, functional and reasonably secure basis for controlling a satisfactory future for itself. In Habermas's understanding, it is only affluent societies in Europe, Canada, Australia and Aotearoa New Zealand that might be determined as being somewhat successful on the path of secularisation given that requirement.[6]

If secularism is marked by a decline in religiosity and religious power and influence, then the imperative for a post-secularism is informed by a realization that the power and influence of religious perspectives cannot be ignored or denied. Habermas observes a global religious resurgence characterized by 'missionary expansion', 'fundamental radicalisation' and the 'political instrumentalization of the potential for violence innate in many of the world religions'.[7] The impact of this resurgence in highlighting the ongoing role of religious perspectives, even in secular contexts, is demonstrated in the attribution of certain global conflicts to religious differences,

---

5. Jürgen Habermas, 'Notes on Post-Secular Society', *New Perspectives Quarterly* 25 (2008), pp. 17-29 (17-18).
6. Habermas, 'Notes', p. 17.
7. Habermas, 'Notes', p. 18.

the continuing significance of religious voices in debates on certain moral and ethical issues (e.g. abortion and euthanasia) and the 'painful process of transformation' of secular societies into 'postcolonial immigrant societies'.[8]

In that context, then, for Habermas, a move to post-secularism is required by two imperatives of democratic, civil society. First, citizens must be able to express themselves in the political domain from their own contexts and perspectives and in their own languages in a civil, democratic manner. Second, 'the democratic state must not preemptively reduce the polyphonic complexity of the public voice'.[9] Such a post-secularity requires the state to 'guarantee its citizens equal freedom … under the proviso they no longer barricade themselves within their … communities'.[10] Similarly, '[a]ll sub-cultures, whether religious or not, are expected to free their individual members from their embrace so that these citizens can *mutually recognise* one another in civil society as members of *one and the same* political community'.[11] In this way, 'democratic government, civil society and subcultural self-maintenance' must seek to work together to balance the 'universalist project of political secularism' with the 'particularist sensibilities of a correctly conceived multiculturalism'.[12] For Habermas, these contrasting impetuses operate in mutual complementarity in a properly constituted contemporary post-secular state.[13] Such a state legally implements and publicly justifies all norms in 'a language that all citizens can understand' without precluding 'the permissibility of religious utterances within the political public sphere, as long as the institutionalized decision-making process at the parliamentary, court, governmental and administrative levels remains clearly separated from the informal flows of political communication and option formation among the broader public of citizens'.[14] The would-be secular state in a post-secular context is confronted by the necessity of maintaining a singular political identity that is informed by a multiplicity of perspectives. All actors within that state are equally confronted by the need for ambiguity in operating from *particular perspectives* for the sake of the state's *universal* politic, and from *a universal perspective* for the sake of the *particularity* of subcultures within it. Such a complex mode of operating defies simplistic dichotomization that informs much of human meaning-making.

8. Habermas, 'Notes', p. 20.
9. Habermas, 'Notes', pp. 28-29.
10. Habermas, 'Notes', pp. 22-23.
11. Habermas, 'Notes', pp. 22-23.
12. Habermas, 'Notes', pp. 22-23.
13. Habermas, 'Notes', pp. 22-23.
14. Habermas, 'Notes', p. 28.

Identity, Dualism and Ambiguity

From a post-structuralist perspective, identities are formed through a process of being defined against other identities: 'I' am not 'you'; 'we' are not 'they'. Identities, then, are inherently dualistic and construct socio-linguistic worlds that are inherently dualistic without that dualism being actually found in the 'reality' to which they purport to refer.

Multiplicity, ambiguity and diversity disrupt set dualisms and force re-alignments of meanings and worlds. Identities remain dualistic in their origins and are constantly tempted into dualistic solidifications. Thus, attention to complexity is a means of preventing any meaning system from solidifying in an inherently false re-presentation of an extraordinarily complex 'real'.

In these two previous paragraphs, I offer a very brief summary of the theory that underpinned my doctoral thesis, supervised by Elaine Wainwright. The thesis explored the disruption of identities defined within patriarchal theological systems, where the inherent duality worked against the non-masculine, non-heterosexual and complex interpretations of subjectivity, both individual and communal. Under the nomenclature of 'poetic reading', I proposed a theological methodology and method for the ongoing disruption of potentially solidifying dualisms, providing several examples of the use of the method. These examples included readings of biblical texts, a re-development of a postmodern theological understanding of God and a strategy for providing an inclusive space for community development, Christian or otherwise.[15]

One of those examples explored the disruptions of identity found in the Matthaean story of the Canaanite woman (Mt. 15.21) based on Wainwright's textual work.[16] At the time of working on that piece, my second supervisor, Francie Oppel, a philosopher, asked Elaine and me about the role of the dog in the story. Two and a half decades later, I am returning to that question. The role of dogs in the Gospel of Matthew offers a fruitful focus for a poetic reading and the destabilization of solidified readings of the text that may entrench injustice.

The Story of the Canaanite Woman

In the centre of the Gospel of Matthew (15.21-28) and away from his home geographic location, Jesus encounters a woman. The woman is identified

15. Anita Monro, *Resurrecting Erotic Transgression: Subjecting Ambiguity in Theology* (London: Equinox, 2006).

16. Elaine Wainwright, 'A Voice from the Margin: Reading Matthew 15:21-28', in Fernando F. Segovia and Mary Ann Tolbert (eds.), *Readings from This Place, Volume 2: Social Location and Biblical Interpretation in Global Perspective* (Minneapolis, MN: Fortress Press, 1995), pp. 132-53.

as a Canaanite, an anachronistic designation to previous inhabitants of the land. She addresses Jesus in Jewish religious language as 'Lord' and 'Son of David'. She cries out for mercy for her demon-possessed daughter. Jesus does not respond. The disciples urge Jesus to send her away. Jesus indicates that his mission is directed to Israel ('the lost sheep'). The woman entreats Jesus again to help her. Jesus indicates that children's food is not for dogs. The woman argues that even dogs get leftovers. Jesus praises her faith and announces that what she wants will occur. The text reports that the daughter is healed.

This brief textual outline provides the background for unpacking the role of the dogs in this story in Matthew.

The Identity of the Dogs

In *Christianity, Globalization, and Protective Homophobia*, Kapya Kaoma identifies the defining of 'particular groups as unwelcome strangers in society' through a process of dehumanization by the naming of these groups in animalistic terms, such as 'pigs', 'dogs' and 'cockroaches'. Kaoma writes in the complex context of a postcolonial 'protective homophobia', which relies on the leftover influence of colonial institutions enhanced in their power by the increasing democratization of African societies. In this context, homophobia, connected with Christian belief, is justified in terms of homosexuality being deemed 'un-African', as complex pre-colonial, post-colonial and neo-colonial influences play off one another.[17] The enduring message of the process of dehumanization is that the 'other' is always defined as 'not me'; or in a public political context, 'not us' to the point of not being of the same substance as I am or we are. The process, its message and result are similar whether the unwelcome group is being defined by colonial status, pre-colonial identity, neo-colonial political location or sexuality.

Similar to Kaoma's observation about the dehumanization of 'unwelcome strangers' in African contexts, Amy-Jill Levine identifies the use of the term 'dogs' in Mt. 15.26-27 as a 'standard insult' found across ancient cultures.[18] As outlined briefly above, in a post-structuralist context, this kind of 'me/other' dichotomization is understood as integral to the formation of language, meaning-making and identity. 'I' am not 'the other'.[19]

---

17. Kapya Kaoma, 'Is Homosexuality an African or Un-African Human Rights Issue?' in *Christianity, Globalization, and Protective Homophobia: Democratic Contestation of Sexuality in Sub-Saharan Africa* (Cham: Springer International Publishing AG, 2017), pp. 1-13.

18. Amy-Jill Levine, 'Gospel of Matthew', in C.A. Newsom, J.E. Lapsley and S.H. Ringe (eds.), *Women's Bible Commentary* (Louisville, KY: Westminster John Knox Press, rev. edn, 2012), pp. 465-77 (474).

19. Monro, *Resurrecting Erotic Transgression*, pp.58-85.

However some interpreters choose to soften their accounts of the meaning of this passage,[20] the passage clearly invokes a contestation of power and identity using the tool of dehumanization. As Levine points out, the woman does not contest her own dehumanization. She accepts the use of the term 'dog' directed at her.[21] She is more preoccupied with the dehumanization of her daughter through demon possession. Her concern is for an 'other', her daughter. Jesus's words are the tool of the dehumanization of the woman. The woman is seeking the rehumanization of her daughter. Jesus affirms the woman's faith, but it is unclear whether she has gained human status or even joined the 'lost sheep' (v. 24). Her acceptance of herself as 'dog' not 'master' is not disputed, although the rehumanization (or at least un-demonization) of the daughter is achieved. The exchange carries strong patronizing overtones with the woman being praised for a faith that accepts her own subordinated position. The dualism between insider and outsider remains, and yet it is disrupted because the woman proves to be more faithful as an outsider 'dog' persisting in her entreaties than the disciples (and perhaps even Jesus) as insider 'sheep' ready to send the woman away or at least ignore her.

There is a profound human-animal dualism embedded in the derogatory use of the term 'dog' in this narrative. Stephen D. Moore acknowledges 'the deep logic of the narrative' and then powerfully deconstructs it by attending to the juxtaposition of the use of animal references throughout the Gospel of Matthew. Moore describes the scene as 'intensely racialized and eroticized—and ... temporarily out of joint', where 'slavish Canaan, represented as a woman, debases herself before Israel, represented by the Son of David, submissively picking up the humiliating dog epithet hurled at her' so that the 'paragon of masculinity' is then responded to appropriately by 'a social and ethnic inferior' with 'fawning obeisance'.[22]

Yet while, in this pericope, Jesus encounters the woman 'as a beast, as a dog, as a dog-woman',[23] elsewhere in the Gospel, 'the animality of the Son of Humanity'[24] is also heightened. For Moore, the 'humanity' of the Human

---

20. The reference to 'dogs' in this passage is often read as a diminuitive noun, i.e. 'little dogs', 'pet dogs' or even 'puppies'. Craig S. Keener, e.g., writes, 'Jesus probably refers to the children's pet dogs; well-to-do Greeks, unlike most Jews, could raise dogs as pets and not view them as merely troublesome rodents' (*The Gospel of Matthew: A Socio-Rhetorical Commentary* [Grand Rapids: Wm. B. Eerdmans, 2009], p. 416).

21. Levine, 'Gospel of Matthew', p. 474.

22. Stephen D. Moore, 'The Dog-Woman of Canaan and Other Animal Tales from the Gospel of Matthew', in F. Lozada and G. Carey (eds.), *Soundings in Cultural Criticism: Perspectives and Methods in Culture, Power, and Identity in the New Testament* (Minneapolis, MN: Fortress Press, 2013), pp. 57-71 (59).

23. Moore, 'Dog-Woman', p. 61.

24. Moore, 'Dog-Woman', p. 64.

One (traditionally, Son of Man) is clearly questioned in the Matthaean text. Matthew's Jesus is more homeless than foxes and birds (Mt. 8.20); an animal 'betrayed into human hands' (Mt. 17.22), eaten (Mt. 26.26) and sacrificed: 'The atrocious abuses to his person that he must endure (20:18-19; 26:67-68; 27:26-50) will threaten to cause him to slide off the lower end of the ancient Mediterranean honour/shame gradient altogether, beyond "slavish" femininity and into abject animality'.[25]

Moore connects the stories of the centurion of Capernaum (Mt. 8.5-13) and the Canaanite woman. Both characters are Gentiles who address Jesus as 'Lord', ask for healing for their children, hear a statement about Israel and are lauded for their faith. However, whereas, for Moore, Jesus's encounter with the centurion is a depiction of a meeting with 'a fellow elite male' where the authority of each is affirmed, the woman does not dispute her status as beast.[26] The centurion's humiliation before Jesus for the sake of his slave is on a different level from that of the woman, already animal, who asks for healing for her daughter. Nevertheless, both characters are involved in acts of abasement in order to achieve their desires. The centurion, an elite male as part of the Roman colonial power structure, humbles himself before Jesus, a member of a colonized people. These acts of abasement as acts of faith form part of the lead-up in Matthew to the abasement of the crucifixion of the 'Son of Man'.

Reading the contrasting comparison of the centurion and the Canaanite woman alongside Derrida's *The Beast and the Sovereign*,[27] Moore highlights the issue of sovereignty undergirding these gendered encounters. Self-sovereignty 'encapsulates the elite Greco-Roman concept of masculinity'.[28] It cannot belong to the Canaanite woman as woman. Despite Moore's assertion, it may not belong to the centurion in the act of abasement before Jesus. Ultimately, in Moore's reading, it does not belong to the 'one like a human being', the Matthaean 'Son of Man'.

Here Moore refers to the importance of the 'Son of Man' imagery in the Gospel of Matthew, translating the phrase 'Son of Man' as 'one like a human being' (also referred to as the 'Human One'). Moore traces this imagery specifically to the context of Daniel 7. Daniel dreams of 'four great beasts' brought before 'an Ancient One' who exacts judgment upon them. 'One like a human being' then presents themself before the 'Ancient One' who grants great power to this new 'beast'. The beasts and the 'one like a human being' are hybrid characters, mixtures of animal (including human)

25. Moore, 'Dog-Woman', pp. 63-64.
26. Moore, 'Dog-Woman', p.61.
27. Jacques Derrida, *The Beast and the Sovereign, Vol. 2: Seminars of Jacques Derrida 2* (trans. G. Bennington; Chicago: University of Chicago Press, 2011).
28. Moore, 'Dog-Woman', p. 62.

attributes – a lion with eagle's wings; a bear with tusks; a four-headed, four-winged monster; a multi-horned, multi-eyed creature; and the 'one like a human being'. For Moore, this hybrid 'one like a human being' is the bestial model for the Matthaean 'Son of Man', 'the real locus of abomination' in the text.[29] This 'Son of Man', like the 'one like a human being' in Daniel 7, is a manifestation of the 'hyphen between the animal, the angelic, and the divine'.[30]

For Moore, the Human One descends into the animality of cannibalistic sacrifice in Matthew's passion narrative (Mt. 26–27). This 'inhuman abomination' is executed by torture via a 'savage scourging' and 'cruel crucifixion' following 'being eaten alive by those who are closest to him' in the Last Supper scene.[31] This ultimate abasement of the expected self-sovereign male is integral to the 'anti-imperial' present/future 'imagined according to logics that lie outside the paradigmatic markers of Roman life experience': a 'queer temporality' which defies expected social conventions. Matthew's overthrowing of the expected order of power proclaims that to save and be saved from the oppression of conventionality, one must be abased or abase oneself, that is, one must become a dog. Thus, in Matthew, the master becomes beast in order to upset the order of the masters and accentuate the solidarity of the Human One with the socio-political dogs. The beast who abases itself for its child achieves the elevation of both. The identities of the masters and the dogs are completely confused in the Gospel where there are no clear conventions relating to power differentiations, and indeed where apparent contravention of previous conventions is rife.

This overturning, or at least complicating, of notions of masters and dogs in the Gospel of Matthew is reinforced if the reading of Mt. 7.6 follows the line suggested by Duffield. Duffield reads Mt. 7.6 against Mt. 7.1-5—a warning against judgmentalism—to propose that Mt. 7.6 is a development of that admonition. The 'holy things' mentioned in v. 6 are either other members of the Christian community humiliated by judgment, or what may be considered wise words of judgment by the giver that, when given, result in the giver's humiliation. Duffield cites Eduard Schweizer and Henri Nouwen in affirming that freedom from judgment and/or classification of others is key to the message of Jesus.[32] In the context of Moore's reading of animality in Matthew, the role of the dogs in both Mt. 7.6 and 15.26-27 is thus an abstract reference to the judgmental categories of an imperialist or rigid regime (religious or political) which have no significance,

29. Moore, 'Dog-Woman', p. 66.
30. Moore, 'Dog-Woman', p. 61.
31. Moore, 'Dog-Woman', p. 65.
32. Ian K. Duffield, 'Difficult Texts: Matthew 7.1-6', *Theology* 119.2 (2016), pp. 117-20.

either in the face of another's needs or with the realization that judgment on another brings judgment on oneself. The Canaanite woman challenges Jesus's words of judgment at the same time as appearing to accept them, and the 'one like a human' concedes her point. The one judged becomes the ultimate judge who declares that all are worthy. The master allows themself to be mastered and refuses to lord it over another character who crosses the boundaries between humanity and animality.

The Church in (Post)Secular Society

What, then, does all this mean for the role of the Christian church in a (post)secular society?

Lidija Novakovic considers the subversion of the dichotomies of 'the conventional distribution of power' in the Gospel of Matthew in the context of contemporary economic globalization.[33] She asserts that, in a 'world governed by military and political power and divided across ethnic and religious lines, Matthew's Gospel offers a new vision of human relationships'.[34] For Novakovic, 'Matthew 15:21-28 encourages the excluded by giving them hope that they can have equal share in the abundance of God's grace'.[35] Conversely, Duffield's reading of Mt. 7.6 falls into Novakovic's assessment of Matthew's warnings that 'those who manage to improve their conditions and find themselves in a position of power should not replicate unjust relationships'. Novakovic exhorts Christian individuals and communities to 'participate in the formation of social policies and/or elect the political structures that support the economic order that aims at serving the general well-being instead of serving just a few at the top'.[36]

While Novakovic's encouragement does not presume overt political power for the church or individual Christians, it does presume that both have the moral high ground. In contemporary Australian society, that is not the case, both in terms of historical abuses and the expectations of secularism. The unique contribution of the Christian church to contemporary public debate in Australia (notwithstanding the important research contributions of church agencies) does not conform to secular principles. It is theological, not scientific; it brings myth, belief and relational values into the public realm; and it does not adhere to an anthropocentricism that believes that we have a reasonably secure basis for controlling a satisfactory

---

33. Lidija Novakovic, '"Yet Even the Dogs Eat the Crumbs That Fall from their Masters' Table": Matthew's Gospel and Economic Globalisation', *HTS* 65.1 (2009), pp. 574-80.

34. Novakovic, 'Matthew and Economic Globalisation', p. 580.

35. Novakovic, 'Matthew and Economic Globalisation', p. 578.

36. Novakovic, 'Matthew and Economic Globalisation', p. 578.

future. Furthermore, this contribution must be conscious that the judgment of others will only result in its self-humiliation on the basis of historical and potentially ongoing abuses perpetrated by its own theology and practices. The role of the church in this context defies simplistic dichotomizations and pre-emptive judgments, particularly by the church itself.

I accept that Mt. 7.6 is a warning against judging others lest that judgment backfires, and Mt. 15.21-28 is an account of Jesus's apparent judgment on the woman and her predicament being subverted by both the woman's acceptance of and implicit challenge to that judgment. The epithet of 'dog', then, in its derogatory implications, must be one that is accepted, rejected and re-interpreted simultaneously by the church as it engages in public debate in a post-secular society. Such an approach begins in humility with respectful listening and engagement based in openness to others and to transformation in and by the process.

Gabriel Flynn explores the ongoing relevance of the 'public vision of *ressourcement*' from mid-twentieth century Catholic theology for the role of the church in a pluralistic world. *Ressourcement* refers to a 'broad confluence of intellectual and spiritual movements of renewal' within the Catholic Church during the mid-twentieth century and most notably associated with the work of Vatican II.[37] Flynn describes *ressourcement* as offering 'a living vision or renewal, dialogue, and constructive engagement with the world in every age'.[38] His final assessment focuses on the three source materials of renewal and regeneration of thought and practice, retrieval of relevant wisdom from the tradition, and attention to ecumenical voices as companions on the ecclesial journey. Flynn identifies three significant theological themes as arising from these sources: the pursuit of a communion of solidarity in love and service across the *ekklesia* (church), a hermeneutic of generosity across the *oikumene* (world), and the hope of a reconciliation that does not demand the diminishment of any in such a complex dialogue.[39] Flynn's themes are highly focused on the church and its assumed pre-eminent role even in a pluralist post-secular society. Nevertheless, they offer a significant set of theological motifs for the church engaged in such a society.

A humble openness to the other in the context of contemporary post-secular Australian society forces the church to confront its own complexity and complicity—its own animality—even as it seeks to reckon with both the animality of the other and the wider societal drive to re-examine the nature of animality. In the context of the animality of the Human One in the Gospel of Matthew, all parties must be prepared to reckon with the com-

37. Gabriel Flynn, 'The Church in a Pluralistic World: The Public Vision of *Ressourcement*', *Religions* 10.11 (2019), p. 595.
38. Flynn, 'Church in a Pluralistic World', p. 604.
39. Flynn, 'Church in a Pluralistic World', pp. 608-18.

plexity of self and others, and the possibility that animality is both redemptive as well as identity-threatening.

René Girard, in his work on mimetic theory and the motif of scapegoating in Christian theology, offers further insight. For Girard, the sacrifice of Christ is the sacrifice *of* the deity, not a sacrifice *to* the deity. This important distinction, he argues, subverts the mimetic violence that continually demands scapegoats for the sake of enforcing singular identities and perpetuating itself. For Girard, Judeo-Christian narratives, in contrast to Graeco-Roman mythology, expose the innocence of the projected scapegoat and incriminate the 'persecuting community'. Thus,

> unlike in myths, where the dramatic resolution is invariably harmonious and 'constructive', since it reflects the cathartic, purgative effect of violent unanimity, collective violence in Judeo-Christian texts produces disunion, especially emphasized in the Gospels ... The sudden intrusion of the truth destroyed a social harmony that depended on the lie of unanimous violence.[40]

The implication of Girard's assessment for ecclesial participation in the public realm aligns with the action of the Canaanite woman accepting her animality while demanding its recognition. It also accords with the action of Jesus accepting the woman's rebuke and acceding to her request. Furthermore, it supports Duffield's reading of Mt. 7.6 as a warning against judging others. Girard articulates the implications as follows: 'Each time a potential rival makes unreasonable demands of us, or what seem to us to be unreasonable demands, instead of treating him in the same manner one must yield on the issue in dispute; one must avoid escalating violence, which leads directly to scapegoating'.[41]

Now, from a feminist perspective and in recognition of the gendered nature of violence, it is important that Girard's analysis is treated carefully. Girard is actively arguing against the reinforcement of scapegoating through the use of a narrative about a vindicated scapegoat with agency, a divine-human hybrid. The narrative becomes associated with a set of religious rites. Citing Luce Irigaray, Martha Reineke notes that two substitutions occur in the construction of this sacrificial economy: 'a sacrificial victim always lies hidden from view beneath the body of another victim who is visible'[42] and religious rites (rehearsals of the sacrifice) overtake

---

40. René Girard, *The One by Whom Scandal Comes* (trans. M.B. De Bevoise; East Lansing, MI: Michigan State University Press, 2014), pp. 37-38.

41. Girard, *Scandal*, p. 41.

42. Martha Reineke, 'The Mother in Mimesis: Kristeva and Girard on Violence and the Sacred', in David R. Crownfield (ed.), *Body/Text in Julia Kristeva: Religion, Women, and Psychoanalysis* (Albany, NY: State University of New York Press, 1992), p. 67.

language (words).[43] In the context of the dualistic development of identity, conventional scapegoats are generally without agency, that is, they are always 'other'. In a dualistic gendered context, the conventional, powerless (and usually unrecognized) scapegoat is normally female. A narrative about a scapegoat with agency, who potentially functions as the victim who hides the victim, has the potential to reinforce the scapegoating mechanism if the depth of the narrative is not recognized. For this reason, accepting Girard's account of the mechanism for overturning mimetic violence by 'yielding' may be quite dangerous in a dualistic gendered context. Demanding acquiescence from a powerless victim is a tool for continued oppression. Only those who have the agency to yield may choose to do so. Further interrogation of Girard's analysis is required.

Girard's analysis holds the divine figure at the centre of the exposure of mimetic violence. The divine is scapegoated unfairly. The one with power must forgo power in order to demonstrate the futility of the power games of mimetic violence. This action of forgoing (or yielding) is a strategy for overturning the dualistic nature of singular identities and exposing their complexity. However, it is a strategy conducted from a position of power.

The scapegoated victim whose innocence is neither exposed nor even assumed finds themselves in a rather different situation. Here, the story of the Canaanite woman offers two different perspectives on the subversion of mimetic violence. If Jesus acquiesces to the demands of one less powerful, then the woman dares to claim justice by acknowledging her powerlessness to achieve it on her own. Both Jesus and the woman are displaced in this narrative, and they accept their displacement for the sake of being open to a greater complexity. In this process, the nature of the Christic presence is diffused:

> In the story, Jesus is out of place and not simply geographically. As Wainwright points out, he also does not conform to the *basileia* vision previously enunciated … The woman, displaced herself, holds the vision and re-imparts it to Jesus, performing the role of Christ herself.[44]

The result of this encounter is not mimetic violence 'without end, for no reason'.[45] but rather the exposure of that violence 'now comically reduced to an ingenious process deliberately invented to dispose of a gift, the victim, whom its givers cannot themselves hand over to a recipient, the divinity, who is forever absent'.[46] Drawing on the work of Julia Kristeva, Reineke recognizes this encounter as a 'poetic mimesis' that transgresses singular

43. Reineke, 'Mother in Mimesis', p. 68.
44. Monro, *Resurrecting Erotic Transgression*, p. 154.
45. Cf. Julia Kristeva, *Powers of Horror: An Essay in Abjection* (trans. Leon S. Roudiez; New York: Columbia University Press, 1982).
46. Girard, *Scandal*, p. 41.

identity through a process of anamnesis; this process exposes the nature of mimetic violence in a more complex way,[47] by identifying the usual (and normally hidden) scapegoated victim as the feminine other.[48] The disciples act as foils in the story to allow this exposure to occur. They are the potential narrative scapegoat victims, the 'lost sheep', rejected in favour of the actual victim, the woman/dog. The role of animality is key in displacing both the characters of Jesus and the Canaanite woman to enable this exposure to occur.

Conclusion

The church, of course, is neither divine nor an innocent victim. It behaves kyriarchally. Yet, in the context of a secular society, it is treated as 'other'. Its identity is ambiguous, rightfully so, as all identities must be understood to be.

In secular society, then, the church can only claim rightful participation and no more. Its history has provided considerable privileges that remain (e.g. property wealth), even if the political power it held in previous eras has gone. Religious perspectives were diminished in the process of secularization. In a post-secular context, the church, along with a multitude of perspectives, previously diminished on other grounds (e.g. race, gender, sexuality and socio-economic status), must rightfully voice its needs and acknowledge that it cannot participate in and of itself alone. However this simultaneous rightful voicing and acceptance of culpability (to a certain extent deserved) must be done in the context of recognizing the ambiguity of all identities in the public realm.

So, in the context of public debate, if the church seeks to follow the *basileia* vision of Jesus, enacted in the exposure of mimetic violence in the passion narrative, it must be prepared to own its ambiguity, its animality— that is, its participation in power games that have victimized others, as well as its victimization in the context of secular discourse that rejects mythological contributions. The church must recognize its right to participate as well as its inability to belong apart from the belonging of others. The church is called to operate in an intentionally relational way beyond the easy dualistic mechanisms of the legacy of mimetic violence.

47. Julia Kristeva, *Revolution in Poetic Language* (trans. Margaret Waller; New York: Columbia University Press, 1984), p. 60.
48. Reineke, 'Mother in Mimesis'.

4

THE GREATEST IN THE KINGDOM OF HEAVEN: INNER TEXTURE ANALYSIS OF MATTHEW 18.1-5

Carlos Olivares

Introduction

In the Gospel of Matthew, Jesus's disciples ask him who is the greatest in the kingdom of heaven (Mt. 18.1). Jesus responds by placing a child in their midst, inviting his disciples to become like children; otherwise they will never enter the kingdom of heaven (18.2-5). Getting in or out of the kingdom is a serious matter in Matthew (e.g. 5.3, 10, 20; 7.21; 23.13), therefore understanding what Jesus means by 'becoming like children' is significant to the Matthaean account.

Because one keyword in this pericope is 'children', scholars usually explain the passage by focusing on ancient stratified societies that locate infants at the lowest level.[1] In antiquity, they argue, children were regarded as incomplete humans,[2] subordinated and marginalized.[3] In the Graeco-Roman world, words denoting children were also used to designate slaves,[4] thus expressing the idea of obedience and submission.[5] Consequently, scholars propose that the phrase 'become like children' means that Jesus's disciples must imitate such a lack of status, adopting an attitude of dependence and humility so as to be part of the kingdom of heaven (cf. 18.4; 19.14).[6]

---

1. Susanna Asikainen, *Jesus and Other Men: Ideal Masculinities in the Synoptic Gospels* (BibInt, 159; Leiden: E.J. Brill, 2018), pp. 95-99.

2. Ulrich Luz, *Matthew 8–20* (Hermeneia; Minneapolis, MN: Augsburg, 2001), p. 428; Gustavo Gutiérrez, 'Gratuidad y fraternidad: Mateo 18', *Páginas* 25 (2000), pp. 28-36 (29).

3. Warren Carter, *Households and Discipleship: A Study of Matthew 19–20* (JSNTSup, 103; Sheffield: JSOT Press, 1994), pp. 95-113.

4. E.g. παῖς and παιδίον. See BDAG, pp. 750-51; Franco Montanari (ed.), *The Brill Dictionary of Ancient Greek* (Leiden: E.J. Brill, 2015), pp. 1521, 1523.

5. Don B. Garlington, 'Who Is the Greatest', *JETS* 53 (2010), pp. 287-316 (292-94).

6. E.g. Craig S. Keener, *The Gospel of Matthew: A Socio-Rhetorical Commentary* (Grand Rapids, MI: Eerdmans, 2009), pp. 447-48; R.T. France, *The Gospel of Matthew*

This interpretation rests on historical and socio-scientific critical grounds, establishing a literary and sociological comparative framework between Jesus's statement and ancient conventions. I do not intend to criticize these findings and their methods but to complement them by using the inner-textual approach of Vernon Robbins, who proposes listening 'to the words themselves' to explore and decode texts with the purpose of deriving meanings.[7] For my analysis of Mt. 18.1-5, I will examine how words and descriptions related to infants operate in Matthew's story, seeking to determine how the exegetical exposition of the phrase 'become like children' in the selected pericope can be built from the wider narrative itself, rather than through a historical critical lens alone.[8]

The Greatest Is the Child (Matthew 18.1-5)

Mt. 18.1-5 opens with the temporal expression, 'At that time the disciples came to Jesus and asked'(18.1).[9] This formulation links the previous scene (17.24-27), in which Jesus asks Peter about tax exemption for the children of the kings of the earth (17.25-26), with the next, where Jesus's disciples question him about the greatest in the kingdom of heaven (18.1).[10] Narratively, the disciples' enquiry emerges because Jesus has spoken earlier about the privileges of some children in the earthly realm. If there are differences between royal families and common citizens, then hierarchical distinctions also exist in the kingdom of heaven (17.24-26).[11] This raises

(NICNT; Grand Rapids, MI: Eerdmans, 2007), pp. 676-67; Warren Carter, *Matthew and the Margins: A Socio-Political and Religious Reading* (JSNTSup, 204; Sheffield: Sheffield Academic Press, 2000), pp. 362-63; Grant R. Osborne, *Matthew* (ZECNT; Grand Rapids, MI: Zondervan, 2010), p. 669; Donald A. Hagner, *Matthew 14–28* (WBC; Dallas, TX: Word Books, 1995), pp. 517-18.

7. Vernon K. Robbins, *Exploring the Texture of Texts: A Guide to Socio-Rhetorical Interpretation* (Valley Forge, PA: Trinity Press International, 1996), pp. 7-39.

8. I dedicate this article to Professor Elaine Wainwright, who was my PhD supervisor at the University of Auckland, New Zealand. I thank Elaine for all the critical and engaging dialogues and also for her pastoral and emotional support during the years I had the privilege to study under her tutelage.

9. All Bible quotations, unless otherwise indicated, are taken from the New Revised Standard Version (NRSV) translation.

10. Eunyung Lim, 'Entering the Kingdom of Heaven Not like the Sons of Earthly Kings (Matthew 17:24–18:5)', *CBQ* 83 (2021), pp. 425-45; John Nolland, *The Gospel of Matthew* (NIGTC; Grand Rapids, MI: Eerdmans, 2005), pp. 730-31; R.T. France, *The Gospel according to Matthew: An Introduction and Commentary* (TNTC; Leicester: Inter-Varsity Press, 1985), p. 273; idem, *Gospel of Matthew*, 675.

11. Charles L. Quarles, *Exegetical Guide to the Greek New Testament: Matthew* (Nashville, TN: B&H Academic, 2017), p. 206.

an important question for the disciples: is their status lower than that of the sons of earthly kings?

The Jesus of Matthew replies to their question by using the image of a child, warning his disciples that, unless they do not change and become like children, they will never enter the kingdom (18.3). In the statement, Jesus speaks a Greek word, παιδίον (18.2-5), that in the Hellenistic corpus designates a male or female child, 'normally below the age of puberty',[12] and roughly up to seven years old.[13]

For Jesus, therefore, to be transformed into children means that Jesus's disciples must humble themselves like little children, and only then will they be the greatest in the kingdom of heaven (18.4). The image of a child, in consequence, 'is an example of humility, not of innocence, nor of purity, nor of moral perfection'.[14] Contextually, Jesus himself first exemplifies the unpretentious attitude that his disciples must have in the episode of Mt. 17.24-26, by submitting to be taxed even though, as a royal son, he was technically exempt (17.25).[15] This explains why, in Jesus's view, whoever receives the childlike in his name also receives him (18.5). These 'childlike' people have become Jesus's representatives,[16] making them the greatest in the kingdom.

For Jesus, this is a serious matter. Because if people do not become like little children, they can be excluded from the kingdom of heaven (18.2, cf. 7.21-23; 21.43). Although it is not my intention to discuss the precise meaning of the phrase 'kingdom of heaven', which is difficult to determine in Matthew's Gospel, some NT scholars would agree that its 'basic emphasis is on the actual rule of God as an activity, rather than on the realm or territory over which he rules'.[17] However, since the phrase 'kingdom of heaven' in Matthew is basically equivalent to the kingdom of God (cf. 12.8; 19.24;

---

12. BDAG, p. 749.

13. Montanari, *Brill Dictionary of Ancient Greek*, p. 1521; Henry George Liddell and Robert Scott, *A Greek-English Lexicon* (Oxford: Clarendon Press, 1996), p. 1287.

14. Francis W. Beare, *The Gospel According to Matthew* (Peabody, MA: Hendrickson, 1987), p. 375.

15. Alfred Plummer, *An Exegetical Commentary on the Gospel according to S. Matthew* (London: Robert Stock, 1928), p. 248.

16. France, *Gospel of Matthew*, 679.

17. Barclay Moon Newman and Philip C. Stine, *A Handbook on the Gospel of Matthew* (New York: United Bible Societies, 1992), p. 58. For other views about the topic, see Jonathan T. Pennington, *Heaven and Earth in the Gospel of Matthew* (NovTSup, 126; Leiden: E.J. Brill, 2007); John Christopher Thomas, "The Kingdom of God in the Gospel According to Matthew," *NTS* 39 (1993), pp. 136-46; Elaine M. Wainwright, *Habitat, Human, and Holy: An Eco-Rhetorical Reading of the Gospel of Matthew* (Earth Bible Commentary, 6; Sheffield: Sheffield Phoenix Press, 2016), pp. 57-58, 72-73, 120-22.

21.31, 43),[18] the expression cannot be associated only with the present (e.g. 5.3, 10, 19; 10.7; 12.28) but also with God's eschatological sovereignty, underlying its future presence (e.g. 5.20; 7.21; 8.11; 12.31).[19]

Children in Matthew's Gospel

The above suggests the need for examining Greek terms and literary portrayals associated with children in Matthew's story, so as to understand why the Matthaean Jesus illustrates greatness in the kingdom, using a child as an example. For this analysis, I have divided this section into two parts, split around Mt. 18.1-5.

Children Mentioned before Matthew 18.1-5

Matthew's Gospel starts with a genealogy of Jesus (1.1-17). Readers learn that generations of children were begotten and born, becoming ancestors of the protagonist of the Gospel, Jesus.[20] Matthew then connects them to the story of Jesus's birth (1.18-25). After Jesus is born, Joseph, his adoptive father (1.18-24), names him (1.25). This might imply that Joseph imposes parental authority over Jesus and takes responsibility for his care. Joseph becomes Jesus's protector when later, for example, Joseph takes the boy and his mother Mary to Egypt because Herod was killing infants in and around Bethlehem, where Matthew's Jesus is initially located (2.13-23). Matthew's infancy narrative depicts Jesus in this last scene using the Greek lexeme παιδίον (2.8-9, 11, 13-14, 20-21), a term that, as I have said, signifies little children. In all these instances, Jesus the παιδίον is displaced to different locations by Joseph (2.14-15, 21-23), revealing that because of his age he depends on his parents and lives under their tutelage. Although Jesus's dis-

---

18. The expression 'kingdom of God' also occurs in Mt. 6.33. However, from a textual critical viewpoint, it is disputed. NA[28] and UBS[5] place the phrase τοῦ θεοῦ ('of God') in square brackets, establishing that there is uncertainty about whether or not it can be regarded as part of the text. For a more detailed discussion of the issues, see Bruce Metzger, *A Textual Commentary on the Greek New Testament* [Stuttgart: United Bible Societies, 2000], pp. 15-16.

19. Thomas J. Ramsdell, 'The Kingdom of Heaven in the Gospel of Matthew', *The Biblical World* 4 (1894), pp. 124-33 (124, 131-33).

20. This genealogy is redacted to emphasize Jesus's Davidic and/or royal heritage (cf. Mt. 1.1). However, in the account, all those named by Matthew are Jesus's descendants. See Jeremy Punt, 'Politics of Genealogies in the New Testament', *Neot* 47 (2013), pp. 373-98 (381-86); Keener, *Gospel of Matthew*, pp. 73-83; R.P. Nettelhorst, 'The Genealogy of Jesus', *JETS* 31 (1988), pp. 169-72; John Nolland, 'Genealogical Annotation in Genesis as Background for the Matthean Genealogy of Jesus', *TynBul* 47 (1996), pp. 115-22.

placement happens because of political circumstances (2.13, 16, 19-23), he does not have a say with regard to these relocations.

Once an adult, Jesus compares 'this generation' to little children (παιδίοις) who are shouting to each other while sitting in the marketplace (11.16):[21] 'We played the flute for you, and you did not dance; we wailed, and you did not mourn' (11.17). The illustration evokes children playing in a public place, a detail that hints to readers about a life with no adult responsibilities. Jesus's description does not necessarily establish a historical view (i.e. without child labour exploitation)[22] but probably alludes to the immaturity of a child's worldview and their lower status in Matthew's account.

Two additional allusions that occur before Matthew 18 reveal children's social standing in Matthew's Gospel. After Jesus feeds two multitudes on two distinct occasions (14.13-21; 15.32-39), the Matthaean narrator uniquely explains to readers that those who ate were five and four thousand men, 'besides women and children' (14.21; 15.38). Matthew's narrative arranges children after women, possibly because in Matthew's world, they occupy the last and lowest position.

The first time that the Matthaean Jesus uses a child to illustrate his teaching is in the Sermon on the Mount (Mt. 5–7). Jesus compares human parents to God, establishing through a metaphor that, although parents are evil, they still provide good things to their children (7.7-11). Here, Jesus employs two Greek words when telling this story: υἱός (son) and τέκνον (child) (7.9, 11). In context, both terms refer to little children.[23] Thus, since parents supply food for their children, these two words evoke a sense of parents' responsibility and children's reliance on adults.

Something similar can be implied when examining the story of a synagogue leader who comes to the Matthaean Jesus, asking him to lay hands on his daughter who has just died (9.18). Matthew designates her as θυγάτηρ, a Greek term used here to depict 'a human female in relation of child to par-

---

21. There is a textual variant in the last part of Mt. 11.16. Instead of τοῖς ἑτέροις ('to others'), a few manuscripts render τοῖς ἑταίροις αὐτῶν ('to their companions') (e.g. KJV, NKJV). In my reading I follow NA[28], which accepts the first textual option as better (cf. UBS[5]).

22. Christian Laes, 'Child Slaves at Work in Roman Antiquity', *Ancient Society* 38 (2008), pp. 235-83; Keith R. Bradley, 'Child Labour in the Roman World', *Historical Reflections* 12 (1985), pp. 311-30.

23. Cf. Mary gives birth to a son (υἱόν) (Mt. 1.21, 25), which in context refers to an infant. Likewise, after Herod killed all the infants (παῖδας) in and around Bethlehem, Matthew quotes a text from the prophet Jeremiah, in which Rachel weeps for her children (τέκνα) (Mt. 2.16-18), associating the term παιδίον with τέκνον (see also Mt. 3.9; 15.26; 18.25). On the other hand, in other contexts, τέκνον and υἱός depict adult children (see Mt. 21.28; 22.2).

ent'— in other words, a daughter.[24] Attentive readers, however, may notice that the Matthaean Jesus also calls her κοράσιον, a diminutive Greek locution for 'girl' (9.24-25). Although the age implied by the words θυγάτηρ and κοράσιον needs to be verified by context (e.g. 9.22; 10.35, 37; 14.6, 11; 15.22, 28),[25] Matthew probably portrays a scene here between an anguished father and his little daughter.

Though readers may recognize the difficulty of decoding the girl's age in this Matthaean episode, they will still observe that the scene portrays parents craving for their children's presence and well-being. This indicates that, regardless of their children's age, progenitors and guardians regard them as 'little ones', rather than grown-ups. If this assumption is correct, becoming like children in Matthew entails developing a similar parent–child relationship, which implies emotional dependency and ongoing care.

This view can also be seen in two other episodes describing parents going to Jesus for help. In one scene, a father asks Jesus to help his possessed son (υἱός) (17.15, 18), while in another a mother does the same for her daughter (θυγάτηρ) (15.22). In the first story, however, the narrator of Matthew calls the boy παῖς (17.18), a Greek noun that in this context describes a young person 'normally below the age of puberty'.[26] In doing so, Matthew's narrator clarifies that the man's son is a little child (cf. 2.16; 21.15).

For the purpose of this study, it is significant that the word παῖς can also refer to slaves in Matthew (e.g. 8.6, 8, 13; 12.18; 14.2).[27] Etymologically, several hypocoristic diminutives are derived from παῖς,[28] like the terms παιδίον and παιδίσκη. In Matthew the term παιδίον denotes only a boy (2.13-14, 20-21; 11.16; 14.21; 15.38); παιδίσκη refers to a female slave (26.69).[29] This ambiguity of παῖς in Matthew may serve to link the obedi-

---

24. BDAG, p. 460. Cf. Montanari, *Brill Dictionary of Ancient Greek*, p. 953.

25. From a canonical or redaction critical approach, readers can infer from Mk 5.42 and Lk. 8.42 that the θυγάτηρ in Matthew's Gospel is twelve years old. However, the method used in this chapter limits such an assumption.

26. BDAG, p. 750; Johannes P. Louw and Eugene Albert Nida, *Greek-English Lexicon of the New Testament: Based on Semantic Domains* (New York: United Bible Societies, 1989), p. 110.

27. The Identity of the centurion's παῖς of Mt. 8.5-13 needs to be identified by context, which in my view points to a slave. See Carlos Olivares, 'The Identity of the Centurion's *Pais* in Matthew 8:5-13: A Narrative Approach', *JAAS* 13 (2010), pp. 103-12; France, *Gospel of Matthew*, pp. 311-12, *pace* H.F.D. Starks, 'The Centurion's Παῖς', *JTS* 42 (1941), pp. 179-80; Theodore W. Jennings and Tat-siong Benny Liew, 'Mistaken Identities but Model Faith: Rereading the Centurion, the Chap, and the Christ in Matthew 8:5-13', *JBL* 123 (2004), pp. 467-94.

28. Robert Beekes and Lucien van Beek, *Etymological Dictionary of Greek* (Leiden: E.J. Brill, 2010), pp. 1142-43. See also BDAG, pp. 749-50.

29. Montanari, *Brill Dictionary of Ancient Greek*, p. 1521; Liddell and Scott, *Greek-English Lexicon*, p. 1287.

ent status of children with slaves, a literary relationship that suggests to the reader that the humility needed to enter the kingdom of heaven entails assuming the low social standing of slaves.

Children Mentioned after Matthew 18.1-5

After affirming the importance of becoming like children (18.1-5), Jesus warns his disciples against putting 'a stumbling block before one of these little ones' (18.6). Jesus defines 'little ones' as people who believe in him (18.6), referencing the humility of little children (18.1-5). The genitive plural μικρῶν τούτων ('of these little ones') in Mt. 18.6 occurred previously in ch. 10. There, Jesus affirms that 'whoever gives even a cup of cold water to one of these little ones [μικρῶν τούτων] in the name of a disciple—truly I tell you, none of these will lose their reward' (10.42). Jesus's statement not only anticipates what he asserts in Mt. 18.5 about welcoming childlike disciples, but also identifies the genitive phrase μικρῶν τούτων with Jesus's disciples (18.6; cf. 18.10, 14). If this analysis is accurate, in Mt. 18.6-9 Jesus pronounces woes against any disciple who causes childlike disciples to stumble (σκανδαλίζω).[30] For the Jesus of Mathew, these admonitions are no joking matter. It would be better, Jesus warns, for those who put a stumbling block before the little ones, 'if a great millstone were fastened around' their neck and be 'drowned in the depth of the sea' (18.6).

This figurative interpretation, however, cannot prevent readers from decoding the occurrence of children's social situation in Matthew's world. Moving beyond the metaphor, Jesus might also be condemning disciples who sexually abuse children and commit other atrocities.[31] This suggests that the 'little ones', as a symbolic representation of children, are as vulnerable as any child. As children, the little ones can be despised, forgotten, and even physically or emotionally harmed. This explains why Jesus alerts the disciples not to despise the little ones, and to search for those who go astray as lost sheep (18.12-14).

The fact of calling the disciples by the Greek adjective μικρός (little) reminds readers of what Jesus says in Matthew 11. In this chapter, Jesus considers that no one born of women is greater than John the Baptist, except 'the least [μικρότερος] in the kingdom of heaven', who are greater (μείζων) than John (11.11).[32] Jesus reveals the identity of the least (μικρότερος) in

30. W.D. Davies and Dale C. Allison, *A Critical and Exegetical Commentary on the Gospel according to Saint Matthew* (3 vols.; Edinburgh: T. & T. Clark, 1988), II, pp. 752-80; W.F. Albright and C. S. Mann, *Matthew* (AB, 26; New York: Doubleday, 1984), pp. 215-19; France, *Gospel of Matthew*, pp. 680-84; Osborne, *Matthew*, pp. 666-82; Keener, *Gospel of Matthew*, pp. 447-52.

31. Lorne R. Zelyck, "Matthew 18,1-14 and the Exposure and Sexual Abuse of Children in the Roman World," *Bib* 98 (2017), pp. 37-54.

32. To interpret why John the Baptist is not greater than the least in the kingdom

Matthew 18 by proclaiming that the greatest (μείζων) in the kingdom are the little ones (μικρός), who, while still adults, have become like children (18.1-5). Since the word 'little' (μικρός) in these contexts specifies a disciple becoming a child, one might wonder whether it is feasible that Matthew has Jesus's infancy narrative in mind, thus construing Jesus's discipleship around Jesus's own story as a child.[33] Although impossible to demonstrate, the fact that in Matthew 25 Jesus identifies himself with the least (ἐλάχιστος) in importance (25.37-40, 42-45)[34] might lead readers to perceive that the Matthaean Jesus identifies marginalized or low-status people as little ones.

In the same vein, as an echo of Mt. 18.1-5, the narrator in Mt. 19.13-15 recounts people bringing children to Jesus so he can lay his hands on them and pray (19.13). The disciples, however, scold them, to which Jesus retorts that the kingdom of heaven belongs to the little children (19.14-15). Jesus again uses the image of a child as a paradigm of what it means to be like children.[35] Jesus's disciples appear to treat the children as inferior beings for not having the same social value as adults. However, Jesus inverts this assumption, expressing children's social worth. In doing so, Jesus metaphorically links the figure of children, who do not have status in the world, with the disciple who will enter the kingdom of heaven.[36]

A final scene in which the Jesus of Matthew links children and the kingdom occurs in Matthew 21. After defending his authority before the religious leaders (21.23-27), Jesus tells the parable of a father and his two children (τέκνα). While the father orders both to go and work in the vineyard, only one obeys (21.28-32). Since the Matthaean Jesus designates these two people with the generic word τέκνον, readers cannot determine their age. However, what is significant in the parable is that the good child obeys his father. Ironically, at the beginning of the parable, the obedient child says he will not go, but afterwards he changes his mind and goes to the vineyard (21.28-29). For Jesus, the complaisant child in the parable represents the marginalized, such as tax collectors and prostitutes, who are going into the kingdom of God ahead of the religious leaders (21.31-32). In Jesus's view,

---

goes beyond the scope of this article. For further discussion, see, for example, Benedict T. Viviano, 'The Least in the Kingdom: Matthew 11:11, its Parallel in Luke 7:28 (Q), and Daniel 4:14', *CBQ* 62 (2000), pp. 41-54; Beare, *Gospel According to Matthew*, pp. 259-60; France, *Gospel of Matthew*, pp. 428-49; Keener, *Gospel of Matthew*, pp. 337-39.

33. Élian Cuvillier, 'Jésus enfant, Jésus et les enfants dans le premier évangile: und christologie du "petit"', *Lumen Vitae* 62 (2007), pp. 19-31.

34. The word ἐλάχιστος can be understood in the sense of being of the least importance. See Louw and Nida, *Greek-English Lexicon*, p. 110; BDAG, p. 314.

35. Douglas R.A. Hare, *Matthew* (IBC; Louisville, KY: John Knox Press, 1993), p. 224.

36. J.C. Fenton, *The Gospel of St. Matthew* (Harmondsworth: Penguin Books, 1963), p. 312.

therefore, childlike disciples act like the submissive child, doing the will of the Father (21.31).

Conclusion

An inner texture analysis of Matthew 1–17 depicts children being submissive to adults and relying on them for care and protection. With regard to social status, adults surpass children, and Matthew locates children last in the social hierarchy. Greek words related to children can also designate slaves, possibly evoking a low social rank of both groups in Matthew's world. In a number of texts following Mt. 18.1-5, an inner textual examination of Matthew's narrative evidences a world in which children are abused and treated as socially unimportant. For the Jesus of Matthew, they are little ones, and they metaphorically function as a paradigm of Jesus's disciples. Therefore in Matthew, Jesus's disciples need to submit to the Father's will, becoming like little children. This is the attitude that will allow them to enter the kingdom of heaven.

5

'The Lord Needs Them' (Matthew 21.3): The Gospel of Matthew's Beasts and Sovereign Christ

Tat-siong Benny Liew

Even from its very beginning, Matthew's Gospel distinguishes Jesus as one with regal pedigree and status.[1] As if introducing Jesus as 'the son of [King] David' (1.1; cf. 1.6) in Jesus's genealogy is not enough to signify his royal connection, Matthew adds in the birth narrative that Jesus himself 'has been born king of the Jews' (2.2) and moves the plot immediately into a duel between sovereigns, in which King Herod dies after failing to eliminate Jesus (2.3-20). As the Gospel concludes, Matthew's resurrected Jesus will declare majestically that '[a]ll authority in heaven and on earth has been given to [him]' (28.18). It is not an exaggeration to suggest that Matthew's Jesus is a sovereign Christ.

Perhaps surprisingly, Matthew's sovereign Christ also compares himself to animals; in fact, he presents them as faring better than he himself: 'foxes have holes, and birds of the air have nests; but the Son of Man has nowhere to lay his head' (8.20). While Martin Heidegger has famously made distinctions among the 'worldless' stone, the 'poor in world' animal, and the 'world form- ing' human,[2] Matthew's Jesus is emphasizing here his own homelessness, which may be related to his experience of being hunted by his opponents like prey. Homelessness or not feeling 'at home' for a thinker/philosopher, accord- ing to Jacques Derrida, is comparable to Heidegger's assumption that animals lack attunement to the world in which they exist.[3] Derrida does this in the

---

1. An earlier version of this chapter appears in Jione Havea (ed.), *Dissension and Tenacity: Doing Theology with Nerves* (Lanham, MD: Fortress Academic/Lexington Books, 2022). Thank you to the publisher for permission to reuse. All rights reserved.

2. Martin Heidegger, *The Fundamental Concepts of Metaphysics: World, Finitude, Solitude* (trans. William McNeil and Nicholas Walker; Bloomington, IN: Indiana Uni- versity Press, 1995), p. 177.

3. Jacques Derrida, *The Beast and the Sovereign* (ed. Michel Lisse, Marie-Louise Mallet and Ginette Michaud; trans. Geoffrey Bennington; 2 vols.; Chicago: University of Chicago Press, 2009-2011), II, pp. 93-118.

final seminar that he offered before his death—titled *The Beast and the Sovereign*—where he critiques the long and pervasive philosophical assumption that differentiates humans and animals, and also faults the 'Graeco-Judeo-Christiano-Islamic' tradition for denigrating animals.[4] Arguing that an emphasis on human sovereignty and superiority over non-human animals has led not only to the hurting and the domesticating of animals but also to the dehumanizing of other humans (particularly women, slaves, children and Indigenous people or foreigners),[5] Derrida proceeds to question what humans tend to assume about themselves, including the rigid difference between humanity and animality, and he points to the need for humans to rethink our relations with other living creatures. With the seminar taking place shortly after 9/11 in 2001, one can also see Derrida trying to think and talk about sovereignty in these pages in relation to the military aggression of the United States against Iraq. Since Derrida also suggests that a particularly strong understanding of sovereignty is 'theological', I will interrogate in this chapter how Matthew's sovereign Christ relates to animals, animality and ipseity (or the power of one's self-identity as an autonomous, self-determining subject). Following Derrida and the public conversations that his work has helped bring about, my purpose in doing so is to critique anthropocentrism and to assert the value of animal lives, especially in a time when the anthropocene has led to the ongoing mass extinction of species—what Elizabeth Kolbert has called 'the sixth extinction'.[6] For Derrida, a better way to do so is not to deny the difference between humans and animals but to multiply differences that exist among humans and among animals.[7] Most of all, he does so by challenging

---

4. Jacques Derrida, *The Animal That Therefore I Am* (trans. David Wills; New York: Fordham University Press, 2005), p. 55. Derrida's long list of targets include Aristotle, Descartes, Kant, Heidegger, Levinas and Lacan. Derrida does name a few whom he sees as being better able to complicate this rigid separation between humanity and animality, such as Plutarch, Porphyry, Montaigne, Rousseau, Bentham and Freud, though Derrida does not see any of them as having spent the time to think through the animal question.

5. Derrida, *Beast and Sovereign*, I, pp. 20, 33; II, p. xiv. See also Judith Still, *Derrida and Other Animals: The Boundaries of the Human* (Edinburgh: Edinburgh University Press, 2015), pp. 182-357; and Donna Haraway, *Simians, Cyborgs, Women: The Reinvention of Nature* (New York: Routledge, 1991), pp. 11-12, 19.

6. Elizabeth Kolbert, *The Sixth Extinction: An Unnatural History* (New York: Henry Holt and Company, 2014).

7. Derrida, *Animal*, p. 35. Derrida therefore invents the French word *animot* for 'animal' to emphasize not only the plurality within what is assumed to be singular (since the invented word sounds like the French plural for animals, *animaux*) but also the artificiality of the (unnatural) distinction that humans make between themselves and non-human animals. Derrida also uses the term 'limitrophy', or the growth, multiplication, or pluralization of limits, to describe this emphasis.

if humans 'can ever possess the *pure, rigorous, indivisible* concept' of sovereignty.[8]

Incidentally or not, questions of animality appear right after Matthew tells us about Jesus's birth, his being taken to Egypt, and his new home in Nazareth after Herod's demise in Matthew 2. In Matthew 3, John the Baptist shows up in the wilderness to 'prepare the way of the Lord' (3.3) by announcing God's judgment and calling the people to repentance. What is intriguing in light of Derrida's seminar is the Baptizer's appearance, diet, location and vocation. He is wearing 'clothing of camel hair with a leather belt around his waist' (3.4). Dressed in animal hair and animal skin, in other words, John the Baptist comes across as a savage, or a man in an animal state. While 'locusts and wild honey' (3.4) are in keeping with Jewish purity laws, they are, for lack of a better term, 'raw food,' which puts John closer to non-human animals, especially given his whereabouts. The presence of the Baptizer in the wilderness and around the Jordan, both indicators of geographical and symbolic boundaries in biblical literature, puts John on the verge between humanity and animality, but John is also presented as someone who has a special relationship to God's salvation.[9] Most significant for our consideration is the fact that Matthew's Jesus, in the words of the Baptizer, 'com[es] after' John (3.11) and travels to this boundary region to be baptized by this animal-like prophet, and receives the Holy Spirit descending and alighting on him 'like a dove' (3.13-17). Matthew's Jesus comes out of his water baptism, then, with a bird—a non-human animal—attached to him. Then he is led by the Spirit—still in the form of a bird?—further into the wilderness to be tempted by the devil (4.1)—yet another contest of power or struggle for sovereignty for Matthew's Jesus?—before he begins his proclamation, calls his disciples and heals the sick (4.12-25).

Before the publication of Derrida's seminar on *Beast and the Sovereign* in two volumes, his interest in questions about humanity's relations with non-human animals had already become obvious in *The Animal That Therefore I Am*. As is well known, the French title of this earlier book by Derrida can also be translated as *The Animal That Therefore I Follow*. In the book, Derrida reads the creation stories in Genesis 1–2, pointing out that the human who names the animals was actually created *after* the animals and asking if priority is given to the human or to the animals in these chapters.[10] In fact, Derrida recounts in this book his experience of being seen naked by

8. Derrida, *Animal*, p. 135, emphasis original.

9. This is not surprising given the long and frequent associations between animals and deities in the Graeco-Roman world. See, e.g., Emma Aston, 'Part-Animal Gods', in Gordon Lindsay (ed.), *The Oxford Handbook of Animals in Classical Thought and Life* (New York: Oxford University Press, 2014), pp. 366-83.

10. Derrida, *Animal*, pp. 14-18.

his cat and how the gaze of this animal in this unexpected encounter embarrassed him by making him aware of his nudity.[11] If, as humans have long assumed, animals are different because they don't know their nakedness and hence have neither feelings of embarrassment and shame nor need for clothing, Derrida wonders what being human means if a cat brought about his humanity by causing him to have these supposedly human realizations of nakedness and feelings of shame.

I am suggesting that something similar is going on with Matthew's sovereign Christ. He follows both a beastly John and a bird-like Spirit into a liminal space to get himself ready to assume his kingship, lordship and sovereignty. Animality in these early chapters of Matthew appears positively as a herald and a guide; it is something close to the divine, close to holy, or simply *is* divine and holy. 'Famished' after fasting for 'forty days and forty nights' (4.2) in the wilderness, Matthew's Jesus seems to be in an animal state himself. He has no home, no food and no one to converse with besides the devil. At the same time, he begins to demonstrate his sovereignty in the wilderness. Should or could we say that animality is a requirement or a kind of preparation for Matthew's Jesus before his assumption of sovereignty?

Rejecting the devil's three proposals, Matthew's Jesus shows that he is not controlled by rapacious appetites as animals are often assumed to be (though we know that animals, even the most ferocious kind, may give up their prey to avoid dangers that they are able to perceive). Instead, he can govern his appetite, his aspiration and his ambition to retain his freedom from the devil (4.1-11). Rather than using his mouth to consume food when he is in extreme hunger (4.2-3), Matthew's Jesus uses his mouth to cite Scriptures and speak back to the devil (4.4-10) and, after emerging out of the wilderness and moving to Capernaum, to proclaim repentance in light of the coming kingdom of heaven (4.13-17) and to call disciples (4.18-22).

Seeing what he calls 'interiorizing "devourment"' and 'exteriorizing "vociferation"' as complementary rather than contradictory, Derrida points out that *apophantics* (the language of declaratory assertion or discourse of judgment) is understood by many philosophers as absent from animals but characteristic of sovereignty.[12] If so, then the sovereignty of Matthew's Jesus seems to be firmly established by his Sermon on the Mount in Matthew 5–7. From his pronouncements of beatitudes to his repeated uses of the 'you-have-heard-that-it-was-said ... but-I-say-to-you' formula to render judgment on various topics, Matthew's Jesus comes across as one who knows and makes things known. Matthew's Jesus is, of course, known for delivering five long discourses (5.1–7.27; 10.5-42; 13.3-52; 18.1-35; 24.4–

11. Derrida, *Animal*, pp. 3-12.
12. Derrida, *Beast and Sovereign*, I, pp. 23, 65, 168; II, pp. 216, 227-30.

25.46) to rival the Pentateuch that has been attributed to Moses.[13] In that sense, one can even say Matthew's Jesus is the sovereign who lays down the (new) law. He also announces that what he says will take place, and that, unlike heaven and earth that will pass away, his words will not (24.34-35). Although Gunther Bornkamm only looked at Mk 4.35-41 and Mt. 8.23-27 in his short article that effectually began what we now know as redaction criticism, he was on good grounds to argue that the disciples in Matthew no longer see their Jesus as a mere 'teacher' (as the disciples in Mark do in Mk 4.38) but as 'Lord' (Mt. 8.25).[14]

In his authoritative discourses, Matthew's sovereign Christ frequently employs parables, which basically make up one of his five long discourses (13.3-52). In *Beast and the Sovereign*, Derrida mentions how 'the essence of political force and power' often 'passes via fables, i.e., speech that is both fictional and performative'.[15] The parables of Matthew's Jesus may well be understood as fables under this definition, especially as he tells them to establish his identity as a sovereign. Some of these parables also portray an imperious household lord or master with absolute power over his slaves (e.g. 13.24-30, 44-52; 14.45-51; 25.14-30). Plutarch, who was a vegetarian, had famously compared treatment of slaves to treatment of animals.[16]

Readers of Matthew should notice how animals are often woven into the texture of the *apophantics* of Matthew's sovereign Christ. He talks about not giving something that is holy to dogs and not throwing pearls before swine (7.6), for instance, and he affirms that a human being is more valuable than a sheep (12.11-12). He repeats this affirmation by telling his twelve disciples that they are more valuable than 'many sparrows' (10.31), because these 'birds of the air ... neither sow nor reap nor gather into barns' (6.26). Whether birds really do not do these things or if this falls into the category of what Derrida calls 'the fabular' as 'a simulacrum of knowing',[17] I am not able to tell. Instead, I will focus on Derrida's repeated arguments in his seminar that, since difference between humans and animals justifies cruelty against animals, 'in the place of the beast, one can put, in the same hierarchy, the slave, the woman, the child'.[18] If the household lord in the parables mentioned above is referring to Matthew's Jesus, does it mean

13. Benjamin W. Bacon, *Studies in Matthew* (New York: Henry Holt, 1930).

14. Gunter Bornkamm, 'The Stilling of the Storm in Matthew', in Gunter Bornkamm, Gerhard Barth and Heinz-Joachim Held (eds.), *Tradition and Interpretation in Matthew* (Philadelphia: Westminster, 1963), pp. 52-57.

15. Derrida, *Beast and Sovereign*, I, p. 217.

16. Derrida, *Beast and Sovereign*, I, pp. 22-23; Still, *Derrida*, p. 274. See also Stephen Newmyer, *Plutarch's Three Treatises on Animals: A Translation with Introductions and Commentary* (Milton: Taylor and Francis, 2020).

17. Derrida, *Beast and Sovereign*, I, pp. 34-35.

18. Derrida, *Beast and Sovereign*, I, p. 33.

that his followers are slaves who can be treated as animals? We know that Matthew's Jesus tells his disciples that they must 'become like children' to enter the kingdom of heaven (18.3). While humility and not animality (e.g. deficiency in understanding) is highlighted as 'becom[ing] like children' (18.4), Matthew's Jesus does use animal imagery to talk about not only himself but also his followers. When he delivers his discourse on mission to the disciples, Matthew's Jesus says he is sending them out 'like sheep into the midst of wolves' so they have to be 'wise as serpents and innocent as doves' (10.16). While Thomas Hobbes is known for using the wolf to talk about threats between humans, Derrida points out that this was perhaps first done by Plautus, a Roman playwright of the third and second century BCE, and that while fox, wolf and lion all tend to appear in political discourse, wolf is the animal that appears most extensively.[19] Matthew's Jesus further stresses these subtle threats between humans by telling his followers to be aware of false prophets, who 'come to you in sheep's clothing but inwardly are ravenous wolves' (7.15). When he affirms that his disciples are more valuable than 'birds in the air' (6.26) such as sparrows (10.31), he is in effect promising them the protection and care that they should both desire and require. Elsewhere, Matthew's Jesus will once again refer to Israelites, including his followers, as leaderless or lost sheep and to himself or to God as a shepherd (9.36; 18.10-14). In other words, the imagery of sheep underscores the importance of Matthew's Jesus and/or God to people/disciples who are needy and vulnerable. The subordination of sheep to shepherd functions analogically to the subjection of slaves to household masters or the reliance of children on adults. Not to be missed in these imageries is the not-so-subtle alignment of the sovereignty of Matthew's Jesus with the providence of God. This exaltation of God's providence brings us back to what Matthew's Jesus says about birds. If he is bringing in the birds as an object lesson for his disciples to learn, is he indirectly asking the disciples to become (like?) birds by not worrying about tomorrow, especially if one of the assumed differences between humans and animals is the latter's lack of foresight (such as the possibility of death)?[20]

Immediately before Jesus's discourse on mission, Matthew provides the names of the twelve disciples: they are all men. Does Matthew's Jesus think that women would hamper his sovereignty? Is that why, following a conversation about divorce, he talks about some men making themselves eunuchs 'for the sake of the kingdom of heaven' (19.3-12)? While the same discourse also characterizes Israelites to whom the disciples are sent as sheep, Matthew's Jesus uses the same imagery to talk about the people of Israel when a Canaanite woman asks him to cure her daughter. When the

19. See, e.g., Derrida, *Beast and Sovereign*, I, pp. 11, 61, 80-82.
20. Still, *Derrida*, p. 212.

woman continues to ask him for help, however, Matthew's Jesus makes a
change to refer to the Israelites as 'children' and employs a different animal
imagery for the Canaanite women: namely, dogs (15.21-26). Perhaps Matthew's Jesus is being consistent with his earlier statement about not giving
something holy to dogs (7.6); he tells the Canaanite mother that food should
be reserved for children and not given to dogs. Despite being denied her
and her daughter's humanity, the Canaanite mother willingly plays a servile
role and turns herself and her daughter effectually into domesticated dogs.
'Yes, Lord', she says, 'yet even the dogs eat the crumbs that fall from their
masters' table' (15.27). Judging from these passages, animality does not
preclude inclusion in the community of Matthew's Jesus, but it certainly
helps institute the structural sovereignty of Matthew's Jesus in the community. Calling other people animals, be it sheep or dogs, is not only powerful
but also performative when it is done by Matthew's Jesus.

So far, I have been arguing for the importance of animality for the emergence of Matthew's Jesus and the establishment of his sovereignty. Now I
want to propose that animality is also crucial for the continuation of Jesus's
sovereignty in Matthew, because his sovereignty is in many ways beastly.
As I have pointed out in the discussion of his encounter with the Canaanite
mother, calling people animals is an injurious and insulting form of dehumanization. Derrida connects the sovereign with beast because both imply
force and brutality. More specifically, Derrida discusses how sovereignty
rules by emphasizing fear and threatening violence.[21] It is rather telling that
each of the five long *apophantic* discourses by Matthew's Jesus ends by
promising reward to those who obey and punishment to those who don't
(7.24-27; 10.40-42; 13.47-52; 18.23-35; 25.31-46). I will focus on two endings that assume the power of humans over animals to elaborate on what
seems to be a carrot-and-stick approach of Matthew's Gospel, but let me
just mention that, among the three endings that I will not take up, one features the power of a king over his slaves (18.23-35). The very last parable
in the discourse of parables promises that 'at the end of the age', bad fish
that have been caught in the net of the kingdom of heaven but do evil will be
fished out, separated from the good fish, and thrown out into the 'furnace of
fire' (13.47-52). At the end of the apocalyptic discourse is the well-known
parable of the sheep and the goats, where Matthew's Jesus is presented as
a shepherd, as well as someone who sits on the throne and judges all the
nations. Depending on how they treat 'the least of these', some (the sheep)
will inherit the kingdom and receive eternal life while others (the goats) will
be sent away into eternal punishment (25.31-46).

Both of these parables are about inclusion and exclusion; they also make
clear that current inclusion in the community of Matthew's Jesus is not

21. See, e.g., Derrida, *Beast and Sovereign*, I, pp. 39-43, 217.

necessarily permanent, since everything cannot be known until a time of future judgment. Furthermore, exclusion is not its own punishment; instead, exclusion implies ongoing pain and total destruction. The choice is therefore either to be wiped out by Matthew's Jesus or to be included as his faithful slaves or domesticated animals. The dynamics become even more difficult because Matthew's Jesus shows that the final judgment will overtake people by surprise. In his apocalyptic discourse, Matthew's Jesus states that the final judgment will come 'at an unexpected hour', and that no one except God will know 'on what day your Lord is coming' (24.36-44; cf. 25.1-13). Derrida begins the very first session of his seminar on *Beast and the Sovereign* by referring to the stealth movements of a wolf: 'to walk without making a noise, to arrive without warning, to proceed discreetly, silently, invisibly, almost inaudibly and imperceptibly ... to surprise a prey, to take it by surprising what is in sight but does not see coming the one who is already seeing it, already getting ready to take it by surprise, to grasp it by surprise'.[22] Derrida's description of the wolf here seems to me to be applicable to Matthew's Jesus. The shepherd who is supposed to protect the sheep from the wolves turns out to be another ravenous (male) wolf in disguise (cf. 7.15), who will not hesitate to consume some of those under his charge by separating them out as goats or as bad fish. Is he protecting the sheep from other wolves to save the sheep for his own devourment? Or is he eating them so no sheep will develop into a competing wolf or a rival sovereign? Matthew's sovereign Christ is in this sense also a beast indeed: his sovereignty can be base and brutal.

Two more animals appear in Matthew in a passage that also implies the beastly sovereignty of Matthew's Christ. Before what has traditionally been known as his triumphant entry into Jerusalem, or what can be seen as a great and public celebration of his sovereignty, Matthew's Jesus sent two disciples to fetch a donkey and a colt (21.1-2). In a way that is rather mysterious or perhaps appropriately majestic for a sovereign, he tells the disciples to just untie and take the animals without asking anyone for permission. He does, however, add that if anyone asks what they are doing, they should simply say, 'The Lord needs them', and then they will be able to carry out what he wants them to do without obstruction.

One of the reasons why Derrida connects beast with the sovereign is their outlaw status. While animals are often viewed as below the law, the sovereign is above it.[23] Here we see once again that the words of Matthew's Jesus come across as their own laws. His agents are on this occasion granted permission to take without asking and, by repeating his words, they can stop anyone from getting in their way (even or especially when those words do

22. Derrida, *Beast and Sovereign*, I, p. 2.
23. See, e.g., Derrida, *Beast and Sovereign*, I, pp. 17-18.

not actually explain his or his disciples' action). If might is right and the sovereign can break the law whenever he sees fit, then it is rather apt that Matthew's sovereign Christ ends up being crucified between two criminals as 'the king of the Jews' (27.29, 37-38; cf. 26.55).

After successfully bringing the donkey and the colt to Matthew's Jesus, the disciples use their cloaks to provide a kind of padded seat for Matthew's Christ to ride into Jerusalem. A large crowd blankets the way before him with their own cloaks and tree branches, praising him out loud as one who is coming in God's name, as Matthew's Jesus performs a circus act by riding on two different animals simultaneously (21.6-9). This passage in Matthew has been much discussed by scholars because, as many have pointed out, Matthew does not seem to understand that the Hebrew Scripture he cites here (to underscore his Jesus as the fulfilment of God's promises) is Hebrew poetry. Since Hebrew poetry works by parallelism and not by rhythm, Zech. 9.9 should not be taken literally as referring to two different animals.[24] Instead of reading this passage as a mistake, I argue that the passage is revealing how Christ's sovereignty is dependent on animality. As Niccolò Machiavelli suggests in *The Prince*, the sovereign, in addition to keeping his promises as a human should, must also have the strength of a lion and the cunning of a fox. That is to say, a sovereign is not only a human-and-animal hybrid but also a chimera animal.[25] This is precisely the picture of Matthew's sovereign Christ as he rides on two different animals in this crowning or clowning scene. Here, Matthew's Christ is what Derrida calls 'the spectacle of a spectrality', because the scene literally shows the

> haunting of the sovereign by the beast and the beast by the sovereign, the one inhabiting or housing the other, the one becoming the intimate host of the other ... In the metamorphic covering-over of the two figures, the beast and the sovereign, one therefore has a presentiment that a profound and essential ontological copula is at work on this couple.[26]

In other places, Derrida will use the language of prosthesis or that of grafting to describe this coupling of or copula between the beast and the sovereign.[27] Let me, however, emphasize the adjectives used by Derrida in

---

24. See, e.g., John P. Meier, *The Vision of Matthew: Christ, Church, and Morality in the First Gospel* (New York: Paulist, 1979), pp. 19-21; W.D. Davies and Dale C. Allison, *Matthew 19–28* (New York: Bloomsbury, 2004), pp. 120-21; Herbert Basser with Marsha B. Cohen, *The Gospel of Matthew and Judaic Traditions: A Relevance-Based Commentary* (Leiden: E.J. Brill, 2015), p. 530; Max Harris, *Christ on a Donkey: Palm Sunday, Triumphal Entries, and Blasphemous Pageants* (Leeds: Arc Humanities, 2019), p. 106.

25. Derrida, *Beast and Sovereign*, I, pp. 77-92.

26. Derrida, *Beast and Sovereign*, I, p. 18.

27. See, e.g., Derrida, *Beast and Sovereign*, I, pp. 26-28, 39-43, 70.

the sentences I cited. The 'profound and essential' coming together of beast and sovereign is perfectly and openly confessed by Matthew's sovereign Christ when he says in reference to himself and the two animals, 'The Lord needs them'.[28]

If his celebratory or crowning entry into Jerusalem turns out to be a disappointment, Matthew's Jesus will secure his sovereignty through his death and resurrection. If one follows the distinction that Heidegger makes between human dying and animal perishing (because animals, according to Heidegger, lack anxiety and the fear of death that humans have),[29] then the episode of Matthew's Jesus in Gethsemane can be read as proof of the distance between Matthew's Jesus and animality (26.36-46). Following Heidegger to argue against Heidegger, Derrida proposes that anxiety may have a benumbing effect that highlights the animality of humans, since benumbment is an animal characteristic for Heidegger.[30] Matthew's Jesus is

---

28. Numerous studies on Matthew have been devoted to the phrase 'Son of Man' that Matthew's Jesus tends to use to refer to himself. See, e.g., Ulrich Luz, 'The Son of Man in Matthew: Heavenly Judge or Human Christ', *JSNT* 48 (1992), pp. 3-21; David C. Sim, *Apocalyptic Eschatology in the Gospel of Matthew* (New York: Cambridge University Press, 1996), pp. 93-109; Leslie W. Walck, *The Son of Man in the Parables of Enoch and in Matthew* (New York: Bloomsbury, 2011). Many studies have also been done to point to the potential connection between this phrase in Matthew and in the book of Daniel in the Hebrew Scriptures (Dan. 7.13). See, e.g., H. Daniel Zacharias, 'Old Greek Daniel 7:13-14 and Matthew's Son of Man', *Bulletin for Biblical Research* 21.4 (2011), pp. 453-61; Brendon Robert Witte, *'Who Do You, Matthew, Say the Son of Man Is?' Son of Man and Conflict in the First Gospel* (PhD diss., University of Edinburgh, 2016), pp. 223-29; Erin Runions, *The Babylon Complex: Theopolitical Fantasies of War, Sex, and Sovereignty* (New York: Fordham University Press, 2014), pp. 231-35. While the NRSV does not use this phrase to translate Dan. 7.13, it does add a note to acknowledge the possibility that 'human being' can be alternatively translated as 'son of man'. Besides depicting four chimera beasts, Daniel 7 affirms that this mysterious figure—who is 'like a human being'—will be given 'dominion and glory and kingship' (Dan. 7.13-14) over these chimera beasts. As Stephen D. Moore (*Gospel Jesuses and Other Nonhumans: Biblical Criticism, Post-Poststructuralism* [Atlanta, GA: SBL Press, 2017], pp. 67-70) carefully and correctly observes, however, at least two of these chimera beasts also have human-like features: the first beast has a human mind and stands on two feet like a human (Dan. 7.4), and the little horn on the fourth beast has human eyes (Dan. 7.8).

29. Martin Heidegger, *Being and Time* (trans. John Macquarrie and Edward Robinson; Oxford: Blackwell, 1962), pp. 284-85, 290-92. See also Jacques Derrida, *Aporias* (trans. Thomas Dutoit; Stanford, CA: Stanford University Press, 1993), p. 35; Stuart Elden, 'Heidegger's Animals', *Continental Philosophy Review* 39 (2006), pp. 273-91.

30. David Farrell Krell, *Derrida and our Animal Others: Derrida's Final Seminar, The Beast and the Sovereign* (Bloomington, IN: Indiana University Press, 2013), pp. 107-109, 118. See also Gerard Kuperus, 'Attunement, Deprivation, and Drive: Heidegger and Animality', in Corinne Painter and Christian Lotz (eds.), *Phenomenology*

clearly struggling with the prospect of death, asking God three times if he may bypass the cross. What I want to point out is how this anxiety causes Matthew's Jesus to feel torn and ambivalent, not only about God's will (he wants to do God's will and his thrice-repeated prayers suggest that he is not sure if the cross is really God's will for him) but also about what to do with his disciples. In Gethsemane, Matthew's Jesus seems to both fear and desire solitude, which is, as it has often been pointed out, a characteristic or a cost of being a sovereign.[31] Taking his disciples to Gethsemane, he leaves them but goes on farther with Peter, James and John. He then goes away from these three disciples to pray and returns to them three times, as if he cannot decide whether he wants to be alone or in their company. Matthew's Jesus, even if only for a short period of time in Gethsemane, seems like a benumbed animal, dazed and confused by anxieties and fear. After Gethsemane, with all of his male disciples gone (26.56) and a few female disciples 'looking on from a distance' (27.55), Matthew's Jesus dies the death as a lone wolf howling on the cross, 'My God, my God, why have you forsaken me?' (27.46).

The death and resurrection of Matthew's sovereign Christ are, therefore, not separable from animality. Referring to Hebrew Scriptures, he compares his upcoming death and resurrection to Jonah being eaten and spending three days and three nights in the belly of a 'sea monster' (12.39-41; cf. 16.4).[32] Matthew's Christ really does need all kinds of animals to be(come) 'Lord', who will in some unknown day and hour move in like a wolf to surprise his followers and all nations with his judgment.

Derrida suggests in *Beast and the Sovereign* that claims and desires to be unique, superior and absolute in knowledge, authority and judgment are *bêtise*—a French word implying both stupidity and animality, which the translator of the seminar has generally left untranslated, but which the translator of Derrida's *The Animal and Therefore I Am* translates as 'asinanity'.[33] I think 'asinanity' or 'asininity' is a good translation in light of the entry into Jerusalem on a donkey and a colt by Matthew's Jesus. The asininity of any assumption of superiority over animals or of sovereignty over others, including the sovereign's claim of having power over life and death, is clearly shown in the reality of death.[34] By repeatedly asking a rhetorical question on the distinction between a 'who' or a 'what', Derrida points out that every human needs an-other to take care of their own dead body, and

---

and the Non-Human Animal: At the Limits of Experience (Dordrecht: Springer, 2007), pp. 13-28.

    31. See, e.g., Derrida, *Beast and Sovereign*, II. pp. 1-8.
    32. The book of Jonah also ends, as Jione Havea kindly reminded me, with a verse implying that the fate of humans and animals are tied together (Jon. 4.11).
    33. Derrida, *Animal*, p. 18.
    34. Derrida, *Animal*, p. 28.

no dead human can really dictate what others do with their own corpse even if there is a will established before their death.[35] After all, burial practices are generally regulated strictly by cultural and governmental forces. We see this being played out in the death of Matthew's sovereign Christ (27.57-61). Joseph of Arimathea must ask Pilate's permission for the corpse of Matthew's Jesus, a request that Pilate has the authority to grant or to refuse. Getting the green light from Pilate, Joseph makes the decision to wrap the corpse of Matthew's Jesus in a clean linen cloth and then bury the wrapped body in the tomb that Joseph has prepared for himself. As Derrida writes,

> The other appears to me as the other as such, *qua* he, she, or they who might survive me, survive my decease and then proceed as they wish, sovereignly, and sovereignly have at their disposal the future of my remains, if there any.[36]

We don't know if Joseph's actions match the desire of Matthew's sovereign Christ, who does affirm an unnamed woman's anointing of him at Bethany as preparing his body for burial (26.6-13). We also know that Matthew's Jesus asks his twelve disciples to take and eat his body at the Passover meal the night of his arrest (27.26), though what he means by that is cryptic. When he claims to have received 'all authority in heaven and on earth' to send his disciples to 'go ... and make disciples of all nations' (28.18-19), is he not in effect transferring or dividing his sovereignty to multiple parties? Here is yet another case that 'the Lord needs them' (21.3), just as a master or a king in Matthew's parables still needs his slaves to reap or collect the harvest (13.24-30; 21.33-41), to invite people to or kick people out of his banquet (22.1-14), to run his household (24.45-51), or to invest his property (25.14-30).

We must remember that, as the prayers of Matthew's Jesus in Gethsemane make clear, his death is the result of God's will rather than his own. Matthew's sovereign Christ does not dare oppose God's will. Similarly, the resurrection of his dead body is done by God, who is arguably the ultimate Other. Matthew's sovereign Christ is a marionette being bobbed down and up by God. Derrida's explanation that the word marionette is a derivative from the name of the Virgin Mary further reminds us that God has been pulling the strings to bring about the birth of Matthew's Jesus.[37] Matthew's God is then the sovereign behind Matthew's sovereign Christ who alone knows when the final judgment will take place. In that sense, the 'perfect' Father God (5.48) of Matthew's Jesus is the invisible and imperceptible wolf who

35. Derrida, *Beast and the Sovereign*, I, pp. 61-62, 137-38, 205-206; II, pp. 119-46. See also Michael Naas, *The End of the World and Other Teachable Moments: Jacques Derrida's Final Seminar* (New York: Fordham University Press, 2015), pp. 64-74.

36. Derrida, *Beast and Sovereign*, II, p. 127.

37. Derrida, *Beast and Sovereign*, I, p. 188.

devours even his own son, who can, in turn, send those among his followers into 'outer darkness' or a 'furnace of fire, where there will be weeping and gnashing of teeth' (8.12; 13.42, 50; 22.13, 51; 25.30). In Matthew's Gospel, this alpha wolf is one who comes in its son's clothing (cf. 7.15).

Matthew's Gospel does seem to multiply the differences among animals and among humans. Doves and sheep, for instance, are presented more positively than pigs and dogs. One can say that the Gospel recognizes the difference between a donkey and a colt, as well as the diversity of birds with its mention of doves and sparrows. Similarly, as I have repeatedly pointed out, the power differential between household masters and slaves is clearly acknowledged. Matthew's sovereign Christ is ushered onto the stage by animality, talks about and treats others as animals, and embodies animality in himself. While he moves and acts with followers calling him 'Lord' and he himself claiming sovereignty, he is also passively controlled by and merely reacting to his Father God. Though called a king at his birth, his birth was orchestrated by God; he was then taken from place to place by his father Joseph (Mt. 2.1-23). At his death and resurrection, his body was again taken care of by Joseph of Arimathea and then raised up by God. The beastly ways of Matthew's sovereign Christ include his becoming a benumbed beast of burden. Sovereignty and animality function in a codependent relationship in Matthew's Jesus, but sovereignty is, in the end, a phantasm even for this king and Lord. Claiming and clinging to sovereignty to assert control over self, animals and different others as animals is not only atrocious but also asinine. This realization is important for any public conversations about sovereignty and about whose or what lives matter.

6

GLIMMERS OF LIGHT BEYOND CLOSED DOORS:
A FEMINIST EXPLORATION OF THE PARABLE OF THE
TEN VIRGINS IN MATTHEW 25.1-13

Barbara E. Reid, O.P.

It is a great privilege to contribute to this Festschrift in honour of Elaine
M. Wainwright, RSM. We first met in Washington, DC, in 1986 while both
attending a meeting of the Catholic Biblical Association of America. We
discovered we had mutual friends and many common interests, including a
passion for learning how to read the New Testament with feminist lenses, in
order to offer liberative pathways toward an egalitarian world and church.
In the intervening years, we have had wonderful opportunities to stay connected, not only at annual meetings of the Society of Biblical Literature,
but especially during extended times together in Auckland and Chicago.
I have learned so much from Elaine's insights in her writings, her papers
presented at scholarly conferences, and from informal exchanges—not only
how to read with feminist lenses, but also with ecological ones, connecting the well-being of women and humankind with that of the cosmos and
other-than-human beings. Knowing Elaine's predilection for the Gospel of
Matthew, I offer this feminist interpretation of the parable of the ten virgins
(Mt. 25.1-13) in her honour, with deepest gratitude for our long friendship
and colleagueship.

The Symbolic Universe of the Parable

While most commentators approach the parable of the ten maidens by
explaining its literary context in Matthew's eschatological discourse (24.1–
25.46) and its resounding call for preparedness for the end times, Elaine's
brief examination of the parable in *Searching the Scriptures* begins by calling
attention to the symbolic universe of Matthew's eschatological discourse.
She observes that chs. 21–25 are 'dominated by male characters, most
particularly the Jewish leaders with whom he [Jesus] comes into conflict as

well as the disciples, of whom twelve males have been specifically called and missioned'.[1] She notes as well that

> the symbolic universe created by this section of the narrative is significantly androcentric, and the vehicle for this construction is the imagery of the parables. It is drawn from the agricultural world—a man with two sons working a vineyard; a householder with servants, who lets out his vineyard to tenants—the political world—a king giving a wedding feast for his son; a king pronouncing judgment—and the economic realm—a man entrusting his property to agents. It is a world in which female experience is not seen as symbolic of the *basileia* being preached.[2]

Elaine signals one exception: the parable of the ten virgins in 25.1-13, 'which draws on female experience—but female experience in a patriarchal world. The women are at the service of the bridegroom, and the bride is invisible in the scene.'[3]

Elaine rightly observes that it is unlikely this parable, along with the one other parable that draws on imagery from female experience—the woman hiding leaven in bread dough (13.33)—has any significant impact on the symbolic universe that the Matthaean narrative constructs. She asserts, however, that these parables offer hidden clues that point to an alternative symbolic universe, providing 'the possibility for imagining a more extensive world of women that could be described in parables in relation to the inclusive *basileia* Jesus was preaching'.[4] Building on Elaine's insights, I would like to probe more deeply into the elements of the parable that can open the way to just such an alternative symbolic universe.

Bridesmaids and Weddings

The main characters in the parable are a bridegroom and ten παρθένοι, translated variously as 'bridesmaids', 'maidens' and 'virgins'.[5] The Greek word παρθένος denotes 'a woman of marriageable age, without focus on virginity'.[6] In the context of a wedding, ten bridesmaids paint a picture of

---

1. Elaine M. Wainwright, 'The Gospel of Matthew', Elisabeth Schüssler Fiorenza (ed.), in *Searching the Scriptures. Volume Two: A Feminist Commentary* (New York: Crossroad, 1994), pp. 635-77 (657).

2. Wainwright, 'The Gospel of Matthew', II, p. 657. The Greek word βασιλεία is usually translated 'kingdom'. Because of its male monarchical connotations, many feminists prefer to use the transliteration *basileia*.

3. Wainwright, 'The Gospel of Matthew', p. 657.

4. Wainwright, 'The Gospel of Matthew', p. 657.

5. E.g.: 'bridesmaids' in NRSV; 'virgins' in NABRE, NKJV; 'maidens' in Warren Carter, *Matthew and the Margins. A Sociopolitical and Religious Reading* (The Bible and Liberation; Maryknoll, NY: Orbis Books, 2000), p. 484.

6. BDAG, p. 777.

the strength of friendship and kinship among women as they surround the bride with support when she enters into the second of three traditional stages of a woman's life: virgin, wife and mother, and wise elder. However, in the parable, there is no mention of the bride; the women attend the groom. It is he whom they go out to meet, he whom the five ready virgins accompany into the wedding banquet. The women's focus is on the man at the centre of the celebration. Moreover, a possible circle of female solidarity is broken when the ones who have oil refuse to share with those who do not.

The image of virgins awaiting a groom evokes a world in which a woman's value[7] and definition derives from her relationship to a man. In antiquity, as well as in some contemporary cultures, young unmarried women are under the control of their fathers. When they marry, they come under the control of their husbands. This pattern is disrupted in Matthew's first chapter, where the mother of Jesus is a virgin (παρθένος, 1.23), not only when she conceives Jesus, but remains so until after his birth.[8] However, as Mary Foskett observes, some feminists have associated Mary's virginity with 'a misogyny that reifies male power over women, subordinates female sexuality and creativity to a virginal ideal, and perpetuates the notion of femininity as passive receptivity'.[9] Other feminists call attention to the problems created by exalting Mary's virginal conception, thereby diminishing the esteem for women who bear children in the usual ways. Still others see in Mary's virginity 'a positive expression of female autonomy and power'.[10] A virgin, unfettered by the cultural constraints imposed on wives and mothers, is an icon of self-containment and singularity, making her powerful and even dangerous.

Probing further into the symbolic universe evoked by virgins, we may recall ancient Greek virgin goddesses such as Athena and Artemis,[11] who exhibited the power women have when they are able to act in ways that

---

7. Marie-Eloise Rosenblatt, 'Got into the Party After All: Women's Issues and the Five Foolish Virgins', in Amy-Jill Levine (ed.) with Marianne Blickenstaff, *A Feminist Companion to Matthew* (FCNTECW, 1; Sheffield: Sheffield Academic Press, 2001), pp. 171-95, observes that if the delay in the parable is due to protracted negotiations over the price of the bride, it could cut two ways: on the one hand, the woman is recognized as being very valuable in her father's eyes, but on the other hand, she is little more than a commodity to be traded for which the groom haggles to get the best deal.

8. The meaning of ἕως οὗ in Mt.1.25 continues to be debated. The NRSV translates it 'until' ('but had no marital relations with her until she had borne a son').

9. Mary F. Foskett, *A Virgin Conceived: Mary and Classical Representations of Virginity* (Bloomington, IN: Indiana University Press, 2002), p. 2.

10. See further Foskett, *A Virgin Conceived*, pp. 63-68.

11. Athena was not only the patron of Athens; her cult also spread to other cities. Artemis was one of the most widely venerated ancient Greek deities, along with Diana, her Roman equivalent.

move outside of the usual strictures on women.[12] Virginity is also linked to the gift of prophecy, as virgins were regarded as pure and receptive to the oracular spirit. In Delphi, for example, the Pythia who delivered Apollo's oracle was a virgin; likewise the vestal virgins of Rome who tended the sacred fire. In the New Testament, the notion of virgins' single-minded devotion and availability to God is evident in Paul's exhortation to virgins to remain unmarried and so be solely 'anxious about the affairs of the Lord', in contrast to married women who are 'anxious about the affairs of the world, how to please her husband' (1 Cor. 7.34). Also, Philip's four daughters, who had the gift of prophecy, were virgins (Acts 21.9). Another woman whose virginal power was widely known throughout Asia Minor was Thecla, a rich aristocratic woman who renounced her family, fortune and fiancé to accompany Paul in his missionary work. In Orthodox tradition, she is venerated as 'apostle and protomartyr among women' and 'equal to the apostles in sanctity'.[13] Her story is recounted in the apocryphal *Acts of Paul and Thecla*, written in Asia Minor in the late second century,

These nuances of virginal power are absent, however, from the parable in Mt. 25.1-13. The virgins' attention is wholly centred on the bridegroom who has the power to admit them or shut them out. There is no challenge to patriarchal patterns in this parable. In fact, the literary context links the virgins with slaves who are ever ready to do the master's bidding.

Slave Readiness

The eschatological discourse (Mt. 24.1–25.46), in which the parable of the ten virgins is imbedded, emphasizes the need to be ready for Jesus's return, the time of which is unknown (24.36, 42, 44, 50) and delayed (24.48). Immediately preceding the parable of the ten virgins is the parable of the faithful and wise slave who is put in charge of the master's household (24.45-51). The word φρόνιμος links the two parables (24.45; 25.2). The implication is that the five wise virgins are like the wise slave.

Using the slave–master metaphor for the relationship of disciples to Jesus is highly fraught, most especially for women. As Elizabeth Johnson observed, 'the master–slave relationship, now totally abhorrent in human society' is

---

12. See Foskett, *A Virgin Conceived*, pp. 65-66.

13. See Sheila E. McGinn, 'The Acts of Thecla', in Elisabeth Schüssler Fiorenza (ed.) with the assistance of Ann Brock and Shelly Matthews, *Searching the Scriptures* (A Feminist Commentary, 2; New York: Crossroad, 1994), pp. 800-828; idem, *Exploring the Acts of Thecla* (Rhetoric of Religious Antiquity; Atlanta, GA: SBL, forthcoming); Susan E. Hylen, *A Modest Apostle: Thecla and the History of Women in the Early Church* (New York: Oxford University Press, 2015).

> no longer suitable as a metaphor for relationship to God ... Slavery is
> an unjust, sinful situation. It makes people into objects owned by others,
> denigrating their dignity as human persons. In the case of slave women,
> their masters have the right not only to their labor, but to their bodies,
> making them into tools of production and reproduction at the master's wish.
> In such circumstances the Spirit groans with the cries of the oppressed,
> prompting persons not to obey but to resist, using all their wiles.[14]

While it may be possible that reflection on the Gospels' slave parables
can galvanize believers to work toward abolishing modern-day forms of
slavery—such as persons detained against their will in inhuman working
conditions, those forced into prostitution, and young girls and women victims used as sex slaves by terrorist groups—the greater likelihood is that
these parables continue to support a spirituality of subservience and servitude. Other metaphors to illustrate faithful readiness to divine manifesta-
tions must be found.

Bride of Christ

Equally problematic is the metaphor of bride or bridesmaid and bridegroom
to speak of a disciple's relationship with Christ, or Israel's relationship with
YHWH. This metaphor is pervasive in both Testaments of the Bible. Isaiah,
for example, speaks words of comfort to Israel at the end of the exile, casting
their maker as their husband, who, for a brief moment, abandoned them
and then called them back like a wife forsaken (Isa. 45.5-8). Similarly, as
Jeremiah prophesies hope to the exiles, he promises a new covenant: 'It will
not be like the covenant that I made with their ancestors when I took them by
the hand to bring them out of the land of Egypt—a covenant that they broke,
though I was their husband, says the LORD' (Jer. 31.32). Similarly, Hosea
speaks about Israel's infidelity, punishment and redemption, concluding
with the promise from Yhwh, 'And I will take you for my wife forever; I
will take you for my wife in righteousness and in justice, in steadfast love,
and in mercy' (Hos. 2.19). It is highly problematic that when this metaphor
occurs in the Scriptures, the wife is always cast as the unfaithful one. This
is all the more ironic given that, in most instances of marital infidelity, it is
the husband who strays.[15]

---

14. Elizabeth A. Johnson, *Truly Our Sister. A Theology of Mary in the Communion
of Saints* (New York: Continuum, 2003), p. 255; Jennifer Glancy, *Slavery in Early
Christianity* (New York: Oxford University, 2002); Sandra R. Joshel and Sheila
Murnaghan, *Women and Slaves in Greco-Roman Culture: Differential Equations*
(London: Routledge, 1998).

15. The 2006 American General Social survey showed that nearly twice as many
married men as women admitted to having had sexual relations with someone other than
their spouse. A survey done in 2000 in the United Kingdom found that 15 percent of men

In numerous New Testament texts, Jesus is spoken of as a bridegroom. Elsewhere in Matthew, in addition to Mt. 25.1-13, Jesus casts himself as bridegroom when he responds to the question about why his disciples do not fast, 'The wedding guests cannot mourn as long as the bridegroom is with them, can they? The days will come when the bridegroom is taken away from them, and then they will fast' (Mt. 9.15).[16] While in many contemporary societies brides and bridegrooms understand their relationship in terms of equal partnership with shared responsibility and mutuality, this was not the case in biblical times. Brides and wives were to be subject and submissive to their husbands, obeying them in everything.[17]

Woman Wisdom

One possible way to redirect the symbolic universe of the parable of the wise virgins is to link the virgins to Woman Wisdom and to the strong overtones of Wisdom Christology in Matthew, rather than to the wise slave in 24.45-51.[18] The allusions to Woman Wisdom can be found most explicitly in the parable of the children in the marketplace (11.16-19). The parable begins with Jesus comparing 'this generation' to 'children sitting in the marketplaces and calling to one another' (11.16); this is evocative of the way that Woman Wisdom cried out 'in the street; in the squares she raises her voice' (Prov. 1.20). As the parable continues, it is not the children who are like Wisdom, but Jesus. Just as Wisdom called out, inviting all to her banquet (Prov. 9.3), John likewise called out his invitation in the desert (Mt. 3.3) and Jesus called out his message for anyone with ears to hear (Mt. 13.9).

Wisdom's invitation to learn from her is cast in terms of eating her bread and drinking her wine (Prov. 9.5). So too, banqueting with Jesus is symbolic

---

had had 'overlapping' relationships in the previous year, but only 9 percent of women had. https://www.bbc.com/news/magazine-18233843.

16. See also Jn 3.29; 2 Cor. 11.2; Eph. 5.21-33; Rev. 21.2, 9; 22.17.

17. See the critique by Elisabeth Schüssler Fiorenza (*Ephesians* [WCS, 50; Collegeville, MN: Liturgical Press, 2017], p. 93) on the husband-wife metaphor for the relationship of Christ to the church.

18. See Celia Deutsch, *Hidden Wisdom and the Easy Yoke: Wisdom, Torah and Discipleship in Matthew 11.25-30* (JSOTSup, 18; Sheffield: JSOT Press, 1987); idem, *Lady Wisdom, Jesus, and the Sages* (Valley Forge, PA: Trinity Press International, 1996); idem, "Jesus as Wisdom: A Feminist Reading of Matthew's Wisdom Christology," in Amy-Jill Levine (ed.) with Marianne Blickenstaff, *A Feminist Companion to Matthew* (FCNTECW, 1; Sheffield: Sheffield Academic Press, 2001), pp. 88-113; J.M. Suggs, *Wisdom, Christology and Law in Matthew's Gospel* (Cambridge, MA: Harvard University Press, 1970); F.T. Gench, *Wisdom in the Christology of Matthew* (Lanham, MD: University Press of America, 1997); Elisabeth Schüssler Fiorenza, *Jesus: Miriam's Child, Sophia's Prophet* (London: SCM Press, 1994).

of responding to his invitation to discipleship (e.g. Mt. 8.11; 9.11; 14.13-21; 15.27, 32-39; 22.1-14; 25.10; 26.17-29). And just as Wisdom's invitation is rejected by the foolish (Sir. 15.7-8; see also Prov. 1.23-25; Sir. 15.7-8; Wis. 10.3; Bar. 3.12), so too that of Jesus, who is accused of being 'a glutton and a drunkard, a friend of tax collectors and sinners' (Mt. 11.19a). The final phrase of the verse, 'Yet wisdom is vindicated by her deeds' (11.19b), clinches the identification of Jesus with Woman Wisdom. That Jesus's deeds or works (ἔργων) reveal his relation to God (11.5, 19) calls to mind Wisdom's participation in God's works (ἔργα) at creation (Prov. 8.22-31). Moreover, the verb ἐδικαιώθη ('is vindicated', 'is justified') carries echoes of Wisdom, who walks in the way of righteousness (δικαιοσύνη, Prov. 8.20) and speaks with all righteousness (Prov. 8.8).[19]

As Elaine well observed, the linking of Jesus with Wisdom imagery is transgressive, able 'to subvert the ideological sex/gender system as it has functioned not only to make meaning of Jesus but also of the lives of Christians', opening up the 'possibilities of *poiesis* that can draw on additional female symbols and metaphors in constructing christologies that will, in their turn, contribute to developing female and feminist subjectivities'.[20] Commenting on the deeds of Wisdom, equated with the deeds of Jesus, she observes that Wisdom's deeds are not only salvific or liberating (see Wis. 10–19), they are also creative. The divine creative work, done by Wisdom at the very shaping of the universe (Prov. 8.22-21; Sir. 24.1-22; Wis. 9.9), is continued in Jesus:

> A new creation is being wrought in the works of righteousness, the reordering of resources and relationships, whereby Wisdom is rendered right or just in the sight of humanity … For contemporary feminist interpreters, this points toward new possibilities of meaning-making and storytelling that will shape a consciousness adequate to the response necessary for the reordering of life for the sake of the planet and all its species—a creative and liberating praxis.[21]

---

19. There are other parallels between Woman Wisdom and Jesus in the Gospel. Like Wisdom's search for a resting place (Sir. 24.7), Jesus tells a potential disciple, 'Foxes have holes, and birds of the air have nests; but the Son of Man has nowhere to lay his head' (Mt. 8.20). As well, Jesus's invitation to his disciples to take up his yoke and learn from him (Mt. 11.28-30) parallels the invitation to come for instruction and submit to Wisdom's yoke (Sir. 51.13-20).

20. Elaine M. Wainwright, *Shall We Look for Another? A Feminist Rereading of the Matthean Jesus* (The Bible and Liberation; Maryknoll, NY: Orbis Books, 1998), p. 77. The word *poiesis* is derived from the Greek verb ποιεῖν, which means 'to make'. *Poiesis* is the activity by which a person brings something into being.

21. Wainwright, *Shall We Look for Another?* pp. 77-78.

Phronimos Wisdom vs. Sophia Wisdom

While allusions to Woman Wisdom and strains of Wisdom Christology open up new horizons in Matthew, the possibilities are slim that the parable of the wise and foolish virgins could lead us in that direction. As Vicky Balabanski points out, there is a difference between the wisdom of Sophia (the Greek name for Woman Wisdom, as well as wisdom more generally) and *phronimos* wisdom (the word used of the five virgins). The former 'has a broad scope, which spans not only the quest for truth and grappling with finitude, but also everyday instruction on human interaction . . . [and] is fundamentally relational'.[22] *Phronimos* 'is more limited. It refers to the sort of cleverness or prudence required for self-preservation, or for fulfilling one's appointed role',[23] like the prudent builder who builds his house on rock (7.24), the watchful slave in 24.45 and the disciples who are told by Jesus to be as prudent or clever as serpents when they go out on mission (10.16).[24]

The five *phronimoi* in Mt. 25.1-13 do not exhibit *Sophia* wisdom, but the cleverness or shrewdness needed for self-advancement. As Balabanski notes,

> Their actions do not model an appropriate ethic for an 'eccesial-logy of liberation'.[25] Their 'wisdom' is not the sort that is needed in the struggle to move beyond patri/kyriarchy, for it is not a *relational* wisdom. Rather, it is one which sets the goal or end above the means, and is prepared to sacrifice the different or 'foolish' young women to reach those ends.[26]

Binary Oppositions

The parable sets up a binary opposition between the two groups of virgins. Other places in the Gospel where Matthew sets up a choice between 'two

22. Vicky Balabanski, 'Opening the Closed Door: A Feminist Rereading of the "Wise and Foolish Virgins" (Mt. 25.1-13)', in Mary Ann Beavis (ed.), *The Lost Coin. Parables of Women, Work and Wisdom* (The Biblical Seminar, 86; London: Sheffield Academic Press, 2002), pp. 71-97 (80, 82).

23. Balabanski, 'Opening the Closed Door', p. 80.

24. In each of these instances, the term Matthew uses is *phronimos*. Luke also uses it of the unjust steward (16.8) whose shrewd actions were for self-preservation. Balabanski, 'Opening the Closed Door', p. 81, observes, 'The person characterized by this sort of "wisdom" is not necessarily ethical, but one of those who "play their cards well"'.

25. This is a term coined by Elisabeth Schüssler Fiorenza in *Discipleship of Equals: A Critical Feminist Ekklesialogy of Liberation* (London: SCM Press, 1993) to describe a liberating *ekklēsia* (church) of women characterized by a feminist ethics of solidarity, which fosters respect and befriending between women.

26. Balabanski, 'Opening the Closed Door', p. 81.

ways' are in Jesus' instructions to disciples to enter the narrow gate that leads to life rather than the easy, wide road that leads to destruction (7.13-14); the two persons in the field and the two women grinding meal, one of which will be taken and the other left behind (24.40-41); and the division at the end times between sheep and goats, separating those who will enjoy eternal life from those who will go to eternal punishment (25.31-46). Feminists have long noted that this manner of setting up binary oppositions serves to maintain patriarchal and kyriarchal power. Constructions such as wise/foolish, male/female, divine/human set up 'a system of allegiance and rejection, whereby the former is defined as good and the latter as evil'.[27] While the parable wants us to side with the astute virgins, to do so is problematic.

Not Giving to Others

Though the wise virgins' preparedness is laudatory, we cannot accept their lack of relationship and care for their needy sisters. Their behaviour, as well as that of the bridegroom, bears little resemblance to the compassion Jesus shows throughout the Gospel toward those who are in need or to those who have missed the mark. It is hard to see how the five wise virgins who refuse to share their oil can be examples to emulate, given that Jesus has taught his disciples, 'Give to everyone who begs from you, and do not refuse anyone who wants to borrow from you' (5.42). The suggestion of the so-called wise virgins that the needy ones go to the dealers and buy oil themselves is akin to the disciples' solution to 'send the crowds away so that they may go into the villages and buy food for themselves' (14.15) when they and Jesus faced a hungry crowd. In that instance, Jesus had shown that to leave everyone to fend for themselves is not the solution. Nor can it be in Mt. 25.1-13.

More often than not, commentators smooth over this difficulty by interpreting oil as a symbol for good deeds, something that cannot be shared. They see an equation between light and good deeds in the Sermon on the Mount, where Jesus enjoins his disciples to let their light 'shine before others so that they may see your good works and give glory to your Father in heaven' (5.16). Also frequently cited is a rabbinic reference in which the phrase 'mixed with oil' means study of Torah mingled with good deeds (*Num. R.* 13.15-16).[28] From a feminist perspective, this explanation

---

27. Balabanski, 'Opening the Closed Door', p. 80.

28. E.g. John R. Donahue, *The Gospel in Parable* (Philadelphia: Fortress, 1988), p. 104; K. Donfried, 'The Allegory of the Ten Virgins (Matt 25:1-13) as a Summary of Matthean Theology', *JBL* 93 (1974), p. 427. In my own work (*Parables for Preachers. Year A* [Collegeville, MN: Liturgical Press, 2001], pp. 195-96), I previously accepted this interpretation, which I now question.

fails to satisfy. We must grapple with the selfishness of the so-called wise virgins and their 'complicity . . . in the patri/kyriarchal *dénouement* of the story'.[29] As Vicky Balabanski observes, if this is to be

> a story in keeping with the broad sweep of the ministry of Jesus of Nazareth, we can do nothing but reply to this kyriarch, '*We* do not know *you*'. This bridegroom cannot symbolize for us Jesus Christ, the liberator. Rather, this bridegroom symbolizes for us all kyriarchs who first make the rules, then use them to exclude others.[30]

Women as Faithful Disciples

One aspect of this parable that is heartening to feminists is that those who embody faithful, prepared disciples are women.[31] In the Gospel of Matthew, there are two strands of tradition that stand in tension regarding women and discipleship. On the one hand, as Elaine observes,

> the Matthean Gospel constructs a symbolic universe that is androcentric and encodes the patriarchal constructs present in its sociohistorical location. The text creates a world in which the male norm is coterminous with the human, and this presupposition finds expression in the grammatical and narrative strategies of the text resulting in the marginalization of women.[32]

Only men are called (4.18-22; 9.9), sent as apostles (10.1-4) and commissioned (28.16). On the other hand, there are texts in which women strongly emerge as faithful disciples, often in contrast to their male counterparts.

The clearest examples of female disciples in Matthew are the Galilaean women who appear at the end of the Gospel (27.55-56, 61; 28.1-10). In the crucifixion scene, Matthew notes that many women were there, having followed (ἠκολούθησαν) Jesus from Galilee and having 'provided for him' (διακονοῦσαι, which is more properly rendered 'served, ministered'; 27.55-56). These two actions are characteristic of disciples. Like the fishermen Peter, Andrew, James, John and the tax collector Matthew who followed Jesus (4.20, 22; 9.9), so too did many Galilaean women, including Mary Magdalene, Mary the mother of James and Joseph, and the mother of Zebedee's sons. Matthew does not mention these female disciples until the crucifixion scene (27.55), but he says that they had been following (ἠκολούθησαν) all along (the verb is in the imperfect, indicating continued or repeated action in the past).[33] In addition to following, Matthew says

29. Balabanski, 'Opening the Closed Door', p. 73.
30. Balabanski, 'Opening the Closed Door', p. 96.
31. Warren Carter, *Matthew on the Margins,* p. 485, notes this.
32. Wainwright, 'The Gospel of Matthew', p. 637.
33. Cf. Lk. 8.1-3, which explicitly places women followers of Jesus alongside the men much earlier in the narrative.

they had been serving or ministering (διακονοῦσαι). They are emulating the actions that Jesus enjoined on the all-male twelve, asserting that his own mission was to serve (διακονῆσαι), not to be served (διακονηθῆναι, 20.28).

In the passion narrative, the faithfulness of these women disciples is set in stark contrast to the betrayal of Jesus by Judas, one of the twelve (26.47) and the flight of male disciples, including Peter and the two sons of Zebedee, when Jesus is arrested (27.56). The faithful discipleship of the Galilaean women continues as Mary Magdalene and 'the other Mary' watch as Jesus's body is placed in the tomb (27.61). They then return to the tomb on the first day of the week, where they are the first to be entrusted with the message of Jesus's resurrection and are the first to encounter the risen Christ directly (28.1-10).

This contrast between the responses of women and the male disciples has been growing in the second half of the Gospel. Two episodes in particular cast the male disciples in opposition to a woman whose actions Jesus affirms. In one, Jesus acclaims the great faith of a Canaanite woman (15.28), something his male disciples sorely lack (Mt. 6.30; 8.26; 14.31; 16.8; 17.20). As Elaine observed, 'the great faith of this woman … acts as a foil to the lack of understanding of the disciples who would have sent her away without compassion (15:23)'.[34] Not only that, the Canaanite woman acts in the way Jesus has instructed his disciples: not to return insult for insult (5.43-48). After Jesus has called her a dog (15.26),[35] she answers respectfully, calling him *kyrios* (most likely to be understood as 'Sir' rather than 'Lord') as she cleverly turns his slur around (15.27).

Another woman, who remains anonymous, plays a key role at the outset of the passion narrative. Two days before Jesus is handed over (26.2), she comes with a very costly jar of ointment and anoints Jesus's head while he is at table (26.6-13). Once again, the disciples play an oppositional role, angrily criticizing 'this waste' and declaring, 'this ointment could have been sold for a large sum, and the money given to the poor' (26.9). Jesus defends her, interpreting her action as 'a good work' that is preparing him for burial. The male disciples repeatedly reject Jesus's declarations about his passion, whereas this woman understands that the time for his death is near and she anoints him for burial, a ritual that is denied victims of crucifixion. Anointing on the head is a prophetic act, emphasizing Jesus's kingship, much as Samuel anointed Saul and David (1 Sam. 9–10, 16). The episode

34. Wainwright, 'The Gospel of Matthew', p. 653.

35. Just as commentators gloss over the disturbing selfishness of the five wise virgins, so many try to explain away Jesus's insult, asserting, e.g., that κυνάριος was an endearing term for a pet. Others suggest that Jesus is repeating a common saying of his day that reflected the animosity of Galilaeans toward the people of Tyre and Sidon who took their grain (e.g. see 1 Kgs 5.10-11; Acts 12.20). These explanations, however, mask the gross insult of calling the woman a dog.

concludes with Jesus declaring solemnly, 'Truly I tell you, wherever this good news is proclaimed in the whole world, what she has done will be told in remembrance of her' (26.13). As Elaine observes, this statement of Jesus 'links the remembering of her action inextricably with the remembrance of him and his actions. . . The preaching and telling of both comprise the gospel, which will be proclaimed in the whole world.'[36]

Although these women act as exemplary disciples, commentators and preachers often assert that women were not, in fact, disciples of the historical Jesus because there are no 'call' stories for them such as those found in Mt. 4.18-22 and 9.9. This is a rather strange argument, since there are at least two figures in the New Testament, one of whom is a woman, who are explicitly called a disciple (μαθητὴς) of Jesus, and for whom we have no call stories: Joseph of Arimathea (Mt. 27.57; Jn 19.38) and Tabitha (Acts 9.36). Moreover, there are many other characteristics of discipleship, such as following Jesus and serving or ministering, as illustrated above.[37]

It is also entirely possible that there were early call stories of women disciples circulating that are now lost to us given the Gospel authors' androcentric tendency to privilege the male twelve. If Elaine is correct, we may see evidence for one such story in the Matthaean version of the episode with Simon's mother-in-law (Mt. 8.14-15).[38] Elaine has proposed that the original account of this story was a call story with a healing motif. In the final form, however, the healing story overshadows the call story. Elaine shows the verbal and formal similarities between the call of Matthew (Mt. 9.9) and the story of Simon's mother-in-law. In both, Jesus takes the initiative. This is a standard feature in call stories (e.g. see the call of Peter, Andrew, James and John in 5.19, 21, and Matthew in 9.9). By contrast, in healing stories, the ill person or an advocate for them takes the initiative. Another similarity is that in both stories, Jesus 'sees' (εἶδεν, 8.14; 9.9) the one he is calling, who then directs their response to Jesus alone (αὐτῷ, 8.15; 9.9; contrast Luke's plural αὐτοῖς, 'them', 4.39). The story of Simon's mother-in-law concludes with her ministering (διηκόνει, 8.15) to Jesus, the

36. Wainwright, 'The Gospel of Matthew', p. 663.

37. See further Barbara E. Reid, 'The Happy Few Plus a Few More', in Vincent T.M. Skemp and Kelley Coblentz Bautch (eds.), *The Figure of Jesus in History and Theology. Essays in Honor of John Meier* (CBQI, 1; Washington, DC: Catholic Biblical Association of America, 2020), pp. 114-26, where, in addition to following and serving, I show that discipleship also entails exercising hospitality, enduring suffering for the sake of the gospel, and hearing and acting on the word. There are New Testament women who fulfil all these qualifications.

38. Elaine M. Wainwright, *Towards a Feminist Critical Reading of the Gospel According to Matthew* (BZNW, 60; Berlin: de Gruyter, 1991), pp. 177-91. See also Elaine M. Wainwright, *Women Healing/Healing Women. The Genderization of Healing in Early Christianity* (Bible World; London: Equinox, 2006), pp. 143-46.

ideal response of a disciple who shares in Jesus's own mission to serve (διακονῆσαι), not to be served (διακονηθῆναι, 20.28).[39]

A further indication that there were female disciples of Jesus is found in Mt. 12.46-50. Jesus has been speaking to the crowds when he is told that his mother and brothers (ἀδελφοί) are standing outside wanting to speak with him. He replies with a query, 'Who is my mother, and who are my brothers [ἀδελφοί]?' He then points to his disciples and says, 'Here are my mother and my brothers [ἀδελφοί]! For whoever does the will of my Father in heaven is my brother and sister [ἀδελφὸς καὶ ἀδελφή] and mother'. In vv. 46, 48, and 49, the masculine plural ἀδελφοί is ambiguous—it can denote a collection of male siblings or a group with both brothers and sisters. The masculine ἀδελφός and the feminine ἀδελφή in v. 50 make explicit that both men and women are in the group of disciples to whom Jesus points in v. 49.[40]

Despite these clear indications of female disciples in the Gospel of Matthew, their role and importance is overshadowed and diminished by the prominence Matthew places on the male disciples. It is male disciples who are the ones explicitly called (4.18-22; 9.9) and sent (10.1-4); they are the recipients of his instruction (11.1); they are the ones who will sit on twelve thrones judging the twelve tribes of Israel when the Son of Man is seated on the throne of his glory (19.28); they are taken aside for special instruction about his passion (20.17); they share his Last Supper (26.20); and they are the ones (minus Judas) who are commissioned to go forth and make disciples of all nations (28.16-20). Moreover, leadership of the disciples is entrusted to Peter, not the faithful women (16.17-19).[41]

An Open Door

Although the symbolic universe of the Matthaean Gospel is overwhelmingly androcentric, the persistent insertion of stories that feature women, especially

39. Deborah Krause comes to a different conclusion in her essay 'Simon Peter's Mother-in-Law—Disciple or Domestic Servant? Feminist Biblical Hermeneutics and the Interpretation of Mark 1.29-31', in Amy-Jill Levine (ed.), with Marianne Blickenstaff, *A Feminist Companion to Mark* (FCNTECW, 2; Sheffield: Sheffield Academic Press, 2001), pp. 37-53. See also Barbara E. Reid and Shelly Matthews, *Luke 1–9* (WCS, 43A; Collegeville, MN: Liturgical Press, 2021), pp. 153-58, where we come to a similar conclusion for Luke's account.

40. See Luise Schottroff, '"Behold, These Are my Sisters" (Matt 12:49): Female Disciples of Jesus the Messiah in the Major Cities of the Roman Empire', in Mercedes Navarro Puerto and Marinella Perroni (eds.), *Gospels: Narrative and History* (The Bible and Women: An Encyclopedia of Exegesis and Cultural History, 2.1; Atlanta, GA: SBL Press, 2015), pp. 53-68.

41. Rosenblatt, 'Got Into the Party After All', p. 185, calls attention to the lack of leadership and powerlessness among the ten virgins in Mt. 25.1-13.

those that show them to be faithful disciples, disrupts the prevailing male-centred symbol system and opens a way where both women and men can be seen to follow and serve, to receive the fruits of the *basileia*, and to be central to the mission of spreading the gospel.[42]

The parable of the ten virgins offers glimmers of women as faithful disciples—virgins who could evoke possibilities of the exercise of female power and prophecy, and wise women who could point toward Woman Wisdom and Jesus's embodiment of her. Despite these slim openings, the parable keeps us firmly in the world of women's slavish readiness to serve males who stand at the centre, with these so-called wise males showing craftiness rather than wisdom as they ensure their own interests. It is a world in which binary oppositions keep kyriarchal systems steadily in place.

Nonetheless, the last word in the Gospel is not the closed door that seemingly locks out the five foolish virgins forever (25.10), but, rather, the open entrance to the tomb of Jesus (28.2) and the opened tombs of the saints who were raised at Jesus's death (27.52-53).[43] This denouement to Matthew's Gospel leaves us with hope beyond reason that even the most firmly closed doors and entrenched patterns of exclusion toward women and other disadvantaged persons can be pried open by God and all who follow Wisdom's lead, effecting life to the full for all. As Elaine urges, this flourishing of life for all must not remain in the realm of eschatological hope, but, rather, the watchfulness that the parable of the ten virgins calls for is a vigilance that points us toward 'the urgency of living an ecological ethic in this now because it is from this moment that the future potential is seeded'.[44]

42. Wainwright, 'The Gospel of Matthew', pp. 666-67.

43. Balabanski, 'Opening the Closed Door', pp. 96-97, notes that the same word, θύρα, is used for the door in 25.10 and for the entrance to Jesus's tomb in 27.60.

44. Elaine M. Wainwright, *Habitat, Human, and Holy: An Eco-Rhetorical Reading of the Gospel of Matthew* (Earth Bible Commentary, 6; Sheffield: Sheffield Phoenix Press, 2016), p. 196.

HABITATS BEYOND MATTHEW

7

Beyond the Paradigm of Stewardship: Making Right Relationship Happen with God, People and Earth

Kathleen P. Rushton

Introduction

It is an honour to contribute to this Festschrift which acknowledges the contribution of Elaine Wainwright to feminist and ecological biblical interpretation. Elaine has been very significant in my journey. Like many women of my generation, I began my formal biblical and theological education in mid-life. I was blessed to meet Elaine in 1992 when she visited Aotearoa New Zealand, a few months before I left to study at Katholieke Universiteit Leuven. At that time, I was questioning the wisdom of that decision. Elaine's reassurance and support, however, affirmed me. She was about to go on sabbatical, which included in the summer of 1993 being Dublin-based with Veronica Lawson, who was doing her doctorate at Trinity College. I was invited to join them. Eventually, I went to Brisbane, where Elaine became my doctoral supervisor. Elaine, Veronica and I are Sisters of Mercy. I acknowledge Elaine's immense contribution to biblical and theological reflection in our congregation internationally.

I have been aware of critiques of the paradigm of stewardship in biblical studies generally. The impetus, however, to explore this paradigm more deeply has simmered within me for some time because several years ago my religious congregation, Nga Whaea Atawhai o Aotearoa Sisters of Mercy New Zealand, adopted stewardship as the term for the ministry of the administration of our temporal goods. I want to acknowledge that many Christian institutions use this paradigm, and the ways it is used are not homogeneous. The following is a short statement that is representative of what human stewardship of the other-than-human creation is commonly understood to mean in Christian usage:

We all share and depend on the same world, with its finite and often non-renewable resources. Christians believe that this world belongs to God by creation, redemption and sustenance, and that [God] has entrusted it to humankind, made in [God's] image and responsible to [God]; we are in the position of stewards, tenants, curators, trustees or guardians, whether or not we acknowledge this responsibility. Stewardship implies caring management, not selfish exploitation; it involves a concern for both present and future as well as self, and a recognition that the world we manage has an interest in its own survival and wellbeing independent of its value to us ... Good stewardship requires justice, truthfulness, sensitivity and compassion.[1]

The paradigm of stewardship is also found in secular cultures, where it has been co-opted by a consumerist logic. H. Paul Santmire points out, for example, that problems 'with consumerism may lead Christians to project the idea of responsible stewardship as an alternative'.[2] He warns that stewardship 'has its own troublesome ambiguities, which we neglect at our own theological peril'.[3] He continues that the term stewardship *'resists normative theological definitions'*.[4] He finds that stewardship 'is unambiguously a sign of the church's cultural captivity, and that it should be publicly rejected and abandoned'.[5] Murray Rae points out that stewardship lacks explicitly theological reference,[6] while Celia Deane-Drummond states, 'I remain to be convinced as to how far stewardship can be grounded in a theological paradigm, even if it is useful in setting boundaries of restraint'.[7]

1. Board of Social Responsibility of the General Synod of the Church of England, 1991, quoted by Richard Bauckham, *The Bible and Ecology: Rediscovering the Community of Creation* (Waco, TX: Baylor University Press, 2010), pp.1-2. For summaries of contemporary Christian views of stewardship, see 'Beyond Stewardship', University of Exeter, https://theology.exeter.ac.uk/research/projects/beyondstewardship/topics/views/ (accessed 26 May 2022).

2. H. Paul Santmire, 'From Consumerism to Stewardship: The Troublesome Ambiguities of an Attractive Option', *Dialog: A Journal of Theology,* 49.4 (2010), pp. 332-39 (333).

3. Santmire, 'From Consumerism to Stewardship', p. 333.

4. Santmire, 'From Consumerism to Stewardship', p. 333. Italics original. For an overview of his reservations about the stewardship construct, see H. Paul Santmire, *Ritualizing Nature: Renewing Christian Liturgy in a Time of Crisis* (Minneapolis, MN: Fortress, 2008), pp. 251-58.

5. Santmire, 'Consumerism to Stewardship', p. 337. He states in n. 28 that the American Catholic Church is 'now apparently trying to "catch up" to the long-established Protestant stewardship fundraising practices and exploring the theological rationale for those practices'.

6. Murray Rae, 'To Render Praise: Humanity in God's World', in R.J. Berry (ed.), *Environmental Stewardship: Critical Perspectives—Past and Present* (London: T. & T. Clark International, 2006), pp. 291-314 (293).

7. Celia Deane-Drummond, review of R.J. Berry (ed.), *Environmental Stewardship:*

At this time, when care for our common home is better understood as necessarily a central dimension of Christian faith, this chapter is a step toward addressing my concern that many Christian institutions uncritically employ the ambiguous paradigm of stewardship to name their relationship with property and finance. This paradigm has been critiqued from theological, scriptural, ethical, environmental, evolutionary and secular perspectives.[8] In this chapter, I will first focus on the lack of scriptural foundations for Christian use of the paradigm of stewardship. Following this, I shall give a brief theological overview of stewardship within the Catholic tradition. By doing so, I seek a way forward toward whakawhanaungatanga/ making right relationship happen with God, people and the Earth. Let me begin by outlining the origins of stewardship.

Origins

In 1967, historian of science Lynn White argued that Christianity was responsible for the ecological crisis because it promoted 'man's' unlimited mastery over nature.[9] Although he does not refer to specific verses of the biblical creation story, he based his assertion on the scriptural justification arising from commonly held interpretations of 'dominion' in Gen. 1.26: 'Let us create humankind in our image, after our likeness, and let them have dominion over the fish of the sea and over the birds of the air and over the cattle and over all the earth and over every creeping thing that creeps upon the earth'. According to White, this passage allowed Christians to claim that humans are mandated by God to use the earth as their possession. White asserted that Christianity was the most anthropocentric religion the world has seen.

In response, Christian theologians, and especially biblical scholars, set out to defend their tradition against White's condemnation. Many argued that the term 'dominion' had been misinterpreted not only by White but also within the Christian tradition. God gives humanity the responsibility to care for the earth. This does not, however, mean humanity has unlimited mastery over creation. Consequently, they argue, the 'correct' biblical view

Critical Perspectives—Past and Present, in *International Review of Systematic Theology* 9.3 (2007), pp. 375-78 (378).

8. Clare Palmer, 'Stewardship: A Case Study in Environmental Ethics', in R.J. Berry (ed.), *Environmental Stewardship: Critical Perspectives—Past and Present* (London: T. & T. Clark International, 2006), pp. 63-91 (75).

9. Lynn White Jr, 'The Historical Roots of our Ecological Crisis', *Science* 155 (1967), pp. 1203-1207. For an overview of White, see R.J. Berry, 'Introduction. Stewardship: A Default Position?', in in R.J. Berry (ed.), *Environmental Stewardship: Critical Perspectives—Past and Present* (London: T. & T. Clark International, 2006), pp. 1-13 (4-6).

of the human relationship to the natural world is that of stewardship, which is *not* about ownership. God is 'the lord of creation', and human beings must account for their caretaking role. Since the 1980s, many Christian churches have become more aware of environmental issues. According to Willis Jenkins, stewardship 'emerged as a discrete theological discourse in the 1980s, supporting a public Christian environmentalism especially associated with evangelical Protestants'.[10] Hilary Marlow points out that some calls to responsible stewardship are apologetic in tenor.[11]

Biblical Critiques of Stewardship

My concern is to critique the use of stewardship in Christian discourse by demonstrating the lack of biblical and theological foundation for this paradigm. As mentioned earlier, at issue is the interpretation of aspects of Genesis 1, which gives an ordered account of God creating the various elements of creation, culminating with the creation of humanity. Nowhere is humanity explicitly depicted as the steward of creation. Many readers interpret the Hebrew imperative 'subdue' (*kabash*, which is often translated as 'dominion') to mean 'stewardship'. Yet the word 'stewardship' is not, in fact, actually found in this verse: 'Let us make humans in our image, according to our likeness, and let them have dominion over the fish of the sea and over the birds of the air and over the cattle and over all the wild animals of the earth and over every creeping thing that creeps upon the earth' (Gen. 1.28).[12] To critique the basis for stewardship that depends on this passage, I shall draw on the five main criticisms of stewardship that Richard Bauckham offers in his book *The Bible and Ecology*.[13] Then, I shall move to the New Testament.

10. Willis Jenkins, *Ecologies of Grace* (Oxford: Oxford University Press, 2008), p. 78.

11. Hilary Marlow, *Biblical Prophets: Contemporary Environmental Ethics* (Oxford: Oxford University Press, 2009), p. 83.

12. Calvin DeWitt, e.g., in *The Green Bible* (New York City: HarperOne, 2008), I, p. 26, asserts that the Bible 'shows that dominion means responsible stewardship. God gave humans a special role and responsibility as stewards of his creation'. Later, in the concluding 'Bible Studies' section of the *Green Bible*, it is stated that the 'stewardship role is important enough that it is mentioned several times in the creation narrative' (p. 1226). On the verb *kabash*, which 'has all the connotations of heavy-handed control', see Norman Habel, *The Birth, the Curse and the Greening of Earth: An Ecological Reading of Genesis 1–11* (Earth Bible Commentary; Sheffield: Sheffield Phoenix Press, 2011), pp. 39-40. In the Septuagint, *kabash* is translated as *katakyrieusate* ('subjugate', 'rule', 'become lord') and in the Vulgate as *dominamini* ('have dominion').

13. I draw on the chapter 'Stewardship in Question' in Bauckham, *Bible and Ecology*, pp. 1-36

Stewardship in the Old Testament

1. *Stewardship as Hubris (Pride or Arrogance).* The common Christian idea of stewardship, understood as an interpretation of the human
   dominion over other creatures given to humans by God in Gen. 1.26 and
   28 (hereafter Christian stewardship), implies that humans are in charge
   of the whole Earth and its destiny. This human role need not be exploitative. It can be responsible and caring. Any control that humans have,
   however, is partial and must be placed in the context of what we do not
   know and will not know.[14] The ecological crisis of our times has its roots
   in the many well-meaning technological and productive advances of the
   past few centuries that have given obvious benefits to our everyday lives
   but have also resulted in catastrophic effects.

   Christian stewardship is a distorted view of stewardship in the Old
   Testament. This 'totalizing' reading of dominion is a peculiarly modern
   one, in that it is not found in the reception history of Gen. 1.26 before the
   modern period,[15] and is also typically modern in its aspiration 'to reject
   all limits on human power and activity, to throw off all the constraints
   of nature, [and] to remake the world according to human design'.[16] The
   modern projection of dominion is hubristic, in that it rejects limits placed
   on human beings and claims the kind of control which was always held
   to belong to God alone.

   Christian thought has usually placed all human action within a larger
   framework of divine providence in which God's created order is structured in a certain way. Human beings violate this at their peril. Interpretations of dominion are problematic and lack a biblical basis because Gen.
   1.26 and 28 have been isolated from the wider context of Scripture to
   define the God-given relationship of humans to the rest of creation.

2. *Stewardship Excludes God's Own Activity in the World.* A second criticism links with the first in that the concept of human stewardship overlooks God's ongoing involvement in creation. It appears to work on the
   assumption, whether consciously or not, that God has delegated governance of the world to humans. Humans were created on the sixth day at
   the end of God's creation. God could now rest, having placed the world

---

14. For an overview of James Lovelock on this, see Bauckham, *Bible and Ecology*,
pp. 2-5.

15. I use the term modern to indicate the change of mindset that arose because of
assumptions about 'dominion' in the Genesis text which authorized human control over
nature, the project of scientific knowledge and technical exploitation. This understanding contrasts with that of mediaeval Western Christianity, which held such control had
previously always been thought to belong to God alone. See Bauckham, *Bible and Ecology*, pp. 5-7.

16. Bauckham, *Bible and Ecology*, p. 6.

in human hands. In this view, humans problematically assume the role of God in relation to creation. This, however, is the exact opposite of the biblical view wherein God's continuing sovereignty over creation is never ceded. The perception that God is in some sense absent is indeed problematic.

3. *Stewardship Lacks Specific Content.* Stewardship has proved to be a very flexible term. Is it hands-on or hands-off? Stewardship implies that the other-than-human creation needs humanity to protect, preserve and repair it. Yet creation, in fact, fared very well without human intervention for millions of years. Some scientists engaged in biotechnology see dominion as a mandate to control the evolutionary process.

4. *Stewardship Sets Humans over Creation, Not within It.* A fourth criticism of the notion of stewardship is that it presents the relationship of humans to creation on a vertical axis without a related horizontal dimension:

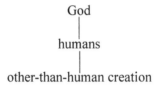

This hierarchy obscures the fact that humans are also creatures in our common home. Stewardship places humans in authority over rather than in community alongside and with creation. This model assumes an anthropocentric relationship. Humans rule and care for creation. Creation is a passive receiver of our care. The vertical focus of dominion or stewardship thus gives rise to the ideological driving forces of the modern technological project of dominating nature. Modern Western people have arguably forgotten their creatureliness, their embeddedness in the creation and their interdependence with the other-than-human. While stewardship may be one way of decentring domination and exploitation, it nonetheless assumes a vertical, one-way relationship. However, there needs to be a reciprocal relationship, which acknowledges humankind's dependence on the other-than-human.

5. *Stewardship Tends to Isolate One Scriptural Text.* As noted earlier, stewardship relies for its biblical support on Gen. 1.26 and 1.28. These two verses 'have been isolated as the only part of Scripture used to define the God-given relationship of humans to the rest of creation'.[17] Obviously this text cannot be left aside, nor should it be lifted out from its context in the canon of Scripture. From a canonical perspective, it is to be inter-

17. Bauckham, *Bible and Ecology*, p. 7.

preted by other texts and offers one theme among many in the Bible for imagining our relationship within the rest of creation. Consequently, we need to rediscover other important biblical texts about the community of creation (such as Job 38–41; Ps. 104) in which the human place in creation is 'completely unconcerned with dominion and that do[es] not set humans above other creatures'.[18]

Stewardship in the New Testament

'Christian stewardship' is assumed to have the authority of Jesus. This assumption arises principally from two of his parables (Lk. 16.1-9; Mt. 25.14-30) where 'stewardship' is associated with the organizational structure of the Graeco-Roman household. This involves three components: the master, the steward and the master's possessions or household for which the steward was responsible. A steward was usually a slave whose responsibilities were over the household on behalf of the master. This involved oversight of all labour, including its products, maintaining a household (both production and consumption) and application of the craft of household management. This idea of stewardship comes from a society based on slavery, a human relationship that is now officially condemned, even though it still exists today in practice. Clare Palmer points out that the 'political message encoded in stewardship is one of power and oppression; of server and served'.[19] An added problem of stewardship, as we saw earlier, is the idea of an absent owner.

In the Gospels, the Greek words denoting stewardship are found only in the Parable of the Unjust Steward (Lk. 16.1-9) and in the saying of Jesus on watchfulness and faithfulness (Lk. 12.42). The three Greek words—administrator (of a household) or steward (*oikonomos*); to administer (*oikonomeō*); and the office of administrator (*oikonomia*)—are confined to the Parable of the Unjust Steward (Lk. 16.1-9). The noun (*oikonomos*), which denotes a person, is found in 16.1, 3; the noun for the office (*oikonomia*) in 16.2, 3, 4; and the verb (*oikonomeō*) in 16.2.[20] In the NRSV, these terms are translated as 'manager' and 'management', while the RSV, as can be seen in the text below, uses 'steward' and 'stewardship'.

18. Bauckham, *Bible and Ecology*, p. 37; for biblical passages on the community of creation, see his chapters 2–5.

19. Palmer, 'Stewardship', p. 69.

20. The words for 'household' (*oikos*), 'steward' (*oikonomos*) and 'inhabited world' (*oikoumēnē*) link with economics, ecumenism and ecology, giving us a new consciousness of the household of God, because three interconnected household (*oikos*) words come into our daily language through the German *oekologie*: ecology, economics and ecumenism.

16 Then Jesus said to the disciples, 'There was a rich man (*anthropos*) who had a manager (*oikonomos*), and charges were brought to him that this man was squandering his property. ² So he summoned him and said to him, "What is this that I hear about you? Give me an accounting of your management (*oikonomia*), because you cannot be my manager (*oikonomeō*) any longer." ³ Then the manager (*oikonomos*) said to himself, "What will I do, now that my master (*kyrios*) is taking the position (*oikonomia*) away from me? I am not strong enough to dig, and I am ashamed to beg. ⁴ I have decided what to do so that, when I am dismissed as manager (*oikonomia*), people may welcome me into their homes." ⁵ So, summoning his master's (*kyrios*) debtors one by one, he asked the first, "How much do you owe my master (*kyrios*)"? ⁶ He answered, "A hundred jugs of olive oil". He said to him, "Take your bill, sit down quickly, and make it fifty". ⁷ Then he asked another, "And how much do you owe"? He replied, "A hundred containers of wheat". He said to him, "Take your bill and make it eighty". ⁸ And his master (*kyrios*) commended the dishonest manager because he had acted shrewdly; for the children of this age are more shrewd in dealing with their own generation than are the children of light. ⁹ And I tell you, make friends for yourselves by means of dishonest wealth (*mamona*) so that when it is gone, they may welcome you into the eternal homes (*skenas*).' (NRSV)

16 He also said to the disciples, 'There was a rich man (*anthropos*) who had a steward (*oikonomos*), and charges were brought to him that this man was wasting his goods. ² And he called him and said to him, "What is this that I hear about you? Turn in the account of your stewardship (*oikonomia*), for you can no longer be steward (*oikonomeō*)". ³ And the steward (*oikonomos*) said to himself, "What shall I do, since my master (*kyrios*) is taking the stewardship (*oikonomia*) away from me? I am not strong enough to dig, and I am ashamed to beg. ⁴ I have decided what to do, so that people may receive me into their houses when I am put out of the stewardship (*oikonomia*)." ⁵ So, summoning his master's (*kyrios*) debtors one by one, he said to the first, "How much do you owe my master (*kyrios*)"? ⁶ He said, "A hundred measures of oil". And he said to him, "Take your bill, and sit down quickly and write fifty". ⁷ Then he said to another, "And how much do you owe"? He said, "A hundred measures of wheat". He said to him, "Take your bill, and write eighty". ⁸ The master (*kyrios*) commended the dishonest steward for his shrewdness; for the sons of this world are more shrewd in dealing with their own generation than the sons of light. ⁹ And I tell you, make friends for yourselves by means of unrighteous mammon (*mamona*), so that when it fails they may receive you into the eternal habitations (*skenas*).' (RSV)

In Lk. 12.42, the noun for the person (*oikonomos*) appears in a question Jesus asks concerning watchfulness and faithfulness: 'Who then is the faithful and prudent manager (*oikonomos*) whom his master (*kyrios*) will put in charge of his slaves (*doulos*), to give them their allowance of food at the proper time'? (NRSV). The RSV, NAB and JB render *oikonomos* as 'steward' rather than 'manager', as those three translations also do in the Parable of the Unjust Steward. The outcome of substituting management language for stewardship language in the NRSV has led to the perception that the concept of stewardship is used more widely in the Gospels. An example is found in the Parable of the Talents (Mt. 25.14-30). A man (*anthropos*) hands over talents to his slaves (*doulos*); however, none of the three Greek stewardship words appear.[21] Some translations of Jn 2.8-9 have Jesus offering directions about the wine to the 'chief steward'. The Greek word there is better translated 'master of the feast' (*architriklinos*). In the Epistles, 'steward' is used metaphorically to denote ecclesiastical offices and functions (e.g. 1 Cor. 4.1).[22] Santamire points out that 'stewards of the mysteries of God' and 'like good stewards of the manifold gifts of grace' (1 Pet. 4.10) may *appear* to take us beyond the anthropocentric but actually continue to drag us back.[23]

Jesus says many things about money, wealth and the dangers of wealth, which we do not encounter in the theological and cultural discussions of these two parables. Stewardship is 'generally about the management and the opportunities of wealth, not about the problems of wealth itself'.[24] Nowhere in the Bible is it explicitly mentioned that a steward was or is responsible for the natural world. In other words, there is no 'biblical' concept of the stewardship of nature. As mentioned earlier, the terms 'steward' (*oikonomos*) and 'stewardship' (*oikonomia*) do not appear in the Septuagint creation narratives.

Summary
The paradigm of Christian stewardship does not have a biblical basis. Nowhere is humanity explicitly given the role of stewards of creation. There are theological problems related to God's presence and action in the world because stewardship infers that God is absent. Politically, the problem encoded in stewardship is one of power and oppression, server and served, thereby assuming the normativity of hierarchical models of governance. In the light of evolutionary science, moreover, the notion that earth is

---

21. The International Theological Commission document *Communion and Stewardship: Human Persons Created in the Image of God*, which I refer to later, states, 'They act in the place of the master as stewards' (cf. Mt. 25.14ff.).
22. See *EDNT*, II, p. 499.
23. Santmire, 'Consumerism to Stewardship', p. 334.
24. Santmire, 'Consumerism to Stewardship', p. 335.

to be managed by humanity does not make sense. Overall, stewardship in its Christian and secular usage is anthropocentric, not ecological, and can in some cases be used to perversely support and legitimate increased exploitation of the natural world.

The Catholic Tradition

Like other Christian traditions, Catholicism rarely reflected on the Earth *in se* for nearly two millennia.[25] The Earth was perceived as the place of human existence and part of God's divine creativity. All was created to provide for 'man' made in the image of God in two ways. First, the Earth was the *setting* where human persons worked toward their salvation in a better world to come; and second, the Earth was the *supplier* of the requirements of life and resources needed for earthly existence. The understanding of the 'common good' that prevailed described the well-being of the human community. While influential theologians Augustine (354–430) and Thomas Aquinas (1225–1274) subscribed to the view that Earth and Earth's creatures did not have an independent value beyond supplying the needs of human persons and the working of the universe, they did 'teach that earth's goods should be distributed in such a way that the needs of all people would be met'.[26]

Even though church leadership valued the life and teaching of Saint Francis of Assisi, a twofold doctrine—namely that all people's needs should be met and all creation exists to provide those needs—persisted, thereby limiting Catholic environmental teachings until the late twentieth century. This twofold doctrine was developed in Catholic social teaching. Pope Leo XIII issued the first papal social encyclical, *Rerum novarum* ('On the Condition of Worker Classes'), in 1891. Set out for the first time was an analysis of social issues, especially economic injustice. However, in addressing the place of humankind in creation, Leo XIII set out the traditional view that 'man' is positioned over all creatures, since the human soul 'bears the express image and likeness of God', and 'there resides in it that sovereignty through the medium of which man has been bidden to rule all created nature below him and to make all lands and seas serve his interests'.[27] Traditional attitudes toward the Earth, other creatures and resources continued in church teaching and are found in the documents of the Second Vatican Council (11 October 1962–8 December 1965) as I shall now show.

25. For an overview, see John Hart, 'Catholicism', in Roger S. Gottlieb (ed.), *The Oxford Handbook of Religion and Ecology* (Oxford: Oxford University Press, 2006), pp. 65-71.

26. Hart, 'Catholicism', p. 69.

27. Pope Leo XIII, *On the Condition of the Working Classes: Rerum Novarum* (NCWC translation; Boston, MA: Daughters of St. Paul, 1942), p. 35, §57.

Stewardship

In the Catholic tradition, the understanding of stewardship is a consequence of human beings having been created in the image of God (Gen. 1.26); this is known as the doctrine of the *imago Dei*.[28] Although the term 'steward-ship' is not found in the 1965 Vatican II document *Gaudium et spes*, its roots are arguably there with the emphasis on the human world (§2) and humanity whose creation in the image of God 'received a mandate to subject to him-self the earth and all it contains, and to govern the world with justice and holiness' (§34; cf. §12).[29]

A significant shift was signalled by John Paul II in his 1990 World Day of Peace Message, 'Peace with God the Creator: Peace with All of Creation'. Even though there is 'retention and affirmation' of traditional perspectives, there is no explicit mention of stewardship. He speaks of 'a new ecological awareness' (§1) emerging and states that 'Christians, in particular, realize that their responsibility within creation and their duty towards nature and the Creator are an essential part of their faith' (§15).[30] John Paul II, however, entitles a 2001 General Audience 'God Made Man Steward of Creation'.[31] After referring to Gen. 1.28, he quotes from his 1995 encyclical, *Evange-lium vitae*: 'Man's lordship however is not absolute, but ministerial: it is a real reflection of the unique and infinite lordship of God. Hence man must exercise it with wisdom and love, sharing in the boundless wisdom and love of God' (§52).[32] He continues: 'We must therefore encourage and support the "ecological conversion" [because] ... Man is no longer the Creator's "steward"'. (§4).[33]

The International Theological Commission document *Communion and Stewardship: Human Persons Created in the Image of God* (2000–2002) addresses the challenges posed by 'the explosion of scientific and techno-

28. Statements about humanity being made in the image of God are rare in the Old Testament (Gen. 1.26-27; 5.3; 9.6; Wis. 2.23; cf. Ps. 8).

29. For an overview on Vatican II (1962–1965) retaining 'traditional attitudes towards earth, earth's other creatures, and earth's good (resources)', see Hart, 'Cathol-icism', pp. 73-74.

30. Pope John Paul II, World Day of Peace Message, 'Peace with God the Creator: Peace with All of Creation', 1 January 1990, http://www.vatican.va/content/john-paul-ii/en/messages/peace/documents/hf_jp-ii_mes_19891208_xxiii-world-day-for-peace.html. The next sentence is, 'As a result, they are conscious of a vast field of ecumenical and interreligious cooperation opening up before them'.

31. John Paul II, General Audience, 17 January 2001, http://www.vatican.va/content/john-paul-ii/en/audiences/2001/documents/hf_jp-ii_aud_20010117.pdf.

32. In §3 he quotes from §52 of his 1995 encyclical, *Evangelium vitae*, http://www.vatican.va/content/john-paul-ii/en/encyclicals/documents/hf_jp-ii_enc_25031995_evangelium-vitae.html.

33. John Paul II, General Audience, 17 January 2001.

logical capability in modern times' (§1).[34] Stewardship is presented as one of the two main themes emerging from the theology of the image of God. The document repeatedly explains and appeals to stewardship, especially in chapter 3, entitled, 'In the Image of God: Stewards of Visible Creation', where it states the following:

> Human stewardship of the created world is precisely a stewardship exercised by way of participation in the divine rule and is always subject to it. Human beings exercise this stewardship by gaining scientific understanding of the universe, by caring responsibly for the natural world (including animals and the environment), and by guarding their own biological integrity. (§61)

This document also draws on the New Testament passages mentioned earlier, inferring incorrectly that the stewardship words are there; for example, 'God appoints man as [God's] steward in the manner of the master in the Gospel parables (cf. Lk. 19.12)' (§58).

Laudato Si'

Significantly, the term stewardship is found explicitly only once in the 2015 encyclical of Pope Francis, *Laudato Si': On Care for our Common Home*, where it is footnoted to a colloquium sponsored by the Federation of Asian Bishops' Conference (§116).[35] Francis is discussing the 'excessive anthropocentrism' of modernity, an 'inadequate presentation of human anthropology' and 'a Promethean vision of mastery over the world'. He continues, 'Instead, our "dominion" over the universe should be understood more properly in the sense of responsible stewardship'. I shall look now at *Laudato Si'* (hereafter *LS*) in the light of four terms Francis employs and which suggest that he is moving beyond the paradigm of stewardship: our common home, interconnectedness, love language and integral ecology.

Some scholars such as Jonathan Boston point out that, '[a]lthough the idea of stewardship is certainly implicit in much of the encyclical, Pope Francis places his primary emphasis on the idea of caring for "our common home"'. There is a shift 'from the ethical management of nature to the ethical management of human behaviour'.[36] The encyclical speaks of the

---

34. International Theological Commission, 'Communion and Stewardship: Human Persons Created in the Image of God', https://www.vatican.va/roman_curia/congregations/cfaith/cti_documents/rc_con_cfaith_doc_20040723_communion-stewardship_en.html. An additional resource that helpfully explains Catholic perspectives on the environment is Agneta Sutton, *Ecology and Stewardship: What Catholics Believe about the Environment* (London: Catholic Truth Society, 2012).

35. *LS* §116, n. 94 cites *Love for Creation: An Asian Response to the Ecological Crisis*, Declaration of the Colloquium sponsored by the Federation of Asian Bishops' Conference (Tagatay, 31 January–5 February, 1993), 3.4.2.

36. Jonathan Boston, *'Laudato Si'*: A Plea from Pope Francis to Protect "Our Com-

Earth, 'our common home', being 'like a sister with whom we share our life and a beautiful mother who opens her arms to embrace us' (§1). *Laudato Si'* personifies nature. The pope's reference to 'mother' and 'sister' is significant. It is more than simply a rhetorical device. It highlights humanity's close relationship with the rest of nature.

Celia Deane-Drummond argues that although traditional Roman Catholic approaches have emphasized 'primacy of human dignity ... taking proper account of interconnectedness requires a significant paradigm shift in what dignity signifies and challenges human exceptionalism'.[37] Ecology and anthropology need to be combined. She also emphasizes how Francis returns to a more holistic way of thinking about the world and human relationship within it and insists that Indigenous people should be 'principal dialogue partners' (*LS* §146).[38] The creation accounts in the book of Genesis suggest that human life is grounded in three fundamental and closely intertwined relationships: with God, with our neighbour and with the earth itself. According to the Bible, these three vital relationships have been broken, both outwardly and within us. This rupture is sin. The harmony between the creator, humanity and creation as a whole was disrupted by our presuming to take the place of God and refusing to acknowledge our creaturely limitations. This in turn distorted our mandate to 'have dominion' over the earth (cf. Gen. 1.28) and to 'till it and keep it' (Gen. 2.15). As a result, the originally harmonious relationship between human beings and nature became conflictual (cf. Gen. 3.17-19; *LS* §66). Furthermore, rather than the possibly hierarchical, managerial implication of the stewardship model, Francis stresses the mutuality of the relationship between humans and the non-human world: 'Each community can take from the bounty of the earth whatever it needs for subsistence, but it also has the duty to protect the earth and to ensure its fruitfulness for coming generations' (*LS* §67).

Mark Graham understands that the love language of *LS* departs significantly from the stewardship paradigm, which he suggests results in anthropocentrism that 'breeds a robust interventionism'. He finds Francis's love language to be 'a breath of fresh air and the beginnings of potential alternative cosmology and anthropology that could result in qualitatively different environmental ethic'. Graham notes that, at the beginning of the document, the love language prevails, but in the middle, it trails off as Francis focuses

---

mon Home"—A Sympathetic Critique', *Stimulus: The New Zealand Journal of Christian Thought and Practice*, 24.2 (2017), n. 13, https://hail.to/laidlaw-college/publication/cGDYGRc/article/fDRykT0#_edn10. For example, stewardship is inferred in *LS* §67.

37. Celia Deane-Drummond, 'A New Anthropology? *Laudato Si'* and the Question of Interconnectedness', in Robert McKim (ed.), *Laudato Si' and the Environment: Pope Francis' Green Encyclical* (Routledge New Critical Thinking Series in Religious, Theology and Biblical Studies; London: Routledge, 2020), pp. 189-201 (189).

38. Deane-Drummond, 'A New Anthropology?' pp. 196-97.

on specific environmental issues, and by the end it is uncertain if 'his love language or the traditional stewardship paradigm is guiding his analysis'. [39]

Anna Rowlands and Robert E. Czerny highlight that 'integral ecology' affirms the interrelationships that exist because 'everything is closely related' and 'today's problems call for a vision capable of taking into account every aspect of the global crisis'.[40] Nature 'cannot be regarded as something separate from ourselves or as a mere setting in which we live. We are part of nature ...' (*LS* §139). Francis challenges us to hear 'both the cry of the earth and the cry of the poor'(*LS* §49). In combining care for our common home with the long-held tradition of the corporal and spiritual works of mercy, Francis takes his readers beyond the usual way of thinking about being merciful to people and invites them to be merciful to a river or trees. In addition, Rowlands and Czerny point out that to *care* goes beyond the relationship of good stewardship, as a steward does not have to love. Parents love and care for their children even if it means sacrificing themselves. Home, therefore, is more than something useful. Home is where we are 'nurtured, kept safe, and learn our distinct cultural identity'. Likewise, Earth, our home, cares for us. Francis, with Francis of Assisi and many Indigenous peoples, understands and recognizes that God sustains us through our sister, Mother Earth.[41]

Conclusion

This chapter is a first step in addressing my concern that many Christian institutions uncritically employ the ambiguous paradigm of stewardship to define their relationship with property and finance. I have examined the lack of scriptural foundations for the Christian use of the stewardship paradigm. I have also explored how traditional attitudes toward the Earth, other creatures and resources continued in the teachings of the Catholic Church in a twofold doctrine—namely that all people's needs should be met, and all creation exists to provide those needs. Recently, a significant shift, arguably beyond stewardship, is identifiable in the light of four terms Pope Francis employs in *Laudato Si'*: our common home, interconnectedness, love language and integral ecology.

These findings prepare the way for a next step, outside the scope of this chapter, which is to move beyond the paradigm of stewardship based

---

39. Mark Graham, 'Pope Francis's *Laudato Si'*: A Critical Response', *Minding Nature* 10.2 (2017), pp. 57-64 (58). https://www.humansandnature.org/pope-francis%E2%80%99s-laudato-si-a-critical-response.

40. Anna F. Rowlands and Robert E. Czerny, 'The Eight Works of Mercy', *Thinking Faith*, 19 February 2018, https://www.thinkingfaith.org/articles/eight-works-mercy.

41. Rowlands and Czerny, 'The Eight Works of Mercy'.

on misinterpretations of the Genesis creation texts and assumptions perceived to be found in the New Testament. This will also require some wider research because, as Clare Palmer points out, 'Stewardship of the natural world, whether Christian or otherwise, then, remains profoundly anthropocentric and un-ecological, legitimating and encouraging increased human use of the natural world'.[42] A way forward is found through the 'integral ecology' of *Laudato Si'*, which affirms the deep connections found in the creation accounts and suggests that 'human life is grounded in three fundamental and closely intertwined relationships: with God, with our neighbour and the earth itself' (§66). This resonates in my context, because Māori, the first people of Aotearoa New Zealand, have an evocative verbal form: whakawhanaungatanga, or making right relationship happen. In this understanding, right relationship is a verb, an action. The causative prefix, whaka suggests 'making' and turns the noun, whanaungatanga (right relationship), into the verb whakawhanaungatanga, meaning 'making right relationship' in a series of interconnected relationships with God (Atua), people (tangata) and land (whenua).[43]

---

42. Palmer, 'Stewardship', p. 75.

43. On Atua, tangata and whenua, see Henare Tate, *He Puna Iti i te Ao Mārama: A Little Spring in the World of Light* (Auckland: Libro International, 2012), pp. 39, 58, 71-72.

8

INTRODUCING DECOLONIZING HERMENEUTICS IN AUSTRALIA

Norman Habel and Anne Pattel-Gray

Preface

It is an honour to contribute to a Festschrift that recognizes the contribution Elaine Wainwright has made to the fields of theology and biblical studies. As editor of the Earth Bible Commentary series, I, Norman Habel, was privileged to read and endorse Elaine's excellent commentary entitled *Habitat, Human, and Holy: An Eco-Rhetorical Reading of the Gospel of Matthew*.[1] Elaine's hermeneutics are a model for all biblical interpreters to celebrate.

As co-author with Uncle Norm (Norman Habel), I, Anne Pattel-Gray, helped develop a hermeneutic that involves decolonizing the biblical narrative. I am a First Nations scholar whose works include *Through Aboriginal Eyes* (1991) and *Aboriginal Spirituality* (1996).

At a Common Dreams Conference in 2019, Uncle Norm gave a presentation on how scholars and churches have ignored the biblical precolonial narratives where Abraham made a treaty with the Canaanites and recognized the Canaanite Creator Spirit, El. Aunty Anne gave a presentation stressing the need, after the release of *The Uluru Statement from the Heart*,[2] for the Australian government to acknowledge the sovereignty of the First Nations people of Australia and to make an appropriate treaty.

In discussions after these presentations, we decided to return to the Bible and explore how together we might decolonize the biblical narrative. In this context, colonialism can be understood as a colonial mindset of individuals,

---

1. Elaine Wainwright, *Habitat, Human, and Holy: An Ecological Reading of the Gospel of Matthew* (Sheffield: Sheffield Phoenix Press, 2016).

2. A historic statement signed by over 250 Aboriginal and Torres Strait Islander delegates in May 2017 petitioning the leaders of Australia to undertake substantial constitutional and structural reforms to empower the First Nations people of Australia. Read the full statement here: https://ulurustatement.org/.

communities or peoples that assumes, claims or activates the fundamental belief or worldview that they have the right to exercise dominion, control or dispossession of other individuals, communities or peoples.

The Colonial Background

Given the long history of reading the Bible from a colonial perspective and the assumption that it justified the colonization of First Nations people, the key question is whether precolonial texts and traditions can be retrieved from the Bible—texts and traditions that are free from colonial language or revisions by colonial narrators and editors, and which speak empathetically to the First Peoples of Australia, or other countries, as fellow human beings. As Steve Heinrichs writes,

> The Bible has been used as a tool of colonialism, xenophobia, exclusion and cultural genocide. It still is. But this does not have to be. For centuries, communities of radical compassion and courage have read and re-read the sacred page in creative and critical fashion, so that these old memories shake the powers from their thrones and bring actual change to those who have been kept down.[3]

At the time I (Norm) was working in Queensland with the Rainbow Spirit Elders in the writing of *Rainbow Spirit Theology*,[4] Michael Prior outlined how the Bible was a powerful factor in the colonial history of Latin America, South Africa and Palestine. In relation to Latin America he writes,

> [Pablo] Richard judges that 'The problem is not the Bible itself, but the way it has been interpreted' (1990, 66). The task of the indigenous peoples, in such a view, is to construct a new hermeneutic which decolonises the interpretation of the Bible and takes possession of it from an indigenous perspective.[5]

In recent years, postcolonial theory has been introduced as a hermeneutical tool for reading the Bible. Many configurations of postcolonial biblical reading are concerned with the socio-political context in which the *voice* of the other is being silenced. A precolonial reading, however, seeks to retrieve the voice of the *other—the precolonial community or people.* In doing so, the voice of the colonial narrator or editor may also be exposed in the context of the biblical text. Lazare Rukundwa declares that 'postcolonial theory

---

3. Steve Heinrichs, 'Preface: Liberating the Bible', in Steve Heinrichs (ed.), *Unsettling the Word: Biblical Experiments in Decolonization* (Maryknoll, NY: Orbis Books, 2018), pp. ix-xvi (xvii).

4. Rainbow Spirit Elders, *Rainbow Spirit Theology: Towards an Australian Aboriginal Theology* (Melbourne: Harper Collins, 2007).

5. Michael Prior, *The Bible and Colonialism: A Moral Critique* (Sheffield: Sheffield Academic Press, 1997), p. 69.

takes into consideration the situation of the colonizer as well as the colonized, in order to reconstruct a negotiating space for equity. Under postcolonial theory, theologians argue that biblical texts have been marked as powerful instruments of imperialism.'[6] According to scholars like Rukundwa, the Bible as a text was produced and circulated under imperial rule to the extent that it was at the service of colonial expansion.

Our precolonial approach does not seek to determine the specific historical colonial context of the narrator or editor of each text; rather, it studies the text's language, rhetoric, innuendoes and force in order to discern whether the text reflects a colonial or materialist thrust; whether a precolonial tradition has been revised using colonial jargon; and whether a precolonial tradition can be retrieved through using the voice of a precolonial narrator.

Recently, Meredith Lake published a relevant volume entitled *The Bible in Australia: A Cultural History*. In Chapter 11, she speaks about 'Indigenising the Bible' and explores the many ways in which the Bible has played a role in colonizing the First Peoples of Australia. She claims that 'the Bible came in a European imperial guise, wrapped up in colonial thought and culture. Various interpretations of the Bible played into the ways the colonists thought about the land they claimed and occupied.'[7] She continues, 'By the mid-twentieth century, there was a significant tradition of Indigenous Australians drawing on the Bible in response to colonialism',[8] and 'by the 1970s and 1980s, an increasing number of indigenous Christians took up the task of reading and interpreting the Bible in an Aboriginal way'.[9] For all these Christians, Lake states, 'the task was to identify the common ground, where indigenous cultures and traditions intersected with Bible teaching'.[10]

In addition to her detailed analysis of how the Bible affected the lives and cultures of First Nations peoples and the various ways in which they sought to relate the Bible to their culture, Lake claims that 'the Bible remains deeply important for Australia today, because it is at once an embedded part of our European inheritance, and a source for subverting colonial power and reconciling the nation. It is a text that crosses and reshapes boundaries.'[11]

'A source for subverting colonial power'! But how?

Can we say instead that the Bible is a source for exposing colonial factors and a means of endorsing precolonial sovereignty in terms of *The Uluru Statement from the Heart?*

---

6. Lazare S. Rukundra, 'Postcolonial Theory as a Hermeneutical Tool for Biblical Reading', *HTS Theological Studies* 64 (2008), pp. 1-9 (2).

7. Meredith Lake, *The Bible in Australia: A Cultural History* (Sydney: New South Publishing, 2018), p. 46.

8. Lake, *The Bible in Australia*, p. 327.

9. Lake, *The Bible in Australia*, p. 332.

10. Lake, *The Bible in Australia*, p. 337.

11. Lake, *The Bible in Australia*, p. 8.

The Decolonizing Procedure

The following outline of the hermeneutical process involved in decolonizing the biblical narrative is a summary of the decolonizing hermeneutic outlined in Volumes 1 and 2 of *De-colonising the Biblical Narrative* published
in 2022–2023.[12]

The interpretation process in relation to *The Earth Bible* commentaries
has been summarized as *suspicion, identification* and *retrieval*.[13] The interpreter suspects/assumes that past interpretations of the text may have been
anthropocentric, the focus being exclusively on human beings and their
relationship with God. The interpreter then seeks to identify with the non-
human components of the text—elements such as Earth, land, forest, waters
and the like—and to ascertain their role in the plot, thought or orientation
of the text. In so doing, the empathetic interpreter may seek to retrieve the
latent voice or message of these non-human elements.

Similar steps will be involved in the hermeneutical process of decolonizing biblical narratives: namely suspicion, exposure, retrieval and response.

Suspicion

The interpreter, one of the First Nations Christians of Australia, or an empathetic reader with a decolonized mind who dares to identify with the worldview of First Nations Australia, will be ready to suspect three colonial factors in previous readings of the biblical narratives.

1. *The Language.* The reader may discover that the language of the text's
   translations in recent generations reflects a colonial orientation rather
   than the orientation of the story in the original tradition. This is immediately obvious in the very first verse of the Bible, where we discover
   colonial translations such as,

   > *In the beginning God created the heavens and the Earth.*

   The original Hebrew in this verse does not refer to the celestial realm
   called the heavens as the abode of a deity or to the domain we call planet
   Earth—this is a cosmology that is part of a much later colonial worldview. The original Hebrew reference in Gen. 1.1 is to 'sky' and 'land',
   not to heaven and Earth. The ancient listener can relate to the visible
   world of sky and land where the narrative is being told. The First Nations

---

12. Anne Pattel-Gray and Norman Habel, *De-colonising the Biblical Narrative.
Volume One: Ancestral Land Narratives of Genesis 1–11* (Adelaide: ATF Press, 2022);
Anne Pattel-Gray and Norman Habel, *De-colonising the Biblical Narrative. Volume
Two: A First Nations De-colonising of Genesis 12–25* (Adelaide: ATF Press, 2023).

13. Norman Habel, *Exploring Ecological Hermeneutics* (Atlanta, GA: SBL, 2008),
pp. 1-8.

listener in Australia is delighted to be able to do the same. A precolonial rendering of this verse would be,

When God began to transform the Sky and the Land, the Land was ...

To discern the colonial colour of a particular word, expression or idiom in the translation, the reader may need to return to the critical text in Hebrew or Greek to ascertain whether the translation reflects a colonial mindset for the original listener. Where a translator is not a member of a First Nations community as such, they will need to try to decolonize the mind and listen empathetically to the voice of First Nations colleagues in the listening process.

2. *The Interpreter*. Virtually all the classic interpretations of the Bible in Australia, whether by academics, clergy or missionaries, reflect the colonial mindset of the interpreter who may well be unaware of his or her colonial mindset. Until recently, relatively few First Nations Australians have been involved in interpreting the original narrative publicly in the light of their traditional Australian culture. In many contexts, the First Nations Australians have been unduly influenced by early missionaries who reflected the colonial culture of the early settlers and, in some cases, claimed to have brought God to the Land of Australia.

   To listen to the narrative as a First Nations Australian, therefore, requires the listener to ignore traditional readings and interpretations and to start from scratch, listening with a decolonized mindset and discerning the language, content and intent of the original narrative tradition, in and of itself.

3. *The Narrator*. An interpretation factor that has rarely been considered in traditional biblical scholarship is the potential colonial orientation of the narrator or editor of the biblical text itself. Despite the conservative tradition that biblical authors were inspired by God, these authors were in fact interpreters of their time who gathered oral traditions from the past and transformed them into relevant narratives or poems. These narratives and poems often reflect the colonial orientation of the Israelite peoples, from the days of Moses to their return from exile in Babylon.

   Listening with a decolonized mind, we can raise again the possibility that the writer/narrator/editor of the tradition was also writing from an ancient colonial perspective which was part of his/her world, even if the context was very different from the colonial orientation of Western peoples of today.

Exposure

The goal of a decolonizing hermeneutic is not only to become aware of past colonial translations and interpretations of the narrative, but also to focus on the specific colonial dimensions of the narrative, be they reflected in the language, the idioms, the content or the theology of the narrative.

This process also involves developing a 'colonial consciousness' that facilitates discerning those traditions that reflect a colonial orientation, however subtle that may be. The *imago Dei* text in Gen. 1.26-28, for example, is replete with the colonial language of dominion and subjugation. According to the text of most English translations, humans are created to reflect God's celestial power, having 'dominion' over living creatures and a mandate to 'subdue/colonize' the Land.

Decolonizing the narrative involves daring, as one First Nations listener stated, to identify the 'curse of colonialism' that has led translators and interpreters to justify the evil of colonialism as a divine right in ancient and modern societies. Our goal is to expose that 'colonial curse' within the text and acknowledge its impact in classic interpretations. First Nations Australians have experienced and continue to be sensitive to the 'curse of colonialism' in their lives.

Retrieval

The process of identifying the colonial dimensions of the narrative also enables the interpreter to retrieve narratives that do not reflect a colonial bias, but which resonate with one or more truths or ancestral narratives of First Nations Australians today.[14]

When we hear the blessing of Melchizedek, the Canaanite priest of Salem, for example, we can immediately recognize a tradition that has survived later editing by colonial narrators. The original indigenous Canaanite blessing formula preserved in Gen. 14.19 reads,

> *Blessed be Abram by El Elyon,*
> *Maker of sky and land.*

This blessing is a Canaanite blessing, not a later Israelite blessing. Not only is the priest a Canaanite, but the God involved is El, the Canaanite Creator Spirit associated with the land of Canaan.

The First Nations listener, moreover, may not only identify the blessing as free from colonial editing, but also may feel inclined to identify with Abraham or Melchizedek and receive a blessing from El, the Canaanite Creator Spirit associated with the Land.

Response

To demonstrate the relevance of decolonizing the original narrative and retrieving narratives free from colonial bias, we have invited fellow First

---

14. In the workshops held with First Nation Australia, we have employed the designation 'Ancestral Narrative' rather than "Dreaming Narrative', because the latter expression can be misleading.

Nations Australian listeners to respond, describing their resonance with the text as a narrative that is in harmony with the ancestral narratives of their country.

Some colonial-oriented texts, however, may also prove offensive and abusive to the First Nation listener, especially if God is portrayed as involved in the colonial bias of the text. It is especially abusive, for example, when First Nations Australians hear the story of Joshua read as a precedent for the invasion and settlement of Australia as the Promised Land.

Narratives that are free from colonial editing, however, such as the commissioning of the first human being to 'serve' and 'preserve' the Land in Eden (Gen. 2.15), resonate with First Nations listeners who believe they are commissioned to be custodians of the Land in Australia and beyond. The process of listening to the subtleties and nuances of the narrative is vital for listeners, whether they be First Nations Australians or empathetic Christians who have decolonized their minds to hear the voice of the ancient storytellers.

The Precolonial Narrative of Genesis 1

To demonstrate the process of decolonizing a biblical text and retrieving a precolonial ancestral narrative we will re-interpret Genesis 1.1-25.

Verses 1-2: The Pre-existing Primordial Cosmos
The opening verse in Genesis 1 is normally translated,

> *In the beginning God created the heavens and the Earth and the Earth was ...*

A common interpretation, reflecting this translation, is that God created the universe (heaven and Earth) out of nothing (*creatio ex nihilo*). A close reading of the Hebrew, with a decolonized mind, reveals that *bara'* ('to create') does not mean 'create out of nothing' but probably 'transform', as suggested by the Rainbow Spirit Elders.[15] As v. 2 makes clear, the Land/Earth (*'erets*) already existed in the primordial Deep.

The rendering of *hashamayim weha'arets* as 'heaven and Earth' is also inconsistent with the traditional Hebrew understanding of the phrase. The basic meaning of this expression is 'the sky and the land'. As the subsequent verses reveal, this narrative of Genesis 1 is about Land, or as the First Nations people acknowledge, Genesis 1 is an Ancestral Land Narrative.

A precolonial rendering of v. 1 is,

> *When God began to transform the Sky and the Land, the Land was ...*

---

15. Rainbow Spirit Elders, *Rainbow Spirit Theology*, p. 76.

Verse 2 describes the nature of the primordial world before the creation/ transformation process begins, before God says, 'Let there be ...'. In that world, the Land is a 'formless mass' that exists in the primordial waters of the Deep, which is covered with darkness.

God is not some celestial being that intervenes from above but exists as a spirit/wind that hovers over the waters of the Deep. While *ruach* may be translated 'spirit', the most common usage of the term refers to 'wind'. The primordial world, before transformation, is a cosmos consisting of waters called the Deep in which the Land is a formless mass hidden in the darkness.

A precolonial rendering of v. 2 is,

> *The Land was a formless mass and darkness was on the face of the Deep.*
> *The wind/spirit of God hovered over the face of the waters.*

Verses 3-5: The Transformation of the Darkness

Verses 3 to 5 describe the origin and function of light in the primordial cosmos. The first creation process is the transformation of the darkness into light and darkness, day and night. The darkness is transformed prior to the transformation of the sky and the Land, thereby making the presence of sky and Land visible.

A precolonial reading of vv. 3-5 has been preserved in most traditional translations, such as,

> *Then God said, 'Let there be light'. And there was light. And God saw the light was good. And God separated the light from the darkness. God called the light Day and the darkness God called Night.*

It is significant that the function of light in this transformation is quite different from the role of the lights in the sky that were designed to provide 'light for the Land' (v. 17). This light is a reality that reveals the presence of the primordial cosmos by the removal of the darkness that covered everything.

Verses 6-8: The Transformation of the Waters

These verses involve the transformation of the primordial waters of the Deep. A 'canopy' in the waters, sometimes translated as a 'firmament', is introduced to 'divide the waters from the waters'. The resulting transformation is a cosmos with waters above the canopy and waters below the canopy.

God then calls this canopy 'Sky'. In colonial translations, the term 'sky' is rendered 'Heaven' even though this is not the abode of God or celestial beings, but the domain where waters are found, waters that would provide sustenance for the Land below.

A precolonial rendering of these verses would be,

Then God said, 'Let there be a canopy in the waters and let it divide the waters from the waters'. So, God made a canopy and it divided the waters under it from the waters above it. And it happened. And God called the canopy 'Sky'.

Verses 9-12: The Transformation of the Land

Contrary to many interpretations of 'Day Three' of the Genesis 1 narrative, God does not say 'Let there be Land/Earth'. As we know from v. 2, Land already pre-exists Deep in the primordial waters. This formless mass is here called *yabbasha*, often translated as 'dry ground', even though it pre-existed in the primordial waters.

A highly significant dimension of this transformation is the specific form of the verb *ra'a*, which is rendered 'appear'—a rendering that is used to describe the 'appearance' of God (as in Gen. 18.2). Earth's transformation first involves its 'appearance' as a massive form from the Deep.

A second image that is reflected in this transformation process is the image of birth. The waters of the Deep are like a primordial womb where the Land resides as an embryo. The separation of the waters is tantamount to the bursting of the waters that enable the 'ground' to appear. When the waters burst and the 'ground' appears, God 'names' the baby 'Land'.

A precolonial rendering of vv. 9-10 would be,

> *Then God said, 'Let the waters below the sky come together into one place and let the ground appear'. And it happened. And God named the ground 'Land'. The waters that came together he named 'Seas'. And God saw that it was good.*

The second transformation of the Land that happens in vv. 11-12 involves the animation of the Land. The Land is transformed from a primordial lifeless mass to animated Land that is the source of rich vegetation. Land is not lifeless matter but animated ground.

A precolonial rendering of v. 11 would be,

> *Then God said, 'Let Land come alive with vegetation, plants yielding seeds and trees bearing fruit in which there is seed, according to its kind upon the Land'. And it happened.*

Verses 14-19: The Transformation of the Sky

The lights placed in the sky transform the sky into a vehicle for facilitating life on the Land, including time, seasons and visibility. The lights in the sky are designed specifically to 'give light to the Land'. Once again, the sky is the source of light, not the 'heavens' as some translations suggest.

A precolonial rendering of vv. 14 and 15 would be,

> *Then God said, 'Let there be lights in the canopy of the sky to divide the day from the night. And let them be for signs and for seasons, for days and*

for years. And let there be lights in the canopy of the sky to give light to the Land.' And it happened.

Verses 20-23: The Transformation of the Waters

The waters of the primordial Deep, once covered in darkness, are now animated with living creatures, as is the sky above. The creatures that swarm in the waters of the sea include 'sea monsters'. The creatures that fly in the sky include 'winged birds' of every kind.

The blessing that follows makes it clear that all living creatures multiply with God's blessing. The blessing of the birds is linked to the Land. The capacity of all living creatures is to 'be fruitful and multiply', which means they are free to live in their designated domains. There is no hint of the later colonial edict that gives humans the right to dominate them or the Land.

A precolonial rendering of vv. 20-23 would be,

> *Then God said, 'Let the waters come alive with swarms of life and let birds fly above the Land across the canopy of the sky'. So, God made great sea monsters and every creature that lives in the waters to reproduce and to fill the sea, according to its kind and every winged bird according to its kind. And God saw that it was good.*
> *Then God blessed them all and said, 'Be fruitful and multiply and fill the waters of the Seas and let birds multiply on the Land'.*

Verses 24-25: The Transformation of the Land

A second transformation of the Land occurs when Land is made the creator of all species of living creatures on the Land—everything from koalas to kangaroos, from lizards to lice. The Land becomes a co-creator!

A precolonial rendering of vv. 24-25 would be,

> *Then God said. 'Let the Land bring forth life, each according to its kind, creeping creatures and Land life, according to its kind'. And it happened. So, God made the Land come alive with life, each according to its kind, animals and creeping creatures, according to their kind. And God saw that it was good.*

The Centrality of Land

The First Nations Australians appropriately designate this precolonial narrative in Gen. 1.1-25 an Ancestral Land Narrative. That the Land is the central theme of this narrative becomes apparent when we recognize that

- Land is a pre-existing formless mass beneath the primordial waters of the Deep.
- When the formless mass emerges from beneath the waters, God names the newborn reality 'Land'.
- The Land comes alive and produces vegetation of all kinds.

- Lights are located in the sky to provide signs, seasons and especially light for the Land.
- Land becomes a co-creator when Land brings forth living creatures of all kinds.

The centrality of the Land in this Ancestral Land Narrative resonates with the centrality of the Land as a living reality that First Nations Australia have sustained as custodians for thousands of years. They have also celebrated the presence of the Creator Spirit in the Land.

The Colonial Addition

To the precolonial Ancestral Land Narrative of Genesis 1.1-25, an editor, with an overt colonial worldview, added a text that describes the so-called *imago Dei*.

A colonial rendering of vv. 26-28 is,

> *Then God said, 'Let us make humankind in our image, according to our likeness, and let them have dominion over the fish of the sea, over the birds of the sky, over the domestic animals, over the Land and everything that creeps on the Land'.*
> *So God formed human beings in his image, in the image of God he formed them, male and female he formed them.*
> *Then God blessed them and said to them, 'Be fruitful and multiply and fill the Land and subdue it and have dominion over the fish of the sea and over the birds of the sky and over every living thing that creeps on the Land'.*

This addition (vv. 26-28) is diametrically at odds with the precolonial narrative that preceded it. These radical differences can be summarized as follows:

- Two different gods! In the precolonial primordial, God is introduced as a 'spirit' that is hovering in the midst of a dark cosmos yet to be transformed. In the colonial addition, God is portrayed as a celestial being who consults with a heavenly council about the creation of a species that is 'like us'—that is, like celestial beings.
- Two different worlds of living beings! In the precolonial world, all living beings—from birds in the sky to monsters in the Sea—are blessed with the capacity to multiply freely. In the colonial addition, human beings are given a mandate to 'rule' over other living creatures like colonial overlords.
- Two different understandings of Land! In the precolonial narrative, Land is the source of life and all living beings, a living reality at the centre of creation. In the colonial addition, humans are given a second mandate to 'crush/subdue' the Land as if it were a dangerous domain.

The two verbs 'rule' and 'subdue' are reflections of a superior colonial attitude. To 'rule' is to have dominion like lords and emperors (1 Kgs 4.24;
5.16). To 'subdue' means to crush violently (Mic. 7.19). It even means
'rape' in some contexts (Neh. 5.5). In this colonial addition, humans are
given colonial control both of the Land and of life on the Land. Humans
become the colonial landlords of the Land, bearing the image of celestial
beings.

First Nations Response

In workshops with First Nations Australians, we invited them to respond to
the precolonial narrative we have retrieved from Genesis 1. The Rainbow
Spirit Elders, for example, maintain that the Creator Spirit has been speaking through Aboriginal culture from the beginning.[16] In an appendix to their
book *Rainbow Spirit Theology*, the elders declare that

> The image of the Land as a given (Gen. 1.2), waiting to be *transformed*
> into land and sky as we know them, is also typical of the picture of 'land
> at the beginning' in Aboriginal dreaming stories … The imagery of verse 2
> makes excellent sense as Land covered with water, waiting for the Crea-
> tor Spirit, in whatever form, to commence *transforming the scene* … The
> picture is not one of a deity descending, in spectacular fashion, from some
> heavenly abode, to create a world out of nothing. Rather, the Creator Spirit
> is portrayed as a wind moving across, and closely linked with, the Land
> from the beginning.[17]

It is significant that at a workshop in 1996, the Rainbow Spirit Elders of
Queensland anticipated our decolonized reading of Genesis 1 and discerned
a precolonial narrative in the text that resonated with the ancestral narratives of First Nations Australia.

The Challenge

The challenge before us is to move beyond traditional colonial approaches to
interpreting the biblical text and dare to decolonize the narrative to retrieve
an ancient narrative that is not only free from colonial bias but resonates
with the spirit of the Ancestral Narratives of First Nations Australians and
Indigenous peoples across the globe.

To meet this challenge, I (Anne Pattel-Gray) and Uncle Norm (Norman Habel) have prepared two volumes of a series we have entitled *De-
colonising the Biblical Narrative*. Volume 1 in the series is entitled *Ances-*

16. Rainbow Spirit Elders, *Rainbow Spirit Theology*, p. 11.
17. Rainbow Spirit Elders, *Rainbow Spirit Theology*, pp. 76-77. Italics original.

tral Land Narratives of Genesis 1–11). Volume 2 is tentatively entitled *Ancestral Narratives Retrieved from Genesis 12–25.*

We invite First Nations peoples from other continents also to meet this challenge; by cooperating with empathetic biblical scholars, they can likewise use the decolonizing hermeneutic we have introduced to retrieve precolonial ancestral narratives or poems that are relevant for their people.

9

THE WISDOM OF THE OSTRICH (JOB 39.13-18)

James E. Harding

In the first of the divine speeches in the book of Job, the LORD tells Job about a bird known as רננים, usually understood since Jerome to be an ostrich hen (Job 39.13-18).[1] The difficulties of this passage are well known,[2] and there have been a number of proposals for emending parts of the text. The meaning of several words is uncertain, and there is doubt both about the correct identification of the bird in question and about the place of Job 39.13-18 in the book. It was not translated in the Old Greek, and it has been argued, on both contextual and text-critical grounds, that it is a secondary insertion. It does appear here in the Masoretic Text, however, and one must therefore assume that it plays some role in the final form of the Hebrew text of the book of Job. The purpose of this chapter is to explore what that role might be. Why does the LORD apparently take such pride and delight in a bird whom he has caused to forget wisdom, to whom he has given no share in understanding? And what might Job need to learn from such a creature?

The noun רננים is a *hapax legomenon* in the Hebrew Bible. It appears to be related to the verb רנן, 'give a ringing cry',[3] 'call loudly, shrilly', 'rejoice',[4] 'cry'[5] (cf. Job 29.13; 38.7), an association that undoubtedly lies behind the later Greek and Syriac translations,[6] as well as to the cognate nouns רנה,

---

1. On the origins of Jerome's rendering of כנף רננים as *pinna strutionum*, see H.-P. Müller, 'Die sog. Straußenperikope in den Gottesreden des Hiobbuches', *ZAW* 100 (1988), pp. 90-105 (94-95) and cf. n. 28 below.

2. For a survey of the pertinent issues, which cannot be addressed in detail here, see David J.A. Clines, *Job 38–42* (WBC, 18B; Nashville, TN: Thomas Nelson, 2011), pp. 1074-78.

3. BDB, p. 943a-b.

4. *HALOTSE*, pp. 1247b-48b.

5. *DCH* VII, p. 502b.

6. Thus Édouard Dhorme, *A Commentary on the Book of Job* (trans. H. Knight; Nashville, TN: Thomas Nelson, 1967), p. 603. See further Müller, 'Die sog. Straußen-perikope', pp. 91-93, 97.

'ringing cry',[7] 'cry',[8] and רננה, 'exultation, rejoicing',[9] 'cry'[10] (cf. Job 3.7; 20.5). It would seem to be associated with the sound characteristically made by the bird, hence 'bird of piercing cries, i.e. ostrich'.[11] The noun is masculine plural, but the verbs (apart from הקשיח)[12] and pronominal suffixes that follow are feminine singular, assuming a female bird as the antecedent.[13] The noun כנף is feminine, of course, and is the subject of the verb נעלסה (appar. 'rejoices'), which might lead one to wonder whether כנף רננים, 'wing of piercing cries', is some sort of poetic name for the bird.

The description of the bird seems to be based on the popular, albeit false,[14] notion of the ostrich being careless of its young. This notion may also be found in Lam. 4.3, where the poet laments that the people of Jerusalem have become cruel, like 'ostriches'[15] in the wilderness, on account of the fact that they no longer treat their children with the tender care that even jackals

7. BDB, p. 943b.

8. *DCH* VII, pp. 501b-2b.

9. *HALOTSE*, pp. 1248b-49a.

10. *DCH* VII, p. 504b.

11. BDB, p. 943b, though BDB prefers the option of emending the text to יענים cf. Lam. 4.3). Robert Gordis has suggested a comparable etymology for the noun יענה, which he associates with IV ענה, 'sing' (*The Book of Job: Commentary, New Translation, and Special Studies* [Moreshet, 2; New York: Jewish Theological Seminary of America, 1978], p. 458). Ibn Ezra does not identify the bird, but takes רננים to be the name of a bird that is perhaps so named on account of the charm of its voice (אולי נקרא כן בעבור נועם קולו) (Mariano Gómez Aranda, *El Comentario de Abraham Ibn Ezra al Libro de Job* [Madrid: Consejo Superior de Investigaciones Científicas: Instituto de Filología, 2004], pp. 80*, 301-2).

12. Unless this is either to be emended to the feminine (Müller, 'Die sog. Straußenperikope', p. 101 n. 55) or repointed as infinitive absolute (John E. Hartley, *The Book of Job* [NICOT; Grand Rapids, MI: Eerdmans, 1988], p. 509 n. 7, following Heinrich Ewald, *Commentary on the Book of Job* [trans. J. Frederick Smith; London: Williams and Norgate, 1882], p. 306).

13. The KJV translates thus: '*Gauest thou* the goodly wings vnto the peacocks, or wings and feathers vnto the Ostrich?', with '*the feathers of the Storke and Ostrich*' as an alternative for the second line. If I have understood the KJV translation correctly, the noun רננים is taken to mean 'peacocks' and the feminine noun נצה to mean 'ostrich', which then becomes the subject of the feminine verbs that follow.

14. Marvin H. Pope, *Job: A New Translation with Introduction and Commentary* (AB, 15; New York: Doubleday, 2nd edn, 1973), pp. 309-10; Izak Spangenberg, 'Who Cares? Reflections on the Story of the Ostrich (Job 39.13-18)', in N.C. Habel and S. Wurst (eds.), *The Earth Story in Wisdom Traditions* (The Earth Bible, 3; Sheffield: Sheffield Phoenix Press, 2001), pp. 92-102 (98-100). On the problem of reading popular ideas of this sort back into Job 39.13-18, see Arthur Walker-Jones, 'The So-called Ostrich in the God Speeches of the Book of Job', *Bib* 86 (2005), pp. 494-510 (504-506).

15. Both יענים (Lam. 4.3) and רננים (Job 39.13) were understood by G.R. Driver to refer to ostriches ('Birds in the Old Testament. II. Birds in Life', *PEQ* 87 (1955), pp. 129-40 (137-38).

can be expected to offer their young. The word used there is כיענים (qere).[16] Thus a number of scholars would prefer to emend רנים in Job 39.13 to יענים.[17] This would be related to the feminine noun יענה, which has also been advanced as a possible alternative to רננים.[18] Elsewhere in the Hebrew Bible, however, we only find בת יענה in the singular,[19] or בנות יענה in the plural, as in Job 30.29.[20] In Job 30.29, Job is lamenting that, as a result of God's appalling treatment of him, he has become a brother to jackals and a companion to *bᵉnôt yaʿănâ* (אח הייתי לתנים ורע לבנות יענה), that is, he is now treated as an outcast from human society. There is, however, considerable doubt as to whether the birds referred to as בנות יענה are indeed to be identified with the ostrich rather than, say, with some kind of owl.[21] Perhaps the most preferable option in the case of Job 39.13 is to see רננים (or possibly כנף רננים) as a poetical name for the ostrich, named thus on account of the cries it emits.[22] This would work rather well here, because even if the verb נעלסה (II עלס niphal, another *hapax legomenon*) is understood to mean 'become agitated, vivacious'[23] (subj. כנף, 'wing') rather than 'rejoice' (a by-form of עלז or

16. The kethib reads כֵּן עֵנִים, but the qere is surely to be preferred.

17. E.g. Edward L. Greenstein, *Job: A New Translation* (New Haven, CT: Yale University Press, 2019), p. 172 n. 45.

18. See the suggested reconstruction of the text in Julius Boehmer, 'Was ist der Sinn von Hiob 39.13-18 an seiner gegenwärtigen Stelle?', *ZAW* 53 (1935), pp. 289-91 (290).

19. Lev. 11.16; Deut. 14.15. The reference in each case is to a species of bird that is to be avoided as unclean. The Babylonian Talmud cites the opinion of Rabbi Hezekiah, to the effect that בת היענה in Lev. 11.16 refers to the egg of the יענה, thereby justifying the prohibition against eating a non-kosher egg. There follows a discussion, based on a number of scriptural passages (Lam. 4.3; Mic. 1.8; Isa. 13.21; 43.20), as to whether בת היענה might be the name of the bird. The conclusion is that Scripture refers to the same bird as both יענה and בת היענה, but the scribe must have had a reason for writing two words instead of one in this case, thus justifying the prohibition against eating the non-kosher egg (*b. Ḥull.* 64b).

20. See also Isa. 13.21; 34.13; 43.20; Jer. 50.39; Mic. 1.8 (cf. previous note).

21. Jacob Milgrom, e.g., regards the identification of בת היענה with the ostrich in Lev. 11.16 as untenable, based on the fact that 'ostriches do not haunt ruins, as do owls', and suggests 'eagle owl' instead (*Leviticus 1–16: A New Translation with Introduction and Commentary* [AB, 3; New York: Doubleday, 1991], p. 663, with other scriptural references to בנות יענה in mind; see also the earlier works of G.R. Driver, 'Birds in the Old Testament. I. Birds in Law', *PEQ* 87 (1955), pp. 5-20 (12-13, 20), and George S. Cansdale, *All the Animals of the Bible Lands* (Exeter: Paternoster Press, 1970), pp. 147-49, 190-91).

22. Thus August Dillmann, *Hiob* (KEH, 2; 3rd edn; Leipzig: S. Hirzel, 1869), p. 347; S.R. Driver and G. Buchanan Gray, *A Critical and Exegetical Commentary on the Book of Job* (ICC; Edinburgh: T. & T. Clark, 1921), II, p. 317; Robert Alter, *The Hebrew Bible: A Translation with Commentary* (New York: W.W. Norton, 2019), III, p. 569.

23. *HALOT* p. 836b (II עלס). Contrast I עלס, 'taste' (*HALOT* p. 836a-b), which occurs in the qal in Job 20.18 (par. I בלע qal) and the hithpael in Prov. 7.18. They are

עלץ), it nonetheless echoes עלז, 'exult, triumph'[24] and עלץ, 'rejoice, exult',[25] which would be entirely appropriate following a noun derived from the root רנן. If the verb does mean 'rejoice', though, it may not necessarily be the most appropriate way to describe the cry made by an ostrich hen.[26] In any case, it may be preferable to regard this verse, and the pericope as a whole, as deliberately ambiguous.[27]

For present purposes, I am not interested in the precise identification of the bird named רננים, if indeed a specific kind of bird was meant.[28] My concern is rather with the role of Job 39.13-18 in the wider context of the book of Job as a whole. The poet in Job 39.17 says that Eloah has caused this bird to forget wisdom, and he has allotted it no share in understanding (כי השה אלוה חכמה ולא חלק לה בבינה). This is in stark contrast to Job 38.36, another verse replete with difficulties, in which the LORD apparently asks Job who it was that endowed the ibis with wisdom and the rooster with understanding (מי שת בטחות חכמה או מי נתן לשכוי בינה). To be sure, it is by no means clear that טחות does refer to the ibis and שכוי to the rooster,[29] and Job 38.36 is most

---

treated as a single root in BDB, p. 763a, and may share a sense of delight, or enjoyment. *DCH* VI, p. 429b, lists עלס I 'rejoice', but is uncertain (1) whether Job 20.18 and Prov. 7.18 belong under this root or under *עלס II 'taste'; and (2) whether Job 39.13 belongs under עלס I, or under either *עלס III 'be restless' or *עלס IV 'be weak'.

24. *HALOTSE* pp. 831b-32a.

25. *HALOTSE* pp. 836b-37a.

26. On this point see Walker-Jones, 'The So-called Ostrich', p. 500. I am leaving aside the possibility that the verb should be emended to נעלה, 'be raised up' (subj. כנף) (see Müller, 'Der sog. Straußenperikope', pp. 97-100, 102).

27. Müller refers to 'an essential ambiguity [*wesenhafte Mehrdeutigkeit*] of poetic-mythical texts, to which the divine speeches of the book of Job belong' ('Die sog. Straußenperikope', p. 90; cf. pp. 104-105).

28. F.S. Bodenheimer follows N.H. Tur Sinai in denying that Job 39.13-18 has anything to do with the ostrich. In Tur Sinai's opinion, this passage was derived from an older fable about two birds, denoted by names that are grammatically masculine and feminine respectively, which abandon their young. See Tur Sinai [H. Torczyner], *The Book of Job: A New Commentary* (Jerusalem: Kiryat Sepher, 1957), pp. 542-47; F.S. Bodenheimer, *Animal and Man in Bible Lands* (Collection de travaux de l'Académie Internationale d'Histoire des Sciences, 10; Leiden: E.J. Brill, 1960), I, pp. 59-60. Walker-Jones has suggested that רננים refers to the sand grouse ('The So-called Ostrich'). Müller (pp. 94-96), followed by Walker-Jones (pp. 497-98), traces the identification of רננים as 'ostrich' to a passage in the *Physiologus* that incorrectly identifies the 'stork' (Heb. חסידה [cf. Job 39.13b]; Gk. ἀσιδά) of Jer. 8.7 with the 'ostrich' (Lat. *struthio*; cf. Job 39.13a [Vulg.]). See *Physiologus* (trans. M.J. Curley; Austin, TX: University of Texas Press, 1979), pp. 55-56. This passage could well be a later addition to the *Physiologus* (thus Müller, *inter alios*), and may itself be both largely dependent on a Greek rendering of Job 39.13-18, and later than Jerome (Müller, 'Die sog. Straußenperikope', pp. 95-96).

29. For the interpretive options, see Clines, *Job 38–42*, pp. 1065-66. The arguments in favour of 'ibis' and 'cock' as the correct renderings of the Hebrew words were laid

likely intentionally ambiguous; but it would make good poetic sense for there to be contrasting verses in different parts of the first divine speech, one referring to the divine bestowal of wisdom on two sorts of bird (Job 38.36) and the other referring to the divine withholding of wisdom from a different sort of bird (Job 39.13).[30] This contrast between the ibis and the ostrich in respect of the gift of wisdom would presumably then be related, in some way, to the concern in the dialogue with the accessibility of wisdom.

Access to wisdom is, in much of the book of Job, a very human concern. Job is introduced in the opening verse of the book as 'one who fears God' (ירא אלהים) (Job 1.1). The fear of the LORD is an important theme in a number of biblical traditions, in some of which it is strongly identified with wisdom.[31] In the Hebrew Bible, only Abraham and Job are explicitly identified as 'fearing God' (ירא אלהים),[32] though the proper attitude of 'one who fears God' is also a concern in Qoh. 7.18. Later on in the book of Job, we are told that God has said to humans that the fear of the Lord is wisdom, and to turn away from evil is understanding (יראת אדני היא חכמה וסור מרע בינה) (Job 28.28).[33] In the present form of the book, this forms an *inclusio* with Job 1.1, and the entire dialogue between Job and his three friends (Job 4–27) falls in between. A major concern of this dialogue is with the possibility of humans having access to wisdom. Whatever else the book of Job may be about, it is concerned with the fear of God and its relationship to the acquisition of wisdom.

It is unclear whether it is Eliphaz, or the mysterious voice that whispered in the night, who says of human beings that 'they will die, but without wisdom' (ימותו ולא בחכמה) (Job 4.21b). The sentiment is broadly in line with the ambiguous rhetorical question in Job 4.17, which seems to cast doubt on the possibility of human righteousness before God. Subsequently, Zophar says to Job, 'But if only Eloah would speak ... and make known to you the secrets of wisdom' (מי יתן אלוה דבר ... ויגד לך תעלמות חכמה) (Job 11.5a, 6a). Zophar seems to be saying that God has access to all wisdom, yet he has hidden it from human beings. If he were to make the secrets of wisdom known, it would become clear to Job that God had caused him to forget

out clearly by Édouard Dhorme in *A Commentary on the Book of Job*, pp. 591-93. John Barclay Burns offers a cogent defence of these renderings in 'Is the Ibis Yet Wise? A Reconsideration of Job 38.36', *PEGLMBS* 21 (2001), pp. 131-36 (132-33), but his argument for placing this verse just prior to Job 38.41 is not wholly compelling.

30. Thus Greenstein, *Job*, p. 170 n. 30.
31. Isa. 11.2; 33.6; Ps. 111.10; Prov. 1.7; 9.10; 15.33; esp. Sir. 1.11-30.
32. Gen. 22.12; Job 1.1, 8; 2.3.
33. Cf. the texts cited in n. 31 above. In Job 28.28 the fear of the Lord *is* wisdom, whereas in Prov. 1.7 it is the *beginning* or the *first part* (ראשית) of wisdom, as in Ps. 111.10. Perhaps the wording of Job 28.28 is meant to evoke the saying found in Prov. 1.7, so that the reader is led to ask what the reason is for the difference between the two.

some of his sin (ודע כי ישה לך אלוה מעונך) (Job 11.6c). It is one of the many ironies inherent in the way the poet brings different perspectives into dialogue that Zophar is, in effect, claiming the sort of knowledge he believes that God has withheld from Job. If I have interpreted this difficult verse correctly, and if Zophar is at least partially right in what he has said, then Job has something in common with the ostrich hen. For just as God has caused the ostrich hen to forget wisdom, he has caused Job to forget some of his sin,[34] something Job does not know because he does not have access to the secrets of divine wisdom.

Job and his friends do seem to claim some kind of wisdom for themselves. In his response to Zophar, Job criticizes his friends by saying, with studied sarcasm, 'Truly, you are [the] people // and wisdom will die with you' (אמנם כי אתם עם ותמות חכמה עמכם) (Job 12.2). Job claims that he, too, has an intellect, and is not inferior to his friends (גם לי לבב כמוכם לא נפל אנכי מכם) (Job 12.2a-b). Traditionally, wisdom was associated with the aged, which is perhaps why Proverbs defines the fear of the LORD as the 'beginning' (ראשית) of wisdom (Prov 1.7): a child has a lifetime to acquire wisdom, provided he begins with the fear of the LORD.[35] Job seems to be quoting a well-known aphorism when he says, 'Wisdom is among the aged // Length of days is understanding'[36] (בישישים חכמה וארך ימים תבונה) (Job 12.12). This belief was certainly known to Eliphaz (Job 15.10), and to Elihu. Indeed, it was this that had held Elihu back from speaking in the presence of his elders (Job 32.4, 6-7).

Also well known is the idea that it is God who ultimately possesses wisdom, which Job apparently affirms when he says, 'With him are wisdom and power // To him belong counsel and understanding' (עמו חכמה וגבורה לו עצה ותבונה)[37] (Job 12.13). For Job, what Zophar has said in Job 11.6a is a truism that adds nothing to what he, like everyone else, already knows. It is of no help to him in dealing with his plight. Perhaps this is why Job goes on to deride the words of his friends, which claim to bear a wisdom they simply do not have: 'If only you would be quiet // And let [that] be wisdom on your part' (מי יתן החרש תחרישון ותהי לכם חכמה) (Job 13.5). And if it is indeed Job

---

34. If the MT is correct, then Job 11.6c and 39.17a are the only occurrences of נשה hiphil in the Hebrew Bible.

35. I am indebted here to Michael Fox's interpretation of Prov. 1.7: '*Fear of the LORD* is the ground for wisdom to grow in; it is essentially conscience. In its most basic form, in the untutored child, it is unreflective fear of consequences. As wisdom develops, fear of God becomes a cognitive awareness of what God wants and does, and this type of fear is equivalent to knowledge of the LORD (2.5)' ('Proverbs', in A. Berlin and M.Z. Brettler [eds.], *The Jewish Study Bible* [New York: Oxford University Press, 2nd edn, 2014], pp. 1437-87 [1439]).

36. The JPS *Tanakh* translation treats this as a rhetorical question.

37. The antecedent of עמו is unspecified, but is surely to be understood as God.

who is speaking in Job 26.3, he says, sarcastically, 'How you have coun-
selled one without wisdom // And made prudence abundantly known' (מה
יעצת ללא חכמה ותושיה לרב הודעת).[38] Job's recognition that the defence of God
offered by his friends is both devoid of wisdom and impious is partly what
convinces him to turn away from them and to bring his protest before the
judge of all the earth himself (Job 13.1-16).

The idea that it is with God that wisdom ultimately belongs also lies
behind Eliphaz's attack on what he believes to be Job's hubris. He asks,
'Have you listened in the council of Eloah? // Or have you seized wisdom
for yourself?' (הבסוד אלוה תשמע ותגרע אליך חכמה) (Job 15.8). So while Job
and his friends do seem to claim some sort of wisdom for themselves, they
criticize one another for claiming to be wise, and they assume that God possesses wisdom in some way that human beings do not. There is perhaps a
variation on this theme in Job 32.13, where Elihu seems to be imagining the
three elders saying that they have found wisdom, but only El can refute Job
(פן מצאני חכמה אל ידפנו לא איש). This can be translated as follows: 'Lest you
say, "We have found wisdom // El will defeat him, not a man"'. This is part
of Eliphaz's case that age does not, after all, bestow the sort of wisdom needed
if one were to rebut Job and defend God. Ironically echoing Job's words
in response to the first cycle of speeches from his friends (Job 13.5), Elihu
ends his first speech by saying, 'Be silent, so that I may teach you wisdom!'
(החרש ואאלפך חכמה) (Job 33.33b).

When the words exchanged between Job and his three friends have finally
run out, a poem from an unknown voice waxes lyrical about the inaccessi-
bility of wisdom. It asks, 'But from where is wisdom to be grasped? // And
where is the place of understanding?' (והחכמה מאין תמצא ואי זה מקום בינה) (Job
28.12), and, 'Wisdom, where does it come from? // And where is the place
of understanding?'[39] (והחכמה מאין תבוא ואי זה מקום בינה) (Job 28.20). A pouch
of wisdom is better than pearls (ומשך חכמה מפנינים) (Job 28.18). The wisdom poem concludes with words supposedly spoken by the Lord to human
beings, to the effect that wisdom is the fear of the Lord, and to turn from
evil is understanding. As noted above, this forms an *inclusio* with Job 1.1,
and brackets the entire dialogue between Job and his friends (Job 4–27). It
also looks forward to the divine speeches. The verse is Janus-facing: just as

38. Another difficult verse. In the MT, it is part of a speech of Job, but it is addressed
to a singular male, and is sometimes attributed to Bildad.

39. In these verses, the poet is playing on different nuances of the root מצא, using a
literary device known as 'antanaclasis'. The use of the verb בוא, 'come', in v. 20 strongly
suggests that מצא niphal in v. 12 means something like 'be reached', or, by extension, 'be
grasped', though in v. 13b it can only mean 'be found' (ולא תמצא בארץ החיים, 'And it is not
to be found in the land of the living'). See Anthony R. Ceresko, 'The Function of *Antanaclasis* (*mṣʾ* 'to find' // *mṣ* 'to reach, overtake, grasp') in Hebrew Poetry, Especially in
the Book of Qoheleth', *CBQ* 44 (1982), pp. 551-69 (561-62).

the 'fear of the Lord' and 'turning from evil' look back to the opening of the prologue, so the parallel between 'wisdom' (חכמה) and 'understanding' (בינה) points forward to what the LORD says about the ibis and the ostrich hen in the first of the divine speeches (Job 39.17).

Access to wisdom turns out to be a divine concern, too, for when the LORD demands an answer from Job in the first of the divine speeches, he questions Job precisely about wisdom. He opens his response to Job by asking, 'Who is this that darkens counsel with words devoid of knowledge?' (מי זה מחשיך עצה במלין בלי דעת) (Job 38.2). The LORD seems to have Job primarily in mind, though he could just about be referring to Elihu. If so, then the LORD would be driving off Elihu's conceited claim to possess wisdom (cf. Job 33.31-33). The LORD is, however, primarily addressing Job, and he goes on to ask who it is that can number the clouds in wisdom, or pour out the waterskins of the sky (מי יספר שחקים בחכמה ונבלי שמים מי ישכיב) (Job 38.37). Not Job, but God, who has given wisdom to the ibis and understanding to the rooster (Job 38.36), but has caused the ostrich hen to forget wisdom and given her no share in understanding (Job 39.17).

Job progresses from an all-consuming absorption in himself and his suffering to a vision of the cosmos from the perspective of the LORD. Along the way, he not only learns empathy for other sufferers and a divine perspective that encompasses creatures whose lives had formerly meant nothing to him, but also learns to become a child again. When he utters a curse upon the day of his birth, Job says, 'Let the day perish wherein I was born // the night that said *a man* has been conceived' (יאבד יום אולד בו והלילה אמר הרה גבר) (Job 3.3). When a similar curse is uttered in Jer. 20.14-18, what the poet says is less unexpected and less ambiguous. He says ארור היום אשר ילדתי בו יום אשר ילדתני אמי אל יהי ברוך, 'Cursed by the day on which I was born // [The] day my mother gave birth to me, let it not be blessed!', and ארור האיש בשר את אבי לאמר ילד לך בן זכר, 'Cursed be the man who brought the good news to my father, "A male child has been born to you!"' A significant difference between the two is that whereas in Jeremiah the poet refers to himself as 'a male child' (בן זכר), Job refers to himself as a 'man' (גבר). This is not what one would expect in reference to the birth of a baby, even if it is not quite as odd as Eve's statement in Gen. 4.1 (קניתי איש את יהוה, 'I have acquired a man with [perh. 'from', cf. Akk. *itti*] the LORD'). In using the term גבר, the poet is engaging in 'defamiliarization',[40] using a term one would not normally expect in order to slow the reader down and encourage them to engage more deeply with the meaning of the text. Here, the reader

40. See Viktor Shklovsky, 'Art as Technique', in *Russian Formalist Criticism* (ed. L.T. Lemon and M.J. Reis; Lincoln, NB: University Of Nebraska Press, 1965), pp. 3-24 [Russian orig. 1917]. The Russian term is *остранение*.

is being led to question why the poet has chosen this particular word to refer to himself at the moment of birth.

One possibility would be that, throughout the poem, Job reacts to his affliction as an adult might, protesting against and seeking a meaning for his plight in a way that would come naturally to an adult man but not to a child, to whom the experience of affliction would not suggest the problem of theodicy.[41] The noun גבר is used elsewhere to refer to adult men, in contrast with children (טף),[42] and in contrast with women of varying ages.[43] It is also used to refer quite specifically to a man who is suffering,[44] suggesting that the reader may be expected to infer connotations of suffering in Job 3.3. The noun is used elsewhere in Job to refer to a mortal man, in contrast with the deity.[45] This is one indication that the poem is not just about Job, but about every human being, Job serving as a representative of all suffering humanity. The use of the noun גבר perhaps also draws attention to the fact that Job is a human being, not an animal. Job's most intense lament is arguably in Job 30.20-31, where he bemoans the fact that his suffering involves being ostracized from human society and, metaphorically speaking, made to dwell with wild animals. Whether or not there is any connection between בנות יענה in Job 30.29 and רננים in Job 39.13, there is some sort of contrast between Job's resentment at being reduced to a companion of jackals and ostriches (Job 30.29) on the one hand, and the LORD's delight in an untameable bird from whom he has withheld wisdom (Job 39.17) on the other. When the LORD confronts Job with the wondrous order of the natural world (Job 38.39–39.30), he is, in a sense, confronting Job with the fact that he may have radically misunderstood his place in the cosmos.

Job's identity as a 'man' (גבר), as distinct from women, children, animals and the deity, raises significant questions about the place of humans, and his own place, in the cosmos. His opening imprecation (Job 3.3-10) contains a number of echoes of the Priestly account of creation (Gen. 1.1–2.4a), and it has been defined as 'a counter-cosmic incantation', which provides 'a systematic *bouleversement*, or reversal, of the cosmicizing acts of crea-

---

41. Compare Dorothee Sölle's discussion of Jacques Lusseyran in *Suffering* (trans. E. Kalin; Philadelphia: Fortress Press, 1975), pp. 88-93.

42. See Exod. 10.11; 12.37; Jer. 41.16; 43.6.

43. It is used in contrast with נקבה, 'female' (Jer. 31.22), אשה, 'woman' (Deut. 22.5; Jer. 44.20 [pl.]), and עלמה, 'maiden' (Prov. 30.19). The context of Prov. 6.34 strongly suggests that it means 'husband' there.

44. Lam. 3.1, 27, 35, 39 [MT]; Ps. 88.5.

45. In addition to Job 3.3, 23, see Job 4.17; 10.5; 14.10, 14; 16.21; 22.2; 33.17, 29; 34.7, 9, 34. The noun is also widely used in Psalms (Pss. 18.26; 34.9; 37.23; 40.5; 88.5; 89.49; 94.12; 127.5; 128.4) and Proverbs (Prov. 6.34; 20.24; 24.5; 28.3, 21; 29.5; 30.1, 19).

tion described in Gen. i–ii 4a'.[46] Job's suffering is such that he cannot look beyond himself, and he conflates his own birth with the birth of the cosmos. Later on, in Job 7.17-18, he complains about God's obsessive attention to him, in an apparent allusion to Ps. 8.5-6.[47] Rather than honouring human-kind as the pinnacle of God's creation, as Ps. 8.5-6 does (cf. Gen. 1.26-28), the poet alludes to the wording of the psalm in parody and inverts its intent,[48] suggesting that God's attention to human beings may be a sign of hostility rather than blessing. Yet this still implies that human beings are the focus of God's concern. This is, indeed, the tacit assumption of each of the speeches of Job, his three friends and Elihu, even when they allude to God's sover-eignty over the marvels of the cosmos. When the LORD appears, however, he asks Job where he was when he laid the foundations of the earth (איפה היית ביסדי ארץ) (Job 38.4a) and proceeds to respond to Job's imprecation against the birth of the cosmos. In so doing, the LORD confronts Job with the unsettling, yet ultimately liberating, truth that he and his troubles are not the sole focus of divine concern.

The LORD's words to Job in Job 39.13-18 are part of a concerted attempt to get him to recognize his proper place in the cosmos. Job may have a degree of wisdom in his own sphere, but it is not the sort of wisdom that gives order to a cosmos that inspires wonder and terror in equal measure. Nor does wisdom necessarily have the sort of importance Job and his friends

---

46. Michael A. Fishbane, 'Jeremiah IV 23-26 and Job III 3-13: A Recovered Use of the Creation Pattern', *VT* 21 (1971), pp. 151-67 (153). Fishbane's comparison is between Gen. 1.1–2.4a and Job 3.3-13. Karen Langton has further suggested that the poet is drawing on the model of Akkadian birth incantations, and that Job 3.3-10 is a satirical reversal of an incantation meant to ensure the safe delivery of a child ('Job's Attempt to Regain Control: Traces of a Babylonian Birth Incantation in Job 3', *JSOT* 36 [2012], pp. 459-69).

47. The two passages read as follows:

מה אנוש כי תזכרנו ובן אדם כי תפקדנו
ותחסרהו מעט מאלהים וכבוד והדר תעטרהו

What is a man, that you should take note of him, or a mortal man, that you should pay attention to him?
That you should make him only a little less than God [or, angels], and crown him with glory and honour? (Ps. 8.5-6)

מה אנוש כי תגדלנו וכי תשית אליו לבך
ותפקדנו לבקרים לרגעים תבחננו

What is a man, that you should regard him as important, or that you should set your mind on him?
That you should inspect him every morning, test him at every moment? (Job 7.17-18)

48. See, e.g., Fishbane, *Biblical Interpretation in Ancient Israel* (Oxford: Clarendon Press, 1985), pp. 285-86.

have imputed to it. After all, the Lord is rather proud of a bird whom he has caused to forget wisdom. Indeed, it may be that a human being like Job would be rather happier if he were to let go of any desire to strive after wisdom at all. For wisdom, according to the book of Job, is in some way identified with a kind of fear. Wisdom is the 'fear of the Lord', according to Job 28.28, and while this might be taken to refer to piety, or due reverence before the Lord, it may also entail a degree of terror or dread. Job may well be 'one who fears God', but his fear of God seems to entail a dread of what might happen if he were to be less scrupulously observant (see, e.g., Job 1.4-5). This is why he goes on to lament that what he had feared all along has now come upon him (כי פחד פחדתי ויאתיני) (Job 3.23a). The ostrich hen, however, has no fear (לריק יגיעה בלי פחד) (Job 39.16b), because Eloah has caused her to forget wisdom (Job 39.17a). In her case, she has no fear that her labour in raising chicks will prove futile, leaving her eggs to warm in the ground and treating her young carelessly, but this, too, is all part of the Lord's wise and mysterious ordering of the cosmos. Job is of concern to the Lord, to be sure, but he is of no more or less concern to God than the ostrich hen (Job 39.13-18) or Behemoth, whom the Lord has made along with Job (Job 40.15a). Job needs to know and accept his place in the order of things. He must accept that his old attitude toward wisdom had engendered a warped sense of his own place in the divine order, which had, in turn, fostered a dread of what might happen if he were to let go of his attachment to punctilious religious observance. It is perhaps here that the book of Job comes closest to Qoheleth, in which the fear of God comes to mean living a life of moderation, without undue striving for a wisdom one can never hope to attain (Qoh. 7.1-29).

When we turn to the epilogue, following Job's profoundly ambiguous response to the Lord in Job 42.1-6, it seems as though the Lord's speeches have left Job free to receive the blessings of the Lord without undue anxiety. If there is any sense in which Job continues to 'fear' the Lord in the epilogue, it is a fear of God that has been cleansed of anxiety and dread, sharing more with the moderation of the wise man in Qoh. 7.18 than with the apparently infanticidal fanaticism of Abraham in Gen. 22.12. Job is also free to look beyond himself, to encounter the face of the Other, whether they happen to be human or not, without reducing them to figments of a stale ideology. Job had twice demanded that his friends look him in the face instead of interpreting him as living proof of the veracity of the traditional doctrine of retribution (Job 6.28; 21.5),[49] yet he had been no more capable than they were of encountering other people, animals and God as they truly

49. For a slightly different engagement with the implications of these verses, see Tod Linafelt, 'Facing Job', in T. Cohn Eskenazi, G.A. Phillips and D. Jobling (eds.), *Levinas and Biblical Studies* (SBLSS, 43; Atlanta, GA: SBL, 2003), pp. 65-74.

are, in their irreducible singularity. Having once been imprisoned by his piety and content to bury his head in the sand,[50] Job is now free to receive life. And in rediscovering the sheer simplicity of a childlike fear of God, Job has grown up in faith.[51]

50. One of my Modern Hebrew dictionaries gives 'a person who buries their head in the sand' (אדם שטומן ראשו בחול) as a translation equivalent for the English 'ostrich', alongside the more literal יען and בת יענה (Ya'acov Levy [ed.], *Oxford English-Hebrew/ Hebrew-English Dictionary* [Tel Aviv: Kernerman Publishing, 1995], p. 325b).

51. This differs slightly from Michael Fox's understanding of a childlike fear of God (n. 35 above). Perhaps the Job of the prologue had grown up without progressing beyond an 'unreflective fear of consequences'. He needed to grow up *in faith*, and thereby discover a different aspect of what it might mean to be childlike, namely, to have a simple acceptance of the way things are (cf. n. 41 above), yet with a mature wisdom he did not yet have when he blessed God in Job 1.21.

10

A LAND OF DEEP DARKNESS:
AN ECO-RHETORICAL READING OF JEREMIAH 2.1-9
AND ITS COLONIAL REVERBERATIONS

Emily Colgan

In his (in)famous work, *The British Colonisation of New Zealand*, Edward Gibbon Wakefield—who masterminded much of the colonial endeavours in Aotearoa and Australia—rhetorically asked, 'Is it not the will of God that the earth should be replenished and subdued, that the desert should give rise to the fruitful field …?'[1] The rhetoric employed by Wakefield, which sets the fertile field (over) against the desert land, is echoed in the discourse of other nineteenth- and early-twentieth-century British colonists in Aotearoa, who similarly drew on a dualistic wilderness (desert)/garden (fertile field) logic as a powerful symbolic tool of the colonial endeavour. While it is difficult to establish a direct intertextual connection between images of land found in the Bible and the language employed by Wakefield and his ilk, it is plausible these settlers were drawing—whether implicitly or explicitly—on a similar binary found in biblical literature.[2] This chapter uses an ecological hermeneutic and a rhetorical methodology to critically examine one such biblical text where this binary appears particularly pronounced. It will then briefly attempt to trace intertextual echoes of this biblical imagery, noting the role such imagery may have played in dictating the terms of encounter between British settlers and the land of Aotearoa.[3]

---

1. In asking this question, Wakefield quotes 'MA of Trinity College Cambridge' (Edward Gibbon Wakefield, *The British Colonization of New Zealand* [London: John Parker/New Zealand Association, 1837], p. 417).

2. The broad ideas contained in this chapter were first conceived as part of my doctoral dissertation, which was supervised by Elaine. I feel deeply privileged to have been mentored by Elaine, and I will always be grateful that she set me on the path of eco-feminist analysis. Thank you, Elaine.

3. I read as a seventh-generation Pākehā New Zealander and a descendant of early British colonists. I am deeply cognisant of the many ways in which my ancestors were complicit in and benefited from the colonization of Aotearoa (the Māori name for New

Jeremiah 2.1-9: An Eco-Rhetorical Analysis

Jeremiah 2.1-3

Jeremiah 2.1-3 is clearly recognizable as the opening sub-unit of Jeremiah 2, and the presence of paragraph markers in the Hebrew text (a *petuhah* both prior to v. 1 and at the end of v. 3) identify these initial verses as an independent passage. In addition to such markings, these verses are bound together by the conventional formulae of oracular speech, which introduces the pericope in v. 1 ('word of YHWH') and concludes the passage in v. 3 with a balancing claim ('utterance of YHWH'). The content of the verses is mostly poetry, and the unit is separated into two double-lined stanzas (vv. 2b-3). Each line is a bicolon except for v. 2, the first line of which is a tricolon. Within these lines, the land features three times, appearing initially in the first colon of the second line of the first stanza (v. 2c), where the word מִדְבָּר (wilderness) is used to designate the place where Israel, the young bride, lovingly pursues YHWH. The next reference occurs in the second colon of the same line, where the wilderness is qualified as being לֹא זְרוּעָה אֶרֶץ (a land not sown). The final reference in the second colon of the first line of the second stanza is an indirect reference to land as a place of רֵאשִׁית (first fruits) and תְּבוּאָה (harvest).

At first glance, there is an obvious contrast between the images of land in the second line of the first stanza and the first line of the second stanza. While one describes a 'wilderness', a land without crops or vegetation, the other suggests a land that has been carefully tended and which produces an abundance of food for harvest. This contrast, however, appears to go much deeper, assigning value judgments to the images, which are reinforced on both structural and stylistic levels. Symmetrical word clusters and images in each tri/bicolon establish a framework for this poetry, and endow the constituent colons with a value that is either positive or negative:

v. 2

I	a	I remember	the devotion (masc.)
			of your youth (masc.)
	b		the love (fem.)
			of your betrothal (fem.)
	c		your following me
			in the wilderness (masc.)
	d		in an unsown land (fem.)

Zealand). As one of their descendants, I also benefit from and am, at times, complicit in this ongoing colonial legacy. I am committed to the radical decolonization of Aotearoa, and I see this work as part of that broader *kaupapa* (agenda).

v. 3

    II   a′   holy (masc.)
                was Israel (masc.) to Y<small>HWH</small>
        b′   the first fruits (fem.)
                of the harvest (fem.)
        c′   all who ate
                were guilty (masc.)
        d′   evil (fem.) came upon them

The balance that is achieved through the establishment of these symmetrical pairs functions to connect the value judgments associated with the images of one pair with that of its corresponding pair. Through these couplings, relative value is assigned to the words describing land. In this way, the masculine pair labelled 'a' can be identified as a positive image, as can the feminine pair labelled 'b'. The masculine pair in 'c' and the feminine pair in 'd', on the other hand, create a negative image. While this structure is reiterated by symmetrical gender-patterning and by the balanced use of nouns and verbs, it is not sufficient to assume that dualistic hierarchies underlie these images, and thus further analysis of the pairs relating to the land is necessary.

The expression of Israel's אַהֲבָה (love) as Y<small>HWH</small>'s כְּלוּלוֹת (betrothed) is the first metaphor to be coupled with an image of land (the corresponding pair labelled 'b'). The initial keyword, אַהֲבָה, has obvious positive overtones and is used variously throughout the Hebrew Bible to refer to the intimacy of marriage (Song 2.4, 7), the faithful devotion of friends (1 Sam. 18.3; 20.17), a moral ideal (Prov. 15.17; 17.9), and the loyal compassion of Y<small>HWH</small> (Deut. 7.13; 1 Kgs 10.9; Hos. 11.4). These connotations overlay the term as it is used in relation to Y<small>HWH</small>'s young bride, Israel. Regardless of whether כְּלוּלוֹת refers to a time of betrothal or a honeymoon period, as some commentators debate,[4] the underlying rhetoric alludes to an idealized innocence associated with the early days of marriage, where the virginal purity of a young woman holds hope of fertility and the promise of happiness and security. Indeed, the various cognates of the term כלל translate to mean 'complete' or 'whole',[5] upholding this state as the pinnacle of female aspiration and societal expectation.

---

4. William McKane, *A Critical and Exegetical Commentary on Jeremiah: Introduction and Commentary on Jeremiah 1–25* (Edinburgh: T. & T. Clark, 1986), p. 28, argues that this term refers to a 'honeymoon' period, while on the other hand, William L. Holladay, ed., *A Concise Hebrew and Aramaic Lexicon of the Old Testament* (Grand Rapids, MI: Eerdmans, 1988), 158, suggests the term refers to a betrothal or engagement.

5. Holladay, *A Concise Hebrew and Aramaic Lexicon*, p. 159.

Positive imagery continues in the image of Israel as the רֵאשִׁית (first fruits) of YHWH's תְּבוּאָה (harvest). On the one hand, this metaphor reiterates the favour of Israel in days gone by, as the text compares this people to the first fruits of each harvest. Stipulated by Hebrew law to be sacrosanct, these fruits were debarred from secular use and used as a gift of thanks to YHWH as an acknowledgment of YHWH's gracious giving.[6] On the other hand, these images and connections assign particular value to the type of land that produces these fruits, land that is worked by human hands and produces crops for human consumption. This rhetoric gives value to land that is 'useful' to humanity. The word רֵאשִׁית translates literally as 'beginning' or 'first', making an immediate connection with the early days of bridal contentment in the matching colon. In other contexts, the root of this term, ראשׁ, translates to mean 'best' or 'choicest', adding positive association to this fruit and the land on which it is grown.[7] Although the term תְּבוּאָה is used in this context with a third masculine singular suffix (תְּבוּאָתֹה), the root word itself is feminine and, like the promise of the virgin bride's fertility, the image of harvest offers a similar assurance of abundance after the initial first sacred yield.

When viewed side by side, the parallels between the image of the female bride and that of the plentiful land become clear. Their shared purity and potential are implicitly affirmed as being highly attractive qualities—objects of desire for their (male) husband/owner. Both are valued for their fertility and their ability to provide and sustain new life, holding future security within. Thus, the rhetoric surrounding these images appears to be positive, evoking a sense of hope for abundance and pleasure. The symmetry of text ensures that the meaning of each bicolon is enhanced by its alternate pair, leaving no doubt as to the positive value assigned to the type of land implied in the image of first fruits and harvest. As the bridal state was upheld as an ideal, so here the optimistic rhetoric implies an ideal of land as arable, providing abundantly for human consumption.

Aside from the reader's preconceived notions of מִדְבָּר (wilderness), the text, as it stands in Jer. 2.2c, only hints at the value judgments assigned to this image of land. The first clue lies in the verb הָלַךְ (to 'go after' or 'follow'), a term that describes Israel's actions in the wilderness with YHWH. Referring, in other contexts, to a woman who walks after the man with whom she is associated (Gen. 24.5; 1 Sam. 25.42), הָלַךְ recalls the devotion of the idealized bride in the previous line, emphasizing Israel's 'following' as an act of love and loyalty. Here, then, the wilderness serves to foreground Israel's unerring devotion by providing the 'admirable foil' against which such

6. Cf. Exod. 23.19; Lev. 23.10-14; Num. 18.12-13; Deut. 26.1-11.
7. Cf. Gen. 49.3; Exod. 30.23. Holladay, *A Concise Hebrew and Aramaic Lexicon*, p. 330.

fidelity is upheld.[8] It is a place of adversity where Israel's identity as YHWH's people is forged.[9] Indeed, the emphasis on 'leading' and 'following' implies a depiction of wilderness as a trackless waste in which one quickly becomes disoriented. Israel's commitment as YHWH's bride is made even more exceptional in light of the apparent hostility of the surrounding environment.

A second hint as to the value assigned to this image is found by examining the word מִדְבָּר itself. Whether one translates מִדְבָּר as 'wilderness', 'desert' or 'pasture',[10] the term refers to an area of agriculturally unexploited land. This contrasts with the image of the fertile, arable land identified in symmetrical pair 'b'. Elsewhere, the root letters of מִדְבָּר are used to describe, among other things, a place of thorns or the occurrence of pestilence (1 Kgs 8.37; Ps. 91.3; Hos. 13.14), both unfavourable terms whose association with מִדְבָּר supports the mounting evidence of wilderness as a negative image. Confirmation of this suspicion, however, must be sought in the imagery of the corresponding bicolon ('c').

The symmetrical pair to the wilderness depiction signals an unexpectedly harsh turn in the text to a bicolon dominated by the verb אָשַׁם (to be guilty).[11] Here, אָשַׁם refers to the consequences incurred for consuming the sacrosanct first fruits that were dedicated to YHWH. The metaphor works on multiple levels, referring to both the literal eating of the first fruits and to the destruction of those who attempt to 'consume' Israel (cf. Num. 24.8.), but it is with the former that I am primarily concerned. To consume the first fruits was to pervert their proper use, violating YHWH's law and distorting the relationship between Israel and its deity. The rhetoric around this legal infringement and its corresponding punishment is undeniably nega-

---

8. Jack R. Lundbom, *Jeremiah 1–20: A New Translation with Introduction and Commentary* (New York: Doubleday, 1999), p. 250.

9. Some commentators have idealized the notion of wilderness, suggesting that it is a place of refuge and a location for divine revelation. This understanding of wilderness can be observed in the work of Susan P. Bratton, *Christianity, Wilderness, and Wildlife* (Scranton, PA: University of Scranton Press, 1993). In light of the negative associations that accompany the images of wilderness in Jeremiah, however, I maintain that the wilderness is portrayed as a desolate and threatening region, which makes human habitation undesirable and impossible.

10. Robert B. Leal, 'Negativity towards Wilderness in the Biblical Record', *Ecotheology* 10.3 (2005), pp. 264-81 (368), argues that מִדְבָּר refers to land that was unexploited for agricultural purposes, but used for grazing animals. See also Daniel Hillel, *The Natural History of the Bible: An Environmental Exploration of the Hebrew Scriptures* (New York: Columbia University Press, 2006), p. 118. The ASV, KJV, NET and NRSV Bibles translate מִדְבָּר to mean 'wilderness'. The NIV and NJB have 'desert'.

11. McKane, *Jeremiah 1–25*, p. 28, notes that although the root אשם appears in the qal imperfect, it is easier if past tenses are assumed. Biblical translations vary: The KJV and ASV stay faithful to the qal imperfect, while the NRSV, NET, NEB and NIV assume the past tense.

tive, endorsing the negative standing of its parallel pair depicting the wilderness. Through this symmetry, the rhetoric also establishes a connection between the wilderness and punishment for breaking Yhwh's law. Such an association suggests that violation of this law results in the decline of the land's ability to produce, reducing it to a wilderness state.[12] Once again, the contrast between the arable and the non-arable is underlined. The arable land, with its positive associations, is valued over and against the penalty of wilderness, and with this division comes a new understanding of these images in terms of divine reward and punishment.

This negative assessment of the wilderness is endorsed by its qualifying statement in the first bicolon of the final pair ('d'). Here, the text states that this wilderness is a לֹא זְרוּעָה אֶרֶץ (land not sown), a description that suggests a place that is unable to be planted (זָרַע, lit. 'sown') and is thus without vegetation.[13] A second layer of meaning is additionally revealed when one examines the other primary meaning of זָרַע: to be pregnant or to produce descendants (Lev. 12.2; 1 Sam 2.20). Once again, the language recalls the hopeful image of Israel as a young and fertile bride, but the resounding לֹא reminds the reader that this is a barren land where no new growth is possible. In being without seed, the wilderness is defined as 'lacking', and is thus set in opposition to its fertile counterpart. A defining characteristic of wilderness that emerges from this observation, then, is that this is a space of minimal human occupation. Without human or crop 'seed', the wilderness is devoid of human presence. It is an unknown, a place beyond the boundaries of civilized society and thus the antithesis of the arable land.

The corresponding bicolon to the image of the unsown land is an announcement of verdict upon those who violated divine property by eating the first fruits: רָעָה (disaster) came upon them (Jer. 2.3b). Although רָעָה literally means 'evil', like many translators I prefer to render it here as 'disaster'.[14] The consequence of defying Yhwh's law is disaster. As punishment was hinted at in the image of wilderness in the previous matching pair ('c'), this connection is reiterated as disaster and combined with the image of the unsown land. A climax is achieved at this point as the accumulation of wilderness imagery builds to bestow one last association: the unsown wilderness is a place of disaster, a place of death. A final sense of contrast and separation is achieved here, as the abundant life that was associated with the arable land is set against this image of death which is found in the wilderness. In this comparison, a balanced set of dualistic images is completed:

12. See Jer. 48.32-33, where the land's lack of productivity is a sign of Moab's defeat.

13. The GNB translates this passage as 'a land that had not been cultivated'.

14. Cf. CEB, ESV, GNB, NET, NIV and NRSV. See also Exod. 32.14; Judg. 20.34, 41; 2 Sam. 15.14; and Jer. 1.14.

Positive	**Negative**
(Devotion)	Wilderness
(Youth)	Unsown land
Love	Guilty
Bride	Disaster/death
(Holy)	
First fruits	
Harvest[15]	

In these two short stanzas, the text's rhetoric achieves a positive portrayal of the arable land and a contrasting negative depiction of the unsown wilderness. Both these representations will be reiterated and expanded in the following six verses.

Jeremiah 2.4-9

As in the previous oracle, Jer. 2.4-9 is framed by two messenger formulae that introduce the unit in v. 5 ('thus says YHWH') and signal its conclusion in v. 9 ('utterance of YHWH'). In spite of the legal language, the passage fails to display the typical characteristics of the covenantal lawsuit genre.[16] Like Jer. 2.1-3, the oracular formulae suggest that this passage derives its structure from the canons of Hebrew rhetoric. It is an example of a prophetic oracle that at times uses the terminology of a covenantal lawsuit.[17]

While the upper limit of the oracle is demarcated by a *petuhah* prior to v. 4, delimitation of the unit's lower limit relies on formulaic and rhetorical criteria, as a section marker does not appear until the *setumah* in v. 28. Verses 4-9 are well developed, however, by the balancing of words and themes, and by speaker alternation. In addition to this, a chiasmus gives this passage structure, making clear the unit's upper and lower limits and its primary thematic concerns:

v. 5 a Oracular formula
        b Authority figures: your fathers
          Going after הָלַךְ
v. 6   c Where is YHWH? אַיֵּה יהוה
          d In a land בָּאֶרֶץ (three times)

---

15. The bracketed images fall outside the scope of this eco-rhetorical analysis.

16. For an extended discussion on the form of Jer. 2.4-9, see Lundbom, *Jeremiah 1–20*, pp. 257-58.

17. In this identification, I agree with R.P. Carroll, *Jeremiah: A Commentary* (Philadelphia: Westminster Press, 1986), pp. 117-23; William L. Holladay, *Jeremiah 1: A Commentary on the Book of the Prophet Jeremiah Chapters 1–25* (Philadelphia: Fortress Press, 1986), pp. 73-74; Lundbom, *Jeremiah 1–20*, pp. 257-58.

v. 7   d' Land אֶרֶץ (two times)
v. 8   c' Where is YHWH? אַיֵּה יהוה
               b' Authority figures: the priests, rulers, prophets
                    Went after הָלַךְ
v. 9   a' Oracular formula

Appearing at the centre of the chiasm, the land creates something of a
climax, demanding that the ecological reader pay particular analytical attention to these central verses.

A glance at Jer. 2.6-7 is enough to reveal the striking dominance of the
word אֶרֶץ (land) within the central verses of this text:

v. 6   They did not say, 'Where is the Lord
            Who brought us out of the אֶרֶץ of Egypt,
       Who led us in the מִדְבָּר,
            In a אֶרֶץ of deserts and pits
       In a אֶרֶץ of drought and deep darkness
            In a אֶרֶץ that no one passes through,
       Where no one lives?'

v. 7   I brought you into a plentiful אֶרֶץ
            to eat its fruits and its good things.
       But when you entered you defiled my אֶרֶץ
            And made my heritage an abomination.

Well balanced and seemingly selected for their rhetorical power, the terms
describing the אֶרֶץ in these verses create two distinct images of land that
echo those images established in Jer. 2.1-3. The first of these depictions
appears in v. 6, where the negative associations of wilderness from the
previous oracle are developed and expanded. Following the identification
of the wilderness in the third colon of this verse are four identically constructed qualifying cola. Each qualifier begins with בְּאֶרֶץ (in a land of), the
repetition of which gives a sense of foreboding, as the descriptions become
increasingly ominous. This phrase is then followed by two evocative terms
that define the appearance and condition of this wilderness, constructing a
detailed illustration of the image that first appeared in 2.2.

The first synonymous pair following the initial reference to the wilderness describes this as a place of עֲרָבָה (deserts) and שׁוּחָה (pits). One can
surmise that on a physical level, this desert area is a waterless region, supporting the depiction of the wilderness as a place without life, unable to
sustain crops or human occupation. As a fissure in the desert terrain, the
word שׁוּחָה offers new insight into the appearance of the wilderness, suggesting an irregular and difficult landscape, over which travel would be arduous

and fraught with danger.[18] A more metaphorical interpretation of this term sees the desert itself as a pit, or trap, out of which it is difficult to emerge.[19] Closely associated with this idea is an understanding of the desert as שְׁאוֹל (Sheol), a place of death whose root letters are connected to that of שׁוּחָה used here.[20] Once again a connection is made between the desert and death, adding weight to the notion of wilderness as a hostile and dangerous place.

Elaborating further on this emerging image of wilderness, the synonyms in the fifth colon mirror those in the previous line by portraying this land as one of צִיָּה (drought) and צַלְמָוֶת (deep darkness). Alliteration of the *ṣade* in these descriptive terms reinforces the menacing tone of the verse, which makes almost tangible to the reader the imminent threat of this wilderness. The inhospitable hostility of the desert noted in the fourth colon is reiterated by the word צִיָּה, but it is the second synonym that nuances this image of drought and sheds light on the conjectures initially made concerning the meaning of שׁוּחָה (pits). Traditionally, צַלְמָוֶת has been translated to mean 'shadow of death',[21] although recently there has been a shift toward understanding the term to mean 'deep darkness'.[22] Regardless of one's interpretive preference, the term connotes negative imagery of extreme danger (Ps. 23.4), distress (Ps. 44.19), gloom (Jer. 13.16; Ps. 107.10), eyes that are heavy with weeping (Job 16.16), and the world of the dead (Job 10.21-22; 38.17). Darkness is also seen here in its metaphorical sense of utter despair, the polar opposite to the hope associated with the world of light.[23] By combining the negative image of darkness with the representation of wilderness, this land's position on the subordinate side of the dualistic couplings is underlined. These descriptive terms thus serve to nuance the image of

18. This interpretation is supported by Holladay, *Jeremiah 1*, p. 87; Lundbom, *Jeremiah 1–20*, p. 259; McKane, *Jeremiah 1–25*, pp. 31-32, who understand the term in the sense of 'ravine'. The NJB also translates this term as 'ravine'.

19. שׁוּחָה is used in two other places in Jeremiah, both with negative connotations. In Jer. 18.20, where the speaker uses שׁוּחָה metaphorically to mean a 'pit for my life', the term is used in connection with evil. It is used again in 18.22 in what could be either a geographical description or a metaphorical phrase: 'they have dug a pit to catch me'. The blurring of meaning in this context suggests that such ambiguity should be kept in mind in the interpretation of 2.6.

20. Nicholas J. Tromp, *Primitive Conceptions of Death and the Nether World in the Old Testament* (Rome: Pontifical Biblical Institute, 1969), pp. 21, 23-24, argues that as well as referring to the surface of the ground, אֶרֶץ denotes the depths of the Earth and, by extension, can represent the realm of death.

21. This is consistent with the ASV, KJV and NJB translations of the Bible.

22. See the NRSV, NET, NIV and RSV. It is interesting to note that the LXX translates this term to mean 'barren', creating a contrast between the infertile land in this verse and the fertile bride in Jer 2.2. Although unfaithful to the text, the GNB translates this term as 'dangerous'.

23. This contrast between light and dark is seen also in Isa. 9.2; Jer. 13.16; Amos 5.8.

wilderness and support the association of this land with danger and death. It is a place of impenetrable darkness, a land devoid of hope.

Jer. 2.6 concludes with the final details of this wilderness description: it is a place where לֹא־עָבַר (none pass through) and where וְלֹא־יָשַׁב (no one dwells). As if to emphasize the reason for this emptiness, the linguistic play on the similarities between עָבַר (pass through) and עֲרָבָה (desert) in the fourth colon call to mind the ever-increasing list of negative associations with this place. Lack of agricultural opportunities, the dangerous terrain and drought ensure that this is a lonely and isolated place without human presence, a point underlined by the pounding reiteration of לֹא. No longer a description of the land's geographical appearance, these final cola assert the ontological conviction that this is the realm farthest from history, from human existence and, by implication, a place at the very edge of YHWH's reach. By completing the description on this note of deathly isolation the terror of the wilderness reaches mythic proportions, functioning as a model for the absolute antithesis to that which is positive, familiar and safe—an image to which the text now turns.

Jer. 2.7 opens with the image of a fertile land, which is then set in anti-thetical parallel with the image of a polluted land:

v. 7   I <u>brought you</u> into a *plentiful* **LAND**
           to eat its fruits and its good things.
        But when <u>you entered</u> you *defiled* my **LAND**,
           and made my heritage an abomination.[24]

כַּרְמֶל translates literally to mean 'fertile field' but typically refers to a garden, orchard or vineyard (Isa. 10.18; 16.10; 29.17; Jer. 4.26; Mic. 7.14), all places of rich produce.[25] כַּרְמֶל can also specify newly ripened grain (Lev. 2.14; 23.14; 2 Kgs 4.42), and in contrast to the barren dryness of the wilderness, the כַּרְמֶל points to the possibility of bountiful growth in this arable environment. In confirmation of the ongoing wealth of this plentiful land, the כַּרְמֶל is qualified as being full of פְּרִי (fruit), calling to mind the first fruits of Jer. 2.3. Where once this produce was reserved exclusively for the deity, however, the Israelites' faithfulness to YHWH that brought them into this land now allows them to reap the benefits of its fertility. According to this subtext, then, abundant yield is closely related to faithfulness.

---

24. For the purposes of this chapter, I will focus on the image of the fertile field. There is not scope within this project to explore the image of the polluted land.

25. Biblical translations of the term in Jer. 2.7 range from 'fertile land' (GNB, NET, NIV) and 'plentiful land' (ASV, NRSV, RSV) to 'plentiful country' (KJV) and 'country of plenty' (NJB).

These fruits are further qualified by the more generic טוּבָה (good things) of the fertile land. Not only does the vagueness of this concluding phrase imply that there is no end to the abundance of this land, it also gives concrete expression to the apparent goodness of this arable region, which has previously only been implied. If the barrenness of the wilderness makes it inherently bad, the fertility of this garden land makes it inherently good. This goodness is finally evidenced by the repeated emphasis on Yhwh's presence in this land, a presence that is made even more obvious by the divine absence in the previous verse.[26] The first line of v. 7 hints at this presence in its opening phrase, וָאָבִיא ([and] *I* brought), emphasizing that it was Yhwh who brought the Israelites to this plentiful land. This is confirmed in the antithetical parallel of v. 7, where Yhwh describes this place as אַרְצִי (*my* land) and נַחֲלָתִי (*my* heritage). Thus, a connection is established between the 'quality' of the land and Yhwh's presence, or favour.

When read uncritically, the dichotomy between the fertile field and the barren wilderness might pass as a simple description of two distinct types of land. From an ecocritical perspective, however, these nine short verses establish two polarized images of land, with clear value judgments associated with each image. Inherent in these dualistic depictions are a number of rhetorical strategies that enhance the relationship of opposition and exclusion that underlines these images of land. These strategies include—but are not limited to—the backgrounding of wilderness as the stage upon which the divine/human action is played out; the utilization of land as an instrument of reward and punishment; and the valuation of women and land based on their purity and reproductive ability. Having identified the dualistic divisions inherent in this imagery, my investigation shifts briefly from text to context, listening closely for the evocation of biblical memories of wilderness in the colonial rhetoric that shaped the environmental histories of Aotearoa New Zealand.

From Text to Context: An Intertextual Exploration

The majority of references to 'wilderness' found in New Zealand literature appears in the writings of early British settler communities, which began the process of colonization in the mid-nineteenth century. The appearance of these references at this time is unsurprising on two levels. First, prior to European contact—and indeed to this day—there was no equivalent word for or concept of 'wilderness' in Māori cultures. Second, the emergence of these biblically grounded images of land coincides with a period of New Zealand history marked by a strong Christian missionary presence, and

---

26. Although Jer. 2.6 depicts Yhwh as being present with the Israelites in the wilderness, Yhwh does not seem to be present in the wilderness itself.

an increasing number of British settlers who, if not practising Christians, were well versed in biblical teaching by virtue of their heritage. As these groups sought to articulate their encounters with this new land, it is not unexpected that they did so by employing the value-laden categories of their ancient Scriptures. At times it can be difficult to separate the notions of wilderness in the final form of the Bible from the millennia of Christian thought that has built upon these ancient ideas and added new depth to their meanings.[27] Despite the layers of development, I agree with Innes,[28] Leal[29] and Patterson,[30] who all argue that regardless of the embellishing stratum of Christian meaning, the colonial attitudes toward wilderness have their underlying roots in biblical—particularly Old Testament—imagery such as that found in Jeremiah.

In exploring the echoes of biblical images of wilderness, I will critically examine a poem by British settler William Pember Reeves (1857–1932).[31] The rhetoric of Reeves's work is illustrative of a wider colonial attitude mirrored by other settler voices at the time, such as that of Edward Gibbon Wakefield.[32] His extensive poem, 'A Colonist in his Garden',[33] is structured as a conversation in the form of a letter between an Englishman and his friend whom he is urging to return home from the young colony of New Zealand: 'Old Friend, ere darkness falls, turn back / To England, life and art' (line 5).

Allusions to wilderness begin to appear in Wakefield's poem as contrasts are drawn between the English 'homeland' and its untamed antipodean colony. These references become explicit in the description of the New

27. Layers of meaning around wilderness developed particularly out of the synoptic accounts of Jesus's time in the wilderness (Mk 1.12-13; Mt. 4.1; Lk. 4.1). Through these narratives the wilderness came to stand for temptation, spiritual deprivation, evil and times of trial. This is reflected in John Bunyan's classic *The Pilgrim's Progress*, which opens with the phrase 'the wilderness of this world', a place that the Christian must escape to reach the Celestial City. See John Bunyan, *The Pilgrim's Progress from This World to That Which Is to Come* (New York: Lane & Tippett, 1845), p. 1.

28. Keith Innes, 'Aspects of Wilderness', *Theology* 110 (2007), pp. 110-17.

29. Robert B. Leal, *Wilderness in the Bible: Toward a Theology of Wilderness* (New York: Peter Lang, 2004), p. 36.

30. John Patterson, *People of the Land: A Pacific Philosophy* (Palmerston North: Dunmore Press, 2000), p. 78.

31. Reeves's parents were settlers, migrating to Canterbury in 1857, and he was born in Lyttelton, three weeks after their arrival.

32. See the introduction to this chapter.

33. William Pember Reeves, 'A Colonist in his Garden', in *The Passing of the Forest and Other Verse* (Cambridge: Chadwyck-Healey, 2000), pp. 14-18. For reasons of copyright, I am unable to include the text of this poem in its entirety. It is, however, able to be viewed online: http://paperspast.natlib.govt.nz/cgi-bin/paperspast?a=d&d=MEX19041022.2.54.2.

Zealand landscape as 'desert' (lines 57, 64), 'wilderness' (line 65) and full of 'drought' (line 59). Not only is the wilderness designated negatively as hostile, without inhabitant (lines 81, 82), and as a 'silent waste' (line 76), but it is also contrasted with the favourable garden (lines 24, 68, 100), with its orchards (line 26), culture (line 6) and cultivation (lines 103-108). While the immediate evidence is not strong enough to claim unequivocally that Reeves's images allude directly to Jeremiah any more than to, say, Isaiah or Hosea,[34] the intertextual imagery is such that it is plausible to claim that if Jeremiah is not *the* evoked text, it is *an* evoked text. It is on this basis that my analysis proceeds.

By encountering the terms 'desert', 'drought' and 'wilderness' in Reeves's poem, a parallel is evoked between the New Zealand landscape and the wilderness described in the ancient Jeremianic texts. Through the use of such terminology, the poem retains an underlying notion of wilderness as a place of hostility, desolation and darkness. It is the attitude of humanity toward this wilderness, however, that is transposed from a position of fear in Jeremiah to one of aggression in Reeves's text. Indeed, the negativity of the wilderness appears to be the poem's justification for this land's violent transformation. Reeves presents the colonists as the subjects of the violent imagery, engaged in a battle with the land to 'Fight Nature for a home' (line 60). Developing this war-like imagery further, Reeves establishes a dichotomy between conqueror and conquered, as the human agents are 'matched against the desert's power' (line 64), bravely fighting to subdue the untamed land and bring it under human dominion (lines 59-61).

Echoes of the Jeremianic wilderness are not restricted to these initial allusions alone, however. In his description of New Zealand's land as 'Wide, empty plains where shadows pass' (line 82), Reeves's work touches upon the chaos, unfamiliarity and isolation identified as characterizing the wilderness of Jeremiah. An intertextual reverberation is immediately audible in this phrase, as the 'passing shadows' recall the wilderness as a 'shadow of death' in the KJV translation of Jer. 2.6.[35] Like the Jeremianic text, this poem also appears to associate the wilderness with distress and danger primarily on the basis of human absence and its existence outside the domain of civilized society. Once again, the well-established metaphorical dualism, setting light against darkness, enters the text. As in Jer. 2.6, Reeves's poem draws a parallel between the land and the moral equivalent of this shadowy

---

34. Similar imagery can be found in Isaiah, Hosea and Joel, where the wilderness is described as deserted (Isa. 27.10) and desolate (Isa. 64.10; Hos. 2.3; Joel 2.22; 3.19), and portrayed as the negative opposite of the fertile land (Isa. 32.15; 35.1; 51.3; Hos. 9.10).

35. Given that the KJV translation of the Bible was the only translation available to nineteenth- and early twentieth-century Christians in New Zealand, it is reasonable to assert a connection between Reeves' work and this older rendering.

darkness: evil. The darkness of the wilderness stands once more against implied perceptions of 'goodness' and light. Thus, the 'fight' against the wilderness becomes a moral imperative, as this land represents the chaos of that which exists beyond the realm of God and Christendom. The colonial task, therefore, involves conquering both the physical and metaphorical darkness.[36]

Closely associated with the dark hostility of the shadowed land is the depiction of wilderness as a place without inhabitant.[37] Evoking the sentiment of the Jeremianic text which insists that no one dwells in or passes through the wilderness (Jer. 2.6), Reeves claims that the islands of New Zealand are 'Wide, empty plains' (line 82), as 'empty as their deep' (line 10), and that they comprise 'a land without a past' (lines 13, 79), without 'man, nor beast, nor tree' (line 81), where 'none before have stood' (line 58). Like Jeremiah, then, Reeves presents a land characterized by an absence of human occupation, although such emptiness extends here to imply a land preserved for colonial development. By depicting the wilderness in this way, however, both the poem and its Jeremianic memories reject the existence of an Indigenous human population as well as any other-than-human ecosystems in this land.[38] Reeves's denial of these communities thus shifts his depiction from a geographical description of an agriculturally unexploited region to an ethnocentric and anthropocentric ontological assertion that the wilderness lacks 'civilized' communities and their agricultural expertise.

Set in opposition to the civilization desired by the colonists, the desolate wilderness is depicted as standing in benign anticipation, patiently awaiting the imprint of the European master. Consistently defined in terms of characteristics lacking, the land of Aotearoa appears here as a space wait-

36. A connection between the physical darkness and the metaphorical darkness is reflected in the words of the Wesleyan missionary Cort Schnackenberg, who, in 1844, advised Maōri, 'if you find your mind [or] your heart to be a wilderness, cultivate it in the same manner as you do your fields, cut down the bush … spare no sin'. Quoted in Geoff Park, 'After the Scene, After the Fever," in Geoff Park (ed.), *Theatre Country: Essays on Landscape and Whenua* (Wellington: Victoria University Press, 2006), p. 107.

37. Descriptions of the New Zealand land by early settlers present it as a desolate and barren place. Thomas Chapman, e.g., bemoans that 'it has many, many times been grief to mind to see thousands of acres of land lying waste and miles of country desolate and entirely uninhabited'. Quoted in Paul Shepard, *English Reaction to the New Zealand Landscape before 1850* (Wellington: Victoria University Press, 1969), p. 23.

38. For reasons of space, I am regrettably unable to explore the devastating impact this rhetoric had on the Indigenous Māori communities who were also posited on the subordinate side of the dualistic hierarchy. This aspect of the colonial 'wilderness' legacy is explored much more extensively in Emily Colgan, 'To Conquer and Subdue: An Ecological Reading of Wilderness in Jer. 17.5-8 and Beyond', in B.F. Kolia and Michael Mawson (eds.), *Unsettling Theologies: Memory, Identity, and Place* (Oxford: Oxford University Press, forthcoming).

ing to receive—a canvas on which 'we rough architects of State ... paint the hues of life' (lines 74, 78). Yet another intertextual parallel is drawn as the reader recalls the Jeremianic connection between the unsown land and the young bride (Jer. 2.2-3). Both land and woman are depicted as dutifully awaiting 'fulfilment' through conception by their (male) husband/owner in order that they might satisfy patriarchal/anthropocentric expectations and produce abundantly.[39] Reeves's image of land is presented as a passive vessel waiting to be transformed by the products of (masculine) human labour and cultivation.[40]

Extending beyond the world of poetic literature, this notion of wilderness (and its opposite, the garden) appears to have been employed in the construction of colonial projects in Aotearoa New Zealand and appropriated as a justification for European domination. As British settlers began to impose the culturally and religiously loaded term 'wilderness' onto New Zealand's landscape and its unique biotic communities, it was inevitable that this land began to be perceived as lacking the properly ordered character of its European counterparts. The powerful symbolic worlds associated with garden and wilderness that were found in the ancient biblical literature and mirrored in the contemporary contextual literature provided both the framework and the motivation for the actualization of these symbolic realities. Settler communities thus set about transforming the untamed wilderness into a 'friendly' agrarian landscape, modelled on the property regimes and extensive agrarian schemes of Europe. These actions irretrievably altered this country's distinctive land and all but destroyed its diverse other-than-human ecosystems.[41] Swept into an emerging self-understanding of 'honest

39. A contrast between the unsown wilderness and the fertile garden is drawn by the Rev. Richard Taylor in 1849 as he writes, 'This morning I walked over to Mr Chapman's garden. The ground was literally strewed with fallen apples. I took my natives to see them ... [and] bid them compare that fruitful garden with the fruitless wilderness we had passed over, that they might see what civilisation could effect'. Quoted in Shepard, *English Reaction*, p. 31.

40. Similar sentiments are expressed in the poems of Thomas Bracken, particularly 'The Canterbury Pilgrims'. In this poem, early English settlers observed 'plains yearning for the spade and plough', and 'vales waiting to be dressed by man'. See Thomas Bracken, 'The Canterbury Pilgrims', in *Musings in Maoriland* (Dunedin: A.T. Keirle, 1890), pp. 84-85.

41. It is estimated, for example, that since the initial European contact of 1769, over 30,000 different types of flowering and cone-bearing plants have been introduced to New Zealand, mostly as garden plants. See Maggy Wassilieff, 'Gardens—Estate and Homestead Gardens', in *Te Ara: The Encyclopedia of New Zealand* (https://teara.govt.nz/en/gardens/page-3). This alone would result in massive change to the land's biodiversity, but it has also contributed to over one hundred New Zealand plant species being classified as either critical, endangered or extinct.

toil',[42] the colonial campaign began erasing the presence of the land's Indigenous ecological agency and the agency of its other-than-human occupants, to make way for the 'large lawns', 'shrub borders' and 'formal rose beds' of the transplanted English garden.

While the colonial mandate to 'take the wilderness' persisted well into the twentieth century, references to wilderness—as well as their Jeremianic echoes—occur with far less frequency in the literature that began to emerge at this time. Remnants of these attitudes seem to remain in the communal consciousness even in the twenty-first century, however, with land being valued primarily in terms of its economic and instrumental potential to the human master. Ongoing debates relating to sources of energy and housing intensification often prioritize immediate social and economic needs without serious consideration of the long-term ecological ramifications. The anthropocentrism inherent in these debates suggests many New Zealanders continue to be the uncritical heirs of a dualistic reality that sets 'garden' against 'wilderness' and imagines the needs of the land and its Indigenous inhabitants as subordinate to so-called progress and development. Acknowledgment and critique of this inheritance, however, offers an opportunity to interrupt this discourse, and to create space for alternative conversations (and actions)—conversations (and actions) that centre the experience of the land and Māori communities who have been disproportionately impacted by this 'wilderness' thinking. Acknowledgment and critique of this colonial past must be included in the ongoing conversation about what it means to live responsibly on this *whenua* (land) of Aotearoa.

42. Claudia Bell, *Inventing New Zealand: Everyday Myths of Pakeha Identity* (Auckland: Penguin Books, 1996), p. 35.

11

THE YOUNG MAN AND THE SEA: RECONCEIVING ANCIENT WATER RESOURCES

Alan H. Cadwallader

It has become increasingly recognized that the author of Mark's Gospel made a decisive intervention in the toponomy of Palestine by renaming the body of water usually called Lake Gennesaret as 'the Sea of Galilee'. The name has become entrenched in subsequent ecclesiastical and administrative gazetteers and was unable to be rescinded by either Luke's or John's efforts to correct the innovation, conscious as they must have been, like the third-century Porphyry of Tyre, that this small body of water could never qualify as a sea. Mark's decision to refer to the lake as 'the Sea of Galilee' or simply 'the Sea' has struggled to find an explanation beyond a contorted appeal to the semantic range and/or literary evocation of Hebrew antecedents. I suggest that there is a more potent driver for the change contemporary to Mark, running at two levels—one, a parody of Vespasianic militaristic propaganda; the other, an appropriation of a fundamental tenet of Greek and Roman law. The Gospel's highly charged and resistant misappellation profoundly distills a confrontation about the use and abuse of water reserves in first-century Galilee. The confrontation captured in the renaming is not only about restoring an environment to a subsistence reciprocity rather than a mercantile resource, but also about releasing the waters and the life held therein from the destructiveness of economic expropriation. In the analysis, I reconfigure ecological hermeneutics by tracing the origins of anthropocenic toxicity to early imperial intensification of agricultural and aquacultural practices for material gain. My reading will thereby allow a nascent ecological concern to the early Jesus movement, albeit factored into the complexity of socio-economic disruption occurring under the avaricious watch of the Roman sycophant Herod Antipas. The approach will, tangentially, ring a modulation of current ecological hermeneutics.

The Gospel of Mark may have received less attention from patristic commentators, who frequently subsumed to Matthew both in textual assimilation in the course of transmission and in didactic interpretations.[1] But Mark secured one lasting triumph: allocating a toponym to the body of water lying in the northern reaches of Palestine as the main reservoir receiving and feeding the River Jordan. This, according to Mark, was the 'Sea of Galilee'.[2] It is the geographical feature that situated and launched the gathering and expansion of a new movement which draws in Gentile territory (Mk 1.16; 7.31). More frequently, it is distilled into the simplex of 'the sea' (ἡ θάλασσα) (Mk 2.13; 3.7; 4.1 [tres]; 4.39; 4.41; 5.1; 5.13 [bis]; 5.21; 6.47; 6.48; 6.49). In two cases, however, 'the sea' takes on a general, perhaps proverbial connotation of a common, nebulously defined receptor (Mk 9.42; 11.23), though perhaps extrapolated from the Legion destruction of Mk 5.13 where pigs meet an abysmal end. The spectrum of Mark's application of the term 'sea', from toponymic to symbolic, will need to be factored into any explanation of that usage.

Nowhere does Mark call the body of water in question a 'lake' (λίμνη), even though at least one scribe effected the correction when transcribing Mark.[3] The problem of Mark calling the lake a sea was compounded by Mark appearing to tie the Legion pericope (Mk 5.1-20) to the territory of the Gerasenes—Jerash/Gerasa was some 30 kilometres away. As Origen noted in a comment that made its way into catenae in some later manuscripts, καὶ Γέρασα δὲ τῆς Ἀραβίας ἐστὶ πόλις οὐτὲ θάλασσαν οὐτὲ λίμνην

---

1. Willem F. Wisselink, in his sometimes-contested study of assimilation, argues that assimilation is a common feature of Gospel transmission, headed by Matthew rather than Mark's Gospel. Nonetheless, he accepts that assimilation in Mark does occur, especially in certain manuscripts. See Willem F. Wisselink, *Assimilation as a Criterion for the Establishment of the Text* (Kampen: J.H. Kok, 1989), pp. 79-91. By contrast, at least in the period of the second to fourth centuries, Cambry G. Pardee, *Scribal Harmonization in the Synoptic Gospels* (Leiden: E.J. Brill, 2019), p. 423, finds that Mark and Luke are more frequently assimilated to Matthew than any other direction of harmonization. Regardless of transmission, however, it is clear that early commentators used 'the teaching Gospel', namely Matthew, as the baseline for the interpretation of Mark. See Joseph Verheyden, 'The Reception History of the Gospel of Mark in the Early Church. Adventuring in Still Largely Unexplored Territory', in Geert van Oyen (ed.), *Reading the Gospel of Mark in the Twenty-First Century: Method and Meaning* (BETL, 301; Leuven: Peeters, 2019), pp. 395-428.

2. See especially, R. Steven Notley, 'The Sea of Galilee: Development of an Early Christian Toponym', *JBL* 128 (2009), pp. 183-88.

3. So, for example, the eleventh-century minuscule 700 (Gregory-Aland) replaces θάλασσα with λίμνη in Mk 5.1, an adjustment that cannot be credited to Matthaean or Lukan influence. Other manuscripts, such as the fifteenth-century minuscule 69, avoided the problem by adopting the Matthew phrasing which omits any reference to sea or lake. Many more scribes were vexed by the reference to Jerash/Gerasa (εἰς τὴν χώραν τῶν Γερασηνῶν, 'into the country of the Gerasenes'). Alternatives (Gadara, Gergesa) proliferate, reflecting the unease about topographical inaccuracy.

πλησίον ἔχουσα ('And Jerash is a city of Arabia having in its proximity neither a sea nor a lake').[4] If we look to other authors of the period, there is little doubt that 'lake' was the correct term to use for a land-locked hydrological expanse. Virgil named the Larius (modern Lake Como) and Lake Benacus as *lacus tantos,* 'our mighty lakes'.[5] They were indeed large, with surface areas today covering 146 and 370 square kilometres respectively. The Galilaean body of water is of a piece with these expanses. It covers 167 square kilometres and is noticeably shallower. Two geographical informants of the Romans, Strabo and Pliny the Elder, were clear that this was a lake (λίμνη, *lacus*),[6] Lake Gennesar(et). Josephus was likewise in no doubt; he described it as one of two lakes (λίμνη) at the northern and southern end of the Jordan River, the former fresh and productive, the latter salty and barren (Lake Asphaltites), though useful for its salt.[7] He offered two names for the northern lake. The first, the Lake of Tiberias, names it according to the adulatory city toponym given by Herod Antipas to his Roman-style urban construction of c. 19 CE;[8] it was a Romanization that John's Gospel was prepared to adopt (Jn 6.1; 21.1). Josephus's second offering was Lake Gennesaritis, that is, designating the lake by reference to its surrounding plain to the west (cf. Mk 6.53 = Mt. 14.34).[9] Josephus confided that sometimes the locals called it simply Gennesar;[10] this may go back to the general reference to 'the water of Gennesar' (τὸ ὕδωρ τοῦ Γεννησαρ) of 1 Macc. 11.67. But little wonder that Luke's avowal of accuracy (ἀκριβῶς) in the opening dedication for the third Gospel (Lk. 1.3) necessitated an adjustment to Mark's text. For Luke, it was unquestionably 'Lake Gennesaret' (Lk. 5.1). He may have seen Mark as wayward or at least misleading with his toponym. The third-century Neoplatonist Porphyry was snidely dismissive of Mark's inaccuracy. The so-called 'sea' was, in his view from Tyre, no more

---

4. See, e.g., minuscule 773 (tenth century). The quotation comes from Origen's *Commentary on John* 6.41.209. See Cécile Blanc, *Origène: Commentaire sur saint Jean,* II (SC; Paris: Cerf, 1970). Euthymius Zigabenus's twelfth-century commentary on the four Gospels lifted Origen's note, uncredited, into his interpretation of Mt. 8.28-34 (*PG* 129.297).

5. Virgil, *Geo.* 2.159-60.

6. Strabo, 16.2.16; Pliny, *Nat.* 5.71.

7. Josephus, *War* 4.455-56, 515.

8. Josephus, *Ant.* 18.37-38. See Anthony Keddie, *Class and Power in Roman Palestine: The Socioeconomic Setting of Judaism and Christian Origins* (Cambridge: Cambridge University Press, 2019), pp. 53-57; Katia Cytryn-Silverman, 'Tiberias, from its Foundation to the End of the Early Islamic Period', in David A. Fiensy and James Riley Strange (eds.), *Galilee in the Late Second Temple and Mishnaic Periods.* II. *The Archaeological Record from Cities, Towns and Villages* (Minneapolis, MN: Fortress Press, 2015), pp. 186-210 (186-97).

9. Josephus, *Ant.* 18.36; *Vit.* 349.

10. Josephus, *War* 3.463-64.

than a 'small lake' (λίμνη μικρά); indeed, it was barely a 'pond' (λάκκος), hardly something to be magnified into a full-blown maritime panorama for divine epiphanies—of Jesus or anyone else.[11]

A Hebraic Explanation?

Scholarly commitment to reinforce a continuity between the Hebrew and Christian Scriptures has fostered the search for a Hebraic origin to Mark's usage of the term 'Sea of Galilee'. Biblical commentators offer two directions, one symbolic, one toponymic. The symbolic element taps into the mythological dimensions of the chaos of the primaeval water which sometimes reasserted itself in threats to the people of God and sometimes delivered an epiphanic vision.[12] The strongest claim on such traditions in Mark's Gospel comes in the storm on the sea (5.35-41), where 'the sea' loses its identifying epithet. But in the two places where that epithet is provided (Mk 1.16; 7.31) there is no hint of chaos; only aquacultural labour and a cartographical indicator.

The toponymic angle seeks to work from the ambiguity in the Hebrew word ים, which can be translated as 'sea' or 'lake'. Consequently, most commentators effectively imply that when one reads 'sea', assume it means 'lake',[13] though in one recent instance the word is translated constantly as 'lake/sea'.[14] However, in the usual supporting citations listed by commentators—Num. 34.11; Josh. 12.3; 13.27—an epithet is provided, that is כנרת, yielding Lake Chinnereth, even though the various LXX equivalents deliver θάλασσα Χεναρα/Χενερεθ and the Vulgate *mare Chenereth/Cheneroth*. It strains credibility that Mark would pick one word from the toponym without the other.[15] In fact, the Septuagint rarely uses λίμνη; when it does, it is usually in the sense of 'pool' or 'pond' (Ps. 106 (107).35; 113 (114).8; Cant.

---

11. Porphyry, *C. Chr.* 55.

12. See Elizabeth S. Malbon, *Narrative Space and Mythic Meaning* (Sheffield: JSOT Press, 1991), pp. 76-79; Michael J. Thate, *The Godman and the Sea: The Empty Tomb, the Trauma of the Jews, and the Gospel of Mark* (Philadelphia: University of Pennsylvania Press, 2019), pp. 123-27.

13. Robert A. Guelich, *Mark 1–8:26* (WBC; Dallas, TX: Word Books, 1989), p. 50; Adela Yarbro Collins, *Mark: A Commentary* (Hermeneia; Minneapolis, MN: Fortress Press, 2007), p. 157 n. 1 (I suspect a typographical error in giving θάλλασα for the LXX references here).

14. James W. Voelz, *Mark 1:1–8:26* (Concordia Commentary; Saint Louis, MO: Concordia, 2013), pp. 144, 483 and generally.

15. So Notley, 'Sea of Galilee', p. 185. The effort of Gerd Theissen (*The Gospels in Context: Social and Political History in the Synoptic Tradition* [trans. Linda M. Maloney; Minneapolis, MN: Fortress Press, 1991], p. 238) to save the case by arguing that Mark adopts the Semitic style of construction is unconvincing.

7.4; cf. 1 Macc. 11.35), exactly the sort of narrowing that Porphyry flung at the evangelist.

There seems little doubt that Mark wanted the body of water defined by the generic regional name, that is, 'the Galilee'.[16] Even though Steven Notley, against Gerd Theissen, sees the toponym as a Christian invention, he ties the development to another Septuagintal prompt, namely Isa. 9.1, the Galilee of the nations appropriated by Matthew (4.12-16). In Notley's view, the 'path for the sea', 'the Transjordan' and 'Galilee of the nations' were folded into a fateful, innovative sublimation—'Sea of Galilee'—which follows in 4.18 as the setting for the initial call of the disciples. The proximity of ים (sea/lake) and גליל (Galilee) in the Hebrew of Isa. 8.29 became θάλασσα and Γαλιλαία in the Greek of Isa. 9.1 (same verse, different numbering). That proximity became combined into a toponym in 'a pre-Synoptic development' seemingly harvested independently by Matthew and Mark but unknown to Luke, even though, in other ways, Luke possessed some accurate knowledge of the region.[17] Notley's own inventiveness seems to outdo that of the evangelists and their sources and certainly sidesteps the issues of synoptic relationships, where the two explicit mentions of 'Sea of Galilee' in Mark (1.16; 7.31) appear to be the source of their only appearance in Matthew (4.18; 15.29).

I want to suggest that there is a more immediate prompt to the appearance of 'the Sea of Galilee' that recognizes that we are dealing with a construct[18] that owes its probably Markan distillation to the might of Rome. In the last decade, a number of commentaries on Mark have recognized how salient is the literary and material witness of Rome's impact on Judaea, Galilee and Syro-Palestina generally. For that, Josephus is the prime source.[19] But to

16. So Robert H. Gundry, *Mark: A Commentary on his Apology for the Cross* (Grand Rapids, MI: Eerdmans, 1993), p. 66.

17. Notley, 'Sea of Galilee', pp. 185-88.

18. So, in general, Cilliers Breytenbach, 'Mark and Galilee: Text World and Historical World', in Eric M. Meyer (ed.), *Galilee through the Centuries* (Winona Lake, IN: Eisenbrauns, 1999), pp. 75-85 (75-76); similarly, Sandra Huebenthal, *Das Markusevangelium als kollektives Gedächtnis* (Göttingen: Vandenhoeck & Ruprecht, 2018), pp. 156-57.

19. See Martin Ebner, *Das Markusevangeliums: Neu übersetzt und kommentiert* (Stuttgart: Katholisches Bibelwerk, 2009); Bernhard Heininger, '"Politische Theologie" im Markusevangelium. Der Aufstieg Vespasians zum Kaiser und der Abstieg Jesu ans Kreuz', in *Die Inkulturation des Christentums: Aufsätze und Studien zum Neuen Testament und seiner Umwelt* (WUNT, 255; Tübingen: Mohr Siebeck, 2010), pp. 181-204; Gabriella Gelardini, *Christus Militans: Studien zur politisch-militärischen Semantik im Markusevangelium vor dem Hintergrund des ersten jüdisch-römischen Krieges* (Leiden: E.J. Brill, 2016); Stephen S. Kimondo, *The Gospel of Mark and the Roman-Jewish War of 66–70 CE: Jesus Story as a Contrast to the Events of the War* (Eugene, OR: Wipf & Stock, 2018). These studies advance earlier 'political' readings of Mark, such

my knowledge, no commentary correlated this folio of evidence to Mark's toponymic invention that launches his own emphasis on 'the Sea'.[20] This does not require that Mark knew Josephus's first account of the Jewish War. Rather, the study here does assume Mark's knowledge not merely of key turns in the conflict but, more especially, of Roman (Flavian) interpretative turns in the memory-making about the conflict,[21] as well as of the growing imposition of a Roman economic regimen, already in train well before the outbreak of organized hostilities. For this analysis, Josephus is a critical source, even with Mark's primary engagement with, shaping of and contribution to traditions of the Jesus movement.

The Lord of Land and Sea

The aggrandizement of Lake Kinneret was an integral element in the establishment of imperial credentials for Vespasian. Josephus had allied himself with Rome when he prophesied, according to his own fashioning of the encounter with Vespasian at Jotapata, that the general was to become 'Lord ... of land and sea and the entire human race' (δεσπότης ... καὶ γῆς

as Ched Myers, *Binding the Strong Man: A Political Reading of Mark's Story of Jesus* (Maryknoll, NY: Orbis Books, 1988); Herman C. Waetjen, *A Reordering of Power: A Socio-political Reading of Mark's Gospel* (Philadelphia: Fortress Press, 1989); cf. Brian J. Incignieri, *The Gospel to the Romans: The Setting and Rhetoric of Mark's Gospel* (Leiden: E.J. Brill, 2003).

20. I consider Notley's 'pre-Synoptic invention' as an unnecessary speculation. Without necessarily requiring the evangelist to be quarantined from community influences (or 'collective memory' in Huebenthal's terms), I consider, in what follows, that Mark has exercised considerable creativity in re-carving the inherited Gospel traditions according and resistant to contemporary Roman imperial constructions. Thomas Baier ('Flavian Gods in Intertextual Perspective. How Rulers Used Religious Practice as a Means of Communicating', in Neil Coffee, Chris Forstall, Lavinia Galli Milic and Damien Nelis (eds.), *Intertextuality in Flavian Epic Poetry: Contemporary Approaches* [Berlin: de Gruyter, 2020], pp. 305-22 [319]), dubs Mark's enterprise 'a distorting mirror' of Flavian theology. See also Christopher M. Tuckett, 'Christ and the Emperor: Some Reflections on Method and Methodological Issues Illustrated from the Gospel of Mark', in Gilbert van Belle and Joseph Verheyden (eds.), *Christ and the Emperor: The Gospel Evidence* (Leuven: Peeters, 2014), pp. 185-202.

21. Consequently, a postwar date is operative, without necessarily stretching the gap into the 80s, as Merrill Miller entertains in 'The Social Logic of the Gospel of Mark: Cultural Persistence and Social Escape in a Post-War Time', in Barry S. Crawford and Merrill P. Miller (eds.), *Redescribing the Gospel of Mark* (Atlanta, GA: SBL, 2017), pp. 207-399 (254-62). He, as many before him, have relied on Mk 13 to postulate a date. The arguments presented here, I would suggest, provide another fruitful pathway to explore. Compare Christopher Zeichmann, 'The Date of Mark's Gospel apart from the Temple and Rumors of War: The Taxation Episode (12:13-17) as Evidence', *CBQ* 79 (2017), pp. 422-37.

καὶ θαλάττης καὶ παντὸς ἀνθρώπων γένους).[22] The first Roman emperor Augustus (27 BCE–14 CE) had laid the foundation for such Roman imperial propaganda, even though the hubris of such a claim had a far earlier appearance.[23] For Augustus, a full-scale naval victory over pirates on the Mediterranean (*the* 'Sea' for Rome)[24] formed a crucial element of the dawning of a new eschaton of prosperity and peace.[25] Augustus was hailed (like Pompey before him) as lord/ruler of land and sea: αὐτοκράτορα Καίσαρα θεοῦ υἱὸν Σεβαστὸν τὸν <π>άσης γῆς καὶ [πάσης] θαλάσσης ἄ[ρχ]οντα.[26] The predicate ran through almost all emperors thereafter, well into early Byzantine times,[27] attaching to a variety of dominical nouns: ἐπόπτης ('overseer'), δεσπότης ('master'), αὐτοκράτωρ ('imperator/emperor'), κύριος ('lord') and, as just noted, ἄρχων; ('ruler') and appearing on different typologies of inscription, from dedications to building foundations and milestones.[28] Vespasian and Titus could do no less. In fact, one tantalizing, worn inscription from the baths at Olympos in Lycia confers on Vespasian the unique epithet ἐπιφανὴς θεὸς γῆς καὶ θαλάσσης ('The appearing as god of land and sea')—at least as Bulent Iplikçioğlu, after autopsy, provided the new reconstruction.[29] Even the *editio princeps* had conferred a singular reconstruction: δίκαιος κύριος ('the just lord').[30] Some doubt may remain about the exact wording, but the accolade is ambitiously aspirational whatever the reading!

The Flavian mimesis of the founder of Rome's imperial age meant not only a reiteration of Augustus's *Aegypta capta* coins through a long-running series of *Iudaea capta* coins, but the affirmation that Vespasian and Titus

22. Josephus, *War* 3.401-2. The portrayal of Josephus's words as prophecy apparently gained considerable Roman approval; see Tacitus, *Hist.* 1.10; 2.1; 5.13; Suetonius, *Vesp.* 4.

23. Aristotle, *Eth. nic.* 1179a.

24. *mare nostrum*, 'our sea': Sallust, *Hist.* 1.9; Pliny, *Nat.* 6.32.

25. *RGDA* 25.

26. ' For the Imperator Augustus, Son of God, the ruler of the whole earth and sea' *CIRB* 1046; see also *IGR* 4.309; *SEG* 36.1129, 57.1665.

27. Serena Connolly, 'A Grammarian Honors the Emperors', *AHB* 24 (2010), pp. 113-25 (121-25), provides a fulsome list. She misses, among a number of instances, one for Tiberius (*IGR* 3.721) and one for Nero (*SEG* 61.1243), which qualify her claim that the phrase does not appear contiguously until Vespasian and after (p. 115). There is also no reference to the evidence of coins; see, e.g., *RPC online* 4.2.3112 temp. (Commodus, Pergamon); *BMC Phrygia* Laodicea 226 with Caracalla flanked by γῆ and θάλασσα.

28. See, e.g., *SEG* 57.1702, 58.1209bis, 61.1243.

29. Bulent İplikçioğlu, 'Zwei Statthalter vespasianischer Zeit und die "Große" Therme in Inschriften von Olympos (Lykien)', *AAWW* 141 (2006), pp. 75-81.

30. Mustafa Adak and Nihal Tüner Önen, 'Neue Inschriften aus Olympos und seinem Territorium I', *Gephyra* 1 (2004), pp. 59-60, nr. 3.

too had commanded a *Victoria navalis*, a naval victory.[31] Like the coins of Augustus before them,[32] coins were struck with the full-length images of Victory standing on the prow of a ship,[33] often with the legend *Victoria navalis*,[34] or *Victoria Augusti*.[35] Occasionally, Vespasian or Titus appear on the reverse, resting a foot on the prow, holding *Victoria* in one hand.[36] Moreover, the famous triumphal procession depicted in the frieze below the eastern cornice of the Arch of Titus, completed by Domitian, displays, *inter alia*, the carriage of the image of a river-god.[37] According to Josephus, the massive triumphal procession itself paraded a flotilla of ships.[38] There was no question that the triumph in Rome exulting Vespasian and Titus for the victory over the Jewish 'rebels' was to be understood as the symbolic fulfilment of Josephus's prophecy. The new emperor (and his two successor sons) revelled in being Lord of land and sea, and, like Augustus before them, portrayed his/their reign as a new era of prosperity.[39]

And it is Josephus who provides us with a description of the actual maritime battle on which the *Victoria navalis* is based—significantly portrayed as the *second* conflict on the lake, the first victory having been won over a so-called rebel faction at Tiberias by no less than Josephus himself,[40] a pro-

31. Karl Matthaias Schmidt, *Wege des Heils: Erzahlstrukturen und Rezeptionskontexte des Markusevangeliums* (Göttingen: Vandenhoeck & Ruprecht, 2010), pp. 305-306.

32. *RIC* I² 263, 264, 474 (with Victoria on the prow); cf. 265A, 265B.

33. E.g. *RIC* II.1² 697, 777.

34. E.g. *RIC* II.1² 284, 285, 335, 336, 407, 417.

35. *RIC* II.1² 331, 602, 678.

36. *RIC* II.1² 387 (Vespasian); *RIC* II.1² 477, 499 (Titus).

37. For photograph and line drawing see Naomi J. Norman, 'Imperial Triumph and Apotheosis: The Arch of Titus in Rome', in Derek B. Counts and Anthony S. Tuck (eds.), *Koine: Mediterranean Studies in Honor of R. Ross Holloway* (Oxford: Oxbow, 2009), pp. 41-53 (44, 46). It is unknown whether the first triumphal arch, constructed by Titus in the Circus Maximus early in 81 CE, fragments of which have now begun to be recovered, conveyed this element. See Andrea Colletti and Stefania Pergola, 'Nuovi dati per una proposta di ricostruzio dell'Arco di Tito al Circo Maximo', *BCAR* 117 (2017), pp. 201-27. The surviving record of the inscription is found in the ninth–tenth century Codex Einsiedeln 326, fol. 71v. For translation and general description, see Jodi Magness, 'Some Observations on the Flavian Victory Monuments of Rome', in Counts and Tuck (eds.), *Koine*, pp. 35-40 (36-37).

38. Josephus, *War* 7.147.

39. It has now been established that coins that portray a winged caduceus (a symbol of commerce) between two cornucopias (symbols of plenty) belong to the Flavian cultivation of the benefits brought by their dynasty. See Ted V. Buttrey, 'Vespasian's Roman Orichalcum: An Unrecognised Celebratory Coinage', in David M. Jacobson and Nikos Kokkinos (eds.), *Judaea and Rome in Coins 65 BCE–135 CE* (London: Spink, 2012), pp. 163-86.

40. Josephus, *War* 2.635-41; *Life* 163-69.

lepsis of what was to come.[41] When Titus captured Tarichaeae, a number of the inhabitants escaped onto the lake, remaining adrift and out of reach of the Romans.[42] When Vespasian joined his son Titus, he ordered the construction of σχεδίαι.[43] The word can cover a wide range of watercraft, from a wicker skiff to a large pontoon.[44] Shelley Wachsmann suggests that existing boats were lashed together to make a catamaran-type construction.[45] Certainly, the rout of the Jewish insurgents would have required manoeuvrability as well as capacity to carry overwhelming numbers of soldiers. The opposing Jewish skiffs/dinghies (σκάφη) are reconstructed in Josephus's re-telling as craft designed for piracy (λῃστρικά),[46] a fanciful portrait of boats integral to a lake fishing industry, but completely of a piece with Josephus's intent to provide the official version for consumption at Rome. Vespasian had given Josephus access to his own field notes,[47] and Josephus well knew that pirates were a crucial component of both Pompey's and Augustus's claim to fame. Whatever may be argued for Josephus's defence of his own people—'soft notes of self-assertion and resistance'[48]—he was certainly composing, as a 'protégée of Vespasian',[49] a full-blown validation of the emperor's Roman triumph and the imperial dynasty. That demanded a demonstration not only of the lordship of land but also of sea.[50] Josephus had to mute the lake primarily known for its pisciculture in order to turn it into a battleground.[51]

41. On Josephus's concerns to portray his own enhanced military skills, see S. Mason, 'The *Fides* of Flavius Josephus', in Antony Augoustakis, Emma Buckley and Claire Stocks (eds.), *Fides in Flavian Literature* (Toronto: University of Toronto Press, 2019), pp. 45-67 (51-53).

42. Josephus, *War* 3.469, 499-502.

43. Josephus, *War* 3.505.

44. *P.Tebt.* 3.1.701 (Tebtynis, 235 BCE); Herodotus 4.88, 97.

45. Shelley Wachsmann, *The Sea of Galilee Boat: A 2000 Year Old Discovery from the Sea of Legends* (Cambridge, MA: Perseus, 1995), pp. 330-32.

46. Josephus, *War* 3.523.

47. Josephus, *Life* 342, 358. Steve Mason, *Flavius Josephus: Translation and Commentary*, IX. *Life of Josephus* (Leiden: E.J. Brill, 2001), p. 140 n. 1402, considers that Josephus had access to Vespasian's field notes for writing his own account of the Jewish War.

48. John M.G. Barclay, 'The Empire Writes Back: Josephan Rhetoric in Flavian Rome', in Jonathan Edmonson, Steve Mason and James Rives (eds.), *Flavius Josephus and Flavian Rome* (Oxford: Oxford University Press, 2005), pp. 315-32 (332).

49. Jürgen K. Zangenberg, 'Walking along the Lakeshore (Mt. 4.18): Observations on Jesus the Jew Traveling through a Changing Galilee', in Markus Tiwald and Jürgen K. Zangenberg (eds.), *Early Christian Encounters with Town and Countryside: Essays on the Urban and Rural Worlds of Early Christianity* (Göttingen: Vandenhoeck & Ruprecht, 2021), pp. 129-47 (132).

50. Compare Thate, *The Godman and the Sea*, pp. 96-102, who also recognizes the importance of Josephus for Mark's frame.

51. Although Josephus generally avows the fish of the lake as different in taste and

Even though Strabo had noted Tarichaeae as an important centre of fish-salting industries,[52] Josephus nowhere mentions this. Rather Josephus only seems interested in the lake as the context for military engagements; more than that, his use of διαναυμαχέω ('fight a sea battle'), ναυμαχία ('sea battle') of that engagement,[53] and the turning of 'skiffs' (σκάφη and σχεδίαι) into 'warships' (νῆες) in his description of the triumph in Rome suggest that here was a full-scale maritime battle,[54] replete with blood and stinking corpses.[55] This was the justification of the 'sea' element in the celebration of Vespasian (and Titus and Domitian) as Lord of land and sea.

Mark's Mimetic Rejoinder

Nowhere in Mark's Gospel is the sea accented more than in the opening to the parabolic teaching about a different kind of βασιλεία ('empire/kingdom'). Three times in Mk 4.1, the sea (θάλασσα) is mentioned: a setting for teacher, boat and communication about the nature of this new empire.

> Καὶ πάλιν ἤρξατο διδάσκειν παρὰ τὴν θάλασσαν·
> καὶ συνάγεται πρὸς αὐτὸν ὄχλος πλεῖστος ὥστε αὐτὸν εἰς πλοῖον ἐμβάντα
> καθῆσθαι ἐν τῇ θαλάσσῃ,
> καὶ πᾶς ὁ ὄχλος πρὸς τὴν θάλασσαν ἐπὶ τῆς γῆς ἦσαν

> And he began to teach them again, beside the sea;
> and a crowd gathered to him, so large that he boarded a boat
> to sit in the sea
> and the whole crowd were on the land along the sea.

This accent on the sea culminates in Mark's own sea battle in 4.35-41.[56] And, in a flagrant reminiscence of the battle scenes of recent memory, Mark

---

appearance from any found elsewhere (*War* 3.508), the only species he mentions—the coracin—he locates in a freshwater flow near Capernaum, away from the lake itself (*War* 3.519-21).

52. Strabo, 16.2.45. Strabo may simply have been toying with the etymology of the name, which displaced the prior toponymic designation of Migdal/Magdala. Nonetheless, it appears that Migdal-Tarichaeae was a centre for the manufacture of salted fish, even though Lake Kinneret was a freshwater basin.

53. Josephus, *War* 3.466, 469, 522, 531.

54. So Steve Mason, *A History of the Jewish War* (Cambridge: Cambridge University Press, 2016), pp. 29-30. E. Mary Smallwood (*The Jews under Roman Rule: From Pompey to Diocletian: A Study in Political Relations* [Leiden: E.J. Brill, 2nd edn, 1981], p. 309 n. 65) considered the engagement a minor lake skirmish (similarly, Gelardini, *Christus Militans*, pp. 694, 772), but this misses the point. The rhetoric of empire required the presentation of a maritime naval victory, and this was delivered. Compare Ida Ostenberg, *Staging the World: Spoils, Captives and Representations in the Roman World* (Oxford: Oxford University Press, 2009), p. 52.

55. Josephus, *War* 3.530.

56. Gelardini, for all her accent on the political and military resonances of Mark's

depicts others as beneficiaries of Jesus's command of wind and wave (Mk 4.39-41). Here, ἄλλα πλοῖα ἦν μετ᾽ αὐτοῦ, 'and other boats were with him' (4.34b), strikingly parallels Josephus's recounting of his own requisitioning of 230 boats for his daring (as he would portray it) capture of the leading authorities and citizens (2,600 in all) from the city of Tiberias.[57] He claims πλοίων δὲ τὴν λίμνην πᾶσαν ... πλήρη ('the whole lake was replete with boats').[58] But the accent of the evangelist is that the boats 'were *with him*'. Jesus now commands the flotilla (whatever its size) *and* the waters on which they cruise.

Set against the prevalent acclaim of Emperor Vespasian as Lord of land and sea, Mark's insistence on calling Lake Kinneret the Sea of Galilee reeks of the utilization of the masters' language in order to mount a counter-claim—here, a more strident subversion of colonial propaganda than that identified by John Barclay in Josephus's own carefully crafted work.[59] However, a recognition that Mark has adopted the empire's own re-constitution of Lake Kinneret to be the 'sea' upon which *dominium* is demonstrated and which thereby grounds that very affirmation has far greater potential than simply being a demonstration of postcolonial resistance.[60] It goes to the core of Josephus's singular avoidance of the main economic activity associated with the lake, that is, fishing, the very attachment given in Mark's Gospel to the first mention of 'the Sea' (of Galilee, Mk 1.16). To this I turn.

The Control of Lake Aquaculture

About thirty landing places, mooring sites, breakwaters and/or harbours have been discovered around the 53 kilometres (33 miles) of the shoreline of Lake Kinneret, almost all of which seem to have been well established by the First Jewish War.[61] This means that, on average, there was some form of

Gospel, fails to discern either the tie between vv. 1-33 and 34-41 or the specific allusions to the still-vivid memory of the Vespasian 'naval battle' on the lake (*Christus Militans*, pp. 157-58), even though she does accent that Jesus's kingship as shaped by the evangelist is a direct challenge (*Kampfansage*) to that of Vespasian (p. 60).

57. Josephus, *War* 2.635-41.

58. Josephus, *Life* 165. Note that there are variations in Josephus's two iterations of the story.

59. See generally Barclay, 'The Empire Writes Back', pp. 315-32.

60. See also Alan H. Cadwallader, 'Peasant Plucking in Mark: Conceptual and Material Issues', in Robert J. Myles, *Class Struggle in the New Testament* (Lanham, MD: Lexington/Fortress, 2019), pp. 67-87 (80-81).

61. Stefano De Luca and Anna Lena, 'The Harbor of the City of Magdala/Tarichaeae on the Shores of the Sea of Galilee, from the Hellenistic to the Byzantine Times. New Discoveries and Preliminary Results', in Sabine Ladstätter, Felix Pirson and Thomas Schmidts (eds.), *Häfen und Hafenstädte im östlichen Mittelmeerraum von der Antike bis in byzantinische Zeit: Neue Entdeckungen und aktuelle Forschungsansätze* (Istanbul:

dock every two kilometres or so, an intensification rivalling any maximiza-tion of returns from agriculture such as has been underscored by Richard Horsley and others.[62] These included sites familiar from Mark's Gospel: Capernaum, Bethsaida and perhaps Dalmanutha.[63] The home province of the Roman writer on agriculture, Columella, was Baetica in Spain. It could count 100 centres for fish salting (for home consumption and export),[64] along its Mediterranean coastline of about 300 kilometres—about one centre for every three kilometres. A similar intensity is found in the ancient Greek region of Boeotia. So, the harbour patchwork around Lake Kinneret was nothing exceptional in Roman times; indeed, it is emblematic. Earlier dismissals of the size and value of the fishing industry have given way to an appreciation of how widely spread fish and fish products were in the diet of all but the most impoverished (cf. Mk 6.38, 41, 43; 8.7).[65] When Josephus records his requisitioning of 230 boats for his raid on Tiberias, he once lets slip the word for fishing boat, that is, ἁλιάς.[66] He may have simply wanted a stylistic variation from his naval allusion in the use of ναῦται ('sailors'),[67] but it betrays the type of vessels available. Significantly, Josephus closed the gates of Tarichaeae to avoid detection of his planned marine attack on Tiberias six kilometres to the south. Hence, even though the appropriation of boats is expressed as 'from the lake' (ἐπὶ τῆς λίμνης), the number was probably met largely from fishing vessels stationed at Tarichaeae and docks

Ege, 2014), pp. 113-63 (115-19); this represents a significant expansion on the sixteen anchorages charted by Mendel Nun, 'Ports of Galilee', *BARev* 25.4 (1999), pp. 19-31, 64; K.C. Hanson, 'The Galilean Fishing Economy and the Jesus Tradition', *BTB* 27 (1997), pp. 99-111 (103).

62. Richard A. Horsley, *Jesus and the Politics of Roman Palestine* (Columbia, SC: University of South Carolina Press, 2013), p. 33. See also Raimo Hakola, 'The Produc-tion and Trade of Fish as Source of Economic Growth in the First Century CE Galilee', *NovT* 59 (2017), pp. 111-30.

63. Other Gospels show familiarity with other sites among the sixteen better-known harbours and breakwaters: Gergesa, Gadara, Tiberias, Tarichaeae/Magdala, Capernaum, Julias/Bethsaida, Aish, Yabgha, Emmaus, Sennabris, Susita/Hippos, Philoteria, Ein Gofra, Kefar Aqavya, Beth Yerah, Duerban.

64. Brian Campbell, *Rivers and the Power of Ancient Rome* (Chapel Hill, NC: Uni-versity of North Carolina Press, 2012), p. 253.

65. See Dimitra Mylona, *Fish-Eating in Greece from the Fifth Century BC to the Seventh Century AD: A Story of Impoverished Fishermen or Luxurious Fish Banquets* (BAR International Series, 1754; Oxford: BAR Publishing, 2008), pp. 103-12; John T. Fitzgerald, 'Food and Drink in the Greco-Roman World and in the Pauline Communi-ties', in Thomas R. Blanton IV and Raymond Pickett (eds.), *Paul and Economics: A Handbook* (Minneapolis, MN: Fortress, 2017), pp. 205-44 (220-22).

66. Josephus, *War* 2.636.

67. Josephus, *War* 2.635. He also uses σκάφη, so accuracy of classification is not his object.

and breakwaters in close proximity to the north. If the number of captured Tiberians is accurate (2,600), as well as the number of 'sailors' (ναῦται, again avoiding 'fishers') that he gives for each boat (that is, no more than four in one account, in the other, two),[68] then we arrive at an average carriage capacity of 14 to 16 people for each boat.[69] This equates to the size of craft needed to transport Jesus and his narrative band of disciples on a number of lake travels (Mk 4.36; 6.51; 8.10, 13-14). If such craft were moored in the thirty or so stations (doubtless of various sizes and capacities) around the shore, then Lake Kinneret was corralled into a sizable fishing industry.

Usually, this intensification of pisciculture is factored according to commercial returns and taxation.[70] But this leapfrogs the prior issues of territorial demarcation, property ownership and division, and the legal and regulatory control of the industry. When it comes to lake fishing, this extended *into* the waters and was not confined (unlike the aforementioned seacoast of Baetica) to the wharf anchorage, warehousing, industrial value-adding markets and fishing associations that were all situated on and behind the shoreline. These interests ensured that every (Roman) foot of the shoreline of Lake Kinneret was controlled and subject to administrative and commercial oversight that swallowed economic returns.[71] The multiplicity of harbours (and their associated buildings and towers) required careful delineation of their territories, for on this hung governance and financial returns, including taxation. The governing authorities of cities and large villages that included stretches of the shore of the lake within their territory would have been scrupulous in protecting their boundaries. The frequent tensions between neighbouring Taricheae and Tiberias that are manifest at the beginning of the First Jewish War were almost certainly not new outbreaks. The origins are probably to be traced to Antipas's imposition of Tiberias on the coastline several decades earlier. We know of conflict over fishing rights between cities in the Lycus Valley and elsewhere.[72] Such disputes were multiplied down the food chain, with individual fishers disputing another's rights to

68. Josephus, *War* 2.635; *Life* 163.

69. The requisite dimensions match that of the so-called Galilee boat, recovered in 1985, which Wachsmann thinks was scuttled (*Sea of Galilee Boat*, pp. 306-19), but Uzi Leibner (*Settlement and History in Hellenistic, Roman and Byzantine Galilee* [TSAJ, 127; Tübingen: Mohr Siebeck, 2009], p. 217) considers a casualty of the campaign. Arrowheads have been found on the lake floor nearby, but this can be no more than suggestive (Mason, *Life of Josephus*, p. 195).

70. See Keddie, *Class and Power*, p. 142.

71. See the valuable discussion in John Kloppenborg, 'Jesus, Fishermen and Tax Collectors: Papyrology and the Construction of the Ancient Economy of Roman Palestine', *ETL* 94 (2018), pp. 571-99 (586-87).

72. See Tullia Ritti, *Hierapolis di Frigia IX: Storia e istituzioni di Hierapolis* (Istanbul: Ege, 2017), pp. 388-95.

fish by appeal to those controlling the fishing rights[73]—and fishing rights were predicated on territorial allocations. Fishers, whether shore or boat operators (Mk 1.16-18, 19-20), were tied to places, such as Capernaum.[74]

No boundary stones from the Kinneret shoreline are extant to date.[75] Elsewhere, however, these occasionally surface. They are probably an indication of widespread practice. For example, at Lake Kopais in Boeotia, a boundary inscription survives, carved into the rock of a promontory.[76] The attention to boundaries reflects how lucrative the fishing industry could be and how profitable taxation was to the civic and Herodian authorities.[77]

Registration, leases (on everything from boats to equipment to labour), moorings, warehousing and marketing—all with their associated fees— demanded considerable enforcement. Tolls were extensive and detailed, and could include charges on transported passengers.[78] More than mere tax offices were required (cf. Mk 2.14). Surveillance was critical. In part, those granted rights to fish probably delivered a modicum of ad hoc cooperation to the authorities to keep out interlopers and safeguard their own position.[79] But officials were essential. Lake Eğridir in Pisidia, a lake more than double

73. *P. Flor.* 2.119, 275 (Theadelphia, c. 260 CE); cf. *P. Oxy.* 19.2234 (Oxyrhynchus, 31 CE).

74. An inscription from Parion on the Sea of Marmara (*I.Parion* 6) mentions the lease of a tower by a fishing operation (for fish scouting and boat surveillance); this reinforces that fishers were largely tied to specific harbours or breakwaters, most especially those operating in lakes. Kloppenborg, citing *Stud. Pal.* 22.183, points out that boats authorized to fish were given some sort of identification for display ('Jesus, Fishermen and Tax Collectors', 588).

75. Compare however the Hellenistic, possibly Roman, period boundary stones close to Gezer, a small city west of Jerusalem (*CIIP* 2764-76); see also David M. Jacobson, 'Editorial: The Gezer Boundary Inscriptions', *PEQ* 147.2 (2015), pp. 83-85. It should be recognized that many boundary markers were made from wood (and even planted trees) and therefore have not survived. See *Ordines Finitionum* (Arcadius Augustus) in J.B. Campbell, *The Writings of the Roman Land Surveyors: Introduction, Text, Translation and Commentary* (JRSs 9; London: Society for the Promotion of Roman Studies, 2000), p. 259.

76. *IG* 7.2792 (third century BCE).

77. On the tax burden under the Herods and Rome, see Gildas Hamel, *Poverty and Charity in Roman Palestine, First Three Centuries CE* (Berkeley, CA: University of California Press, 1990), pp. 142-63; Fabian E. Udoh, *To Caesar What Is Caesar's: Tribute, Taxes and Imperial Administration in Early Roman Palestine (63 BCE–70 CE)* (Providence, RI: BJS, 2005).

78. *OGIS* 674 = *I.Portes du désert* 67—the 'tariff of Coptos' (on the Nile), dated 90 CE. See Gary K. Young, *Rome's Eastern Trade: International Commerce and Imperial Policy 31 BC–AD 305* (London: Routledge, 2001), pp. 42-44.

79. Such a level of cooperation is clear in the construction of a tollhouse by an association of fishers at Ephesos (*I.Ephesos* 20) and in a joint dedication by 'the masters of the nets and tax-farmers' at Parion on the Sea of Marmara (*I.Parion* 5).

the area of Lake Kinneret, boasted a certain Ares, who was remembered as a πρόοικος, a warden or guardian for 'the Mother'[80] (possibly designating control of the warehouses/emporia and general infrastructure on the land) and ἐπεὶ (= ἐπὶ) λίμνης ἐπιστάτης, a warden/superintendent of boat movements and/or catches.[81] In general terms, he was someone who controlled both offshore and onshore fishing activities.[82] These two aspects of control—the fishing on the lake, the discharge and movements for warehousing and marketing—are represented in two panels of relief on the epitaph.[83] There is no similar inscription from the vicinity of Lake Kinneret, but Zaraza Friedman has identified a boat with a sharp cutwater bow (a *myoparo*?), found in a *Kai su* mosaic in a baths complex in area C at Tarichaeae, as designed to be a policing craft.[84]

These snatches of material evidence support the understanding that, when it comes to lakes and rivers, proprietorial control over the waters was the norm, most especially as regards fishing, but also including the harvesting of reeds and molluscs.[85] And it was lucrative to those who controlled the licences, taxes and fees on fishing, access to towers (*inter alia*, for 'spotting' of schools of fish), allotments of the shoreline for basket traps and 'fish farms', the assignment of labour, landing/mooring posts and so on. Sometimes, an entire lake, if small enough, was leased out by its

80. William Calder, 'A Greek Ephemeris', *CR* 40 (1926), pp. 126-27 (127), called her 'Artemis of the lake'.

81. *SEG* 2.747, ll. 3, 5. It may be that his jurisdiction was limited to the northern part of the lake, known as Lake Hoyran.

82. In Egypt, the comptroller of fishing (including both fishers and their catches) was called an ἐπιτηρητής. See *P. Leit.* 14; *BGU* 15.2468; *P. Oslo* 3.90.

83. The stone is now known only through the sketch accompanying the *editio princeps*: B. Pace, 'I Paesi del Lago di Egherdir," *ASAA* 3 (1916–1920), pp. 47-53 (53 fig. 26), reproduced in Ernst Pfuhl and Hans Möbius, *Die ostgriechischen Grabreliefs* (Mainz am Rhein: Philip von Zabern, 4 vols., 1977), nr. 1129.

84. Zarara Friedman, 'The Ship Depicted in a Mosaic from Migdal, ISRAEL', *JMR* 1.2 (2008), pp. 45-54 (50). For the mosaic in general, drawing the boat simply into apotropaic associations, see Stefano De Luca and Anna Lena, 'The Mosaic of the Thermal Bath Complex of Magdala Reconsidered: Archaeological Context, Epigraphy and Iconographjy', in Giovanni C. Bottini, L. Daniel Chrupcala and Joseph Patrich (eds.), *Knowledge and Wisdom: Archaeological and Historical Essays in Honour of Leah Di Segni* (Milan: Terra Santa, 2014), pp. 1-33.

85. It is difficult to admit the turning of the fishing industry into free-flowing business enterprises as argued by Greg Stanton, 'Wealthier Supporters of Jesus of Nazareth', *JGRChJ* 12 (2016), pp. 99-126; also Hakola, 'The Production and Trade of Fish', pp. 111-30. Compare the castigating critique of the influence of neo-liberal market economics on constructing first-century fishing by Robert J. Myles, 'Fishing for Entrepreneurs in the Sea of Galilee? Unmasking Neoliberal Ideology in Biblical Interpretation', in Myles (ed.), *Class Struggle*, pp. 115-37; see also James Crossley and Robert J. Myles, *Jesus: A Life in Class Conflict* (Winchester: Zero, 2023), pp. 79-84.

public or private owner—one small lake at Hermopolis in Egypt brought in two talents annually.[86] John Kloppenborg has highlighted the enormous variety of monetary extraction from the fishing industry (including taxes on those pursuing the occupation of fishing themselves) found in Egyptian papyri and applied these to the fishing and associated industries located around and on Lake Kinneret, on a controlled assumption that there is a comparable resonance between the two locations.[87] He sees particular significance that the two occupations listed for disciples of Jesus in Mark are fishers and tax collectors—these are conjoined at 'the Sea of Galilee' (Mk 1.16-20; 2.13-14).[88]

The Sea—A Resource in Common

However, as I have shown, the dissonance operating here is not merely that we are dealing with a misnomer of referring to a lake as a 'sea' (even if encouraged by Roman imperial ideology), but that the intensification operating in the fishing industry stands *against* the designation of 'sea'. Michael Thate is correct, even though he did not investigate the legal determinations about the sea—the sea resists 'enclosure'.[89] It may be that there was a similar intensification in the fishing industry across the Mediterranean (as seen along the Baetica coastline mentioned above), so much so that some city economies were fundamentally dependent on it.[90] Indeed, one second-century Roman jurist, serving the very class he represented, held that farmers and fishers should hand over their harvest/catch immediately and return to their work to ensure there was no hiatus in supply to their cities.[91] But hidden here is the recognition that taxation, licences, leases and fees associated with sea fishing were landlocked. Their reach did not extend to the ability of boats and even of shore fishers to ply their trade. Sales, storage, repairs and chains of production were different matters, but the sea was common and accessible to all, relatively without restriction.[92] The distinc-

---

86. *P. Amh.* 100. (198–211 CE).

87. Kloppenborg, 'Jesus, Fishermen and Tax Collectors', pp. 576-77.

88. Kloppenborg, 'Jesus, Fishermen and Tax Collectors', pp. 571-72. He also notes Celsus's vilification of Jesus's followers as 'the most wicked tax collectors and sailors' (p. 573; Origen, *C. Cels.* 1.62).

89. Thate, *The Godman and the Sea*, p. 64.

90. A number of civic bronze coins privilege fish as an indication of the importance of the industry to its economy. Baetica, e.g., sacralizes the importance of fishing by including fish as columns on a tetrastyle temple on some of its coins (*RPC* 1.124, 125, 126). Compare the fish added to the waters beneath the river-god Glaucus at Eumeneia (*RPC online* 6.5635 temp.; cf. *RPC online* 1.1378A, 1379A [Buthrotum]) among many.

91. *Digest* 50.11.2 (Callistratus).

92. See Ephraim Lytle, 'Η θάλασσα κοινή: Fishermen, the Sea and the Limits of

tion between lake and sea in terms of proprietary control was not a Roman invention. It hails back to at least Plato.[93] Consequently, Roman law deemed the principle a *ius gentium*, that is, a law held by all peoples, that all should hold access to the sea and its bounty.[94] There is no reason to doubt that this view was maintained by those who held their control under the auspices of Rome, namely Philip the Tetrarch and Herod Antipas, especially given the prior history of Hellenistic influence.

Kloppenborg recognized this distinction[95] but did not extend the argument to assess Mark's use of the 'Sea of Galilee' and 'the sea' in complete abnegation of the toponymic and geographical realities. If Steve Mason can assert that neither Vespasian nor Titus had concern for proportionality and historical truth but were driven by other concerns (looking 'more Pompeian-Augustan'),[96] then the same assertion can hold for the author of Mark's Gospel. Put bluntly, Mark was asserting that, if the emperor was cultivating a view of the waters of Galilee as a 'sea' for the sake of his imperial credentials as ruler of land and sea, then the legal safeguard on freedom of access for fishing could equally apply. This may help to explain that, in Mark, there is remarkably little reference to the variety of specific delimitations on fishing as a lake industry. The oblique conjunction of fishers and tax officers comes the closest (Mk 1.16-20; 2.13-14), perhaps compounded by the implied hierarchy within the industry as between the brothers Peter–Andrew and James–John (cf. Mk 10.35). There is also the inference from the disciples' monetary response (two hundred denarii!) to the need for the crowd to eat (Mk 6.36, 37b) that even though the lake was close at hand (Mk 6.32; cf. 8.10), fish could only be purchased not caught.[97] The subsistence support of the lake had been usurped. By redefining the waters as 'sea', Mark is restoring the ability of crowds of hungry people to supplement their diet. In commanding his disciples to provide for them (δότε αὐτοῖς ὑμεῖς φαγεῖν, 6.37) the Markan Jesus is implicitly calling the disciples into a new distribution of resources, one not controlled and monetized by a narrow

Ancient Greek Regulatory Reach', *ClAnt* 31 (2012), pp. 1-55; Annalisa Marzano, *Harvesting the Sea: The Exploitation of Marine Resources in the Roman Mediterranean* (Oxford: Oxford University Press, 2013), pp. 235-42; Cynthia Bannon, 'Fresh Water in Roman Law: Rights and Policy', *JRS* 107 (2017), pp. 60-89.

93. Plato, *Leg.* 7.824c.

94. *Digest* 8.4.13 (Ulpian), 41.1.1.1 (Gaius), 47.10.13.7 (Ulpian).

95. Kloppenborg, 'Jesus, Fishermen and Tax Collectors', p. 583. He therefore rejects completely the arguments of Hakola, 'The Production and Trade of Fish', pp. 111-30 (122).

96. Mason, *Jewish War*, p. 30.

97. Mk 1.19 alerts us that nets were probably stowed in the boat, so it would have been theoretically possible for the boat of 6.32, 45 to have been deployed as an alternative to heading for town or village markets (6.36).

cartel of Roman dependants. The freedom of navigation for travel purposes that was protected on lakes and rivers was therefore extended to include the harvesting of the water's produce. Significantly, in response to Peter's avowal that everything (πάντα) had been left in order to follow Jesus (Mk 8.28), Jesus's embellishing of that 'everything' in terms of property and family ties includes house and lands/fields (οἰκία, ἀγροί, Mk 8.29). But it does not include boats and fishing, despite the fact that Peter and the other fishers had 'left their nets' (Mk 1.18, 20). I would suggest that even though Peter the fisher is the Markan spokesperson prompting Jesus's reply, his participation (by fishing rights and leases) in the proprietorial closure of the lake is no longer applicable. The relationship with the lake and its produce was now governed by 'the law of the sea', at least in the fictive construction Mark is distilling in the name 'Sea of Galilee'.

Conclusion

The Sea of Galilee may have become the default toponym for the large body of water in northern Israel. It has proved a problem for historians and biblical commentators because that name appears a novelty. It is neither a sea nor the Sea of Galilee. Efforts to explain its sudden appearance in the Gospel of Mark have remained unconvincing. In this chapter, I have proposed an alternative, one that takes seriously the ubiquitous, though not uninterrogated, influence of Roman imperial ideology and the common inheritance of legal conceptions of 'the sea'. This solution accepts that the author of Mark's Gospel conceives of the traditions of Jesus as having arisen in a context that unavoidably had to deal with overt Roman presence and as carrying potential critically to address aspects of that presence at the time of writing not merely at the time that the narrative assumes. For the author, the 'gospel' which is alternate to that of (Augustan and Vespasianic) Rome (Mk 1.1) has conceptual as well as practical consequences. At the conceptual level, just as with 'the gospel of Jesus Christ' (τὸ εὐαγγέλιον Ἰησοῦ Χριστοῦ), language that had become pervasive in public and civic display and discourse is expropriated to serve other ends.[98] Lake Kinneret is converted into the Sea of Galilee. It is now obedient to another divine ruler, a new 'Lord of land and sea'. But this conversion is not an esoteric semantic but one with real-world consequences. If the body of water is now a 'sea', then, according to the very law upheld by the Romans, it and its produce can no longer be sequestered into private ownership. Those denied access to the fruit of the lake are now admitted to that of 'the Sea'. The Sea of Galilee

---

98. Note the use of εὐαγγελία ('good news') of Vespasian in *War* 4.619 (with festivals and sacrifices). This, I think, reflects Josephus's portrayal that Vespasian was Augustus's successor, including in the celebrations of 'good news'.

therefore stands as one of the most profound challenges to the collapsing of resources into the hands of a few, a toponymic phrase that restores, in its commandeering of Rome's own ideological and juridical resources, provision for the many. It is telling that the name probably invented by Mark has been cemented but its significance frequently eroded.

12

THINKING THE DIVINE ANIMAL?
A BRAIDED READING OF LUKE 2.7

Anne Elvey

Habitat is a concept that connects animals (including humans) with the places and spaces in which we live, breathe, eat and drink, work, interpret signs such as trails, scents and script, tell stories, make marks, cry out, sing and play. Habitat is a word at the heart of the ecological hermeneutics that my friend and colleague Elaine Wainwright has developed in a socio-rhetorical mode.[1] Habitat describes the more-than-human complex of contexts—social, ecological, political—that make up the inter-contextuality in and from which a creature interprets.[2] Inhabitants, their co-inhabitation and their habitats interweave in stories of sustenance, scarcity, sufficiency and, sometimes, abundance and creativity, forming habits that in turn impact habitats, a community's own and others. Habitat is material situation understood by way of enmeshment, where an ecosystem as inhabited (be it a desert, old growth forest, coal mine, post-industrial city or suburban neighbourhood and its nearby creek and beach) is multiply formed and forming across deep time sedimentations into contemporary relationships of more-than-human agency, power and effects, with impacts that reverberate into deep futures. The concept of habitat has aspects of relatedness in common with the First Nations concept of Country; but, as a concept, habitat is thin-

---

1. Elaine M. Wainwright, *Habitat, Human, and Holy: An Eco-Rhetorical Reading of the Gospel of Matthew* (Earth Bible Commentary, 6; Sheffield: Sheffield Phoenix Press, 2016); Elaine M. Wainwright, 'Images, Words, Stories: Exploring their Transformative Power in Reading Biblical Texts Ecologically', *BibInt* 20 (2012), pp. 280-304.

2. I resonate here with Deborah Bird Rose's use of the term 'creature', not in relation to a divine creator but 'to encompass all of us earthlings ... as members of life's creative work'. Rose's description of 'an ontological-ecological terrain' is similar to what I intend by 'habitat', especially where she writes of 'circuits of flow that are local and intimate, and that are connected into wider and wider circuits that ultimately form the substance and continuities of life on Earth'. See Deborah Bird Rose, *Shimmer: Flying Fox Exuberance in Worlds of Peril* (Edinburgh: Edinburgh University Press, 2022), pp. 13, 15.

ner than Country, less culturally embedded, limited but useful, especially for settler readers like myself.[3]

When applied to biblical interpretation, the concept of habitat includes context and setting but is more than these. In Lk. 2.1-20, a birth narrative of the child who will be named Jesus (2.21), the habitats internal to the story world are multifaceted and contain the material situation not only of lands, waters and skies that characters inhabit and traverse, but also inter-human relations shaped materially by cultural, social, religious and political influences, in particular the Roman Empire (2.1-3). In subjection and obedience to this empire, the Lukan Mary and Joseph travel to Bethlehem for a census (2.4-5). The habitat of the road rushes by: do the travellers need to dodge bandits such as exercise violence on the road between Jerusalem and Jericho in 10.30? Do they carry food and water? Where do they find shelter? The reader arrives in Bethlehem, a little breathless perhaps, with Joseph and a pregnant Mary (2.5); and, after an unspecified time, Mary goes into labour—understood as a fulfilment of the time (ἐπλήσθησαν αἱ ἡμέραι) signified by her pregnant body (2.6).

Oftentimes, popular imagining has the labouring Mary trying with Joseph to find somewhere to give birth, but the text hints that they may have already been lodging in the place which is no place.[4] Having found no place (τόπος) in an inn or guest house, as the well-known story goes, they are sheltering in a place where a manger (φάτνη)—a feeding box or trough— suggests the inhabitation of other animals (2.7). In the wider context of the lands, waters and skies of Judea and Galilee and the occupying Roman Empire, two symbols define the temporary habitat of the newborn child and his parents, the absence of a place (τόπος) and the presence of a feeding box (φάτνη). Moreover, these two symbols are in tensive relation with the maternal body.[5] In this chapter, I take up the symbol of the manger

3. For helpful descriptions of the concept of Country, see Garry Worete Deverell, *Gondwana Theology: A Trawloolway Man Reflects on Christian Faith* (Reservoir, Victoria: Morning Star Publishing, 2018), p. 14; Deborah Bird Rose, *Nourishing Terrains: Australian Aboriginal Views of Landscape and Wilderness* (Canberra: Australian Heritage Commission, 1996), p. 6.

4. Lk. 2.6 opens, Ἐγένετο δὲ ἐν τῷ εἶναι αὐτοὺς ἐκεῖ—this signals that the parents (they) are there, already at the place where Mary will give birth. That this labour is couched in terms of fulfilment suggests that this is the right place. With the use of the imperfect ἦν in 2.7, the lack of place in the inn/guest house may not be something the couple have just discovered during Mary's labour but an ongoing situation since their arrival. For Amy-Jill Levine and Ben Witherington III, *The Gospel of Luke* (New Cambridge Bible Commentary; Cambridge: Cambridge University Press, 2018), p. 57, it may signal, rather, that the place of the manger offers privacy for the birth-giving not available in the guest room of a private house, possibly belonging to a relative.

5. I discuss this briefly below and more fully in Anne Elvey, *An Ecological Feminist*

as a focus for the habitat into which the child is born. I practice what I call braided reading, moving between the Lukan text, examples of poets' reception of that text and the call of other animals, to explore how the symbol of the manger suggests a point of intersection between other animals, humans and the divine.[6] Such a braided reading prompts the reader of the text as a material artefact, which has been an agent of colonization among other things, to listen to the voices of contemporary creatures.

Settler Perspectives

My braided reading offers a settler perspective from an Australian context where colonial invasion continues.[7] In this context, the Bible and the symbol of the manger, which has a life beyond the Bible in nativity settings in particular, arrived with the colonizers as material artefacts and agents of colonization.[8] As such, their impact has been ambiguous, and includes both efforts to replace First Nations cultures and instances of enculturation by First Nations in the context of their own knowledge systems.[9] Further, settler poets such as Les Murray, to whom I refer below, have been immersed in a colonizing imaginary and their/our work needs to be read with a hermeneutic of suspicion, especially in relation to its claims for settler ownership of Country.[10]

Reading of the Gospel of Luke: A Gestational Paradigm (Studies in Women and Religion, 45; Lewiston, NY: Edwin Mellen Press, 2005), pp. 124-26.

6. I introduce this notion of braided reading in Anne Elvey, *Reading with Earth: Contributions of the New Materialism to an Ecological Feminist Hermeneutics* (T. & T. Clark Explorations in Theology, Gender and Ecology; London: Bloomsbury T. & T. Clark, 2022), pp. 4-5, 18-20.

7. On the ongoing nature of colonial invasion, see Tony Birch, '"We've Seen the End of the World and We Don't Accept It": Protection of Indigenous Country and Climate Justice', in Nicole Oke, Christopher Sonn and Alison Baker (eds.), *Places of Privilege: Interdisciplinary Perspectives on Identities, Change and Resistance* (Leiden: E.J. Brill, 2018), pp. 139-52 (141).

8. See Anne Elvey, *The Matter of the Text: Material Engagements between Luke and the Five Senses* (BMW, 37; Sheffield: Sheffield Phoenix Press, 2011), pp. 70-77.

9. See, e.g., Diane J. Austin-Broos, '"Two Laws" Ontologies, Histories: Ways of Being Aranda (Aboriginal People) Today', *Australian Journal of Anthropology* 7 (1996), pp. 1-20; David Burramurra and Ian McIntosh, 'Motj and the Nature of the Sacred', *Cultural Survival Quarterly* 26.2 (Summer 2002), https://www.culturalsurvival.org/publications/cultural-survival-quarterly/motj-and-nature-sacred; Graham Paulson and Mark Brett, 'Five Smooth Stones: Reading the Bible through Aboriginal Eyes', *Colloquium* 45.2 (November 2013), pp. 199-214; Lee Miena Skye, *Kerygmatics of the New Millennium: A Study of Australian Aboriginal Women's Christology* (Delhi: ISPCK, 2007), p. 66; Meredith Lake, *The Bible in Australia: A Cultural History* (Sydney: NewSouth, 2018), p. 8.

10. For a critique of Murray in this vein, see Jonathan Dunk, 'The Stump: Look-

Koalas, Kangaroos and Wombats in the Manger

The traditional settler nativity scenes I grew up with in Australia fea-ture often brightly painted plaster statues of (usually pale-skinned) Mary, Joseph, a manger, a baby to be added at Christmas, two or three (again pale-skinned) shepherds with crooks, a cow, a couple of sheep, sometimes also three kings of various skin colours (one of which may be dark-skinned) to be added at Epiphany, and an angel or two, with several of the creatures (but not the other-than-human ones) haloed.[11] In Australian kitsch, there are variants on this, where the actors/statues are koalas or kangaroos, for example.[12] In a similar vein, albeit in the genre of animal fables teaching a human lesson about relationships, Mem Fox's *Wombat Divine* (a children's picture book) places a wombat in the manger/crib in a nativity play in which a variety of Australian native animals take part.[13] Under bossy Emu as cast director, Wombat tries unsuccessfully for every part in the nativity scene, until finally he tries for the part of the baby Jesus and succeeds, even falling asleep during the performance, 'just as a real baby would'. The punchline comes after the play when Emu says to Wombat, 'You were divine, Wom-bat!' The book then closes, 'And Wombat beamed'. The word 'divine' plays at first glance on two levels: (1) the colloquial affirmation of an actor's performance: 'you were divine, darling'; and (2) the reference to the baby Jesus, played by Wombat, as divinity incarnate.

While *Wombat Divine* works via a deliberate anthropomorphism as a fable employing animal characters, there is a level at which Wombat's inhabitation of the manger raises a question concerning the animal (or bet-ter creaturely) nature of the incarnation. Dorothy Hewett's 'Zoo Story' also has this effect when she writes of the birth of a giraffe:

> Behind us in the straw-filled manger,
> the new-born six-foot child wobbles to life,
> its mild eyes luminous.[14]

ing back on the Republic of Murray', *Overland*, 7 June 2019, https://overland.org.au/2019/06/the-stump-looking-back-on-the-republic-of-murray/.

11. Contemporary Indigenous Christians, for example, at Aboriginal Catholic Ministry Victoria, are creating more culturally appropriate nativity scenes, sometimes including a coolamon, a carrier for food or infants, in place of the manger. See Aborigi-nal Catholic Ministry Victoria, https://www.cam1.org.au/acmv (accessed 27 July 2022).

12. See, e.g., Big Christmas, https://bigchristmas.com.au/product/kangaroo-christ mas-nativity-set (accessed 27 July 2022); Bristlebrush Designs, https://www.bristle brush.com.au/aussie-nativity-australian-nativity-scene (accessed 27 July 2022).

13. Mem Fox, *Wombat Divine* (illustrated by Kerry Argent; New York: Scholastic, 1995).

14. Dorothy Hewett, 'Zoo Story', *Meanjin* 32.3 (Spring 1973), p. 269.

Read beside Lk. 2.7, these works pose a question: is the incarnation specific to humankind or is the child Jesus born as creature (a particular instance of animal—of a certain species, gender, culture and time, dwelling in a particular habitat)?[15]

Another question emerging concerns the extent to which literary representations of other animals, especially native animals such as wombats, in the manger indicate something specific about an Australian settler consciousness and aesthetic. For poets and critics Evelyn Araluen and Melody Paloma, this settler aesthetic is a widely employed class of kitsch that functions to elide Indigenous sovereignty.[16] Colonial kitsch works to assert settler legitimacy by a process of nativizing that appropriates native species of animals and plants to settler imaginaries, especially through the emotional appeal of cuteness, which serves further to support a 'settler move to innocence'.[17]

Not only do works like Mem Fox's *Wombat Divine*, where the cute nativizing factor is overt, provide examples of colonial kitsch, but national narratives and tropes such as the ANZAC myth and mateship also carry this settler aesthetic;[18] so too the work of poets like Murray when he writes: 'Swallows flit in the stable as if / a hatchling of their kind, / turned human, cried in the manger'.[19] The poem from which these lines come, 'Animal Nativity', asks about the meaning of the incarnation for other-than-human animals. 'Peopled' by goats, cattle, lambs, turtle-doves, as well as unspecified fish, spiders and dogs, the poem could be set anywhere, but Murray's prominence as an (even in some circles 'the') Australian poet, implies this is an Australian poem, and the imported swallows become interpreters at the site of incarnation. Does this 'animal nativity' focused on creatures other than humans suggest a sharp theological insight, or does it attempt to render

15. Barbara E. Reid, OP, and Shelley Matthews, *Luke 1–9* (Wisdom Commentary; Collegeville, MN: Liturgical Press, 2021), pp. 68-69, gesture toward this possibility in their commentary on Lk. 2.1-7, by including a short vignette on deep incarnation, which sees the incarnation as embedding the divine, corporeally and materially, in and with the whole Earth community.

16. Evelyn Araluen, 'Snugglepot and Cuddlepie in the Ghost Gum', *Sydney Review of Books* (11 February 2019), https://sydneyreviewofbooks.com/snugglepot-and-cuddlepie-in-the-ghost-gum-evelyn-araluen/; Melody Paloma, 'Rupturing Colonial Kitsch, Untangling Myth', *Meanjin* 80.3 (Spring 2021), pp. 198-204.

17. Araluen, 'Snugglepot and Cuddlepie'; Paloma, 'Rupturing Colonial Kitsch', p. 200.

18. For a nationalistic interpretation of the traumatic experience of the Australian and New Zealand forces in World War I, especially at Gallipoli, see 'Anzac spirit', Australian War Memorial, https://www.awm.gov.au/articles/encyclopedia/anzac/spirit (accessed 15 November 2022).

19. Les Murray, 'Animal Nativity', in *Translations from the Natural World* (Manchester: Carcanet, 1993; eBook 2012).

the colonial Christmas story and its adherents innocent of the ongoing invasion in which European Christianity is complicit? In Murray's poem, the infant swallows must become human to be incarnate in the feeding trough; the cattle, too, affirm the necessity of humanity for this incarnational move: 'cattle are content that this calf / must come in human form'. There are poignant passages where dogs, like enslaved humans, go hungry and where the passion and death of Jesus is hinted at in references to 'crux' and 'lamb'. The poem contrasts human insensitivity to the Gospel narrative with a kind of utopian sensitivity to the liveliness of the event (signalled by the word 'vivid'), received through the supposed simplicity of other creatures and a 'girl's' (Mary's) assent. The poet speaker, moreover, adopts a posture of (settler and masculine) innocence in both his appeal—and his implied assimilation—to the imagined 'innocence' of other-than-human creatures and a young woman. Yet the question remains concerning the birth of the human child into the habitat of other animals.

The Manger in the Gospel of Luke

There is no mention of other-than-human animals in Lk. 2.7, although the next verse describes shepherds living in the fields keeping watch over their flocks. They share habitat with their sheep or goats; their lives and livelihoods entwine in the nightly labour of guarding/keeping (φυλάσσοντες φυλακὰς, 2.8). In this they share with the human creature (ἄνθρωπος) of Gen. 2.15 (LXX) the more-than-human labour of working (ἐργάζεσθαι) and keeping (φυλάσσειν) the divinely planted garden. The Lukan story will bring the shepherds and the child into contact, and the manger becomes, through the angelic messengers and the witness of the shepherds, a sign (2.12, 16) of the birth of a saviour (2.11); this 'good news' is celebrated by the heavenly host as a promise of peace over Earth (2.13-14). This peace echoes, and more particularly stands in contrast to, the *pax Romana*, promised by and embodied in the Caesar and his rule, denoted here by an imperial decree (2.1) that provides the socio-political and geographic habitat for the birth.

Drawing on feminist theory, I have argued elsewhere that, in the birth of the child, Mary is born as mother, and the manger represents the separation of child and mother occurring in birth-giving, when Mary places the child away from her body in the manger.[20] But this separation is not absolute, and the maternal body remains a crucial site of relatedness and sustenance. 'In the Bleak of Midwinter', nineteenth-century English-born poet Christina Rossetti describes a crossing between the maternal body and the manger in the more-than-human habitat of the (no) place of birth:

20. Elvey, *Ecological Feminist Reading*, pp. 111-34.

> Enough for Him, whom cherubim, worship night and day,
> Breastful of milk, and a mangerful of hay;
> Enough for Him, whom angels fall before,
> The ox and ass and camel which adore.[21]

This is the third (and middle) stanza of the poem composed of five four-line stanzas. The first stanza paints a picture of an Earth that in winter is hard and ungiving and so highlights the vulnerability of the infant in this habitat; but the poet finds in this site of material scarcity a kind of sufficiency. The (no) place of the 'stable' is 'enough', so, too, the maternal body as source of sustenance and the feed box (manger) as infant bed. For Rossetti, the attention of more-than-human creatures, including angels, ox, ass and camel is likewise sufficient.

A parallel exists in Luke between the parents finding a sufficient place for the child in the more-than-human habitat of the manger and the shepherds living in the fields with the other animals they are keeping (2.7-8). The maternal keeping exercised by the Lukan Mary (2.19, 51) echoes both the work (2.8) and witness (2.15, 17) of the shepherds as they recognize and relate to a material sacred—the ῥῆμα (thing/matter/deed) and ῥήματα (things/matters/deeds) they have heard and seen and to which they witness in and beyond their temporarily shared habitats.[22] The manger symbolizes the 'no place'—outside the socio-cultural space of the empire's elites—which is a shared space of sacred communication and more-than-human sociality.

After so many nativity tableaux and icons depicting human and other-than-human characters together in the scene, the more-than-human sociality of the manger space may seem self-evident. Nonetheless, I revisit the scene. Of the manger (φάτνη), François Bovon writes:

> In large estates, farmers would build costly stables in caves; in farmhouses, 'the feeding place for cattle would often be in the room where the family lived'. Stables would also be located 'in the ground-floor of the house or in annexes, or feeding-troughs outside, e.g., in the farm-yard'. The manger was probably made of stone (perhaps chiseled into the wall of a cave or the face of a rock) or of mud; wood was too expensive.[23]

21. Christina Rossetti, 'In the Bleak Midwinter', Poetry Foundation website, https://www.poetryfoundation.org/poems/53216/in-the-bleak-midwinter (accessed 27 July 2022).

22. On a 'material sacred', see Elvey, *Reading with Earth*, pp. 45-50. The Greek verbs for 'keeping' used in Lk. 2.8, 19, 51 differ, but their meanings resonate with each other.

23. François Bovon, *Luke 1: A Commentary on the Gospel of Luke 1:1–9:50* (ed. Helmut Koester; trans. Christine M. Thomas; Hermeneia: A Critical and Historical Commentary on the Bible, 63A; Accordance electronic edn; Minneapolis, MN: Fortress Press, 2002), p. 90.

For Michael Trainor the manger, as feed-box, has linked ecological and christological meanings:

> There are two insights that come from Luke's reference to the manger, one christological and the other ecological; both are linked. Christologically, the manger is a place of food, nurture and life. It prepares for a dominant theme in Luke-Acts. In Jesus' future public ministry, food, meals and the place of eating will play an important part. Ecologically, the manger affirms Jesus' connection to the land, the human community and non-human creatures. The manger is an important intertext for Luke. From Isa. 1.3 we learn that servile animals were intimately bonded or, literally, tied to it.[24]

As many have noted, the language of laying the child in the manger echoes the language of reclining at a meal, so that arguably a link is implied between this birth and the meal scenes in Luke.[25] By implication, the problem of hunger in connection with communion—of 'communion without communion'—can be asked at the site of the manger.[26] Where many scholars emphasize links between the manger, meals, hospitality and eucharistic themes in Luke, often the manger is read principally as a metaphor for human feeding, eliding its primary relation to other animals. Rather, the manger as a feeding box constructed by humans principally for the sustenance of other animals, even where those animals are serving human needs, renders it a site of intersection between human and other-than-human cultures and interests. As Trainor comments, then, '[a]t a symbolic level [and I would add at a material level], the manger is ... the nexus between the human and non-human world'.[27]

Thinking forward to Luke 15 and the younger son's hungering after the husks he was feeding to the pigs (15.15), I suspect humans in dire circumstances found themselves feeding from another animal's manger. In Xenophon's *On the Art of Horsemanship*, the horseman is advised to situate the manger so that it is as difficult to steal from as it is to steal the master's food from his stores.[28] Is this recommendation made so that poor humans do not steal from another's manger in order to feed their own animals, or to feed themselves, or so that other (possibly 'wild') animals do not steal from the mangers of 'domesticated' animals? In the context of the symbolism of the manger in Luke, it might also be asked: how far does hunger extend? Generally the question of hunger refers to the devastating reality of human

---

24. Michael Trainor, *About Earth's Child: An Ecological Listening to the Gospel of Luke* (Earth Bible Commentary, 2; Sheffield: Sheffield Phoenix Press, 2012), p. 80.

25. The same verb ἀνακλίνω is used at 2.7 for placing the child in the manger and at 12.37 and 13.29 in relation to reclining at a meal.

26. On 'communion without communion', see Elvey, *Matter of the Text*, p. 182.

27. Trainor, *About Earth's Child*, p. 80.

28. Xenophon, *Horse* ch. 5

poverty, particularly on a mass scale, but in a time of biodiversity losses and the thinning of sustaining habitats for many other creatures, not only humans go hungry.

Animal Interests

Several references to φάτνη (manger or crib) in the Septuagint relate to other animal interests. Job 6.5 (NETS) reads: 'Why, will the wild ass bray for no reason? / Is it not rather looking for grain? / Yes, and will an ox break into lowing at its manger (φάτνη) when it has food?' Here, other animals have reasons for their behaviour, and the search for and provision of sustenance is a key. The manger represents fulfilment of a vital need. As noted above, there is a poignancy to this relationship to the manger, for it also represents the other animals being mastered, whether benignly or otherwise, by the human 'owner'. Is it possible to think further about the particular relationships of interdependency and co-agency between humans and other animals in such domestic interspecies arrangements, both in a first-century peasant context and in diverse twenty-first-century forms of agriculture?

Other Septuagint uses of the term φάτνη point to difficult times. Times of stress and destruction for humans (probably due to inter-human conflict) are recognized in, and as, times of stress for domestic animals:

> Heifers have jumped up at their mangers (φάτναις);
> storehouses have been annihilated;
> wine presses have been razed to the ground,
> because the grain has dried up. (Joel 1.17 NETS)

In this situation, the cattle themselves weep (Joel 1.18 LXX). A dire situation for other creatures is articulated in the prophetic warning:

> For a fig tree shall bear no fruit,
> and no produce shall be on the vines;
> the work of the olive will deceive,
> and the plains will yield no food;
> sheep have run out of food,
> and cows are not at the mangers (φάτναις). (Hab. 3.17 NETS).

Habakkuk juxtaposes warning with steadfast response to the divine in difficult times (Hab. 3.18-19 LXX). Elsewhere, times of abundance and well-being for humans are characterized as times of sustenance for their domestic animals: 'and cities for the produce of grain and oil and wine and mangers (φάτνας) for every herd and folds for the flocks' (2 Chron. 32.28 NETS). In such agricultural habitats, the lives of humans and other than humans are deeply interconnected, and the manger is one symbol of this interdependent sociality.

Outside the Lukan birth narrative, only one other reference to φάτνη appears in the Second Testament, and it is also in Luke: 'But the Lord answered him and said, "You hypocrites! Does not each of you on the sabbath untie his ox or his donkey from the manger (φάτνης), and lead it away to give it water?"' (13.15). This reference recalls that animals were tethered to their masters' mangers, as Trainor notes, something that appears in writing at least as early as Homer's *Iliad*.[29] Owners would, moreover, in the joint interest of themselves, their households and their animals, see to the animals' needs, for example, for water, even on the Sabbath. So, the vital needs of the other animal, and their intersection with the vital needs of the human, come under the biblical 'choose life' principle that prevails on the Sabbath. In Luke 13, the theme of liberation (ἄφεσις, 4.18) resonates in the loosing of the animals' bonds (so that they may drink, 13.15) and has a parallel, of the kind 'and how much more so', with the loosing of the woman's bondage on account of her infirmity and its effect on her because of sociocultural habits (13.16).

The manger in Luke is, thus, situated at an intersection of human and other-than-human cultures, where humans and their domestic animals are interdependent, but where this interdependence is marked also by human power to bind and to let loose the other animal. Into the space of this complex inter-relationality, the Lukan Jesus is placed as dependent, an infant. The manger itself (probably stone) is a piece of Earth carved from and holding Earth's deep-time material being and situating the swaddled child (Lk. 2.7) as held by Earth.[30] The vulnerability of the newborn child, however, has an ominous reverberation in the vulnerability of the subjugated man under the violence of empire. As Trainor notes, the manger and the swaddling clothes echo in advance, and are echoed in, the burial narrative.[31] Death and life intersect in this more-than-human symbol of the manger.

As a more-than-human symbol, the manger crosses creaturely cultures, so that constructed by humans, it is assimilated to the intents and knowledges of other animals, for example, heifers and oxen (Joel 1.17; Job 6.5). It forms a marker both of difference and of similarity between creatures distinguished as wild and domesticated; the former will not be tethered to a manger (Job 39.9) while both kinds will seek the kind of sustenance the manger signifies and, when well-tended by humans, provides (Job 6.5). That both kinds vocalize when in want of food unsettles any easy distinction between wild and tame (Job 6.5). But while retaining its symbolic force, the capacity of the manger to act as a material site of nourishment can be upset (usually temporarily) by a creature's (a dog's perhaps or a human's) repurposing of the feeding box.

29. Homer, *Iliad* 6.506; Trainor, *About Earth's Child*, pp. 195-96
30. See Trainor, *About Earth's Child*, p. 83.
31. Trainor, *About Earth's Child*, pp. 83-84.

In Aesop's short fable 'The Dog in the Manger', a dog lies in the manger, barks, and does not allow the horse to eat.[32] This story appears also in the *Gospel of Thomas* to critique religious leaders who will neither act for their own nurture nor allow others to be nourished, and in Lucian's *Timon* as a symbol of the misanthrope.[33] In the complexity of the symbol of the Lukan manger, there is irony: when Jesus is placed in the manger, his presence, like the fabled dog's, may temporarily prevent from eating the animals for whom the manger is their feed box.

In contrast to the barking dog, the newly born child is more vulnerable, needing the protection of others to shield him from other creatures that might snuffle at the feed box. The narrative does not relate whether the manger provides a bed of straw for the infant (as popular settler piety suggests) or if it has been cleared out, feed left in an alternative space for other animals, and other matter used to support the swaddled child. But the situation of Jesus at the site of human and other-than-human interdependencies and relations of power and vulnerability suggests that the dualistic splitting of human and other animal, as if humans are not also animals, may not have been central to Luke's worldview.[34] Nonetheless, a hierarchy is also suggested in Luke paralleling but favouring human over other-than-human interests (12.2-7, 22-29; and 13.15-16).

While Lk. 2.7 provides a human-centred tableau in which the animals that would have fed from the particular manger in which the Lukan Mary lays her newly born child are not named, the manger itself suggests their presence. Moreover, the manger, as both place of more-than-human provision of nourishment (e.g. feed provided through the agency of humans, soil, rain, sun and plants) and symbol of the servitude of tethered animals, becomes a material site of the complex interdependencies and shared labour of human animals and their other domesticated animals, such as cattle, oxen and the Samaritan's pack animal of 10.34. The fate of these animals is entwined with human intentions, so that, for example, in Lk. 15.23, the father's compassion for his returning son finds expression in the slaughter of the 'fatted calf' for a celebratory feast. The description of the calf as 'fatted' indicates that, from a human perspective, the purpose of the calf and its nourishment has been for an end such as this. The manger signals not only the nourishment of the other animal but the whole habitat of the 'domesticated' animal as it is shaped by human interests, nurture and power.

---

32. Aesop, 'The Dog in the Manger', Library of Congress, https://read.gov/aesop/081.html (accessed 28 July 2022).

33. *Gos. Thom.* 102; Lucian, *Tim.* 14.

34. Later parts of Christian tradition recollect that humans are animals. See the discussion in Stephen D. Moore, 'From Animal Theory to Creaturely Theology', in Stephen D. Moore (ed.), *Divinanimality: Animal Theory, Creaturely Theology* (New York: Fordham University Press, 2014), pp. 1-16 (9-10).

Conclusion: Sacrifice and the Other Animal

Framed by the domestic human action of emptying a hot-water bottle, the 'mangered harbour' of a cow in Bruce Beaver's poem 'The Killers' is a sign of contentedness that is also bondage.[35] Amid a dense build-up of imagery, the poet narrates a boyhood memory of human violence to other animals in nightly rabbit hunting. Human warfare echoes in the language of the poem. The masculine rite of passage of rabbit hunting with ferrets and rifles contrasts with the rabbit 'warren's / Complex of womb-dark and mothering earth'. The cow's bondage signals a kind of safe habitat denied to the wilder rabbits inhabiting an earthy underground that reminds the poet of his mortality as a human animal: 'Beneath us the illuminated burrows / We must return to'. The cows themselves are interconnected with the cosmos, through the imagery of 'the moon's / Long let of milk light'. Beaver's 72-line poem closes with reference to the death of Jesus; as the hot-water bottle empties, the poet witnesses 'This flow of blood and water from the side of the past'. Deftly, the poet interweaves the human capacity to sacrifice both the other animal and the self in the one act of killing not only for sustenance but also for an imaginary of salvation, here under a patriarchal trope of making boys into men. Against this imaginary is the possibility of recognizing Earth as a nurturing but not always safe habitat for more than humans.

It is not clear to me whether the cow of Beaver's poem is a lone bovine or one of a larger milking herd on a small farm. In a contemporary context, while cows in such circumstances are subject to human power over their lives, deaths and capacities to feed and protect their own offspring (who may well become fatted calves), a distinction needs to be made with the instrumental fate of animals in industrialized agriculture, effectively defined by a construct of imposed sacrifice. Against this context and reading Lk. 2.7 braided with 15.23 and Beaver's poem, I ask: to what extent is the feeding imagery of the manger, with its incarnational and eucharistic nuances, infected by and unsettling of the killing of the other animal, both in industrialized commercial contexts and attendant on divine hospitality, as symbolized in the character of the compassionate father of Lk. 15.11-32? Can Luke's human saviour be a saviour for other creatures, or is the other animal sacrificed to the Christian idea, and ultimately doctrine, of incarnation? What might the fatted calf, or the cow in its 'mangered harbour', voice to the manger-inhabiting infant?

---

35. Bruce Beaver, 'The Killers', in *New and Selected Poems 1960–1990* (St Lucia: University of Queensland Press, 1991).

13

FEEDING 5,000 IN THE SLUMS OF BETHSAIDA (LUKE 9.10-17)

Robert J. Myles

This chapter juxtaposes Luke's version of the miraculous feeding of 5,000 men[1] against the socio-economic changes taking place in Palestine in the lead up to the initial organizing of the early Jesus movement. It considers the likely environmental impacts of Herodian building projects, and the disruptions caused to established life patterns, both human and more-than-human, that would have taken place as a consequence. Specifically, I argue that the socio-economic and environmental upheavals around the Sea of Galilee during the early decades of the first century CE generated a perception—if not a lived experience—of food insecurity among non-elite human populations. This milieu of economic hardship and environmental exploitation forms the immediate material backdrop to Jesus's miraculous multiplication of loaves and fishes and should facilitate the critical reader to generate new meanings and meaning effects with the biblical text.

Adopting a historical materialist lens,[2] my analysis is further enhanced by an exploration of 'habitat'. Elaine Wainwright's important work on the

---

1. Luke retains Mark's emphasis on 'men' (ἄνδρες) rather than 'people' (ἄνθρωποι). Only Matthew adds 'besides women and children', thereby increasing the total number of people fed. Some scholars have suggested that, while women and children are rendered invisible by Luke, we can presume they were 'present and active' in the story, as in Matthew's Gospel. See, e.g., Barbara E. Reid and Shelly Matthews, *Luke 1–9* (Collegeville, MN: Liturgical Press, 2021), p. 280. However, the androcentric focus, in addition to Jesus's instructions for the men to 'sit down in companies of about 50 each' (Lk. 9.14), may also have militaristic overtones of Jesus feeding an army of (male) soldiers, thereby giving the story a completely different twist. See Hugh Montefiore, 'Revolt in the Desert? (Mark VI.30ff.)', *NTS* 8 (1962), pp. 135-41. Reference to a 'crowd' (ὄχλος), which appears in Lk. 9.12 and in v. 11 in plural form, carried strong political connotations in Graeco-Roman and Jewish usage. The LXX often explicitly connects the term to military affairs (e.g. Isa. 43.17; Ezek. 16.14; 17.17; 23.24, 46, 47; Dan. 11.13, 25, 43). See further Robert J. Myles, 'Crowds and Power in the Early Palestinian Tradition', *JSHJ* 18 (2020), pp. 124-40 (130).

2. Historical materialist approaches typically frame phenomena in terms of

Gospel of Matthew in particular has helpfully introduced the analytic of 'habitat' to ecological biblical interpretation. Habitat refers to 'the dynamic context and contextualizing of interrelationship/s between the material, temporal, spatial and social' such that materiality is 'inextricably linked to sociality'.[3] It is a much broader concept than *setting* or even *context*, given its focus on interconnectedness, albeit in my understanding it also fruitfully draws on these adjacent categories. Thus, within a narrative framework, setting generally denotes 'the background against which the narrative action takes place', 'contributes to the mood of the narrative' and 'highlight[s] the religious, moral, social, emotional, and spiritual values of the characters'.[4] These factors will be important for interpreting the feeding of the 5,000 in light of rapidly changing habitats, as we shall observe below.

The path of navigation is as follows: I begin by introducing historical and material changes that were taking place in Palestine through the early decades of the first century CE, assessing their socio-economic as well as environmental impact. This leads me to a discussion of Luke's unique description of the narrative setting of the feeding of the 5,000 as occurring simultaneously within 'a deserted place' (v. 12) and 'a city called Bethsaida' (v. 10). In unpacking this tension, I suggest the 'desolate' habitat of the urbanized Bethsaida—in which hungry crowds are required to draw on the material resources of the surrounding fields and villages in order to satisfy human needs—exposes not only the damaging cycle of economic and environmental exploitation by this newly raised *polis*, but also the inherent contradiction of a *polis,* which cannot adequately provide for its own mass of inhabitants. I suggest this contradiction is resolved ideologically in the text via Jesus's miraculous multiplication of the loaves and fishes, in which he provides an abundance of food without depleting natural resources from the surrounding fields or marine environment. From an ecological perspective, however, this 'utopian' solution is left wanting, for it problematically infers that it is only through divine intervention, rather than a tectonic shift in mode of production, that economic and environmental problems can be overcome in the longer term.

---

longer-term material and technological changes leading from one mode of production to another, i.e. feudalism to capitalism or, in my case, agrarianism to feudalism. Marxist and ecological approaches do not always sit comfortably together. For the complexities and possible resolutions, see Jonathan Hughes, *Ecology and Historical Materialism* (Studies in Marxism and Social Theory; Cambridge: Cambridge University Press, 2000).

3. Elaine M. Wainwright, *Habitat, Human, and Holy: An Eco-Rhetorical Reading of the Gospel of Matthew* (Sheffield: Sheffield Phoenix Press, 2017), pp. 21-22.

4. James L. Resseguie, *Narrative Criticism of the New Testament: An Introduction* (Grand Rapids, MI: Baker Academic, 2005), pp. 87-88; cf. Mark Allan Powell, *What Is Narrative Criticism?* (Minneapolis, MN: Fortress Press, 1990), pp. 69-83.

The Early Jesus Movement and Feeding 5,000 in an Agrarian Context

From a historical materialist perspective, the prominent ideas, perceptions and activities of the early Jesus movement can be explained in part as a reaction to the socio-economic upheavals and class conflicts in Palestine during the early decades of the first century CE.[5] These conflicts involved not only the dynamic shifts and rhythms that characterize the agrarian mode of production generally but also the intrusion of considerable disruptions to the normal functioning of daily life.

The basic outline of this social formation should be familiar to most biblical scholars, but I here briefly rehash it for the benefit of those who are not: within pre-feudal and agrarian societies, the smaller propertied class, by virtue of its control of the means of production, appropriated surplus off the larger class group made up of those who mostly worked the land and water. Exploitation usually took its form in unfree labour (including slavery, serfdom and debt bondage), as well as in the form of taxes and tribute, and the letting of land and house property to leasehold tenants in return for rent paid either in money, kind or services.[6] In the ordinary workings of the world, resources were produced and consumed unevenly, leaving many to go without. In the Roman world in particular, vast inequalities of wealth and power meant that, for many people, procuring adequate nutrition and drinkable water was a daily challenge. Food security was a recurring problem affecting both urban and rural populations.[7]

Anxieties over hunger in Palestine were deemed important enough by the early Jesus movement to warrant frequent and repeated attention. This includes parallel Matthaean and Lukan sayings concerning food insecurity, which, if deemed to derive from *Q*, would go back to a time much earlier in the emerging Palestinian tradition (e.g. Mt. 5.6//Lk. 6.21; Mt. 6.11//Lk. 11.4; Mt. 6.25//Lk. 12.22-23). Jesus's famous miracle of the feeding of 5,000 also appears in all four Gospels (Mt. 14.13-21//Mk 6.32-44//Lk. 9.10-17//Jn 6.1-15), and Matthew and Mark additionally include the feeding of 4,000 (Mt. 15.32-39//Mk 8.1-9). In all six versions, Jesus multiplies a small

---

5. See James Crossley and Robert J. Myles, *Jesus: A Life in Class Conflict* (Winchester: Zer0 Books, 2023).

6. See further G.E.M. de Ste. Croix, *The Class Struggle in the Ancient Greek World* (Ithaca, NY: Cornell University Press, 1981); Roland Boer and Christina Petterson, *Time of Troubles: A New Economic Framework for Early Christianity* (Minneapolis, MN: Fortress Press, 2017).

7. See further Peter Garnsey, *Famine and Food Supply in the Graeco-Roman World: Responses to Risk and Crisis* (Cambridge: Cambridge University Press, 1988); Peter Garnsey, *Cities, Peasants and Food in Classical Antiquity: Essays in Social and Economic History* (Cambridge: Cambridge University Press, 1998).

number of fish and loaves in abundance to satisfy the hunger of a crowd. As we will see, Luke, who probably finalized their Gospel toward either the end of the first century or early in the second, preserves, distorts and embellishes earlier material in various, sometimes contradictory, ways. However, it appears a kernel of the feeding miracle goes back much earlier in the life of the Jesus movement. Luke's source in Mk 6.30-44 itself appears to be based on an earlier Palestinian tradition written in a Semitic language before being later translated into Greek.[8]

Historical Materialist and Environmental Impacts of Herodian Urbanization

The major economic drivers in Galilee during the reign of Herod Antipas (4 BCE–39 CE)—beyond the usual patterns of agrarian production of the land and water that sustained local populations (or not)—included a small number of sizable building projects. This was part of a broader and longstanding pattern in Herodian Palestine under a policy of Roman imperial development which attempted to bring these habitats into the empire's orbit in order to appropriate its surplus more efficiently through such mechanisms as tribute, taxes, rents and loans. Antipas's father, Herod the Great, was well known for inaugurating several building projects in Judea, most notably the refurbishment of the Jerusalem Temple, the construction of fortresses, and the founding of the *polis* of Caesarea Maritima. Antipas himself, following in his father's footsteps, sponsored at least two major urbanization projects in Galilee as Jesus was growing up there: the rebuilding of Sepphoris and the building of Tiberias.

Sepphoris had been destroyed by the Romans in 4 BCE during the turmoil surrounding Herod the Great's death. After he became tetrarch, Antipas had the city rebuilt and refortified to the extent that Josephus could later refer to it as 'the ornament of all Galilee' (*Ant.* 18.27). Sepphoris served as Antipas's capital until some years later when he founded the even grander city of Tiberias on the western shore of the Sea of Galilee. Tiberias was completed around 20 CE and named in honour of the Roman emperor Tiberius (*Ant.* 18.35-6). As Jonathan L. Reed notes, 'No area of Galilee lies outside a 25-km radius of these new urban centers'.[9] Accordingly, through the construction of these two cities, Antipas was able to extend his strategic and administrative influence over the entirety of Galilee, incorporating previ-

---

8. See Roger David Aus, *Feeding the Five Thousand: Studies in the Judaic Background of Mark 6:30-44 Par. and John 6:1-15* (Lanham, MD: University Press of America, 2010).

9. Jonathan L. Reed, *Archaeology and the Galilean Jesus: A Re-Examination of the Evidence* (Harrisburg, PA: Trinity Press, 2000), p. 96.

ously self-sustaining and independent villages and towns into a more tightly integrated imperial economy.

The development of these cities obviously came at a cost. From a class perspective, that cost was disproportionately borne by the non-elite human population. Sepphoris, for instance, had complete dependence on the countryside for agricultural goods, which it was incapable of producing itself. This placed additional demands on local producers: surrounding villages (like Nazareth) would have to contribute additional labour-power to sustain it. Surplus could be expropriated 'through outright seizure, forced services, taxes, rents, interest on loans, or fees for various services offered by the cities, including market and exchange services'.[10] Similar inequitable dynamics between city and countryside structured the flow of resources and wealth in Tiberias. These urban settlements functioned as concentration points for the upward flow of wealth and resources.

From an ecological perspective, the environmental cost of these building projects should not be underestimated. While the productive technologies of earlier social formations like agrarianism are arguably less damaging to the environment than under capitalism—especially given capitalism's perpetual drive toward accumulation, self-expansion and exponential growth—moves toward urbanization in the Hellenistic and Roman periods clearly involved an intensification of the productive forces, nonetheless. Indeed, Antipas's large-scale urbanization efforts in Galilee are only comprehensible in terms of the depletion of natural resources. The need for raw materials for the ornamentation of Sepphoris and construction of Tiberias were, of course, mined or harvested from deposits in the surrounding countryside. With the development of the water system, including from the time of Antipas, Sepphoris also dominated water resources in the area.[11] Forests and wildlife had to be cleared and land reallocated to make way for the changes. As the trees were hacked to death, animals, birds and insects lost their habitats. Josephus's chilling account of the building of Tiberias explicitly refers to the forced and violent displacements that took place as a consequence; he remarks that the new settlers, many of whom were Galilaean and poor, were 'by compulsion and with violent force' relocated to this new city to be its inhabitants (*Ant.* 18.36-38). Although Josephus's comments were intended to apply only to human inhabitants, we can extend them to include more-than-human inhabitants who were also undoubtedly caught up in these upheavals when they were forcefully moved or killed to clear the path for Herodian progress and development.

10. William E. Arnal, *Jesus and the Village Scribes: Galilean Conflicts and the Setting of Q* (Minneapolis, MN: Fortress Press, 2001), p. 147.

11. Sean Freyne, *Jesus: A Jewish Galilean* (London: T. & T. Clark, 2004), pp. 46-47.

In addition to harvesting mineral deposits, depleting forests and displacing wildlife, the urbanization of Galilee also led to longer-term structural changes to natural ecosystems around the region. Given the proximity of Tiberias to the lakeshore of the Sea of Galilee, for example, the impact on the marine environment was likely considerable. Waste produced by the city's large influx of inhabitants would have leached into the soil and the lake, resulting in changes to marine biodiversity. For millennia, fishing on the lake had been a largely local, self-reliant and seasonal affair. The founding of a major urban settlement like Tiberias suddenly enabled better-connected elites to dominate the lake economy and its ecosystems. This would have placed additional demands on local fishermen in small villages like Capernaum through the strategic installation of tax farmers like Levi, and led to an overall rise in extractive activity.[12] This increase in production introduced new environmental imbalances, possibly contributing to the depletion of the lake's fish supply. Although speculative, we might see hints of overfishing in Luke's account of the miraculous catch of fish (Lk. 5.1-11), wherein the fishermen disciples are said to have 'worked all night but have caught nothing' (v. 5).

All in all, the material world was significantly altered by these Herodian building projects. Human-driven changes to local habitats transformed both the 'social' (that is interconnections within the human community) and 'sociality' (as the web of interconnections between humanity and the more-than-human) of the Galilaean landscape, including around the Sea of Galilee where the early Jesus movement initially began to organize their millenarian response to Herodian and Roman power.

Habitats of Jesus's Miraculous Feeding in Luke

When people respond to shifts in material forces, whether consciously or not, they do so by using cultural (including religious) language and symbols to communicate those responses. As a Jewish social and religious move-

---

12. Recent excavations in Tarichaea (sometimes identified as 'Magdala') have also uncovered a sizeable harbour complex and several fish processing workshops from the Hellenistic and Roman periods. The Greek word Tarichaea literally means 'pickled fish', gesturing to the large-scale fishing operations and processing work that was situated there. At the time of the early Jesus movement in the late 20s CE, the settlement would have been a thriving hub of activity, second only to Tiberias. See further Robert J. Myles, 'Fishing for Entrepreneurs in the Sea of Galilee? Unmasking Neoliberal Ideology in Biblical Interpretation', in Robert J. Myles (ed.), *Class Struggle in the New Testament* (Lanham, MD: Lexington Books/Fortress Academic, 2019), pp. 115-38; Richard Bauckham, 'Magdala and the Fishing Industry', in Richard Bauckham (ed.), *Magdala of Galilee: A Jewish City in the Hellenistic and Roman Period* (Waco, TX: Baylor University Press, 2018), pp. 185-268.

ment, the early Jesus movement had access to a substantial repository of cultural knowledge and traditions through which they could interpret their changing world and construct a compelling narrative of a loyal God who intervenes in human history, sometimes through intermediary agents and messianic figures. Indeed, the theme of God coming to the aid of Israel and meeting basic material needs is attested through the Hebrew Bible (e.g. Exod. 16.4; Ps. 68.5-6). This theme was taken up and developed in its own way by the Gospels, such as in the key petition in the Lord's Prayer to 'give us this day our daily bread' (Mt. 6.11//Lk. 11.4//*Did.* 8.2), as well as the feeding miracles, the miraculous catches of fish (Lk. 5.1-11//Jn 21.1-14) and the widespread provision of healthcare. Stories like these provided hope and reassurance to those suffering under the changes instigated by Herodian building programmes, that no matter how much their material world was changing, God would ultimately intervene to take care of his loyal subjects.

The 'Polis' of Bethsaida

Luke's account of the feeding of the 5,000 uniquely takes place in 'a city called Bethsaida' (Lk. 9.10). Quite why Jesus 'slips quietly into' Bethsaida is not explained by the Lukan text. Commentators sometimes set aside the detail as a remnant of the author's underlying Markan source, which has the disciples travel by boat to Bethsaida immediately following the parallel episode (Mk 6.45).[13] According to Barbara E. Reid and Shelly Matthews, 'the Lukan literary context suggests that Jesus wants to escape Antipas ([Lk.] 9.7-9) by going into the territory ruled by Philip, another of Herod the Great's sons'.[14] Indeed, immediately before this pericope, Antipas had expressed a chilling desire to 'see' Jesus for himself upon hearing about 'all that had taken place' (v. 7). This meeting will ultimately take place during Jesus's trial before Herod Antipas, an encounter unique to Luke (23.6-12).

Bethsaida literally means 'house of the fisherman' and, according to Jn 1.44, was the original homeplace of three of Jesus's male disciples, including the fishermen brothers Simon and Andrew.[15] Located on the north shore

13. Heinz-Wolfgang Kuhn, 'Bethsaida in the Gospels: The Feeding Story in Luke 9 and the Q Saying in Luke 10', in Rami Arav and Richard A. Freund (eds.), *Bethsaida: A City by the North Shore of the Sea of Galilee* (Kirksville, MO: Truman State University Press, 1995), I, pp. 247-48; Michael D. Goulder, *Luke* (Sheffield: Sheffield Academic Press, 1989), p. 433; Joseph A. Fitzmyer, *The Gospel According to Luke I–IX* (New York: Doubleday, 1981), p. 765.

14. Reid and Matthews, *Luke 1–9*, p. 279. Other commentators obfuscate these political drivers behind the withdrawal. For example, Fitzmyer writes, 'Jesus is depicted retiring to Bethsaida for seclusion, as v. 10b suggests, not to avoid an "encounter" with Herod' (*Luke I–IX*, p. 766).

15. See further Sean Freyne, 'The Fisherman from Bethsaida', in Helen K. Bond

of the Sea of Galilee, the settlement fell outside the territory of Galilee[16] and was instead within the region of Gaulanitis in the tetrarchy of Philip, who ruled the region from shortly after Herod the Great's death in 4 BCE until 34 CE. Like both his father and brother, Philip is remembered for instigating a building programme during his long tenure. Not only did he re-found the city of Panias in 2 BCE, renaming it Caesarea after the Roman emperor and making it his strategic capital,[17] but, according to Josephus, Philip also raised the small fishing village of Bethsaida into the status of a city (πόλεως), increased its population considerably, strengthened its fortifications and renamed it 'Julias' after Augustus's daughter, Julia, in homage to the Roman power that lay behind his own (*Ant.* 18.28).[18]

Exactly when this urbanization of Bethsaida took place is not clear. If Josephus's tradition about renaming is accurate, then it presumably took place early, specifically, before Julia was exiled in 2 BCE (*Ant.* 18.27-28). However, the more likely option is that Josephus got the details wrong, and that the city was named after Livia, Augustus's wife, whose name was changed to Julia Augusta in 14 CE and who died in 29 CE. This would mean that Philip renamed Bethsaida after the mother of Emperor Tiberias in around 30 CE. Hence, the city probably would have been under construction during the late 20s CE when the early Jesus movement was initially organizing.

In any case, similar socio-economic and environmental changes would have occurred in Bethsaida as had taken place in Galilee, albeit the level of urbanization appears to have been on a smaller scale when compared to the significant development at Tiberias.[19] Nevertheless, land would have had to be deforested or razed in the surrounding areas to make room for agriculture and animal grazing, the need for raw materials for the construction of new buildings and fortifications would have had to be mined and transported, and an overall increase in productive and extractive activity would have put further strain on natural resources and especially the marine environment. Frequent reports of lake crossings in the Gospels (e.g. Mk 4.35-36; 5.1, 2; 6.45, 53) also attest to the interconnectedness of these various lakeside settlements. The integration of the lake and its surroundings into the wider Roman imperial network facilitated the ease of fish exports (such as *garum* or fermented fish paste) to service wealthy connoisseurs in the various cities

and Larry W. Hurtado (eds.), *Peter in Early Christianity* (Grand Rapids, MI: Eerdmans, 2015), pp. 19-29.

16. See Jn 12.21, where the author erroneously locates Bethsaida in Galilee.

17. Jesus travels through the villages surrounding this city in Mk 8.27 (cf. Mt. 16.13) where it is referred to as 'Caesarea Philippi' (lit. 'Philip's Caesarea').

18. It is not clear why Luke retains the name 'Bethsaida'.

19. This is true of either of the major contenders for the archaeological sites of biblical Bethsaida, namely Et-Tell or Al-Araj.

of the empire. The construction of Bethsaida would have thus generated increased economic activity on the lake. Although the Gospel of John is not generally to be relied upon for historical detail, it has been suggested by at least one scholar that the upheaval of the fishermen brothers from their original homeplace in Bethsaida (Jn 1.44) to the quieter and rustic Capernaum (cf. Mk 1.21) could have been related to these increased demands of the Herodian political-economic expansion around the lake.[20]

Crucially, increased extractive activity combined with rapid population growth as a consequence of raising Bethsaida to a *polis* would have placed additional demands on local resources, especially the production of food. The famished crowds presupposed by Luke's account of the feeding of the 5,000 should be therefore understood as a human-made catastrophe: a consequence of poor urban planning, increased production for export, unsustainable changes to natural ecosystems and the foreseeable gap between a finite level of resources and the ballooning appetite of a rapidly growing human population.

'A Deserted Place', or the 'Slums' of Bethsaida

Luke offers a secondary—possibly ironic—habitat for the feeding of the 5,000 that appears to contradict the first. In setting up Jesus's miracle, the Twelve approach Jesus and (sarcastically?) declare, 'we are in a deserted place [ὧδε ἐν ἐρήμῳ τόπῳ ἐσμέν]' (Lk. 9.12). In his ecological commentary, Michael Trainor highlights this geographical tension and the interpretive questions it raises:

> Is this a reflection of Luke's urban auditors? Is their Greco-Roman urban experience like being in a desert wilderness? Or is the need of Luke's urbanites to come into the wilderness, a characteristic withdrawal that Jesus has in his communion with God in this natural environment?[21]

While some commentators attempt to soften this apparent contradiction by suggesting that Jesus's movement 'to' (εἰς) Bethsaida was more of a 'direction ... than the destination',[22] I prefer to tease out the hard implications in terms of the meaning effects it potentially generates, albeit I take a different route from Trainor who ultimately explains the urban-wilderness tension as

20. Fred Strickert, 'The Founding of the City of Julias by the Tetrarch Philip in 30 CE', *JJS* 61 (2010), pp. 220-33 (225).

21. Michael Trainor, *About Earth's Child: An Ecological Listening to the Gospel of Luke* (Sheffield: Sheffield Phoenix Press, 2012), p. 158.

22. François Bovon, *Luke* (Hermeneia; Minneapolis, MN: Fortress Press, 2002), p. 354.

another hangover from Luke's Markan source re-contextualized for Luke's urban auditors.[23]

In the context of food production and consumption, the 'deserted' habitat elicits multiple associations. On the one hand, for instance, the Greek noun ἔρημος (wilderness, desert) obviously evokes for the biblically literate reader associations with Israel's desert sojourn and, in the context of feeding miracles, manna falling from heaven (Exod. 16.22).[24] It is, accordingly, an appropriate habitat for God to come to people's aid in their time of need.

On the other hand, the desert imagery possibly evokes a deforested landscape. Whereas trees and natural vegetation protect water and soil quality and replenish water supplies, from an agrarian economic perspective, the desert features as a kind of 'third-space', outside the formal cycles of production and consumption. Within a spatial analysis of the ancient economy, for instance, a parasitic urban-rural relation largely took place between the *polis* and *chôra*: the *chôra* here refers to the productive countryside with its rural villages and fields supplying food and resources to the *polis*, or urban environment, in order to sustain it.[25] From the anthropocentric perspective of the *polis*, then, the desert or wilderness falls beyond the hinterland deemed to be economically productive and valuable.

If taken in an ironic sense, then, the Twelve appear to appropriate this latter connotation of the desert and turn it on its head: the 'city called Bethsaida' is, in fact, 'a deserted place'! It is incapable of providing sufficient nourishment to its newly assembled mass of inhabitants. Instead, the proposed solution of the Twelve is to have the crowd dispersed, 'so that they may go into the surrounding villages and countryside, to lodge and get provisions ...' (v. 12). In other words, to resort to the parasitic urban-rural relation where the resources of the *polis* are appropriated from the *chôra*. But this response only further entrenches agrarian imbalances and lacks hospitality so apparently it will not do. Accordingly, Jesus replies in v. 13 that, instead, the Twelve should themselves give the crowd something to eat. However, they retort: 'We have no more than five loaves and two fish—unless we are to go and buy food for all these people'. Their monetary response assumes a level of commodification of food and an alienation

---

23. Trainor writes the 'urban-rural-wilderness tension is the result of Luke maintaining the wilderness location from the original Markan intertext while placing it explicitly within an urban setting more relevant to the gospel auditors' (*About Earth's Child*, p. 158). What I find insufficient about this explanation is that Mark also had predominantly urban auditors, especially if we take Mark's traditional association with Rome into account.

24. Morna Hooker, *The Gospel According to Saint Mark* (London: Hendrickson, 1991), p. 165.

25. Boer and Petterson, *Time of Troubles*, pp. 81-85.

from nature associated with urban habitats in which fish can now only be purchased and not caught and bread only bought and not baked.[26]

My own way of understanding this contradiction of a *polis* that is simultaneously 'a deserted place' is to imagine the gritty underside of Herodian urbanization: the newly created 'slums' of Bethsaida. The metaphor of slums readily calls to mind the environmental consequences of urbanization, such as increased sewage, waste, crime and poverty. Economically too, the appearance of slums at the outskirts or even within the centre of a city is closely linked to the process of urbanization.[27] Rapid urbanization drives economic growth, causing further migrants to seek out opportunities for work in populated areas. However, poor infrastructure, insufficient housing and the reallocation of agricultural land for urban development can result in displaced people with no option but to dwell in slums. With a rapid shift from rural to urban life, poverty also tends to migrate to urban areas: these people arrive with hope but lack shelter and other resources to make it work. Slums are the places of alternative economies, for the problem is often not a lack of material goods or supply of food, but rather inflated prices associated with urban environments.

By referring to the 'city called Bethsaida' as 'a deserted place', the Twelve attempt to diagnose its sickness as a broken habitat—a concentration of wealth, power and resources which, within the context of a hungry mass of people, cannot adequately distribute food or provide shelter for its inhabitants. This underscores the pivotal contradiction between the imperial ideal of the *polis* (how things should be) and the material reality of its slums (how things really are). The conflicting settings of Luke's account of Jesus's feeding miracle thus gestures to the economic and environmental ambivalence of urbanization in which the many riches and benefits of the Herodian political-economic expansion were simply off-limits to those not occupying the apex of the social and economic pyramid. But how to resolve this contradiction of a *polis* unable to feed its hungry inhabitants?

Give Us our Daily Bread!
Toward a Fully Automated Luxury Divine Agrarianism

The solution envisaged by Luke's account of the feeding miracle is, to be sure, fantastical and utopian. Rather than follow the practical strategy offered by the Twelve, which appears to lack hospitality, Jesus instead takes

26. In her reading of the Matthaean parallel account in Mt. 14.13-36, Wainwright asks whether the 'response of the disciples (v. 15) to the *erēmos* and its being peopled by a great crowd is informed by an arrogant rather than an ecological eye, an eye for commodity exchange in an imperial economy as a way of feeding hungry communities' (*Habitat, Human, and Holy*, p. 151).

27. See further Mike Davis, *Planet of Slums* (London: Verso, 2005).

the five loaves and two fish, looks up to heaven, blesses, breaks and gives the pieces back to the disciples to distribute them to the crowd. Remarkably, 'all ate and were filled' (vv. 16-17), and there were even twelve baskets of broken pieces gathered up afterwards. These theatrical actions by Jesus were religiously coded in ways immediately recognizable to those familiar with the language of early Judaism. As Anne Elvey observes, following Jesus's blessing of the food stuffs, the resultant blessing in the form of an abundance of food 'echoes a scriptural tradition of divine blessing of people and land, accompanying a promise of fertility, prosperity and well-being (Deut. 7.12-14; 16.15; 28.3-6)'.[28] The action also re-enacts the Lord's instruction to Moses in the desert regarding the provision of manna falling from heaven: 'I am going to rain bread from heaven for you, and each day the people shall go out and gather enough for that day' (Exod. 16.4).

Materially speaking, this dramatic action by Jesus, with its appeal to divine intercession and abundant blessing of those 'who are hungry now' (cf. Lk. 6.21), depicts a superior system of food production and distribution—a kind of fully automated luxury divine agrarianism—in which human needs are met directly through divine deliverance and a 'short-circuiting' of the agrarian mode of production, with Jesus as prime benefactor. It does not rely on the urban-based exploitation of villages or fields, nor does it plunder natural resources or destroy ecosystems or local habitats. These overall socio-economic relations envisaged by Luke are, as Halvor Moxnes describes them, a

> reversal that implied a central, forced *redistribution* of goods and possessions, prophetically forewarned in the Magnificat (1:51-53). This reversal was an act of God, and the divine redistribution manifested through the acts and speeches of Jesus, the benefactor of humanity.[29]

Within this utopian way of life, every human eats, every human is filled and no further environmental damage is perpetrated. Even the leftover waste is responsibly gathered up into baskets![30]

As a solution to food insecurity and environmental decay, however, Luke's manifesto sounds somewhat naïve and idealist, at least to our modern ears. The feeding miracle only provides an immediate solution to the hunger of the crowd. It does not offer longer-term policy settings or practical solutions that we might implement to solve the technological and eco-

---

28. Anne F. Elvey, *The Matter of the Text: Material Engagements Between Luke and the Five Senses* (Sheffield: Sheffield Phoenix Press, 2011), p. 177.

29. Halvor Moxnes, *The Economy of the Kingdom: Social Conflict and Economic Relations in Luke's Gospel* (Eugene, OR: Wipf & Stock, 1988), pp. 154-55.

30. As Trainor writes, 'more is indicated than simply cleaning up a mess left over by the crowd. It suggests that environmental respect is essential. Nothing is to be wasted' (*About Earth's Child*, p. 161).

nomic imbalances associated with (agrarian) food production or, indeed, the extractive intensification of resource depletion brought about by (Herodian) urbanization. Despite a well-meaning interpretive tradition that emphasizes an ethic of sharing, no such communal arrangements are explored or advocated by this particular text, and the strict communal arrangements practiced later by the community (Acts 2.44; 4.32) required no transformation of the productive forces of society in the here-and-now. From a historical materialist perspective, then, not least among the ideological deficiencies was an inability of the early Jesus movement to think practically beyond an advancing agrarian way of life with all of its anthropocentric trappings. These trappings would only intensify in the transition from agrarianism to feudalism and even more so with the onset of capitalism.

Given their perception of the enormity of the material shifts they were responding to, however, the early Jesus movement likely realized that their great leap forward in resource management could be achieved only via supernatural intervention. Ultimately, it would require the dramatic inbreaking of a radical new administration–the kingdom of God–ruled by or on behalf of Israel's God, and with a decisive bias toward meeting the material interests of the peasantry. While the early Jesus movement's hope for some momentary respite from the pressures of Herodian urbanization was fantastical, it was simultaneously realistic and understandable in its ancient cultural context, because there was no other way the world could be changed so radically to end hunger without the hand of God dramatically intervening and playing some integral part.

With this we should also keep in mind that miracle stories in the Gospels do much more than elevate Jesus theologically. Grounded in the contradictions of real life, and as ideological resolutions to historical and material changes in first-century Palestinian society, they simultaneously attest to 'the sigh of oppressed creature, the heart of a heartless world, and the soul of soulless conditions'.[31] They assume that those first attracted to the early Jesus movement perceived conditions as so hostile to possibilities for human flourishing (not to mention the flourishing of the more-than-human) that only through dramatic divine intervention could things be put right.

31. Karl Marx, 'A Contribution to the Critique of Hegel's Philosophy of Right: Introduction' (1843), https://www.marxists.org/archive/marx/works/1843/critique-hpr/intro.htm.

14

'GIVING HER ALL': AN ECOLOGICAL
FEMINIST READING OF LUKE 21.1-4

Elizabeth Dowling and Veronica Lawson

It is an honour to be contributing to this Festschrift for Elaine Wainwright. Like Elaine, we are Sisters of Mercy. We have worked with Elaine in exploring and breaking open the biblical text, and we have also learnt so much from her. Veronica has been a collaborator with Elaine for more than forty years. Both Elaine and Veronica initially inspired Elizabeth to engage in biblical studies and then encouraged her along her journey. We have chosen to write this article together in an expression of collaboration and solidarity, two features that characterize Elaine's scholarly activities. Our article will focus on the narrative of a Lukan widow in the Jerusalem temple (21.1-4). There is a sense in which this woman can be considered prophetic and as 'giving her all', a fitting scenario for our tribute to Elaine who has also given so much of herself in her biblical studies endeavours and whose scholarship has often challenged us to read the biblical text differently.

Interpretive Stance

Throughout her biblical studies career, feminist interpretation has been at the heart of Elaine's writing. Over the decades, she has widened the pegs of her tent and engaged an ecological hermeneutic. The term 'ecological' is used here in its broadest sense, reflecting the concerns of Earth itself and the entire Earth community, including humans. 'Habitat, human and holy' are the foci of Elaine's interpretive hermeneutic.[1] She describes an ecological reading as 'a critical conversation engaging the principle of *suspicion* in the face of pervasive anthropocentrism and a domination and/or erasure of women, the colonized and the other-than-human'.[2] At the same time, her ecological reading engages in a process of reconfiguration or re-reading that

---

1. This is evidenced by the title of her commentary, *Habitat, Human, and Holy: An Eco-Rhetorical Reading of the Gospel of Matthew* (Earth Bible Commentary, 6; Sheffield: Sheffield Phoenix Press, 2016).
2. See Wainwright, *Habitat*, p. 20.

is attentive to Earth and its community, so that the result is a 'dance between interpretative stances of suspicion and reconfiguration'.[3]

We use such an ecological approach in this chapter, highlighting both the concerns of Earth and of women in our analysis of the Lukan text, while also being conscious of the multidimensional nature of oppressive systems. As Anne Elvey explains, 'Not only do ecological feminists recognize material and conceptual links between oppression of women and destruction of Earth, but these links are impacted by broader frame-works of oppression based not only on gender but also on class, race, sexuality, and species'.[4] Furthermore, our ecological hermeneutic involves attention to all the elements in the narrative: places are not considered simply as settings for a human drama but, rather, as constituent elements of the story that unfolds. As already indicated, habitat is a constitutive element of our discussion as are the human and the holy.

We are all aware that the current global context has been heavily impacted by the Covid-19 pandemic and the ongoing effects of ecological destruction, both social and environmental. We also cannot underestimate the impact of war on the human community and on the environment at this time. The vulnerable are disproportionately affected by these crises, both because they are located in precarious conditions and because they lack sufficient resources to ameliorate the ravages that confront them. A staggering feature of, and issue for, our present time is the extreme inequality between the resources of the rich and those rendered poor.[5] This current context nuances the focus of our gaze as we read the biblical text.

Another Lukan Widow

An earlier story of a widow in the temple, namely the story of Anna in Lk. 2.36-38, also merits attention in this context. Although this earlier narrative is not the main focus of our exploration, the presence of both temple and widow link this story with 21.1-4. We are introduced to Anna as a prophet (*prophētis*, 2.36). Listing 'prophet' before any other identifying markers gives a primacy to this designation. A surprising amount of detail follows Anna's identification as prophet. She is the daughter of Phanuel of the tribe

3. Wainwright, *Habitat*, p. 20.

4. Anne Elvey, 'A Multidimensional Approach in Feminist Ecological Biblical Studies', in Susanne Scholz (ed.), *The Oxford Handbook of Feminist Approaches to the Hebrew Bible* (Oxford: Oxford University Press, 2021), pp. 555-73 (556).

5. Oxfam reported on 17 January 2022 that the ten richest men on the planet at that time held six times the wealth of the world's 3.1 billion poorest people. See their press release, 'Ten Richest Men Double their Fortunes in Pandemic While Incomes of 99 Percent of Humanity Fall', https://www.oxfam.org/en/press-releases/ten-richest-men-double-their-fortunes-pandemic-while-incomes-99-percent-humanity.

of Asher, thus she is identified in relation to her father and his tribe. She was married for 7 years, then widowed for 84 years or until the age of 84, with the numbers here perhaps signifying perfection and completeness.[6] Anna's constancy is a feature of the narrative: 'She never left the temple but worshipped there with fasting and prayer night and day' (2.37). The repeated use of the imperfect in 2.38 indicates that her praising of God and her speaking about the child are ongoing activities.[7]

In effect, the temple has become 'a house of prayer' (cf. Lk. 19.45a) for the widowed Anna who 'gives her all' to God.[8] Anna speaks in the public space of the temple. The public nature of her proclamation is also indicated by the identification of her audience as 'all who were looking for the redemption of Jerusalem' (2.38). Unlike Simeon's words (2.29-32), however, the words of the prophet Anna are not recorded. We know the topic of her speech but not its explicit content. This is consistent with the rhetorical effect of the Lukan Gospel regarding the public speech of women. Lukan women are generally silent in public, and the significance of the words of those who do speak in public is minimized.[9] We will see that Anna's characterization has several links with that of the widow who gives her two coins (21.1-4).

Significance of the Temple

For Barbara Reid, the widows of Lk. 2.36-38 and 21.1-4 'frame the gospel story with their pouring out of their very lives in the Temple'.[10] The location of each of these two women in the temple complex is a significant feature of both pericopes, especially because of the overall importance of the temple in the Gospel of Luke. Following the prologue (1.1-4), the constructed habi-

---

6. For the significance of Phanuel's name, the interpretation issues surrounding '84 years' and the significance of the numbers, see Barbara E. Reid and Shelly Matthews, *Luke 1–9* (Wisdom Commentary Series, 43A; Collegeville, MN: Liturgical Press, 2021), pp. 88, 90.

7. The Greek text in this verse can also be interpreted as Anna speaking about God.

8. On giving one's all as a Lukan theme, see also 9.57-60; 14.33; 18.18-30 and our focus pericope, 21.1-4.

9. See Elizabeth V. Dowling, *Taking Away the Pound: Women, Theology and the Parable of the Pounds in the Gospel of Luke* (Library of New Testament Studies, 324; London: T. & T. Clark International, 2007), pp. 211-13.

10. Barbara Reid, *Choosing the Better Part? Women in the Gospel of Luke* (Collegeville, MN: Liturgical Press, 1996), p. 196. Amy-Jill Levine, 'Luke and the Jewish Religion', *Int* 68.4 (2014), pp. 389-402 (393), suggests a different interpretation of this frame: 'The two women, both apparently childless, symbolize the fate of the institution: there will be no next generation to continue temple piety'. It is difficult to see how Levine can make the assertion of childlessness without explicit evidence from the Gospel text.

tat for the first narrative of the Gospel is the temple complex, specifically the sanctuary (*naos*, 1.9, 21-22). The last verse of the Gospel portrays the disciples continually in the temple (*hieron*) blessing God (24.53).[11] In effect, it is the temple that bookends the Lukan Gospel narrative. Between these literary boundaries, the temple complex is also an integral feature of a succession of stories in the Gospel: the Simeon and Anna narratives (2.25-38); the story of the child Jesus listening to the teachers (2.41-50); the testing of Jesus (4.9-13); the parable of the Pharisee and the tax collector (18.9-14); and much of Jesus's Jerusalem ministry (19.45-21.38), the final verses of which describe Jesus teaching in the temple every day (21.37) with all the people listening to him in the temple (21.38). Officers of the temple police are among those who come to arrest Jesus, and he reminds his captors that he has been with them day after day in the temple (22.52-53). During the crucifixion, the curtain of the temple (*naos*) is torn in two (23.45).

The temple functioned as the centre of Jewish life, shaping the religious, cultural, political and economic life of the people and evoking the experience of God's presence with them.[12] While Luke's Jesus predicts the future destruction of the temple (Lk. 21.5-6), the narrator nonetheless continues to connect the early activities of the disciples after Jesus's ascension to the temple precincts and Jerusalem, thus grounding the beginnings of the early Jesus movement in a Jewish framework.[13] The earliest community members are portrayed as spending time together in the temple (Acts 2.46), the first of many references to the temple in the book of Acts.[14] As Turid Seim argues, however, the centrality of the temple diminishes over the course of Acts, with the shift away from the temple accompanied by an increasing focus on the house as the centre of action.[15] Amy-Jill Levine argues that the importance of the temple decreases over the course of the Lukan Gospel itself: 'Following the nativity material in the first two chapters, the sacred quality of Israel, Jerusalem, and the temple is gradually eroded'.[16] The decreasing focus on the temple in Acts reflects the geographical trajectory of the movement from Jerusalem 'to the ends of the earth' (Acts 1.8).

11. *Hieron* occurs fourteen times in the Lukan Gospel (2.27, 37, 46; 4.9; 18.10; 19.45, 47; 20.1; 21.5, 37, 38; 22.52, 53; 24.53), while *naos* is used on four occasions (1.9, 21, 22; 23.45), likely referring to the inner sanctuary of the temple. See *TDNT* IV, pp. 882, 885.

12. For more on the centrality of the temple and its significance in the infancy narrative, see Joel B. Green, *The Gospel of Luke* (NICNT; Grand Rapids, MI: Eerdmans, 1997), pp. 61-62.

13. See, e.g., Lk. 24.53; Acts 2.46; 3.1-26; 5.12-13, 17-26, 42.

14. *Hieron* occurs 25 times in Acts, 13 times in Acts 2–5 and 12 times in Acts 19–26.

15. Turid Seim, *The Double Message: Patterns of Gender in Luke-Acts* (Edinburgh: T. & T. Clark, 1994), pp. 138-45.

16. Levine, 'Luke and the Jewish Religion', p. 393.

The temple casts an ecological shadow on the Lukan narrative that needs to be acknowledged. This shadow relates, in particular, to the ecological cost of Herod the Great's expansion of the temple mount and the temple's ongoing practices. Michael Trainor notes the 'pillaging of Earth's gifts' in the reconstruction and describes the temple as 'the quintessential setting of sacrifice and death of Earth's animals'.[17] In other words, the natural habitat of Earth and Earth's creatures were conscripted to 'give their all' for the construction and ritual life of the temple.[18] Herod's temple mount was constructed of limestone quarried locally from the mountains around Jerusalem. While stones weighing between two and three tons were used in constructions on the temple mount, some of the cornerstones of the mount itself weighed over 80 tons.[19] Although he has a tendency to exaggerate the numbers, Josephus states that Herod prepared one thousand wagons to transport the stones for the building, which also brings to mind the thousands of animals who would have pulled these wagons. Further, he states that Herod selected ten thousand skilled workers for the building project and bought a thousand priestly garments (*Ant.* 15.390).

Let us consider briefly how the wider Earth community was affected by this construction, which took several decades to complete.[20] First, the mountains around Jerusalem, composed of limestone, were quarried so that their riches could become available for human exploitation. According to Leen Ritmeyer, the process was a combination of chiselling, using a pickaxe, inserting wooden beams and pouring water to provide the pressure required to separate the stone. The large stones were placed on wooden rollers, which were then pulled by oxen.[21] Earth and Earth's creatures bore the cost and bore the load of Herod's temple expansion project.

The grandeur and wealth of the temple are described by Josephus. The exterior of the temple was said to be covered with 'massive plates of gold' (*War* 5.222); treasures of the temple included solid gold vessels and ornaments, precious stones, and large quantities of purple and scarlet garments and sweet spices (*War* 6.387-91). Josephus also informs us that the treasury chambers (*gazophulakia*) contained 'vast sums of money, vast piles of raiment and other valuables' (*War* 6.282). The term *gazophulakion*, which

17. Michael Trainor, *About Earth's Child: An Ecological Listening to the Gospel of Luke* (Earth Bible Commentary, 2; Sheffield: Sheffield Phoenix Press, 2012), p. 69.

18. Elvey (*Multidimensional Approach*, p. 562) makes an important link between critique of biblical sacrifice and contemporary questions around what humans consume or destroy for the purpose of sustenance, comfort and excess.

19. Leen Ritmeyer, 'Quarrying and Transporting Stones for Herod's Temple Mount', *BARev* 15.6 (1989), pp. 46-48 (46-47).

20. These comments on the ecological cost of the construction of the temple could well be said of so many of the world's great monuments, both ancient and modern.

21. Ritmeyer, 'Quarrying', pp. 46-47.

appears in our focus pericope (Lk. 21.1-4), can be understood in different ways: as 'a room in the temple used as a treasury' or as 'a large box in which offerings were placed'.[22] According to *m. Šeq.* 6.5, the temple contained thirteen shofar-chests—trumpet-shaped containers—to collect the offerings.[23]

Earth's resources of gold, precious stones, spices and natural fibres were used for the purposes of ornamentation and treasures in the temple and these similarly came at a cost to Earth.[24] One example of this is the manufacture of the large quantity of purple and scarlet garments that Josephus includes in his list of temple treasures (*War* 6.387-91). The garments would likely be made of linen from the flax plant. The purple dye could be sourced from animals, specifically the sea snail, or from plants.[25] A second example is the use of cinnamon, cassia and other sweet spices for the daily incense offering (*War* 6.390).

The large quantity of coins in the treasury draws attention to the metals, such as silver, copper and bronze that were used to mint these coins. Again, Earth was the source of these riches and was affected by the extraction of these precious metals. Earth was the generous provider, bearing the cost. The temple's celebration of feasts and its animal sacrificial system had an impact on the ecological dynamic of the Earth community; to give just one example, Josephus reports that hundreds of thousands of animals were slaughtered during Passover alone (*War* 6.423-25).[26]

Models of Power

While the Lk. 21.1-4 pericope takes place in the Jerusalem temple precinct, the temple is not simply the backdrop for the human drama. The temple mount, with its history of construction and operating practices, interacts with and becomes embroiled with the human characters in the stories. Usually, when the Jerusalem temple is considered, it is the temple hierarchy that is associated with power. This reflects a traditional understanding of

22. See Johannes P. Louw and Eugene A. Nida (eds.), *Greek-English Lexicon of the New Testament* (New York: United Bible Societies, 1988), pp. 71, 86; François Bovon, *Luke 3: A Commentary on the Gospel of Luke 19:28–24:53* (trans. James E. Crouch; Hermeneia; Minneapolis, MN: Fortress, 2012), p. 94.

23. Bovon, *Luke 3*, p. 93, and Joseph A. Fitzmyer, *The Gospel According to Luke X–XXIV* (AB, 28a; New York: Doubleday, 1985), p. 1322.

24. For a description of the golden vine at the entrance to the sanctuary, see Margaret Daly-Denton, *John: An Earth Bible Commentary: Supposing Him to Be the Gardener* (London: Bloomsbury T. & T. Clark, 2017), p. 191.

25. Ivoni Richter Reimer, *Women in the Acts of the Apostles: A Feminist Liberation Perspective* (Minneapolis, MN: Fortress Press, 1995), pp. 100-105.

26. The lambs slaughtered at Passover were a food source for the large number of celebrants.

power—namely, a hierarchical, pyramidal model that, as Val Plumwood identifies, reinforces a range of dualisms based on race and class, as well as gender and species, in a network of domination.[27] On this vertical power grid—an artificial human construct—first-century Jewish widows would generally be thought to occupy a lowly rank and would be perceived as vulnerable to exploitation from those positioned 'above' or 'over' them, with little or no opportunity to improve their situation. At the same time, the temple was perceived as sacred and holy, and its religious leaders had a privileged position within this hierarchical construct.

The work of Chela Sandoval can give us insights into another way of understanding power. In *Methodology of the Oppressed*, Sandoval describes a postmodern move away from a 'sovereign, pyramidal model of power' with its hierarchical structure and vertical movement: 'Instead, global post-modern power is increasingly figured as a force that circulates horizon-tally, on a lateral and flattened plane, even if many-sided, with deviations occurring at every turn'.[28] In this postmodern model, *all* constituents are understood to have access to their *own form* of social power based on the exchange between their location in multiple horizontal grids, such as race, sexuality, nationality, gender, class and age.[29] Sandoval's grid network can be extended to include grids of species and materiality, allowing the whole Earth community to be drawn into the model.

Sandoval sees the evolution of this horizontal view of power, with its multidimensional elements, as creating new possibilities: 'The growing metaphoric dominance of this newly conceived horizontal grid networking the globe generates a kind of double-reality and double-consciousness of power, with new and old formations at work all at once'.[30] This shift in mod-elling power creates tensions and ruptures, yet also opportunities, 'open-ing space in the order of the real for the previously unimaginable'.[31] Such openings allow us to perceive the widow in Lk. 21.1-4, and indeed other constituents of the narrative, through different eyes as the 'new and old formations' of power operate at the same time. In the hierarchical pyrami-dal model of power, some are considered 'below' or 'inferior' to others and cut off from the power at higher levels unless they move 'up' the scale. In contrast, Sandoval identifies the movement in the horizontal model as from

27. Val Plumwood, *Feminism and the Mastery of Nature* (London: Routledge, 1993), pp. 42-43. For an outline of a pyramidal model of patriarchal Greek democracy, see Elizabeth Schüssler Fiorenza, *But She Said: Feminist Practices of Biblical Interpre-tation* (Boston: Beacon Press, 1992), pp. 114-18.

28. Chela Sandoval, *Methodology of the Oppressed* (Minneapolis, MN: University of Minnesota Press, 2000), p. 73.

29. Sandoval, *Methodology*, p. 74.

30. Sandoval, *Methodology*, p. 75.

31. Sandoval, *Methodology*, p. 76.

'margin to center', or 'inside to outside', opening up exploration of life at the 'interstices' or 'borderlands'.[32]

The Widow with Two Coins (Lk. 21.1-4)

Within the temple setting of extravagance and wealth, Jesus sees a needy widow (*chēran penichran*) throw in two coins (*lepta duo*, Lk. 21.2). A *lepton* was a copper coin with the least value of the coins in circulation.[33] Jesus observes that the rich have contributed 'out of their abundance', but the poor (*ptōchē*) widow has given *panta ton bion hon eichen* (21.4), understood as either all that she had to live on,[34] or, in fact, her whole life.[35] Jesus contrasts the gifts of the rich with that of the widow, highlighting the costly nature of the woman's seemingly small gesture (21.3-4). The pericope is immediately preceded by Jesus's condemnation of the scribes for devouring widows' houses (20.46-47) and is followed by Jesus's prediction of the destruction of the temple (21.5-6). This narrative context leads some readers to interpret the religious leaders as having exploited this poor widow, inducing her to give her all to the temple treasury, and thereby leaving her destitute.[36] In this interpretation, the widow is a victim of unscrupulous operators within the temple system.

There is, however, no explicit connection in Jesus's words between this particular widow's action of 'giving her all' and the actions of the scribes or other religious leaders. As Levine points out, it is the priests, not the scribes, who run the temple.[37] While scribes have earlier been linked with chief priests (Lk. 19.47; 20.19), Jesus associates the scribes who 'devour widows' houses' with the market-places, synagogues and banquets (20.46), rather than the temple.[38] Moreover, Levine posits that, after contributing her last coins, the widow will be relying on support from the temple:

---

32. Sandoval, *Methodology*, p. 74.

33. So Luke Timothy Johnson, *The Gospel of Luke* (Sacra Pagina, 3; Collegeville, MN: Liturgical Press, 1991), p. 316; Fitzmyer, *Luke X–XXIV*, p. 1003. The *lepton* is usually understood to be 1/128th the value of a denarius. See BDAG, p. 592.

34. See the NRSV translation, for instance.

35. See Levine, 'Luke and the Jewish Religion', p. 393, and Reid, *Choosing the Better Part*, pp. 195-96, for this translation.

36. Addison G. Wright, 'The Widow's Mites: Praise or Lament? A Matter of Context', *CBQ* 44 (1982), pp. 256-65, was influential in the development of this interpretation.

37. Amy-Jill Levine, '"This Poor Widow ..." (Mark 12:43): From Donation to Diatribe', in Susan Ashbrook Harvey *et al.* (eds.), *A Most Reliable Witness: Essays in Honor of Ross Shepard Kraemer* (BJS, 358; Providence, RI: Brown University, 2015), pp. 183-93 (190).

38. Levine, '"This Poor Widow ..."', p. 190.

It is not God who will give this woman her next meal; it is rather the Jewish system of *tzedakah*, the contributions that others make to the benefit
of the community as a whole. The very temple to which she gives her last
two coins will be the institution that will provide for her.[39]

With this insight, the widow's contribution need not provoke a critique of
the temple institution, despite Jesus's prediction of the destruction of the
temple immediately following this pericope (21.5-6).

Levine reminds us further that the temple had a complex relationship
with Rome. Pilate's control and the presence of Roman troops were a factor
in the temple's operation.[40] Let us take a closer look at the exercise of power
in relation to the construction and operation of the temple mount. Within a
traditional vertical model of power, Herod would be perceived as having
had extreme power in regard to the construction of the temple mount. In the
functioning of the temple closer to the time of Jesus's death, by which time
Herod the Great was himself long dead and Judea was under direct Roman
rule, the priests held significant power but not necessarily ultimate power,
given the Roman prefect Pontius Pilate's rule and his deployment of the
Roman guard, especially during Jewish festivals. As previously mentioned,
a widow would be considered one of the lowest ranked on this vertical
power grid.

Within Sandoval's horizontal model of power, however, the widow in this
pericope can be located on multiple horizontal grids based on her species,
gender, marital status and economic situation, as well as other factors, such
as her age, that cannot be identified from her characterization. According
to this model, the widow *does* have access to *her own form* of social power.
She can be seen as moving from the margins toward the centre by her action
of contributing the two coins. When she *chooses* to give her last coins—her
living, literally in the Greek 'all the life that she had'—the widow becomes
the centre of Jesus's gaze[41] (and also the centre of the reader's focus). In so
doing, she draws the attention of the Lukan Jesus to the inadequate response
of the rich. She is the subject of Jesus's conversation with his disciples, but
we do not hear her voice.[42] Since the widow does not speak, we cannot be
certain of her motivation in giving the coins. We do know, however, that
Jesus interprets her action as prophetic in the sense that, for him, it constitutes a condemnation of the wealthy who contribute only from their surplus

39. Levine, "'This Poor Widow ...'", p. 186.
40. Levine, "'This Poor Widow ...'", p. 192.
41. Bovon, *Luke 3*, p. 95.
42. This links her to two other nameless Lukan women—the woman who anoints
Jesus and the bent-over woman—who are also the subjects of Jesus's conversation with
men, while their own words are not heard (Lk. 7.44-47; 13.15-16). See Dowling, *Taking
Away the Pounds*, p. 170.

while she contributes 'her whole life' (21.3-4).[43] Like the earlier widow Anna (Lk. 2.36), therefore, she can be considered prophetic, although she is not explicitly labelled as *prophētis*. While Anna does speak without her words being recorded (2.38), this widow remains silent. Effectively, the reader is denied the opportunity to hear the voices of both these widows.

While the widow with her two coins moves away from the margins and further toward the centre as she utilizes her power, the rich lose their position at the centre and diminish in power as they are exposed by the widow's prophetic action and the words of Jesus (21.3-4). We might consider this as an example of 'the previously unimaginable' that is given opportunity and space in Sandoval's model. This movement toward the centre for the widow and away from the centre by the rich evokes previous Lukan reversals of rich and poor, evident in Mary's song of praise (1.51-53), the blessings and woes (6.20-26) and the parable of the rich man and Lazarus (16.19-31).[44]

Just as the widow actively gives her whole life, *panta ton bion hon eichen*, so too will Jesus give his life, according to the passion narrative (Lk. 22.1-23.56), which begins in the following chapter. Some characters in Luke appear to deem this action an utter waste or utter failure (cf. 23.35-39), but Jesus is vindicated by the resurrection (24.1-53). While Luke portrays the plot to kill Jesus as triggered by the chief priests and scribes (22.2), and while the ensuing trials before the Jewish council and then Pilate (22.66-71; 23.1-25) result in Jesus's crucifixion, Jesus is not portrayed narrowly as a victim. His prayer on the Mount of Olives prepares him for what he will face (22.39-46). He makes no attempt to flee from his captors. He chooses to give his life. The widow, by her action of offering 'her life', can thus be aligned with Jesus. She demonstrates agency by her actions. She cannot be subsumed under the label of 'victim'.

Within a horizontal model of power, animals and Earth can also be located on grids based on their species and materiality, so we can consider humans, animals and Earth interacting on a horizontal plane. In the context of this pericope, the Earth community provides resources for the construction and operation of the temple—limestone, precious metals for ornamentation, plant fibres for cloth, metals for coins, animals as part of the building

43. Michael Trainor (*About Earth's Child*, p. 256) names her action as 'a form of prophetic denunciation' of the wealthy. Surekha Nelavala insightfully comments that it is easier to give away all that you have if you only have two coins rather than if you are rich. See Surekha Nelavala, 'Why Make It a Big Deal! Seeing the Widow beyond Her Two Coins (Mark 12:41-44): A Dalit Feminist Perspective', in Peniel Jesudason Rufus Rajkumar, Joseph Prabhakar Davam and I.P. Asheer Vadham (eds.), *Mission at and from the Margins: Patterns, Protagonists and Perspectives* (Regnum Edinburgh Centenary Series, 19; Oxford: Regnum Books International, 2014), pp. 173-78 (178).

44. Anne Elvey, 'Love and Justice in the Gospel of Luke—Ecology, the Neighbour and Hope', *AusBR* 60 (2012), pp. 1-17 (9).

labour and used in the sacrificial system, and so on. Some questions come to mind in this configuration. Are the other-than-human Earth elements positioned on the margins or closer to the centre? If animals are conscripted to provide their labour, for instance, can they be said to have power to move away from the periphery?

Like the widow,[45] Earth can be perceived as vulnerable to unjust practices and able to be exploited until it has nothing more to give. With the current demand on Earth's resources more than Earth can sustain,[46] it would seem Earth is indeed giving its all. But also like the widow, Earth is a subject and agent with its own forms of power.[47] This is evident when we witness, for instance, the power of an erupting volcano or an earthquake. Such events are part of the natural process and bring essential nutrients to the Earth's surface or perhaps contribute to the formation of mountains. It is important to note here that Luke's narrative does not include the significant detail of an earthquake at Jesus's death as we find in Matthew's account (Mt. 27.51). Luke does, however, invoke cosmic agency with mention of darkness coming over the whole Earth (Lk. 23.44). Earth's power can also be seen in less dramatic events, such as the way the roots of trees will search for available sources of water. Earth is not solely a victim.

Concluding Thoughts

We read our Lukan narrative, conscious of and informed by the power and graciousness of Earth to provide resources that have been used by humans in the past context of the Jerusalem temple, and in the construction and ongoing practice of many of the large institutions in our present context. There is a sense in which Earth pours out its life, and renewable resources mean that Earth *continually* pours out its life within the Earth community. Earth is another that can be aligned with Jesus in the act of giving its life. Jesus and the widow with two coins choose to give their life. Does Earth choose to lay down its life? We think not! While Earth may not have the capacity to choose, it nonetheless gives its life. It is the responsibility of the human community to ensure that Earth's gift is sustainable rather than destructive of life itself.

---

45. As in the interpretation of Wright, 'The Widow's Mites', for instance.

46. For information on Earth Overshoot Day, the date each year when humanity has already used as much as Earth can sustain for the entire year, see Global Footprint Network, https://www.footprintnetwork.org/about-us/our-history (accessed 24 March 2022).

47. See the Earth Bible Principles explained in Norman C. Habel and Peter Trudinger, *Exploring Ecological Hermeneutics* (Exploring Ecological Hermeneutics, 46; Atlanta, GA: SBL, 2008), pp. 1-2.

Reading the story of the widow (Lk. 21.1-4) in the light of our current global context, several questions and insights come to mind. With world-wide reported death numbers from Covid-19 at more than six million,[48] a huge number of people have lost family members. Many women have become widows as a result of the pandemic. Similarly, lives lost because of the ongoing effect of war are resulting in an increased number of wid-ows. These women, rendered widows through tragic circumstances, often become physically and financially vulnerable. Like the widow in our story who freely gives her last two coins, these women are not necessarily deprived of agency to determine what they do with the resources still avail-able to them.

The prophetic nature of the Lukan widow's action highlights the vast inequality between the donations of the rich and the poor, as pointed out by Jesus (21.3-4). In this time of pandemic, an increasing number of people have become economically vulnerable, and the divide between rich and poor has widened significantly, as made clear in the recent Oxfam press release: 'The world's ten richest men more than doubled their fortunes from $700 billion to $1.5 trillion … during the first two years of a pandemic that has seen the incomes of 99 percent of humanity fall and over 160 million more people forced into poverty'.[49] Who are the prophets in our times who seek to address such inequities?[50] Like so many Lukan women, the widow of 21.1-4 does not speak. While her actions function as prophetic, her silence cannot be ignored. In Hebrew, widow is *almanâ*, whose root can mean 'silent' or 'unable to speak'.[51] We might also ask, 'Whose voices are not heard in our present time and is this by choice or have their voices been suppressed?'

Our current global context of pandemic, war and ecological destruction result from violence and the exercise of 'power over' others. The widow of Lk. 21.1-4 exhibits a different sort of power as we envisage her moving from the margins to the centre on a horizontal power grid, rather than a ver-tical one. This widow who chooses to 'give her all' is able to exercise the power that she has and to break through all the barriers that might prevent her from exerting influence. Like Jesus, who will also give his all in the fol-lowing chapters, she models a power that is not achieved through violence, a power that is needed in our world today.

---

48. See the World Health Organization COVID-19 website: https://covid19.who.int (accessed 8 June 2022).

49. Oxfam, 'Ten Richest Men'.

50. Economist Kate Raworth may be one such prophetic presence. Her economic framework is designed to meet the needs of the whole human community within the lim-its of what Earth can sustain. See Kate Raworth, *Doughnut Economics: Seven Ways to Think Like a 21st-Century Economist* (London: Random House Business Books, 2018).

51. BDB, pp. 47-48.

15

'THE PLACE THAT MEN CALL PARADISE':
EMILY DICKINSON'S EARTHLY ENGAGEMENT
WITH THE APOSTLE PAUL

Caroline Blyth

Introduction

In one of her poems, Emily Dickinson (1830–1886) describes the Bible somewhat cynically as 'an antique Volume—/Written by faded Men/At the suggestion of Holy Spectres'.[1] Yet in another poem, she alludes to the dangerous potential of this 'antique Volume', referring to it as 'a word/Which bears a sword'.[2] In her writing, Dickinson holds these two seemingly disparate evaluations of the Bible in tension. With her characteristic enthusiasm, she critiques and parries with the biblical traditions, using them to explore her own distinctive spirituality, which sometimes stood at odds with the religious orthodoxies of the day. Challenging the claims of nineteenth-century higher criticism—that the biblical texts holds a single, 'correct' meaning—she preferred to embrace a 'hermeneutic of indeterminacy', recognizing the text's potential to be reshaped and rephrased in ways that would better reflect her own life experiences and spiritual contemplations.[3] Dickinson refused to feel constrained by the authoritative nature of the biblical texts; rather, she looked upon Scripture as 'a flexible textual construct',[4] whose authority was contestable and whose words she was free to parody, remodel and challenge.

---

1. Martha Dickinson Bianchi and Alfred Leete Hampson (eds.), *The Poems of Emily Dickinson* (London: Jonathan Cape, 1937), p. 259. This edition of Dickinson's poems is also available online at Project Gutenberg (http://www.gutenberg.org/files/12242/12242-h/12242-h.htm).

2. Bianchi and Hampson, *Poems of Emily Dickinson*, p. 148.

3. A 'hermeneutic of indeterminacy' is the term used by Alicia Ostriker, 'Re-playing the Bible: My Emily Dickinson', *Emily Dickinson Journal* 2 (1993), pp. 160-71 (165), to describe Dickinson's engagement with the biblical texts.

4. Marietta Messmer, *A Vice for Voices: Reading Emily Dickinson's Correspondence* (Amherst, MA: University of Massachusetts Press, 2001), pp. 162-63.

While Dickinson engaged with many biblical traditions in her writing, I focus in this chapter on her engagement with one particular 'faded man'—the apostle Paul. Dickinson makes several direct and indirect references to Paul in her letters and poetry, often in ways that thoroughly unbalance his spiritual and heaven-centred gaze, thrusting it earthwards as though compelling the apostle to engage with worldly elements, such as friendship, family and the natural world. By taking a closer look at some of her letters and poetry, I explore how Dickinson saw Paul's teachings as being incompatible with her own earth-centred spirituality, particularly her unshakeable delight for a world in which she could encounter her own sense of 'paradise'.[5]

'My Wars Are Laid Away in Books': *Dickinson's Social and Religious Milieu*

Before looking at Dickinson's engagements with Paul, let me first outline the contexts from within which she interacted with the biblical texts. Emily Dickinson was born in the small New England town of Amherst, Massachusetts. Her life coincided with a time of great social and religious upheaval in the United States, including industrialization, scientific discovery, religious revivalism and sectarianism, the rise of the women's suffrage movement and the grimness of a bloody Civil War. This shifting and restless landscape had a considerable impact on Dickinson's writing; although renowned for her self-sequestered lifestyle,[6] her engagement with the socio-political world of nineteenth-century America sings out in her poetry and correspondence, including her literary explorations of the biblical material.[7] It is as though this especially turbulent milieu within which Dickinson existed—cloistered

---

5. This chapter is based on an earlier (and longer) article published in 2019. See Caroline Blyth, 'Bringing the Apostle Down to Earth: Emily Dickinson Wrestles with Paul', *JIBS* 1.1 (2019), pp. 6-25. A German translation of the article was also included in Irmtraud Fischer *et al.* (ed.), *Die Bibel war für sie ein politisches Buch: Bibelinterpretationen der Frauenemanzipationsbewegungen im langen 19. Jahrhundert* (Theologische Frauenforschung in Europa, 29; Vienna: LIT, 2020). When I initially began researching Emily Dickinson's poetry, I was working at the University of Auckland's School of Theology under the leadership of Professor Elaine Wainwright. Over the years, Elaine has been a wonderful colleague and a wise mentor, and it is a pleasure to contribute to her Festschrift. I chose this topic as I think Elaine will appreciate Dickinson's celebration of the natural world, the flowers in her garden, and the loyalty and love of friends and family.

6. By the late 1850s, Dickinson had essentially withdrawn entirely from social life, rarely leaving her family home. But she continued to communicate with close friends and family through her prolific letter writing.

7. Shira Wolosky, 'Public and Private in Dickinson's War Poetry', in Harold Bloom (ed.), *Emily Dickinson* (Bloom's Modern Critical Views; New York: Infobase Publishing, 2008), pp. 169-90 (169-70); see also Wendy Martin, *The Cambridge Introduction to*

as she was—acted as a traumatic catalyst for her literary endeavours, which demanded that she re-evaluate the significance of issues such as war, class, race, death, theodicy and justice.[8]

On occasion, Dickinson also turns her gaze toward her own gendered location, contemplating her place as a woman within the highly patriarchal social milieu of nineteenth-century New England. Yet her flexible and ever-changing voice defies attempts to categorize her as either a 'proto-feminist' or 'anti-feminist'. In a sense, she gives voice to both sentiments; her writings mix and conflate traditional gender stereotypes, which she then presents in new and radical poetic form.[9] She appeared to eschew any involvement in the traditionally masculine spheres of civic and religious life, preferring to embrace her position within the more restrictive domestic realm prescribed by the social gender codes of her day.[10] Nevertheless, behind the trim curtains of her Amherst home, she created for herself a locality that fizzed with literary creativity and social confrontation, using her literary outputs to address, with honesty, both her own private life and faith *and* the public life of American society, religion and politics.[11]

With regard to her religious affiliations, Dickinson never officially professed a Christian faith; yet she was doubtless influenced by the Puritan Calvinist heritage of the Trinitarian Congregational Church, which had seeped indelibly into the warp and woof of eighteenth- and nineteenth-century New England.[12] This Puritan heritage followed the Reformation doc-

---

Emily Dickinson (Cambridge Introduction to Literature; Cambridge: Cambridge University Press, 2007), pp. 24-39, 58-70.

8. Wolosky, 'Public and Private', 173-75. Wolosky offers many examples from Dickinson's poetry that illustrate her engagement with contemporary social issues ('Public and Private', 169-90).

9. David S. Reynolds, 'Emily Dickinson and Popular Culture', in Harold Bloom (ed.), *Emily Dickinson* (Bloom's Modern Critical Views; New York: Infobase Publishing, 2008), pp. 111-34 (128). Bianchi and Hampson, *Poems of Emily Dickinson*, include various examples of Dickinson's poems where she engages with social and religious ideologies of gender, such as 'This World Is Not Conclusion' (p. 195); 'I'm "wife"—I've finished that—' (p. 135), 'She Rose to his Requirement—Dropt' (p. 136), and 'Title Divine—Is Mine!' (p. 154).

10. Wolosky, 'Public and Private', 169; Sharon Leder and Andrea Abbott, *The Language of Exclusion: The Poetry of Emily Dickinson and Christina Rossetti* (Contributions in Women's Studies, 83; New York: Greenwood Press, 1987), p. 151.

11. Wolosky, 'Public and Private', pp. 170-73; *idem*, 'Gendered Poetics', in Eliza Richards (ed.), *Emily Dickinson in Context* (New York: Cambridge University Press, 2013), pp. 169-78 (169-70); Martin, *Cambridge Introduction to Emily Dickinson*, p. 24.

12. Jane Donahue Eberwein, 'New England Puritan Heritage," in Eliza Richards (ed.), *Emily Dickinson in Context* (New York: Cambridge University Press, 2013), pp. 46-55 (46-48). Also see James McIntosh, 'Religion', in Eliza Richards (ed.), *Emily Dickinson in Context* (New York: Cambridge University Press, 2013), pp. 151-59.

trine that salvation could be attained only by a predestined few through faith in the atoning sacrifice of Christ's death, rather than through good works. Humanity was inherently corrupt as the consequence of Original Sin and incapable of salvation without intercession from a transcendent, inscrutable and typically vengeful God. The earthly domain was considered, like humanity, to be eternally stained by sin—an irredeemable and undesirable mess compared to the glorious and numinous heavenly realm.

Living through no fewer than eight Congregational Church revivals in mid-nineteenth-century Amherst, Dickinson saw an increasing number of her family, neighbours and friends undergo the conversion experience. It is likely that she would have felt a certain pressure from those around her to convert; certainly, some of her friends and family wrote to her expressing their concerns that her unconverted state would prevent her from gaining access to heaven.[13] Nevertheless, she also retained a strong desire to preserve the freedom of her own, less conventional, spiritual convictions and refused to 'give up the world' by undergoing any official conversion experience.[14]

Dickinson would also have been influenced by the religious liberalism that was being fostered in many parts of North America during the nineteenth century. Even in conservative corners of Massachusetts such as Amherst, religious life was becoming increasingly complicated by revivals, dissents, schisms and the formation of new churches and movements, all of which fostered an environment of religious multiplicity.[15] Dickinson was certainly familiar with the doctrines of the Unitarian Christian Church, which had a presence in New England, and she preferred its more optimistic views on human nature and the natural world, as well as its stress on the humanity of Christ.[16] She was also drawn to an offshoot of the Unitarian Church—Transcendentalism—which extolled humanity's ability to relate to God directly through meditation, intuition and communing with the natural world, rather than through the intercession of priest or church.[17] As James McIntosh notes, Dickinson had the cultural resources to think about religion—and the biblical traditions—'idiosyncratically and flexibly',

13. Martin, *Cambridge Introduction to Emily Dickinson*, p. 26.
14. Written in a letter to her schoolfriend Abiah Root, 16 May 1848. See Thomas H. Johnson (ed.), *The Letters of Emily Dickinson* (3 vols.; Cambridge, MA: Belknap Press, 1958), I, p. 67. Many of Dickinson's letters are also published in Mabel Loomis Todd (ed.), *Letters of Emily Dickinson* (2 vols.; Boston: Robert Brothers, 1894), which can be found online at the Hathi Trust Digital Library, http://catalog.hathitrust.org/Record/011225228.
15. Rowena Revis Jones, '"A Taste for Poison": Dickinson's Departure from Orthodoxy', *Emily Dickinson Journal* 2 (1993), pp. 47-64.
16. McIntosh, 'Religion', pp. 153-54.
17. Martin, *Cambridge Introduction to Emily Dickinson*, pp. 32-34.

particularly during those traumatic times of war and unrest, when so many of her assumptions and beliefs appear to have been sorely shaken.[18] With the 'boldness of a prophet',[19] she consciously let her very human fluctuations in faith lie in tension with each other, reflecting her own desire to keep belief alive through questioning it, exploring it and confronting it head on. As she says in a letter to her close friend Judge Otis Phillips Lord, written on 30 April 1882, 'We both believe and disbelieve a hundred times an hour, which keeps Believing nimble'.[20]

Dickinson therefore did not consider personal doubts and challenges to be the death knell of faith; rather, they were *essential* to faith. Unwilling to either accept or reject absolutely the traditional tenets of Calvinist Christianity, she was, in the words of Shira Wolosky, 'a poet of religious engagement, whose very criticism of religion reflects her deep involvement in it … Dickinson's work as a whole … at once asserts a possible faith, and no less painfully, questions and denies such faith.'[21] Or, as Roger Lundin so eloquently puts it, 'She wrestled with God all her life'.[22]

In terms of her engagement with the biblical texts, Dickinson was an outsider to the traditionally male-dominated academy of biblical scholarship, with its adherence to the objective and detached rigours of higher criticism. Yet she chose to be a tremendously *engaged* outsider, offering a deeply personal and contextual reading of the biblical traditions that would have grated against the exegetical orthodoxies of her day. Perhaps the conventionally feminine and intensely *familiar* domestic location she occupied gave her the confidence to eschew these orthodoxies, bringing to the text instead her gender, her faith and her socio-historical location—with all their concomitant 'baggage'—and using these to read the Bible from the margins, unencumbered by formal convention. In so doing, Dickinson makes her own radical entry into biblical studies, applying her 'hermeneutic of indeterminacy'[23] in order to bring to the biblical traditions a new pair of eyes—women's eyes— and a fresh breath of humanity.[24]

18. McIntosh, 'Religion', p. 153.

19. Carol J. Cook, 'Emily Dickinson: Poet as Pastoral Theologian', *Pastoral Psychology* 60 (2011), pp. 422-35 (429).

20. Johnson, *Letters of Emily Dickinson*, III, p. 728.

21. Shira Wolosky, 'Emily Dickinson: Being in the Body', in Wendy Martin (ed.), *The Cambridge Companion to Emily Dickinson* (Cambridge Companion to Literature; Cambridge: Cambridge University Press, 2002), pp. 129-41 (132).

22. Roger Lundin, *Emily Dickinson and the Art of Belief* (Grand Rapids, MI: Eerdmans, 2004), p. 4.

23. Ostriker, 'Re-playing the Bible', p. 165.

24. Magdalena Zapedowska, 'Wrestling with Silence: Emily Dickinson's Calvinist God', *American Transcendental Quarterly* 20 (2006), pp. 379-98 (394).

'Earth Is Heaven': Dickinson's Engagement with Paul

Dickinson's complex engagement with her faith and with the Bible is demonstrated effectively in her poems and letters that allude to the Pauline Epistles. As space does not allow me to explore every reference to Paul in Dickinson's writing, I have chosen to focus on one topic that seems central to her engagement with the apostle—that is, her insistence on the paradisiacal qualities of life on earth, including the natural world and the comforting presence of family and friends. I consider how Dickinson's own earth-centred spirituality and faith shape her responses to Paul's more heaven-centred gaze.

Within Dickinson's writings, the reader is offered vivid testimony of her love for the world around her; in both her poetry and her letters, she is vociferous in her praises of nature—the towering mountains, the singing brooks, the voluble sun, the chattering birds, the sociable meadows and the flowers in her beloved garden. While some of her work does echo her hopes for the reality of a *heavenly* paradise, she bears a much more powerful witness to the delights of the senses and the flesh available to her *here on earth*. Indeed, compared with traditional devotional poets of the nineteenth century, who often looked heavenward for the source of their spiritual inspiration, Dickinson gained a sense of the heavenly and the sacred through the blissfully immanent and powerful presence of earthly delights.[25] As Paula Bennett notes, nature was, for Dickinson, 'an alternative religion as well as a source of poetic strength' which took on a revelatory power—'the equivalent of experiencing heaven'.[26] Wendy Martin likewise observes that, for Dickinson, 'Heaven and God become secondary to the natural world and its tiny creatures, and love of nature becomes faith ... Life in its minutest details and briefest experiences is what interests Dickinson as the greatest of treasures.'[27] The beauty of the world was to be experienced and revered as hallowed in its own right.

Thus, in her poem that begins 'Heaven has different signs—to me', Dickinson's garden becomes her 'church' and the birds her Sabbath choir.[28] Throughout the poem, she employs sacred language to summon those

25. Wendy Martin, *An American Triptych: Anne Bradstreet, Emily Dickinson, Adrienne Rich* (Chapel Hill, NC: University of North Carolina Press, 1984), p. 131. See also Roxanne Harde, '"Who Has Not Found the Heaven—Below—/Will Fail of It Above—": Emily Dickinson's Spirituality', in Kristina K. Groover (ed.), *Things of the Spirit: Women Writers Constructing Spirituality* (Notre Dame, IN: University of Notre Dame Press, 2004), pp. 155-80 (156).

26. Paula Bennett, *Emily Dickinson: Woman Poet* (Hemel Hempstead: Harvester Wheatsheaf, 1990), p. 105.

27. Martin, *Cambridge Introduction to Emily Dickinson*, p. 66

28. Bianchi and Hampson, *Poems of Emily Dickinson*, p. 304.

achingly beautiful fixtures of the world in which she saw the paradisiacal. She recalls 'The Orchard when the Sun is on—/The Triumph of the Birds', along with the 'Awe' of the dawn and 'The Rapture of a finished Day—/ Returning to the West', all of which serve to remind her of 'the place/That Men call "Paradise"'.[29] Likewise, in her poem '"Heaven"—is what I cannot reach!' Dickinson identifies 'The Apples on the Tree' and 'The Color on the Cruising Cloud' as 'Heaven'.[30] In 'The Gentian weaves her fringes', she uses the language of liturgy and formal worship to capture the summer morning, ending with the final liturgical response, 'In the name of the Bee—/And of the Butterfly—/And of the Breeze—Amen!'[31] Similarly, in 'These are the days when Birds come back', she employs eucharistic imagery, naming the 'sacred emblems' of 'consecrated bread' and 'immortal wine' that she seeks to partake of in the 'Sacrament of summer days'.[32]

Dickinson also uses religious language to talk about the natural world in some of her letters. Writing to her close friend and confidante, Elizabeth Holland, in early August 1856, she observes, 'If God had been here this summer and seen the things I have seen—I guess that He would think his Paradise superfluous'.[33] Within her writing, Dickinson repeatedly fostered a vision of a world in which the complexity and sacredness of nature were embraced and celebrated. Thus, according to Wendy Martin, 'When trying to imagine how "Heaven" could be more glorious than the earth, Dickinson's imagination fails. She sees the earth's revelations as her senses experience them, instead of imagining potential glories beyond them.'[34] In this sense, Dickinson echoes and prefigures the sentiments of contemporary feminist theologies of embodiment, which refuse to focus exclusively on the otherworldly but instead celebrate the sacredness and sanctity of life here on earth.[35]

Consequently, Dickinson's love of an earthly creation that she could experience in the here and now stood at times in stark contrast to the Puritan Calvinist traditions of nineteenth-century New England, which undermined the earthly as corrupted by sin in favour of the more sacred heavenly realms. Following a certain reading of the Pauline Epistles dominated by the ideological and religious concerns of the Reformation, the Calvinist orthodoxy of Dickinson's religious milieu considered the world to be mere vanity, while the human body and mind were lowly, despicable and prone to

29. Bianchi and Hampson, *Poems of Emily Dickinson*, p. 304.
30. Bianchi and Hampson, *Poems of Emily Dickinson*, p. 42.
31. Bianchi and Hampson, *Poems of Emily Dickinson*, p. 90.
32. Bianchi and Hampson, *Poems of Emily Dickinson*, pp. 106-107.
33. Todd, *Letters of Emily Dickinson*, p. 169.
34. Martin, *Cambridge Introduction to Emily Dickinson*, p. 69.
35. Roxanne Harde, '"Some—Are like my Own—": Emily Dickinson's Christology of Embodiment', *Christianity and Literature* 53 (2004), pp. 315-36 (317).

sin and guilt. Within some of his Epistles (especially those deemed 'authentic' by modern scholars), Paul's line of vision is directed heavenward and his appreciation of the present created order—'groaning' as it was (Rom. 8.22)—tended to be more muted in comparison to his anticipatory adulation for the new heavenly creation that would dawn in an eschatological age.[36] In some of her engagements with Paul's writings, Dickinson therefore takes the apostle to task for what she considered to be his overtly spiritual and heaven-centred gaze, appropriating his own writings in order to challenge him to look earthwards and thus acknowledge the inherent value and paradisiacal delight that could be encountered in *this* world.

Thus, for example, in a letter to Elizabeth Holland written in the early summer of 1873, Dickinson mentions that, on returning from a visit to the Hollands, her sister Lavinia (whom she called Vinnie) had described the beautiful location of their home as 'paradise'.[37] Dickinson tells Holland that she has never believed Paradise to be 'a supernatural site'; contemplating the delights of her own locality that very afternoon, she writes, 'Eden, always eligible, is peculiarly so this noon. It would please you to see how intimate the Meadows are with the Sun.'[38] Dickinson thus sees here the spiritual, the Edenic and the 'heavenly' in the world around her, eschewing any future immortality in favour of that which she can see, taste and feel in the here and now.[39] Dickinson then alludes to the Pauline teaching of the corruptible and perishable nature of this current life in 1 Cor. 15.53, where Paul states that the corruptible 'must put on incorruption' at the time of the resurrection. Speaking of her sister Vinnie and her father, Edward Dickinson, both converts to the Trinitarian Congregational Church, she avers to Holland, 'While the Clergyman tells Father and Vinnie that "this Corruptible shall put on Incorruption"—it has already done so and they got defrauded'.[40] In other words, Paul, the architect of this 'fraud', invites believers like her father and sister to look forward to the imminent coming of the incorruptible kingdom of God, where 'death is swallowed up in victory' (1 Cor. 15.54). Dickinson, however, challenges the apostle's heavenward gaze and insists that Paradise is a divinely created earthly domain, to be enjoyed in the here and now, rather than an unknowable and intangible 'supernatural site' that will only be revealed in some distant, numinous future. As she says in a

36. E.g. Rom. 3.10-11, 23; 5.12-21; 8.7-8, 18-25; 1 Cor. 15; 2 Cor. 4–5; Gal 6.6-16.

37. Johnson, *Letters of Emily Dickinson*, II, p. 508.

38. Johnson, *Letters of Emily Dickinson*, II, p. 508.

39. Similarly, in a letter to her brother Austin on 25 October 1851, Dickinson describes her own home as 'a bit of Eden which not the sin of any can utterly destroy' (Todd, *Letters of Emily Dickinson*, I, 75). This again alludes to the Calvinist traditions of New England Puritanism, which followed the tenet of Original Sin being the cause of humanity's loss of paradise and the inevitable, ongoing degradation of the earthly realm.

40. Johnson, *Letters of Emily Dickinson*, II, p. 508.

poem written to her brother Austin in 1877, 'Earth is Heaven—/Whether Heaven is Heaven or not'.[41]

Similarly, in another letter sent to Elizabeth Holland in the summer of 1856, Dickinson again makes an allusion to a Pauline Epistle in order to affirm her great love of the world around her.[42] In the letter, she expresses her delight in the beauty of the passing summer months: '[I]f God had been here this summer, and seen the things that I have seen—I guess that He would think His Paradise superfluous. Don't tell Him, for the world, though, for after all He's said about it, I should like to see what He was building for us, with no hammer, and no stone, and no journeyman either.'[43] These last remarks allude playfully to Paul's attestations in 2 Cor. 5.1 that, although earthly buildings may decay and be destroyed, God will provide believers with a superior, everlasting home, which will be 'not made by human hands, eternal, and in heaven'. Paul's argument rests upon his oft-visited theme of the lasting supremacy of all things heavenly over the impermanence and perishability of earthly existence. Dickinson, however, teases Paul here by contesting his claims to the superiority of heaven over the delights offered during the earthly summer months. And—tongue firmly in cheek—she questions his claims about the quality of any heavenly home that is apparently built without the benefits of tools, materials or craftsmen. Reading his words quite literally, it is as though she winks playfully at his solemnity, thereby destabilizing his message of heavenly supremacy in order to affirm once more the joys of her earthly existence.

Dickinson's playful appropriation of Paul's own words to present her own contradictory point of view is demonstrated again in another letter, this time to her close friends Samuel Bowles and his wife, Mary.[44] Here, she describes the pleasures of a morning ride she had taken that morning with her brother Austin: 'I rode with Austin this morning. He showed me mountains that touched the sky, and brooks that sang like Bobolinks. Was he not very kind? I will give them to you; for they are mine and "all things are mine" excepting "Cephas and Apollos", for whom I have no taste.'[45] Here, Dickinson quotes from 1 Cor. 3.21-22, Paul's message to the Corinthian Christians concerning unity. In this section of the letter, the apostle urges his audience to avoid having any special loyalty or allegiance to particular human teachers or preachers, insisting that all things in this world are in

---

41. Thomas H. Johnson (ed.), *The Complete Poems of Emily Dickinson* (New York: Back Bay Books/Little Brown and Company, 1960), p. 602. Similarly, in her poem 'Nature Is What We See—' (Bianchi and Hampson, *Poems of Emily Dickinson*, p. 233), she boldly declares that 'Nature is Heaven'.

42. Todd, *Letters of Emily Dickinson*, I, p. 141.

43. Todd, *Letters of Emily Dickinson*, I, p. 141.

44. Todd, *Letters of Emily Dickinson*, I, p. 212. The letter is dated June 1858.

45. Todd, *Letters of Emily Dickinson*, I, p. 212.

the service of the church, gifted by the grace of God through the death of Christ.[46] 'All things belong to you', he avers, dismissing the claims of some Corinthian Christians that they 'belonged' in terms of loyalty or service to a particular apostle (1 Cor. 1.12). Naming three of these apostles—Paul, Cephas and Apollos—Paul then asserts that *they* 'belong' to the church, not vice versa: 'Whether Paul or Apollos or Cephas or the world or life or death or the present or the future—all belong to you' (1 Cor. 3.22). Again, we see Dickinson take but one element of Paul's message here and use it creatively to express her *own* viewpoint and priorities. Her desire is to share the joys of a beautiful morning ride with her friends, and she appropriates Paul's words to validate her right to such a sharing; her mischievous rejection of Cephas and Apollos deflects from the apostle's message of church unity, bringing his words firmly down to earth and situating them within the earthly joys of the soaring mountain skyline and the babbling brook.

As well as being empowered and inspired by the natural world around her, Dickinson's spirituality and faith were also heavily invested in the companionship, loyalty and love of those friends and family whom she held dear. It was in these friendships that she, once again, seemed to find a sense of the paradisiacal; thus, in a letter to her friend Adelaide Hills, written in the spring of 1871, she writes 'to be loved is heaven',[47] while in another correspondence to her beloved cousins Louisa and Frances Norcross in April 1873, she asserts, 'Each of us gives or takes heaven in corporeal person, for each of us has the skill of life'.[48] Such beliefs again led her on occasion to engage with some of Paul's teachings and, in particular, to challenge or subvert what she regarded as his prioritizing of a future heavenly life over humanity's present earthly existence.

Thus, in a letter to her close friend and sister-in-law, Susan Gilbert Dickinson, written on 9 October 1851,[49] Dickinson again selectively paraphrases one of Paul's statements in a way that affirms her own deep regard for human, rather than heavenly, affairs.[50] Singling out a phrase from the apostle's triumphant assertion of the power of Christ's love for humankind (Rom. 8.38-39), she utilizes it instead to champion the very earthly love she feels for her friend. Paul's conviction is rooted firmly in the supremacy

---

46. For further discussion of this passage, see Joseph A. Fitzmyer, *First Corinthians: A New Translation with Introduction and Commentary* (AB, 32; New Haven, CT: Yale University Press, 2008), pp. 208-209.

47. Johnson, *Letters of Emily Dickinson*, II, p. 487.

48. Todd, *Letters of Emily Dickinson*, II, p. 278.

49. Susan Dickinson (née Gilbert) was married to Dickinson's brother Austin and was, for a number of years, one of Dickinson's closest friends. See Alfred Habegger, *My Wars Are Laid Away in Books: The Life of Emily Dickinson* (New York: Random House, 2001), pp. 375-82.

50. Johnson, *Letters of Emily Dickinson*, I, pp. 143-45.

and inexhaustibility of divine love; nothing at all, 'height nor depth, nor anything else in all creation' will be able to separate believers from the love of God that is in Christ (v. 39). Such a heady affirmation is adopted by Dickinson for a much more corporeal purpose—to stress to her beloved sister-in-law that, even when she was away (Susan was in Baltimore), Dickinson was still able to write to her: 'Susie, *did* you think that I would never write you when you were gone away—what made you? ... I should be *constrained* to write—for what shall separate us from any whom we love—not "*hight* [sic] nor depth".'[51] Here, Dickinson once again appropriates a Pauline affirmation to meet her own purposes, which remain very much rooted in the earthly domain; Paul's credo of faith in the all-powerful and enduring love of God becomes, in her hands, an assertion of faith in the precious and equally enduring power of human friendships. As Martin states, Dickinson appeared to believe that 'worship is owed not to God but to friends, especially to her female friends'.[52]

In another instance, Dickinson critically engages with Paul's assertions in 1 Cor. 15.51-53 that the resurrection of Christ leads to the great 'mystery'; that is, the resurrection of the dead and immortality. In a letter to Louise and Frances Norcross written in April 1873, she describes George Eliot (Marian Evans), an author whose writing Dickinson greatly admired, as a 'mortal' who 'has already put on immortality'; 'the mysteries of human nature surpass the "mysteries of redemption"', she states, 'for the infinite we only suppose, while we see the finite'.[53] Here, Dickinson destabilizes Paul's affirmations of human 'corruptibility' and fallibility and rejects his insistence on the superiority of the infinite soul over the finite, physical body. Instead, she boldly states her preference for human nature in all its encounterable corporeality and mortality over an uncertain and unknowable future immortality. For Dickinson, people such as George Eliot had value and worth in the here and now, not just in some unforeseeable heavenly future; Eliot's 'immortality' lay in her glorious writing; her 'mystery' was wrapped up in her human nature, not in any potential redemption she may receive in some unforeseeable time to come.

Dickinson also uses one of her poems to question another of Paul's statements on the fallibility of the flesh in 1 Corinthians 15, thereby again asserting her belief in the infinite worth of human life and human community.[54] This time, she takes to task the apostle's claim in vv. 42-43 that the body is 'sown in dishonour' and 'sown in corruption' prior to its being raised in glory, incorruptibility and power through the resurrection. She thus chal-

---

51. Johnson, *Letters of Emily Dickinson*, I, p. 145.
52. Martin, *Cambridge Introduction to Emily Dickinson*, p. 64.
53. Todd, *Letters of Emily Dickinson*, II, p. 279.
54. Bianchi and Hampson, *Poems of Emily Dickinson*, p. 257.

lenges Paul's supposed adherence to the doctrines (embraced by Puritan Calvinism) of human sinfulness and Total Depravity, and his understanding of human life as inherently corrupt and dishonourable. '"Sown in dishonor"!/ Ah! Indeed!' she exclaims, 'May *this* dishonor be?'[55] Dickinson's tone within this poem is a mix of doubt and incredulity; she cannot accept that this life she so cherishes is rooted in sin and dishonour. Citing the biblical text using her own language of doubt and protest, her emphatic *'this'* in the second line of the first stanza refers perhaps to her own poetic activity here; she recognizes that, in the eyes of traditional Pauline orthodoxy, her earthly 'resurrection' of the apostle's words within this poem may stand accused of being a dishonouring event, tainted by her own inherent human sinfulness.[56]

Yet, Dickinson resists such an appraisal of her activity, as her critique in the second stanza becomes more explicitly directed toward Paul: '"Sown in corruption"!/Not so fast!/Apostle is askew!'[57] Here, she applies the brakes to Paul's assertions of human depravity; humankind is not, in her mind, innately dishonoured, corrupt or sinful. Her brief mention of the 'circumstance or two' that she suggests Paul 'narrates' in 1 Corinthians 15 to substantiate his belief in human corruptibility does nothing to inspire our confidence in his claims.[58] For Dickinson, Paul's promise of an incorrupt body following resurrection is of secondary concern; as in her other writings mentioned earlier, she attempts here to disrupt and destabilize the Pauline prioritization of the heavenly dominion, preferring instead to delight in the pleasures of humanity in this present earthly life.

Conclusion

In this chapter, I have taken a brief journey through some of the complexities of Emily Dickinson's spirituality and faith, focusing on some of her engagements with the apostle Paul. Dickinson quoted Paul often, at times with humour, at other times with a sense of frustration, but always with a consuming interest in what he had to say. Through the language and words of her poetry and letters, she explored, confronted, questioned and—from time to time—engaged playfully with the words of the apostle, in order to give rich timbre to her own unique faith that was deeply embedded in the world around her. At times, she thoroughly unbalances the spiritual and heaven-centred gaze of this 'orator of Ephesus',[59] thrusting it earthwards

---

55. Bianchi and Hampson, *Poems of Emily Dickinson*, p. 257 (original italics).

56. Bianchi and Hampson, *Poems of Emily Dickinson*, p. 257; Linda Freedman, *Emily Dickinson and the Religious Imagination* (Cambridge: Cambridge University Press, 2011), p. 171.

57. Bianchi and Hampson, *Poems of Emily Dickinson*, p. 257.

58. Bianchi and Hampson, *Poems of Emily Dickinson*, p. 257.

59. Johnson, *Letters of Emily Dickinson*, I, p. 92.

to confront elements of human existence, such as family, friendship and the natural world. Through her challenges to Paul's teachings, along with her absolute commitment to her place within this earthly life, Dickinson exudes a spirituality that gives 'full recognition and exploration of lived and felt experience'.[60] Her relationship with Paul is complex, audacious and utterly fascinating in its bold refusal to acquiesce to or accept unquestioningly the apostle's teachings. As a woman writing from the 'margins' of nineteenth-century male-dominated biblical scholarship, she had the freedom to engage with Paul on her *own* terms, recontextualize his words within her own unique location—the gendered spaces of home, garden and family.

---

60. Roxanne Harde, 'Who Has Not Found', p. 174.

LEGACIES

16

MOANA HERMENEUTICS:
CHARTING A NIU DIRECTION

Nāsili Vaka'uta

Having the freedom to ask questions (*fa'a 'eke*) and the courage to 'talk-back' (*kau'i-talanoa/taungutu*) are two fundamental aspects of what I do as a person and a biblical scholar.[1] I see both as *practices of freedom*: one interrogates; the other interrupts. Interrogation and interruption are vital tools for those in the margins and the undersides of texts, church and society. Interrogation keeps those in power accountable; interruption breaks up patterns of control. Both tools serve as the 'oars' that propel the *waka* (canoe) of Moana hermeneutics forward.[2]

I use the term 'Moana hermeneutics' instead of Oceanic hermeneutics for various reasons. First, to situate this talanoa within te Moana Nui a Kiwa, the Great Moana, as the common home for Moana islanders: a home with very rich and diverse cultures, traditions, beliefs and knowledge, yet a home that is abused/violated by the legacies of colonization and racism, the unjust and brutal effects of neoliberalism/economic exclusion, the harsh reality of environmental degradation and climate injustice, and the ongoing problems of domestic violence (against women and children), gender/sexual discrimination and religious intolerance, as well as the proliferation of faith-inspired mis-/dis-information and conspiracy theories (for example, resistance to COVID-19 vaccinations).

Second, I use the term 'Moana hermeneutics' to give this work a name that is inclusive of islands and islanders and that thereby calls for an end to the use of labels like Polynesia, Micronesia and Melanesia, because they are misleading, divisive, belittling and, to an extent, racist. Moana weaves islands and islanders together and strengthens a shared sense of belonging and identity.

---

1. Those were key components of a culture of learning that was nurtured and encouraged during my undergraduate years, but it was frowned upon by many people within the church who were in the power and control business.

2. This chapter is a revised version of my inaugural address at the Havea Lecture series, Uniting Theological College, North Parramatta, New South Wales, 21 May 2022.

Third, and finally, Moana provides an alternative conceptual frame for doing theology and biblical interpretation—a frame that requires a shift from the *land-obsessed* and *land-grabbing mentality* we encounter in colonial and biblical discourses to the appreciation of nature in its totality.[3]

The word *niu* that I use in the title of this chapter is commonly translated as 'coconut', applying both to the tree and its fruits. In Oceania, *niu* is the 'tree of life'. In this work, I am using *niu* in two ways. First, to call for something *new, fresh*, life-affirming and liberating; something that is not dictated by a dead faith tradition (as in Constantinian orthodoxy),[4] but is shaped by a living present reality rooted in the lived experiences of people here and now. Second, to call for something *niu* (as in coconut) and *local*; something that captures the longings of the peoples and islands of the Moana, something that expresses their concerns and symbolizes their hopes; something is-landic, salty and fluid (to use a few of Jione Havea's terminologies).

The title of this chapter implies that the goals for biblical interpretation have changed, the wind of scholarship has shifted, some life-threatening issues have disrupted our lives and affected the well-being of people; so there is a need for a *readjustment* of our 'sails'. Not that we have to go with the flow, but it is important to rechart our course based on the currents/weather of the day.

My task therefore is simple and straightforward. I will offer a very general talanoa on how far we have come vis-à-vis works produced by Moana biblical scholars, especially Jione Havea's publications. I will then lay out a brief proposal for what I think Moana hermeneutics should look like. There is no attempt to prescribe a one-size-fits-all approach. It is rather an admission of where my thinking is at present. I will put the spotlight on key areas for further consideration, hoping to get somewhere in the end.

Moana Hermeneutics

Moana Hermeneutics can be defined as (to borrow from my definition of *island-marking* texts)

---

3. If I may add one more reason: I claim the name because Trinity College (where I work) came up with the name for one of our courses Moana Hermeneutics, a paper within the Moana studies strand of our Bachelor of Theology programme. This undergraduate theology degree is the first to have Moana studies as a major area of specialization.

4. See Wes Howard-Brook, *Empire Baptized: How the Church Embraced What Jesus Rejected* (Maryknoll, NY: Orbis Books, 2016). See also Rodney J. Decker, 'The Bauer Thesis: An Overview', in Paul A. Hartog (ed.), *Orthodoxy and Heresy in Early Christian Contexts: Reconsidering the Bauer Thesis* (Cambridge: Lutterworth Press, 2015), pp. 6-33.

a reading of the bible[5] that arises out of island/Moana contexts, shaped by island/Moana cultures and values, gives privilege to island/Moana knowledge systems (epistemologies) and languages, reads the bible through island/Moana lenses, takes account of critical issues that confront Moana islanders, and serves the interests of the islands and islanders.[6]

The origin of Moana hermeneutics can be traced back to contextual theological proposals in the 1980s, like Sione 'A. Havea's 'coconut theology', and those published in the seminal volume *South Pacific Theology*.[7] These proposals marked a jubilee moment in doing theology in Oceania, as they initiated a departure from 'missionary-positioned' theologies in search of something closer to home that reflects people's ways of being. What was lacking, however, was any proposal with a direct link to biblical studies.

Imagine yourself sitting in a semester-long postgraduate course on Pacific hermeneutics, at a theological institution at the heart of the Pacific, only to find out at the end that there was nothing Pacific about the course at all—not even the lecturer. That was my experience as an MTh student at the Pacific Theological College in Suva, Fiji, in 1995. I felt confused and frustrated by the lack of Pacific components in the biblical studies courses we did.

A few of us in the MTh programme wanted to do something, but we did not know how. It was a bit terrifying to make an attempt, because we had been taught to read texts using traditional methods of biblical interpretation. But hope came when the *Pacific Journal of Theology* published a few of Jione Havea's early attempts to do contextual readings.[8] It took me almost ten years, however, to do something along that line when I did my doctoral research at the University of Auckland. Jione Havea continued to be a source of encouragement and a conversation partner along the way, but apart from him, there was no one on the ground except my two doctoral supervisors: one was a special Australian, Professor Elaine Wainwright (Sisters of Mercy); the other was a very understanding Englishman, the late Dr Tim Bulkeley. Both of them created a friendly space for me to be

---

5. I use 'bible' not 'Bible' throughout this chapter because I consider our own Indigenous 'texts' as scriptural and sacred, and they should therefore be given similar treatment.

6. Nasili Vaka'uta, 'Island-Marking Texts: Engaging the Bible in Oceania', in *Islands, Islanders, and the Bible: RumInations* (Atlanta, GA: SBL, 2015), pp. 57-64 (57).

7. *South Pacific Theology: Papers from the Consultation on Pacific Theology, Papua New Guinea, January 1986* (Parramatta: Regnum Books, 1987).

8. E.g. Jione Havea, 'The Future Stands Between Here and There: Towards an Island(Ic) Hermeneutics', *The Pacific Journal of Theology* 2.13 (1995), pp. 61-68; *idem*, 'Shifting the Boundaries: House of God and Politics of Reading', *The Pacific Journal of Theology* 2.16 (1996), pp. 55-71; *idem*, 'A Resting King David: 2 Samuel 7 and [Dis]Placements. San Francisco, November 22-24 1997', in *Post-Structuralist Research on the Hebrew Bible* (AAR/SBL, San Francisco, 1997); *idem*, 'Numbers', in Daniel Patte (ed.), *Global Bible Commentary* (Nashville, TN: Abingdon, 2004), pp. 43-51.

different in the way I think and express my ideas on biblical interpretation. The result was published as a monograph by the Society of Biblical Literature (SBL) in their then new series International Voices in Biblical Studies (IVBS). The monograph's title is *Reading Ezra 9–10 Tu'a-wise: Rethinking Biblical Interpretation in Oceania.*[9]

The goal of that work was 'to develop ... an "alter–native"[10] approach to biblical interpretation from a Tongan standpoint and to depart, on the other hand, from theories and methods that dominate biblical scholarship'.[11] This alter-native approach puts more emphasis on *contextualizing interpretation* than on the bible itself. The former is about employing contextual or, more specifically, Indigenous categories of analysis for interpretation, whereas the latter is about applying the insights from one's reading to one's situation or tracing correspondence between a text and one's context. One is about methodology; the other is about application.

During my PhD studies, I wanted to prove (first, to myself, and second, to the academy) that a Tongan reading of biblical texts can make a difference in this area of scholarship. I was so passionate about that task that, when it was time for my viva voce, one of the external examiners asked me how I felt about what I did. My response: 'I set out in this journey to do a task, and I think I have done it. So, I don't care if you give me a pass or fail; I've done my job.' (They were generous enough to award the degree, but my supervisor, Professor Elaine Wainwright, who was sitting nervously inside the room, asked me afterwards, 'What were you thinking?')

To me, Indigenous projects like Moana hermeneutics are more than developing a theory of interpretation; they are more than completing a degree; they are more than publishing an article or a book; they are more than talanoa in academic forums. This kind of project has to be driven by a strong desire to survive, because it is about survival: our survival! Survival in this context means an acknowledgment of our existence because we are being ignored and deemed absent. It is about having access to life in its fullness. Any Indigenous project that aims below the desire for survival, for presence and for life is, in my opinion, not worth doing.

A lot of great projects have emerged in the last decade, and most are due largely to the leadership of Havea in encouraging collaboration among scholars from island contexts (the Caribbean for example) and mobilizing Moana islanders (especially from Tonga and Samoa) to get involved in biblical studies forums and book projects.

---

9. Nāsili Vaka'uta, *Reading Ezra 9–10 Tu'a-wise: Rethinking Biblical Interpretation in Oceania* (IVBS; Atlanta, GA: SBL, 2011).

10. The term 'alter–native' indicates that the approach I will develop in this work is not just another approach but seeks to alter existing approaches using native insights, and, if necessary, it will also alter what is native.

11. Vaka'uta, *Reading Ezra 9–10*, p. 2.

These collaborations have led to the following:

- The inclusion of *island reading/criticism* as one of the options for interpretation listed by the SBL.
- The set-up of a unit on 'Islands, Islanders and the Bible' within SBL, which has been part of its annual meetings.
- The establishment of the Oceania Biblical Studies Association (OBSA) alongside Talanoa Oceania to focus on promoting biblical scholarship in the region.
- Partnerships between OBSA and other bodies like the Society of Asian Biblical Studies (SABS) and the Aotearoa New Zealand Association of Biblical Studies (ANZABS).
- The publication of volumes such as *Islands, Islanders, and the Bible*,[12] *Bible, Borders, Belonging(s)*,[13] *The Bible and Art: Perspectives from Oceania*,[14] *Sea of Readings*,[15] *Bible Blindspots*,[16] *Bordered Bodies, Bothered Voices*,[17] and a series of volumes from the Council for World Mission (CWM) Global Forum on Discernment and Radical Engagement (DARE), edited by Jione and published by Lexington Books.[18]
- Contributions to projects like *Voices from the Margin*,[19] the Texts@ Contexts series,[20] minoritized criticism,[21] and several monographs and

---

12. Jione Havea, Margaret Aymer and Steed Vernyl Davidson (eds.), *Islands, Islanders, and the Bible: RumInations* (Atlanta, GA: SBL, 2015).

13. Jione Havea, David J. Neville and Elaine M. Wainwright (eds.), *Bible, Borders, Belonging(s): Engaging Readings from Oceania* (Semeia Studies, 75; Atlanta, GA: SBL, 2014).

14. Caroline Blyth and Nasili Vaka'uta (eds.), *The Bible and Art, Perspectives from Oceania* (London: Bloomsbury T. & T. Clark, 2017).

15. Jione Havea (ed.), *Sea of Readings: The Bible in the South Pacific* (Atlanta, GA: SBL, 2018).

16. Jione Havea and Monica Jyotsna Melanchthon (eds.), *Bible Blindspots: Dispersion and Othering* (Eugene, OR: Pickwick Publications, 2021).

17. Nasili Vaka'uta, 'Kalanga: (Sh)Outing Bodily Abuse in the Bible, Society, and Churches', in Jione Havea (ed.), *Bordered Bodies, Bothered Voices: Native and Migrant Theologies* (Eugene, OR: Pickwick Publications, 2022), pp. 162-72.

18. Jione Havea (ed.), *Religion and Power* (Lanham, MD: Lexington Books/Fortress Academic, 2019); *idem* (ed.), *Scripture and Resistance* (Lanham, MD: Lexington Books/Fortress Academic, 2019); *idem* (ed.), *Vulnerability and Resilience: Body and Liberating Theologies* (Lanham, MD: Lexington Books/Fortress Academic, 2020).

19. Rasiah S. Sugirtharajah, *Voices from the Margin: Interpreting the Bible in the Third World. 25th Anniversary Edition* (Maryknoll, NY: Orbis Books, 2016).

20. Athalya Brenner, *Genesis: Texts @ Contexts* (ed. Archie Chi-chung Lee and Gale A. Yee; Minneapolis, MN: Fortress Press, 2010).

21. Tat-Siong Benny Liew and Fernando F. Segovia (eds.), *Reading Biblical Texts Together: Pursuing Minoritized Biblical Criticism* (Atlanta, GA: SBL, 2022).

graduate theses from Moana students in various theological institutions.

These projects have taken the course of Moana hermeneutics in multiple directions, with emphases on key issues such as migration and citizenship, climate injustice and the legacies of colonialism and slavery. These projects, however, are not products of abstract theoretical endeavours but are part and parcel of a movement that begins from where we are in search of answers to our questions and solutions to our problems.

A Movement

Moana hermeneutics is a movement; it is a journey toward purposeful actions. It dances around to the beat of four fundamental phases (see Fig. 1) reflecting along the way the cyclical Moana worldview and life-world.

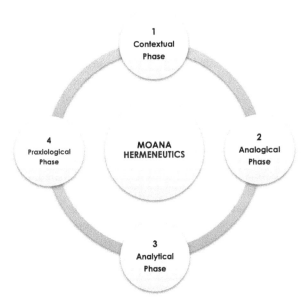

Figure 1: Phases of Moana Hermeneutics

The Contextual Phase

Moana hermeneutics begins at home as a contextual project. This may sound like a cliché, but it is fundamental to any hermeneutical project to have an awareness of its own venue/setting. Where I situate myself becomes the starting point for my hermeneutical dance/movement. I won't be able to tell where I am going without knowing where I am. I can only chart my direction if I know my location.

Moana hermeneutics is situated and rooted within the various Moana cultures and immerses itself in an ocean of opportunities and challenges. Indigenous cultures and local contexts give Moana hermeneutics the 'life-breath' required for its movement. As such, participants in this movement ought to have a clear understanding of the key issues on the ground and be able to know how people are positioned in relation to power and access to scarce resources.[22]

In this phase, Moana hermeneutics seeks to establish answers to basic questions such as: Who am I? Where am I? What is going on around me? Where do I/we need to go?

Close attention needs to be directed at persisting problems like climate injustice, gender injustice, colonialism and racism, to name but a few. It is also essential to understand current issues like data imperialism (the process by which corporations like Facebook claim ownership of data collected from users), digital divide (the gap between groups that have access to modern information and technology), and the impact of artificial intelligence (AI) (computers and machines that are developed to act and behave like human beings). To be ignorant of what affects people and nature in Oceania is detrimental in many ways.

The Analogical Phase

Once the answers to the above questions are established, Moana hermeneutics steps into the analogical phase, which seeks to weave together a framework for interpretation. This phase proceeds from context to text, placing emphasis on what is familiar with readers as maps for engaging texts.

This phase can employ cultural concepts and ideas as metaphors/analogies to guide interpretation; trace correspondences between biblical narratives and local stories/myths and allow the latter to shed light on the former; and juxtapose biblical faith tradition with Indigenous ones, not to evaluate one on the basis of the other, but to let them illuminate each other.

The basic requirements for this phase include acceptance of Indigenous cultures as valid sites for academic discourses; appreciation of local myths

---

22. Generally speaking, acknowledging this phase is largely absent from continental/colonial hermeneutics (as if these hermeneutics approach the interpretive task from an other-worldly setting).

and their role in positioning people in relation to power and access to scarce resources; and the acknowledgment of Indigenous/native beliefs and Scriptures.

For the most part, Moana scholars have done well in this regard. The many publications from Havea and others have employed some interesting analogies. For example:

- The use of island-ocean features as lenses for understanding texts, subjects, meaning and interpretation (Havea).
- The various articulations of the Fijian concept of *vanua,* both from Fijians in Fiji and those in diaspora like Seforosa Carroll[23] and the late Ilaitia Sevati Tuwere.[24]
- The use of Moana art as in *tatau* (Havea)[25] and *ngatu* making (Vaka'uta)[26] as reading markers.
- The employment of Māori categories like *whenua* and *whakapapa* (Beverley Moana Hall-Smith)[27]
- The utilization of traditional wisdom sayings, as in the doctoral research of Moana scholars, two of whom are Brian Fanolua Kolia[28] and Fatilua Fatilua.[29]

23. Seforosa Carroll, 'Reimagining Home: A Diasporic Perspective on Encounters with the Religious Other in Australia', in Heup Young Kim, Fumitaka Matsuoka and Anri Morimoto (eds.), *Asian and Oceanic Christianities in Conversation: Exploring Theological Identities at Home and in Diaspora* (New York: Rodopi, 2011), pp. 169-84.

24. Ilaitia S. Tuwere, *Vanua: Towards a Fijian Theology of Place* (Suva, Fiji: Institute of Pacific Studies, 2009).

25. Jione Havea, 'Tatauing Cain: Reading the Sign on Cain from the Ground', in Caroline Blyth and Nasili Vaka'uta (eds.), *The Bible and Art: Perspectives from Oceania* (London: Bloomsbury T. & T. Clark, 2017), pp. 187-202.

26. Nāsili Vaka'uta, 'Art as Method', in Caroline Blyth and Nasili Vaka'uta (eds.), *The Bible and Art: Perspectives from Oceania* (London: Bloomsbury T. & T. Clark Academic, 2017), pp. 97-116.

27. Beverley Moana Hall-Smith, *Whakapapa (Genealogy), a Hermeneutical Framework for Reading Biblical Texts: A Māori Woman Encounters Rape and Violence in Judges 19–21* (PhD diss., Flinders University, 2017). See also Nasili Vaka'uta, 'It's Whenua, Stupid! A Māori Twist on 1 Kings 21', in Tat-Siong Benny Liew and Fernando F. Segovia (eds.), *Reading Biblical Texts Together: Pursuing Minoritized Biblical Criticism* (Atlanta, GA: SBL, 2022), pp. 221-35.

28. Brian F. Kolia, *Maota Tau Ave: Towards an Australian-Samoan Diasporic Understanding of Wisdom in Ecclesiastes* (PhD diss., University of Divinity, Melbourne, 2021).

29. Fatilua Fatilua, *Seu le manu ae taga'i i le galu: A Socio-rhetorical Inquiry of the Political Economic Context—Steering a Pacific Island Reading of Luke 18:18-30* (PhD diss., Pacific Theological College, Suva, Fiji, 2022).

The main challenge in this phase is how to avoid using Indigenous cultural categories to mask non-contextual ideas. For a *niu* (coconut) cannot be used as an analogy (a mask) for an apple. It can only be explained within the environment in which it grows and flourishes.

The Analytical Phase

This third phase of Moana hermeneutics is about analysis and connecting. In a Tongan context, interpretation is about relevance and relation. Meaning is defined not as an abstract phenomenon but as a point of intersection, where two or more parties meet. Where there is no connection, there is no relevance or meaning. The goal of interpretation, therefore, is not to gather information or find meaning; that is a part of the task, but the end goal is to establish something that is transformative and life-affirming.

This is the methodological phase. It deals with the way we read and interpret texts. It lays out the 'how' and scrutinizes the text accordingly. This is where interrogation and interruption come into play. The analytical phase uses the key aspects of the analogical phase as tools for analysis. It formulates key questions from each category for interpretation.

The key requirements here are to use the Indigenous tools available, think about one's cultural ways of meaning making, and rename alien categories. So far in Moana biblical scholarship, this is the weakest link. Despite the employment of Indigenous categories at the analogical level, many are still comfortable with the master's tools as though we have none in the region, and most of the questions asked in various publications do not really answer what we in Oceania are grappling with.

If we shift our emphasis at the analogical level to Moana metaphors for interpretation, we need to identify the key aspects of those metaphors, trace the kind of questions they would pose to texts, and use those questions as our reading tools, because we need to ask different questions—those that are relevant to us.

Is this possible? Absolutely! And we can no longer claim that we are just reading texts (biblical or otherwise); that is another way of saying we have internalized the ethos of colonial readings without admitting it. We have to be transparent and honest about the way we read because our readings have the power to affect real people within our communities.[30]

The Praxeological Phase

The fourth, and final, phase for the movement of Moana hermeneutics is the praxeological phase.[31] Moana hermeneutics is not merely a theoretical and/

---

30. See Vaka'uta, 'Kalanga', pp. 162-72.
31. Ludwig von Mises in his work *Human Action: A Treatise on Economics*, Volume

or a methodological exercise. It bends toward actions, purposeful actions (*praxis*). It is never satisfied with meanings/information; it seeks to make positive changes with meanings/information.

Moana hermeneutics is interested in justice issues that affect people's lives. Published works from Moana scholars have dealt with many of these issues. I would also emphasize that the following issues deserve serious attention and immediate action. First, the threat posed by data imperialism and privacy rights. People's personal information is collected as a commodity by various online platforms (Facebook, Twitter, Instagram, etc.), not to mention online surveillance by government agencies and corporations the world over. People's exclusive rights to privacy are violated and manipulated. How might we read the bible where God is characterized as all-knowing, ceaselessly surveilling our movements and having access to our innermost secrets, almost like a divine stalker?

Second, the problem of post-truth and mis-/dis-information. We encounter on a regular basis various attacks on information that is vital to our existence and well-being, inspired in many cases by faith communities and their interpretations of Scripture. How might we address this problem through interpretation, when what we seek to interpret (i.e. the bible's grand narrative) is littered with misinformation?

Third, the ongoing struggle against modern-day slavery and supremacist narratives. The legacies of colonization and slavery are still real, though manifesting themselves in new forms. Colonial masters continue to stalk their prey differently. How shall we go about interpreting the bible where slavery is the norm and violent narratives of supremacy become the expressions of God's promises and redemption?

These are 'rough waters'. A collective effort that integrates and aligns the four phases I have just discussed is required to make sure Moana hermeneutics dances toward transformation and life-flourishing situations, where everyone is free to live life to the full.

In Closing ...

There are two tasks that must go hand in hand to ensure *niu*-ness of Moana hermeneutics:

First, it is necessary to develop more Indigenous methods for reading. The problem is that a lot of Moana scholars are still stuck within the fold

---

3 (Eastford, CT: Martino Fine Books, 1940) defines praxeology as the science of human action. The specific method of praxeology is not formal logic or mathematics, but is rather what Mises calls the method of imaginary constructions. An imaginary construction is a conceptual image of a sequence of events, logically evolved from the elements of action employed in its formation (p. 12).

of Western methods. I am not saying this is a bad thing; but if we complain about the malestream and Eurocentric orientations of Western methods, let us develop some Moana ways of interpretation because we have a rich knowledge tradition.

Second, there is a need for cultural and, hence, textual de-valorization. This means we have to lift up our own cultures and texts from the underside of academia and church and give them due appreciation. I am not endorsing a non-critical acceptance of what we have, but we need to say that these are our Moana cultures and Scriptures and they are as valid as European/imperial cultures and Scriptures.

Doing Moana hermeneutics is not about sitting idly on our *waka* drifting with the flow; it is in most cases about paddling against the rough currents, feeling the surface of the waters, tasting the saltiness of the deep, listening to the voices of the waves as we allow ourselves to be lost in the embrace of the Moana, breathing life into us and connecting us together, here and now.

17

Professor Elaine Wainwright's *Silasila Mamao* (Watching from a Distance) and Matthew 27.55-56: Biblical Studies and Women in the Samoan Christian World

Vaitusi Nofoaiga

It is a privilege to contribute an article to this publication to celebrate the great work done by Professor Elaine Wainwright. Elaine is known not only for her outstanding research on the Bible but also for her endeavours to recognize the voices of biblical readers who are marginalized by traditional methods of interpretation.[1] This article recognizes two of the many important aspects of Elaine's work on the Gospel of Matthew: first, her reading approach acknowledges the importance of the reader's context;[2] and second, she explores female discipleship in Matthew.[3] The scope of this article does not allow me to discuss these two important topics in depth. Instead, I will briefly explain them before offering a Samoan reading of Mt. 27.55-56 as an example of a contextual approach to biblical interpretation. My study of this Gospel text serves as my acknowledgment of and debt to her great scholarship.

The Importance of the Reader's Situation in Biblical Interpretation

Elaine has always recognized that biblical readers' contemporary issues, social status and location inevitably inform the interpretative process.[4]

---

1. For example, traditional interpretation of discipleship at the global level overlooks the significance of discipleship at the local level. See Vaitusi Nofoaiga, *A Samoan Reading of Discipleship in Matthew* (Atlanta, GA: SBL Press, 2017).

2. See Elaine M. Wainwright, 'Feminist Criticism and the Gospel of Matthew', in Mark Allan Powell (ed.), *Methods for Matthew* (Cambridge: Cambridge University Press, 2009), pp. 83-117.

3. See Elaine M. Wainwright, *Towards a Feminist Critical Reading of the Gospel According to Matthew* (BZNW, 60; Berlin: de Gruyter, 1991).

4. David Jasper, *A Short Introduction to Hermeneutics* (Louisville, KY: Westmin-

Elaine's approach reflects a gradual shift in biblical interpretation over the past few decades, with a growing number of interpreters adopting structuralist, humanistic and critical approaches to studying the biblical texts, rather than classical hermeneutical epistemology.[5] In other words, in contrast to traditional methods of interpretation that focus predominantly on uncovering the 'original meaning' intended by the text's author, biblical interpretation today also considers the world of the reader, which brings a whole new dimension to the interpretative process.[6] Every reader brings their own perspectives and questions to the text, and these perspectives and questions will shape their analysis. This does not mean that the reader can simply impose their own meaning upon the text. Rather, there is a recognition that meaning-making is influenced by the issues the reader *brings* from their contemporary situation and *takes back* to that situation.

Considering the reader's context to be important, Fernando F. Segovia speaks of the location of meaning as an encounter between text and the 'flesh-and-blood' reader.[7] This differs from the traditional approaches of historical and literary criticism, which primarily locate meaning in the world of the text or the world of the author. Such a shift raises the question: how did practitioners and proponents of traditional methods of biblical criticism overlook the perspectives and agendas of readers whose interpretations are necessarily affected by their socio-cultural, economic, religious and political locations? This oversight began to be remedied in the mid-1970s with the emergence of several biblical studies that foregrounded readers' personal and/or social locations. Through these studies, new ideo-

ster John Knox, 2004), pp. 104-106; Anthony C. Thiselton, *The Two Horizons: New Testament Hermeneutical Philosophical Description with Special Reference to Heidegger, Bultmann, Gadamer and Wittgenstein* (Exeter: Paternoster, 1980), pp. 24-47; Hans-Georg Gadamer, *Truth and Method* (trans. Joel Weinsheimer and Donald G. Marshall; New York: Seabury, 1975), pp. 356-57.

5. The historical outline of the progress of hermeneutics is briefly explained in Jasper, *A Short Introduction to Hermeneutics.* See also the various chapters in Steven L. McKenzie and Stephen R. Haynes (eds.), *To Each its Own Meaning: An Introduction to Biblical Criticisms and their Application* (Louisville, KY: Westminster John Knox Press, rev. edn, 1999), pp. 183-283.

6. This is evident in the emergence of the Islander Criticism approach to biblical interpretation in Oceania and Samoa, where biblical scholars from these parts of the world interpret the Bible using their understanding and experience of issues and situations they encounter in their own contexts.

7. Fernando F. Segovia, 'Cultural Studies and Contemporary Biblical Criticism: Ideological Criticism as Mode of Discourse', in Fernando F. Segovia and Mary Ann Tolbert (eds.), *Reading from This Place: Social Location and Biblical Interpretation in Global Perspective* (2 vols.; Minneapolis, MN: Fortress Press, 1995), II, pp. 1-17.

logical approaches were developed and subsequently institutionalized into the mainstream of biblical studies.[8]

This shift toward the reader is evident in Elaine's feminist studies of the Bible, such as her interpretations of discipleship in the Gospel of Matthew.[9] Feminist criticism, as the most prominent among the newer hermeneutical approaches, is a well-known form of ideological critique which engages the text and challenges dominant methods of interpretation through the filter of women's experience and the critique of patriarchy.[10] Feminist readers whose emphasis is on reading for social or theological liberation—such as the liberation of women in Jesus's ministry—insist on reading discipleship through a lens that opens up the potential for identifying women as also being disciples of Jesus.[11] For example, using the literary-historical method, Elaine's research[12] constitutes a critical reading of Matthew from a feminist perspective, which recognizes and amplifies the voice/s of marginalized women in the text. Thus, her inclusive interpretation of the 'crowd' following Jesus in Mt. 4.25 and its links to the healing of Peter's mother-in-law (8.14-15) and the woman with hemorrhages (9.20-22) is significantly different from the gender-exclusive interpretations of discipleship made by the male European-American scholars

8. See Fernando F. Segovia, 'And They Began to Speak in Other Tongues: Competing Modes of Discourse in Contemporary Biblical Criticism', in Fernando F. Segovia and Mary Ann Tolbert (eds.), *Reading from This Place: Social Location and Biblical Interpretation in the United States* (2 vols.; Minneapolis, MN: Fortress, 1995), I, pp. 1-34. Segovia refers to the approach that signifies the reader's world as 'cultural criticism'. See also R.S. Sugirtharajah, 'Introduction: Vernacular Resurrections', in R.S. Sugirtharajah (ed.), *Vernacular Hermeneutics* (Sheffield: Sheffield Academic Press, 1999), pp. 11-17. Sugirtharajah considers this approach a 'cultural studies approach or vernacular hermeneutics'.

9. Wainwright, *Towards a Feminist Critical Reading*, pp. 27-28.

10. Wainwright, 'Feminist Criticism and the Gospel of Matthew', pp. 83-117, offers an overview of feminist criticism's directions and influence within Matthaean studies.

11. Other examples are Janice Capel Anderson, 'Matthew: Gender and Reading', *Semeia* 28 (1983), pp. 3-27; Elisabeth Schüssler Fiorenza, *Discipleship of Equals: A Critical Feminist Ekklesia-logy of Liberation* (London: SCM Press, 1993).

12. Postcolonial readers also consider the meaning of discipleship in relation to the readers' world, interpreting the text from a postcolonial point of view. For example, Botswanan scholar Musa W. Dube applies postcolonial and feminist lenses to her readings of biblical texts for social liberation. See Musa W. Dube, *Postcolonial Feminist Interpretation of the Bible* (St Louis, MO: Chalice Press, 2000); *idem*, '"Go Therefore and Make Disciples of All Nations" (Matt 8:19a): A Postcolonial Perspective on Biblical Criticism and Pedagogy', in Fernando F. Segovia and Mary Ann Tolbert *Teaching the Bible: The Discourses and Politics of Biblical Pedagogy* (Maryknoll, NY: Orbis Books, 1998), pp. 224-46.

such as Martin Hengel,[13] Gerd Theissen,[14] Stephen Barton[15] and Ulrich Luz.[16] These male-authored studies of discipleship restrict the calling of Jesus's disciples to the all-male twelve, who include the two sets of fishermen brothers named in 4.18-22. Elaine argues that the crowds who 'followed' Jesus in 4.25 are similar to the four fishermen who 'followed' him in 4.20, except that the crowd does not indicate gender differences.[17] Thus, the crowd's following in 4.25 includes both women and men who responded positively to Jesus's ministry.

The story of Peter's mother-in-law (Mt. 8.14-15) is another text that Elaine draws upon to highlight women characters who play important roles in Jesus's ministry; again, her reading differs significantly from some male European-American interpretations. According to Elaine, the healing of Peter's mother-in-law singles out another member of the crowd whose mission is to 'serve' Jesus in her household and beyond.[18] She suggests that, despite its gendered limitations, 'serving' Jesus is nonetheless an action of discipleship. Thus, Elaine regards Peter's mother-in-law as a disciple of Jesus.[19]

Elaine's inclusive interpretation of discipleship in Matthew is explicitly undertaken from her location in the world 'in front of the text' (the world of the reader). She makes sense of the purpose of Jesus's ministry by drawing on her own contextual location as a woman and a feminist. Elaine's reading approach is appropriate to my own search of the Bible for answers to many issues in our Samoan world, such as the issue of women becoming equal leaders in the church. One example of my use of this approach is demonstrated in this chapter. I interpret the presence of women at the crucifixion of Jesus in Mt. 27.55-56 by drawing on the Samoan hermeneutic of *Silasila Mamao*. As will be explored below, the Samoan phrase *Silasila Mamao* metaphorically expresses watching from a distance as a form of profound wisdom. This hermeneutical lens opens new possibilities in the interpretation of Matthew.

---

13. Martin Hengel, *The Charismatic Leader and his Followers* (trans. James C.G. Greig; Edinburgh: T. & T. Clark, 1981); Ulrich Luz, *Matthew 1–7* (trans. James E. Crouch; Minneapolis, MN: Fortress, 2007).

14. Gerd Theissen, *The First Followers of Jesus: A Sociological Analysis of the Earliest Christianity* (trans. John Bowden; London: SCM, 1978).

15. Stephen C. Barton, *Discipleship and Family Ties in Mark and Matthew* (SNTSMS, 80; Cambridge: Cambridge University Press, 1994).

16. Luz, *Matthew 1–7*.

17. Wainwright, *Towards a Feminist Critical Reading*, pp. 80-81.

18. Wainwright, *Towards a Feminist Critical Reading*, pp. 83-87.

19. In other words, this woman's act of serving Jesus makes her a servant or disciple of Jesus. This is reflected in Wainwright's point that this woman's service is an example of 'going beyond'.

Using a Silasila Mamao (Watching from a Distance)
Hermeneutic to Guide the Reading of Matthew 27.55-56

Silasila Mamao depicts my own situation and context as an interpreter of the women characters in the Gospel of Matthew. It is a reading that pursues Elaine's consideration of the importance of women in our families, villages, churches and wider society. As a hermeneutic, *Silasila Mamao* describes the action of seeing an event from a distance, which metaphorically implies the importance of thinking deeply or profoundly about that event. In this way, *Silasila Mamao* is another description of wisdom in our Samoan context: it is wisdom to embrace a love for others, such as those in need. Love is shown by recognizing the need of others and then providing the appropriate help. *Silasila Mamao* is a wisdom that comes with the experience of being in the midst of life for a long time.

A woman or a man who is understood in our Samoan community as having *Silasila Mamao* is someone who has served his or her family and community well and with great wisdom. A man of such calibre has to lead his family and village with love, while a woman with *Silasila Mamao* carries on the roles of being a *feagaiga*,[20] or a covenant, not only in the family to which she was born but also in her husband's family. One of those roles involves leading and embracing peace and harmony within the family. A woman accomplishes this by connecting one family member to another in a mutual relationship, where everyone helps one another with love. She puts into practice her role and responsibility as *feagaiga,* or covenant, as in the sister–brother relationship. She is a healer, a teacher, a peacemaker and a mediator within the family. She works as a *sootaga o le manuia ma le filemu*— a person who brings the family together to continue living in peace and harmony. At the same time, she teaches and shows her family the wisdom of living, working together and respecting one another.

For my reading of Mt. 27.55-56, I will integrate the culture of wisdom as depicted in *Silasila Mamao* with the characterization of the women looking on from a distance in Matthew's crucifixion scene. According to the patriarchal ideology of first-century Mediterranean society, women were generally regarded as a disadvantaged group ranked below men.[21] While the wom-

---

20. Penelope Schoeffel, 'The Samoan Concept of *Feagaiga* and its Transformation', in Judith Huntsman (ed.), *Tonga and Samoa: Images of Gender and Polity* (Christchurch, NZ: Macmillan Brown Centre of Pacific Studies, University of Canterbury, 1995), pp. 85-105.

21. In first-century Mediterranean society, the person with 'honour' was a person with high status either in the external or internal government. He or she had an abundance of land and was born to an elite family. People in first-century Mediterranean society receive and achieve honour when their worth and standing are acknowledged in public in accordance with the public social, cultural, economic and religious expectations.

en's act of standing at a distance from Jesus's crucifixion can be understood as symbolic of their supposedly secondary status, the *Silasila Mamao* hermeneutic raises the possibility that, instead, the women's distance illustrates their thinking deeply about how to ameliorate the purpose of God for the world in and through Jesus's death on the cross. By standing 'at a distance', they are taking on the roles of peacemakers, healers and teachers. They are showing that their presence is important, and their wisdom to deal with the purpose of Jesus's crucifixion needs to be embraced and recognized. Thus, they are a group of faithful disciples who should not be ignored by society, for their wisdom goes back to their following Jesus. It is also important to recognize, however, that their watching Jesus from a distance does not just happen during the crucifixion, but emerges earlier in the Matthaean text. We must, therefore, look at Jesus's relationship with women in his ministry to give some further examples of the *Silasila Mamao* of women. In the rest of this chapter, then, I bring in examples from Elaine's own reading of those moments in her book *Towards a Feminist Critical Reading of the Gospel According to Matthew*. But first, I will briefly describe Elaine's understanding of discipleship in Matthew, which shows the inclusive meaning of becoming and being a disciple.

Women as Disciples in Matthew

As noted earlier, Elaine argues that discipleship in Matthew's Gospel is not restricted to the male 'twelve' and that women characters are also disciples of Jesus. Her interpretation reflects the inclusive meaning of discipleship as described by Fernando F. Segovia. According to Segovia, the many interpretations and claims of what discipleship means in Matthew ultimately led to two general definitions.[22] First, discipleship is a tradition

See David A. deSilva, *Honor, Patronage, Kinship & Purity: Unlocking New Testament Culture* (Downers Grove, IL: Intervarsity Press, 2000), pp. 23-94; John H. Elliott, *What Is Social-Scientific Criticism?* (Minneapolis, MN: Fortress Press, 1993), pp. 130, 133-34. On the other hand, 'shame' is the reverse of 'honour'. Despite the sense of negativity associated with the term, 'shame' was culturally accepted in the Mediterranean world (Halvor Moxnes, 'Honor and Shame', in Richard Rohrbaugh (ed.), *The Social Sciences and New Testament Interpretation* [Peabody, MA: Hendrickson, 1996], pp. 19-40 [31-33]). For example, with regard to gender difference, a dominant view in social scientific research on first-century Mediterranean society is that the public sphere tended to be treated as a masculine space, while the private or domestic realm was the expected place for women to inhabit. These gender codes were also understood to involve cultural assumptions about honour and shame, and further embedded widespread patriarchal assumptions onto women's bodies and spaces (Moxnes, 'Honor and Shame', pp. 21-22).

22. According to Fernando F. Segovia, discipleship has both a narrow and a broad definition: 'In the former sense, it is to be understood technically and exclusively in terms of the "teacher"/"disciples" relationship with all its accompanying and derivative

of following Jesus in accordance with the historical master-disciple relationship established between Jesus and the chosen twelve disciples. Second, in Christian theology and practice, 'discipleship' generally refers to the self-understanding of a Christian believer with their daily practice of the teachings of Jesus.

Segovia's definitions of discipleship show that the First Gospel can be regarded as the author's interpretation of the master-disciple relationship structured to consolidate their audience's faith and to make sense within their daily lives. In this way, the definition of discipleship emphasized by Segovia and reflected in Elaine's study of women as disciples in Matthew takes seriously one's self-understanding and experience as a Christian. This self-understanding of discipleship influences how I see discipleship in our Samoan world that is based on my enculturation in the *fa'aSamoa* (the Samoan way) of serving others. And it is revealed in the meaning of *Silasila Mamao*, which is first learned and practised in the family unit and village community. This understanding is expanded by my recognition of the inclusive nature of Jesus's proclamation, ἡ βασιλεία τῶν οὐρανῶν (the kingdom of the heavens). From this perspective, I will explore how Mt. 27.55-56 presents discipleship as the task of following Jesus in such a manner that invites me, as a follower, to meld and mould my understanding of Jesus's vision of ἡ βασιλεία τῶν οὐρανῶν to accord with the world I live in and encounter to survive—a world made up of both men and women.

Women Disciples in Matthew and
their Relationship to Women in Samoan Society

Elaine's consideration of women as disciples in the Gospel of Matthew influences how I regard the recognition of women in Samoan society. One of the challenges women face in their ministry work is not being recognized as equal to men because of their gender and/or status as women. They are marginalized by gendering and elitism in society. I use the term 'gendering' to refer to a social tradition or belief[23] that defines and shapes how women and men should act and behave. Gendering functions hierarchically within the patriarchal tradition, where men are considered leaders in both the private and public spheres. By 'elitism' I mean the 'advocacy of or reliance

terminology (for example, "following" or "on the way"). In the latter sense, discipleship would be understood more generally in terms of Christian existence—that is, the self-understanding of the early Christian believers as believers.' See Fernando F. Segovia, 'Introduction: Call and Discipleship—Toward a Re-examination of the Shape and Character of Christian Existence in the New Testament', in Fernando F. Segovia (ed.), *Discipleship in the New Testament* (Philadelphia, PA: Fortress Press, 1985), pp. 1-23 (2).

23. Wainwright, *Towards a Feminist Critical Reading*, p. 28, defines the term 'gender' as being distinct from sexuality and as a social construct and belief system.

on the leadership or dominance of a select group'.[24] Elitism is a recognized and respected phenomenon of power and knowledge that controls a society or community. Those considered elite believe they are more deserving of power and authority than other people; therefore, they are the most favoured people by society for undertaking the matters of society. Gendering and elitism affect how some Samoan people make decisions in social, cultural, political and religious circles. For example, in Samoan society, gendering and elitism still influence who has authority to become leaders in families, villages, churches and government.[25] The authorization of women to become leaders in the Samoan world, such as becoming chiefs in families and villages or becoming ministers within the church, has been and continues to be highly contested in the Samoan community. Authorization implies empowerment, a legitimate power, framed by laws or constitutions.[26] Authorization involves giving a person of a particular group or organization a legitimate power to undertake any duty assigned for their position within that group. I have witnessed many women's professional contributions to church administration, education and other projects relating to the development of the church and the government in Samoa, but, still, they are not considered good enough to become equal leaders.[27]

Feminist theologians have spoken about issues regarding the inclusion and recognition of women in social roles, such as church leaders and ordained ministers.[28] As a feminist biblical scholar, Elaine has made a contribution to the critical exploration of those issues in her study of the Gospel of Matthew. Feminist theologians question the patriarchal and androcentric traditions that dominate the interpretation of God's message in the Scriptures and throughout the church's history, including practices that portray men as having sole authority to undertake ministry. Campaigns for women's ordination emerged from feminism's wider struggle for women's liberation in patriarchal society. Two of the causes of that struggle are gender inequity and elitism,[29] which lead to the belief that there is already a more suitable group of people (i.e. men) who ought to be authorized as leaders. Hence,

24. Lesley Brown (ed.), *The New Shorter Oxford English Dictionary: The New Authority of English Language* (Oxford: Clarendon, 1993), p. 800.
25. Schoeffel, 'The Samoan Concept of *Feagaiga*', p. 103
26. Rodney J. Arnott (ed.), 'Authority, Concept and Theory of', in *The Dictionary of Pastoral Care and Counselling* (Nashville, TN: Abingdon Press, 1990), pp. 59-61.
27. The recognition of women as leaders in the Samoan Government is beginning to happen, but not in villages and churches.
28. Schüssler Fiorenza, *Discipleship of Equals,* pp. 24-25.
29. This is the culture of favouritism based on gendering and elitism. From my point of view as a Christian Samoan, the culture of favouritism influences the authorisation of people to undertake ministry in Samoan society, and it is an offspring of Christianity, *faa-Samoa* (Samoan way), and Western influences.

women's capacity to be leaders in a Samoan village and a Samoan church is still regarded as a problem.

The gendering of culture and the elitist attitudes in Samoan society discourage women's hopes of becoming leaders. The Samoan people embracing the culture and mindset that rejects women's claims to leadership justify their views of male-only leadership in families and churches by pointing to Jesus's commissioning of twelve *male* disciples (Mt. 4.18-22). This process of selecting people to be authorized in leadership roles is influenced by elitism. In a society such as Samoa, the elite can be easily identified by their material wealth and status.[30] This is discussed by Elaine, when she writes about the function of Scripture:

> It became clear that while the scriptures provided legitimation for the liberation of all who suffered under oppression, they were also used by many within the Christian churches as a weapon against the poor and marginalised, as a means of 'keeping them in their place'.[31]

Concerning the Gospel of Matthew, for example, Elaine shows that patriarchy and androcentrism are encoded in the text. She explains clearly the difference between patriarchy and androcentrism as they are understood in feminism.[32] On the one hand, patriarchy refers to the socio-cultural system that existed in the biblical period and remains present in our contemporary context. Androcentrism, on the other hand, is part of a worldview in terms of language and ideology, which prioritizes a masculine point of view at the expense of feminine identities, interests and concerns. Elaine's distinction between the two terms is adopted in this essay. Patriarchy as a cultural system and androcentrism as a worldview have slowly nullified the equal and shared roles of men and women in today's world, including our Samoan world; these roles ensure peace and harmony in the community, with both men and women acting together in relation to the interests of their families. Elisabeth Schüssler Fiorenza argues that these processes of gendering contrast with the inclusive purpose of Jesus's ministry.[33] Thus, the refusal to consider women as leaders or ordained ministers in the church does not

---

30. John Garrett (*Footsteps in the Sea: Christianity in Oceania to World War II* [Suva, Fiji: University of the South Pacific, 1992], p. 186) observes that, 'in a Samoan village, two substantial houses belonging to the chief and the pastor (or Catholic priest) often stand out above the rest'. This means that these houses show the wealth of the pastor and the highest chief.

31. Wainwright, *Towards a Feminist Critical Reading*, p. 2.

32. Wainwright, *Towards a Feminist Critical Reading*, pp. 27-28.

33. This problem is stated clearly in Schüssler Fiorenza, *Discipleship of Equals*, pp. 106-16.

reflect the likely historical reality of the early Christian movement, which she reconstructs as a 'discipleship of equals'.[34]

Elaine explores three healings in the Gospel of Matthew that involve women—Jesus's healing of Peter's mother-in-law in her house (8.14-15); the recovery of the woman with hemorrhages (9.20-22); and the healing of the Canaanite woman's daughter (15.21-28). Her readings emphasize the women characters' perspectives and their navigating of societal expectations within a male-dominated society. According to Elaine, these women's healing events have a unique pattern that shows the different approaches women can take to get what they need for themselves and for their communities.

The *Silasila Mamao* hermeneutic recognizes women's great wisdom in knowing how to deal with different life situations according to time and place. For Elaine, the healing of Peter's mother-in-law[35] (8.14-15) depicts a woman who cannot leave her house—her place of belonging according to prevailing social codes of the first-century Mediterranean world. Jesus knows that he must enter this woman's house to help, for she is left helpless therein by patriarchal social and cultural values. By entering the house and healing this woman Jesus shows that he is, after all, the Lord. Elaine interprets Jesus's actions as showing God's breaking down of social and cultural barriers that stop this woman from seeking help beyond her home. According to Elaine, the woman's response to her healing is one significant factor in this healing event. The healed woman stands up and 'serves' Jesus with silence. The verb διακονεῖν is used only three times in the Gospel of Matthew. It is used here and in 20.28 and 27.55. For Elaine, the word has both the symbolic and ongoing nature of service, as seen in the angels' service of Jesus after the temptations (4.11). Jesus's healing of Peter's mother-in-law shows the healer (Jesus) taking the initiative by approaching the sick woman (Peter's mother-in-law) to help her. Thus, the woman's subsequent serving of Jesus makes her a disciple, or a woman with *Silasila Mamao*.

The next healing story that Elaine interprets is the healing of the woman with hemorrhages (9.20-22).[36] Readers are told that the sick woman approaches Jesus, the healer, in public. She takes the initiative by coming to Jesus from behind and touching the fringe of his cloak, after which Jesus heals her. The third healing event discussed by Elaine is when the Canaanite woman approaches Jesus face to face in order to seek help for her daughter (15.21-28).[37]

These three different healing stories thus show a pattern of the women characters' developing confidence to come face to face with Jesus. Jesus

---

34. Schüssler Fiorenza, *Discipleship of Equals*, pp. 105-6.
35. Wainwright, *Towards a Feminist Critical Reading*, pp. 83-87.
36. Wainwright, *Towards a Feminist Critical Reading*, pp. 191-213.
37. See Wainwright, *Towards a Feminist Critical Reading*, pp. 217-52.

takes the initiative in the first healing by approaching Peter's mother-in-law in her house and healing her. She responds by serving Jesus with silence. In the second healing event, the sick woman in public initiates approaching Jesus from behind for help without saying a word, and she is subsequently healed. Then the third healing is initiated by the woman who faces Jesus and talks with him until he gives her what she asks for.

These three healings, as interpreted by Elaine, show the *Silasila Mamao*, or the great wisdom of women in the communities in which Jesus did his ministry. These women demonstrate dealing with different illnesses in ways that would help them support themselves. They did not compel Jesus to give them the healing they sought. Instead, they seek Jesus's help from their subject positions as women within a male-dominated society. For example, Peter's mother-in-law's response shows her status as a woman hosting guests coming to her home. The sick woman who seeks help in public (Mt. 9.20-22) knows she is not supposed to be there, but because she is desperate for help, she tries to touch Jesus covertly without anyone noticing. These are two examples of the women *Silasila Mamao,* or watching from a distance, thinking deeply about what to do according to their situations. As such, they are considered Jesus's disciples, for they respond positively to Jesus's proclamation of the kingdom of heaven. This great wisdom culminates in the women who watch Jesus from a distance at the crucifixion (Mt. 27.55-56).

Many interpretations of Mt. 27.55-56 speak of this moment as showing the women's loyalty and commitment to Jesus's ministry, which started in Galilee. In this part of the chapter, I emphasize one important interpretation of these verses, which I believe sums up the great work done by Elaine. This is shown in R.T. France's interpretation of Mt. 27.55-56, which highlights the vital presence of women in Jesus's ministry as characters who draw connections between events that happen after the crucifixion and Jesus's fulfilment of God's will to save the world. France writes:

> This brief paragraph forms a bridge between the accounts of the death of Jesus and his burial, in that the women were witnesses of both. 'Mary the Magdalene and the other Mary' will reappear in v. 61 and in 28:1, so that they form an important line of continuity through the whole process from death to burial to resurrection. They are therefore the guarantee that when the tomb is found to be empty there has been no mistake: these same women saw him die and saw where he was buried; they would not have gone to the wrong tomb. It will also be they who are the first to meet the risen Jesus in 28:8-10. So this short notice, introducing the focal characters of this latter part of the story of Jesus, deserves to be treated on its own rather than either as an appendage to the account of Jesus' death or as the introduction to the burial.[38]

38. R.T. France, *The Gospel of Matthew* (ICNT; Grand Rapids, MI: Eerdmans, 2007), pp. 1085-87.

France's reading of Mt. 27.55-56 is also reflected in Douglas Hare's interpretation: 'The female witnesses connect the crucifixion with the ensuing scenes of the burial (v. 71) and the resurrection (28:1-10)'.[39] These interpretations of the relevant verses are important, for they express the significant function of women in the ministry of Jesus. Their standing from a distance depicts their preparedness not to leave Jesus unattended following his crucifixion. The women are willing and prepared to carry out these roles, which were expected of them according to Jewish tradition; through their actions, as France and Hare suggest, they help Jesus fulfil his messiahship and bring salvation to the world. It shows that their presence in the fulfilment of God's will in and through Jesus Christ is vital. Thus, the women's act of standing in the distance at the crucifixion is an important continuation of their service and discipleship to Jesus, which began earlier in his ministry.

That interpretation is affirmed by Matthew's use of three particular words: θεωροῦσαι (looking on), ἠκολούθησαν (followed), and διακονοῦσαι (provided for). The words for 'looking on' and 'followed' reflect another characteristic of being a disciple in Matthew. And the Greek word διακονεῖν shows the women continuing to fulfil their role of being true disciples of Jesus. As France states:

> These women are not part of the twelve, but they are described as having 'followed' Jesus, a term which we have earlier seen to denote discipleship in the broader sense (see on 8:18-23). And as disciples they have literally 'followed' Jesus all the way south from Galilee to Jerusalem.[40]

These women's act of *Silasila Mamao,* or watching with wisdom from a distance, is also evident in their presence at Jesus's resurrection, where they became the people to let the twelve know about the resurrection. Not only do they follow Jesus from the beginning of his ministry, but they also have a role in Jesus's fulfilment of God's will. The Gospel of Matthew reveals these women's loyalty and commitment to doing their part in the coming of Jesus the Messiah to save the world. Through her work on women in Matthew, Elaine emphasizes the importance of recognizing these women as disciples of Jesus who help Jesus's fulfilment of his ministry.

In her interpretation of Matthew, Elaine also discusses the patriarchal and androcentric language in the text. In Matthew 27, the story is dominated by male characters such as Pilate, Herod and the centurion. These men of high status represent the elite of the Roman imperial system and its lackeys. They are shown making decisions based on their fears that their status is being threatened by the presence of Jesus among the crowds. In

39. Douglas R.A. Hare, *Matthew* (Interpretation: A Bible Commentary for Teaching and Preaching; Louisville, KY: John Knox Press, 1993), pp. 324-25.

40. France, *The Gospel of Matthew*, pp. 1085-87.

other words, they fear losing their power and money because of Jesus's rising popularity. For example, despite their knowledge of Jesus's innocence, they use the tension between the Jewish leaders and Jesus to make Jesus a criminal, thereby allowing them to maintain their position of power. Pilate set Barabbas free and ordered that Jesus be crucified. However, the patriarchal exercise of Roman imperial power here is disrupted by the appearance of the women watching from a distance (*Silasila Mamao*). The women's silence is the witness of faithful disciples of Jesus preparing to complete their part in the purpose of Jesus's ministry.

I can see in these women's *Silasila Mamao* the great and profound wisdom of Elaine in her many good works helping us (Pacific people) on our side of the world. Elaine's *Silasila Mamao* ensures that we are able to make sense of the meaning of the Bible in our worlds and contexts. I will talk about this further in the following section.

Professor Elaine Wainwright,
a Woman with Silasila Mamao

Elaine's scholarship and research on the Gospel of Matthew led me to find an opportunity to be supervised by her. She did not disappoint me when she accepted my request to work with her on my master's degree, in which I explored the topic of crowds as Jesus's disciples in the Gospel of Matthew. This led to my PhD study under her supervision, where I developed a Samoan reading of discipleship in Matthew.[41] Elaine's support of the type of work I was doing, utilizing my experience and understanding of serving God in our Samoan world to read the Bible, is unforgettable. Her professionalism in dealing with students to ensure they can work to their full potential was outstanding. She encouraged her students with kindness. These are the characteristics of her *Silasila Mamao,* or a woman who watches her students from a distance, a woman who uses her profound wisdom according to the metaphorical meaning of *Silasila Mamao* to ensure they succeed.

Elaine is a biblical and theological scholar who recognizes that the worlds of contemporary Bible readers (the worlds in front of the text) are important to their interpretative journey. She also acknowledges that the biblical text is the basis of interpretation. I consider myself very fortunate to have had the opportunity to be supervised by Elaine. She was able to apply her feminist point of view about the 'other' to the situations and locations of Bible readers from our Samoan worlds—the Pacific world. It is

---

41. Vaitusi Lealaiauloto Nofoaiga, *Towards a Samoan Postcolonial Reading of Discipleship in the Matthean Gospel* (PhD thesis, University of Auckland, 2014). This study was published as a monograph under the title *A Samoan Reading of Discipleship in Matthew* (Atlanta, GA: SBL Press, 2017).

Elaine's *Silasila Mamao*, or wisdom, that I recognize and adore; it allows us to relate to her and she to us—it makes her one of us. We respect this marvellous scholar—an honest, hardworking and caring servant of God. She is an example of a human being, a woman, who has *Silasila Mamao,* the profound wisdom of not only looking from a distance like the women in Mt. 27.55-56 but of looking ahead and beyond things happening to make sure that help is always there for those in need.

One other important characteristic of Elaine's *Silasila Mamao* is her willingness to ensure a connection between her many works and the church. Every work she does is for God in service to the church. From her *Silasila Mamao*, I have learned the importance of remembering our churches in our research. In other words, Elaine asserts the importance of the church in our interpretation of the Bible. We should not, as readers of the Bible in today's world, ignore the church, for the church has shaped the Christian Bible.

Elaine's *Silasila Mamao* has been evident in her recognition of the potential and ability of theological students from Samoa and the Pacific to continue studying and researching the Bible at university level. Her *Silasila Mamao* can also be considered as providing hope for the future of biblical studies in Samoa and the Pacific. Faafetai tele (Thank you very much), Elaine, for your *Silasila Mamao* (great wisdom).

18

SEACHANGES: CREATING AND SUSTAINING A COMMUNITY OF WOMEN SCHOLARS OF FEMINISM, RELIGION AND THEOLOGY IN THE PACIFIC, 1990–2016

Kathleen McPhillips

Introduction: Contexts and Herstories

This chapter[1] addresses the field of feminist studies in religion and theology and will look at the important work that Elaine Wainwright facilitated among women in the Pacific region and in particular her commitment to bring scholars together through the Women Scholars of Religion and Theology association (WSRT). The WSRT emerged from the work of women in universities and theological colleges across Australia and New Zealand in the early 1990s. During its lifetime, WSRT members organized three regional conferences and a journal—*SeaChanges*—to provide an important space for scholars to explore issues facing women in the academy as teachers and researchers, as well as being a creative outlet for theological research and reflection. It was also a supportive space for women entering the academy, especially postgraduate students, where they could be mentored and encouraged in their scholarly pursuits. The association was made possible by the leadership of Elaine Wainwright and her vision for a community of women scholars supporting one another across the diverse cultures of the Pacific region.

Elaine's work is nestled in a number of areas, but in the WSRT her concerns with feminist theology and hermeneutics and her growing engagement with ecofeminist theological discourse were the driving ideas behind

---

1. This chapter is a personal reflection on the Women Scholars of Religion and Theology association, which Elaine was instrumental in establishing in the early 1990s. I draw on Elaine's essay in *SeaChanges* journal, vol. 4, and an interview that I recorded with her in March 2021. I am indebted to Elaine for her vision and generosity in guiding and supporting my own work.

the association's desire for a deeper engagement with the Pacific region. It is important to state from the beginning that Elaine worked in a wholly collegial and collective way, practicing feminist social justice principles of inclusion and sharing the workload. The work that led up to the establishment of WSRT happened over a number of years, involving different communities of women scholars and activists in Australia, Fiji and Aotearoa New Zealand, where a vision for a more formal recognition of the work we were doing could be realized. However, it is also the case that Elaine's vision of bringing women together across the region was a powerful motivator for action. Through the 1990s and into the next decade her scholarship was being recognized in Australia and internationally as a substantial and important contribution to the development of feminist theology.[2] Her position at Brisbane College of Theology (BCT) during the 1990s and then as professor and head of theology at the University of Auckland from 2003 on meant that she was in an institutional position to support the emerging work of other women through undergraduate teaching, postgraduate supervision, co-authorship and regular gatherings. Students who were interested in feminist studies of religion and theology were drawn to BCT, where Elaine organized seminars and supervised many students. At the time, there were relatively few places in Australian universities where women were able to study in the fields of feminism, religion and theology. During the 1990s, as a postgraduate student at the University of Newcastle working in the field of feminist studies in religion, I travelled on numerous occasions to Brisbane to attend meetings and conferences with students and scholars at BCT and the University of Queensland, and I benefitted significantly from this ongoing support and networking.

Networking is a primary tool of feminist engagement and characterized much of the feminist work of that time. Indeed, the 1980s to the 1990s was a dynamic period of social action for women and religion in Australia.[3] Particularly in Christianity, women were active across a number of organizations including Sydney Women-Church, Women and the Australian Church (WATAC), Movement for the Ordination of Women (MOW), Feminism and the Uniting Church (FUN), Ordination of Catholic Women (OCW) and the Australian Feminist Theology Foundation (AFTF). The intense commitment and indeed fight for the inclusion of women in theological, pas-

2. Elaine Wainwright, *Shall We Look for Another: A Feminist Re-reading of the Matthean Jesus* (Maryknoll, NY: Orbis Books, 1998); Elaine Wainwright, *Women Healing, Healing Women: The Genderization of Healing in Early Christianity* (London: Equinox, 2006); Elaine Wainwright, *Towards a Feminist Critical Reading of the Gospel of Matthew* (BZNW, 60; Berlin: de Gruyter, 1991).

3. Kathleen McPhillips, 'Contested Feminisms: Women's Religious Leadership and the Politics of Contemporary Western Feminism', *Journal for the Academic Study of Religion* 29.2 (2016), pp. 134-49.

toral and organizational arenas brought about significant changes in some Christian traditions, particularly the ordination of women in the Anglican and Uniting churches and the rise of women into leadership positions more generally. Significant discussions around gender, sexuality and the inclusion of LGBTQI Christians became ongoing concerns. The emergence of WSRT was a particular initiative to bring women together who were researching, teaching and working across the diverse cultures of Oceania, producing new theological insights and approaches.[4] The aim was to decentre the dominance of Western discourse and make space for the multiple and diverse cultures in the Pacific region.

Women Scholars of Religion and Theology (WSRT)

> Gathering as Women Scholars of Religion and Theology can give identity and purpose from which new possibilities may emerge.[5]

WSRT was formally founded in July 1992 at a gathering in Melbourne of women theologians who were also attending the International Society for Biblical Literature (ISBL) conference at the University of Melbourne.[6] This gathering had its roots in an earlier international gathering at the University of Dunedin in 1991, and both occasions were responding to a deep sense of 'women's isolation as emerging scholars in the South Pacific region and their desire for networking'.[7] While many of the participants were from theological colleges and studying in the field of feminist theology, other scholars of religion from universities and humanities and social sciences disciplines were drawn by the need to connect with one another, share stories of the challenges of working in largely patriarchal institutions and hear one another's scholarship.

The WSRT association also emerged from a dynamic interaction between women in largely Christian traditions to explore and understand the wider Pacific region in which we were living. As theologians, sociologists, liter-

---

4. Anna Halafoff and Kathleen McPhillips, 'Women and Religion in Oceania', in Caroline Starkey and Emma Tomalin (eds.), *The Routledge Handbook of Religion, Gender and Society* (London: Routledge, 2022), pp. 576-92.

5. Elaine Wainwright, '*SeaChanges* Land and Living and Loving: Women Scholars of Religion and Theology over 10 Years', *SeaChanges* 4 (2004).

6. Wainwright, '*SeaChanges*', p. 7. This section draws substantially on an important essay authored by Elaine Wainwright that was presented at the third WSRT Conference in 2004 in Melbourne with the aim of providing the history of WSRT and the *SeaChanges* journal. The presentation was then published in *SeaChanges* 4 (2004). Uppermost in Elaine's thinking was a concern for the need to document this history so it was not 'lost' to the past, as so many women's stories and lives are.

7. Wainwright, '*SeaChanges*', p. 6.

ary scholars and historians, we were keen to bring to our experiences the insights of feminist, postcolonial and ecological perspectives in which we were so deeply engaged via our reading, writing and teaching. From the beginning, postcolonialism as a critical discourse guided our thinking on how to come together in respectful and culturally sensitive ways. We discussed and analysed the damaging impact of colonialism and neocolonialism on Pacific communities, as well as engaging with new and inventive discourses that reflected the resilience and creativity of communities.

From November 1992, a formal association was established under the name Women Scholars of Religion and Theology; it included a directory of interested women, which was funded through a subscription process and managed by a small executive. The association did not adopt a formal constitution and remained primarily a space in which a network of women scholars could meet and interact. It was organic to its central functions of connection and the sharing of knowledge and experience. While WSRT began in Australia, it emerged from shared discussions between women scholars around the Pacific. And when Elaine took up the chair of theology at the University of Auckland in 2003, there began a period of engagement with feminist theologians across the Pacific region that was productive, exciting and challenging.

WSRT Conferences

> What interesting new theology and religious studies might emerge if some of these explorations could be brought into dialogue ... What might emerge if the association of Women Scholars of Religion and Theology could facilitate dialogue between such scholars across cultures?[8]

There were three conferences between 1998 and 2004 sponsored by WSRT. They were organized by the WSRT executive along with the local organizing group and brought together women scholars from across the Pacific and Asia to meet, network and discuss our work.

Brisbane 1998: Gathering the Threads

The first conference was held in Brisbane in January 1998. It benefitted from the 7 years of networking in which the association had been engaged, and 140 participants met to enthusiastically discuss scholarship and future meetings. Participants came from across the Pacific and beyond, including Tonga, Fiji, Papua New Guinea, Aotearoa New Zealand, Australia, India, the Philippines and England. The theme of the conference was 'Gathering the Threads'—an apt metaphor for the ways in which women were seeking

---

8. Wainwright, '*SeaChanges*', p. 12.

to weave together our own work to a wider space.[9] A new executive was elected, and further conferences planned. This move to a higher level of structure and engagement was both exciting and affirming of the original aims to bring women together in both meaningful and culture-specific ways.

Auckland 2001—Sharing the Baskets

The second conference shifted the cultural focus to reflect the cultural and theological concerns of women studying and living in Aotearoa New Zealand. The conference documents were provided in bilingual text, and the theme was explained in terms of Māori cultural/religious traditions. It was the first time that many of us experienced a pōwhiri (welcome ceremony), which was held at the University of Auckland's Waipapa Marae. 'Sharing the Baskets' provided a way of thinking about our multicultural realities and of cultural generosity and knowledge. We were all encouraged to share the contents of our scholarly and cultural baskets and acknowledge the cultural differences as those that bring us together rather than separate us.[10] It was a very powerful coming together and a cultural exposure for many of us from Australia. For myself, I had a profound experience at this conference of cultural immersion and learning from Māori women, whose approach to theology was experience based and embodied. From this conference, other initiatives of women and religion developed, including a book project, *Weavings: Women Doing Theology in Oceania* (2003), and a consultation as part of the South Pacific Association of Theological Schools.[11]

Elaine notes that for herself—and indeed for a number of us—this conference was particularly helpful in linking her own work (which was rooted in Western philosophical and theological traditions) to those engaged with other cultural and methodological traditions. Bringing these multiple perspectives into conversation was challenging at times, but it opened up new thoughts around methodology and theoretical perspectives. The linchpin was a commitment to cultural respect and the importance of postcolonial theory and method which presented challenges to feminist analysis that was particularly reliant on Western perspectives:

> Feminist perspectives are being challenged and nuanced by postcolonialism. This brings with it an attentiveness to hybridity and the multiple languages [both actual and metaphorical] which colonised women have had to learn and the multiple dimensionality of their work for feminist transformation among their colonised people … feminism or feminisms within the region cannot be monolithic but that there will be a blurring of boundaries.[12]

9. Wainwright, '*SeaChanges*', p. 9.
10. Wainwright, '*SeaChanges*', p.10.
11. Wainwright, '*SeaChanges*', p. 11.
12. Wainwright, '*SeaChanges*', pp. 12-13.

The theme of *borderlands* emerged as a key word in describing what the association was trying to achieve:

> Perhaps one of the greatest challenges to our association is the dialogue that recognises hybridity in relation to cultures that constitute this region, to diversities and differences in methodologies for the study of those cultures and their religious and theological traditions.[13]

The hope was to build a conversation that was truly inclusive and open to cultural awareness and transformation; that contained reflexivity of thought and action; that was 'truly postcolonial' in approach; and that was embedded in the *SeaChanges* journal and the association's gatherings.

Melbourne 2004 Peaceworks

The third gathering of the WSRT community took place in Melbourne. It brought together women from across the region and focused on the theme of networking and how to build regional relationships. In particular, we discussed networking with other feminist theological/religious organizations active in the Pacific region and beyond. A number of WSRT members had been attending the Feminist Liberation Theologians Network (FLTN), which gathered every year at the American Academy of Religion conference and was hosted by Mary Hunt and Elisabeth Schüssler Fiorenza, so we were keen to reach out to this group. Over the years the FLTN has been an important space for feminist theologians and religion scholars from the Pacific region to meet and gather, with several meetings featuring speakers from Australia, Japan and Aotearoa New Zealand.

SeaChanges Journal

As WSRT grew in numbers, we could see the value of starting a journal that would provide a voice for the research and creative work produced by women scholars. *SeaChanges* was launched at the 2001 Auckland conference, and by 2016, seven volumes had been published. From the beginning this was an ambitious undertaking, and it took much effort to organize and implement. The philosophy of the journal, as expressed by the first editorial board, was to provide a publicly accessible place for the growing interest in women, religion and theology in the Pacific. We also sought to establish a space where women scholars could continue to engage in the process of listening and hearing each other. Set up as a peer-reviewed journal, it was intended that it be accessible, hence the decision to publish as a free online and open-source journal. The online decision helped keep costs and administration down, but also allowed easy access for communities and schol-

---

13. Wainwright, '*SeaChanges*', p. 13.

ars across the world, particularly the Pacific region. *SeaChanges* aimed to reflect the diversity of members and to encourage scholarly engagement, particularly where women scholars were having difficulty getting their work published in mainstream theological journals. Additionally, Pacific women's stories were largely within an oral tradition, so writing was a practice that involved cultural adaption; *SeaChanges* provided a medium for this process. As Elaine stated,

> Oral tradition is a powerful medium among all the Indigenous peoples of this region and it will continue to grow strong, but Indigenous women are also seeking a public voice and using the written medium as well.[14]

The Weaver's Writing Workshop in April 2001 discussed the differences between writing and oral practices, and in the subsequent publication, *Weavings: Women Doing Theology in Oceania*,[15] it was clear that women's writing projects were an important part of the articulation of experience and communication. Elaine suggested that the Weaver's workshop and publication could be a model for WSRT by encouraging the voices of women to be heard in multiple forums and formats, and *SeaChanges* could be used as one site of dialogue. She stated that, 'For many women in the region for whom the discursive is not their primary mode of theologizing or creating religious traditions, an electronic journal which allows for more creative articulations than print media may be a very important vehicle'.[16]*SeaChanges* did not develop enough to include more creative formats, such as art, music and poetry, but these formats were certainly recognized as valuable expressions of theology and were present at the conference gatherings.

The essays published in *SeaChanges* focused on the engagement of religion and theology as specific to the historical and current concerns of women's lived experience in the Pacific region. There were also articles reflecting individual scholars' areas of interest and expertise not specifically related to the region. Thematically, the journal was intended to be an interdisciplinary project in which scholars from the region could explore the connections between theology and biblical studies and other disciplines, such as literature, sociology, anthropology and history, as well as exploring the lived experience of being an embodied scholar living and working in this region. A commitment to diversity and difference as key principles shaped the journal's orientation from the very beginning. The journal was also a place in which experienced scholars, new scholars and postgraduate students alike could contribute to and share their work. Postgraduate stu-

---

14. Wainwright, '*SeaChanges*', p. 15.

15. Lydia Johnson and Joan Alleluia Filemonie-Tofaeono (eds.), *Weavings: Women Doing Theology in Oceania* (Suva, Fiji: University of South Pacific and Weavers, South Pacific Association of Theological Schools, 2003).

16. Wainwright, '*SeaChanges*', p. 16.

dents were particularly invited to contribute their work, both in recognition of the cutting-edge approaches with which they were engaging and also as a means of encouraging publication pathways and connection with wider networks of scholars. Volumes 6 and 7 of *SeaChanges*, edited by Kathleen McPhillips, were opportunities for postgraduate students to showcase their work. These two issues provided a group of students the opportunity to experience the process of submitting to a peer-review journal in a safe and encouraging space.

The journal was managed by an editorial board comprising Dr Angela Coco (Southern Cross University), Dr Anita Monro (Grace College, University of Queensland), Dr Kathleen McPhillips (University of Newcastle) and Prof. Elaine Wainwright (Professor Emerita, University of Auckland). Kathleen McPhillips remains the managing editor, and Anita Monro has carefully managed the website since its inception. The journal remains publicly available and free of charge.

Over the 7 published volumes, there were 33 contributors and 40 published articles. Articles were principally engaged with theological thematics, including feminist ecotheology, feminist theology, feminist ecclesiology, feminist biblical hermeneutics, historical analysis of biblical texts, histories of women's religious communities and spiritual women, and sociological and philosophical feminist accounts of religion. While Christianity was the central religious tradition discussed in the journal articles, contributors also wrote of the history of Buddhism and women in Australia, Tibetan Buddhism and Muslim women. A number of essays also addressed Indigenous women in the Pacific. In short, the journal offers an eclectic collection that reflects the varied concerns of women scholars in this region.

Elaine Wainwright: Understandings of Body, Self and Community.

In her theological work, Elaine has prioritized the experience of women within the wider historical, cultural and social spaces in which they live. Her work also seeks to be embodied and local. She states,

> Attentiveness to body and to space are two of the key categories I am using as I seek to give subjectivity to the healing women of antiquity, situating them not only in human communities but in the broader ecological system of their day.[17]

The importance of the sea and the seascape was foremost in Elaine's reflections as she moved across the Tasman Sea to the University of Auckland. She strived to recognize that the region, comprised of islands within

17. Wainwright, *'SeaChanges'*, p. 3.

the wide sea of the Pacific, was the source by which identity and self are shaped by the movement and meaning of water. In Auckland she found that she needed to re-frame her sensory awareness of space and land, and water in particular, where 'my awareness of the sea ... turns attention to a recognition of sea changing living in so many material ways for the women of this region'.[18] This impacted Elaine's methodological focus on feminist hermeneutics, which is key to her theological approach to understanding women's experiences, both in antiquity and in current times. She states, 'Within a feminist hermeneutic that begins with experience, women's experience, interpretations of texts and traditions and analyses of women's religious experiences and spiritualities within the region will vary considerably as sea changes living in its multidimensionality'.[19]

Elaine's experience in Auckland and her commitment to understand more about the Pacific region and its fundamental role in shaping her own theological orientation drove her work with the WSRT and other regional events and initiatives. Elaine wanted to engage her theological praxis with multicultural perspectives and, in particular, Māori contexts.[20] Underlying it all was a deep sense of obligation to social justice and gender equity for women in the Pacific region and beyond.

Conclusion

After the last conference in Melbourne, WSRT produced a 2005 issue of *SeaChanges*. Following this, the association lost wind and scaled back. There were two further issues of *SeaChanges* (2013, 2016), both of which were edited by Kathleen McPhillips, and which, as noted above, focused on the work of postgraduate students across Australia and New Zealand.

It is hard to say what led to the diminishment of WSRT; the association has not met since Melbourne, 2005. Certainly, busyness played a factor, with the editorial board and the WSRT executive all engaged in full-time academic work. The tyranny of distance meant that we only met together at conferences. Elaine considered that the reliance on a single organization rather than building smaller networks might have been at fault.[21] But it may also be that the timing of the association's rise and fall coincided with the fall of women's activism in religious spaces and more generally. The turn to conservatism politically and socially, both in Australia and globally, had a damaging impact on feminist activism, and this only began to recover

18. Wainwright, '*SeaChanges*', p. 3.
19. Wainwright, '*SeaChanges*', p. 3.
20. Interview with Elaine Wainwright, March 2021.
21. Interview with Elaine Wainwright, March 2021.

with the rise of the #MeToo movement in 2017.[22] A new sharper focus on gendered violence and its consequences has begun to inspire new feminist activisms among theologians and religion scholars and is leading to better understandings of what living in patriarchies means.[23]

Women Scholars of Religion and Theology played a small but important role in providing a space for women across the Pacific to meet, talk and listen to one another's experiences. Our teaching and research was shaped by this process, breaking down isolation and building resilience. The cultural interchange was very productive, with the meetings and conferences being rich spaces for many participants. From the very beginning, Elaine took a leading role in bringing WSRT to birth as a scholar, colleague and friend, providing leadership, vision and insight into the development and formation of this association and the work it undertook in taking the issue of gender justice forward.

22. McPhillips, *Contested Feminisms*, pp. 144-45.
23. Kathleen McPhillips and Sarah-Jane Page (eds.), 'Religion, Gender and Violence', Special Issue, *Religion and Gender* 11.2 (2021) and 12.1 (2022).

Index of References

Index of Authors

Harland, P.   30n53
Harris, M.   64n24
Hart, J.   93n25, 93n26, 94n29
Hartley, J.E.   113n12
Havea, J.   56n1, 66n32, 212, 214, 217
Havea, S.'A.   212
Haynes, S.R.   222n5
Heidegger, M.   56, 65
Heininger, B.   144n19
Heinrichs, S.   100, 100n3
Hengel, M.   224
Herrmann, P.   20n14, 21n16, 25n35,
     26n41
Hewett, D.   162
Hillel, D.   128n10
Holladay, W.L.   126n4, 126n5, 127n7,
     130n17, 132n18
Hooker, M.   180n24
Horsley, R.A.   151n62
Howard-Brook, W.   211n4
Huebenthal, S.   144n18
Hughes, J.   172n2
Hylen, S.E   72n13

Incignieri, B.J.   145n19
Innes, K.   135, 135n28
İplikçioğlu, B.   146n29
Irigaray, L..   44

Jacobson, D.M.   153n75
Jasper, D.   221-22n4
Jenkins, W.   87, 87n10
Jennings, T.W.   52n27
Jobling, D.   122n49
Johnson, E.A.   72, 73n14
Johnson, L.   241n15
Johnson, L.T.   191n33
Johnson, T.H.   199n14, 200n20,
     203nn37-38,40, 204nn41-45,
     205nn47,50, 206n51, 207n59
Jones, R.R.   199n15
Joshel, S.R   72n14

Kaoma, K.   38
Kearsley, R.   24n28
Keddie, A.   142n8, 152n70
Keener, C.S.   47n6, 50n20, 53n30,
     54n32
Kittel, G.   4n11
Kimondo, S.S.   144n19

Klancher, N.   33n2
Kloppenborg, J.   152n71, 153n74, 155,
     156
Kolbert, E.   57
Kolia, B.F.   137n38, 217
Konradt, M.   18n2, 19n11
Krause, D.   81n39
Krell, D.F.   65n30
Kristeva, J.   35, 45-46
Kuhn, H.-W.   177n13
Kuperus, G.   65n30

Laes, C.   51n22
Lake, M.   101, 101n7-11, 161n9
Langton, K.   121n46
Lawson, V.   xxiv
Leal, R.B.   128n10, 135, 135n29
Leibner, U.   152n69
Lemon, L.T.   119n40
Lena, A.   150n61, 154n84
Levine, A.-J.   38-39, 71n7, 74n18,
     81n39, 160n4, 186n10, 187n16,
     191, 192
Levy, Y.   123n50
Liddell, H.G.   49n4, 52n29
Liew, T-s.B.   xxi, 52n27, 214n21
Lim, E.   48n10
Linafelt, T.   122n49
Loughrey, G.   xxv
Louw, J.P.   52n26, 54n34, 189n22
Lovelock, J.   88n14
Lundbom, J.   128n8, 130n16, 130n17,
     132n18
Lundin, R.   200
Luz, U.   4n10, 8n32, 14n38, 18n3, 47n2,
     224
Lytle, E.   155n92

Machiavelli, N.   64
Magness, J.   147n37
Malbon, E.S.   143n12
Mann, C.S.   53n30
Marlow, H.   87, 87n11
Martin, W.   197-98n7, 198n11, 199nn13,
     17, 201, 202n34, 206n52
Marx, K.   183n31
Marzano, A.   156n92
Mason, S.   148n41, 148n47, 149n54,
     156n96

Milton Keynes UK
Ingram Content Group UK Ltd.
UKHW010228080224
437389UK00005B/198